In France Profound

Also by T. D. Allman

As Author

Finding Florida: The True History of the Sunshine State
Rogue State: America at War with the World
Miami: City of the Future
Unmanifest Destiny: Mayhem and Illusion in
American Foreign Policy

As Coauthor or Contributor

Anatomy of a Coup: Cambodia: The Widening War in Indochina
Reporting Vietnam: American Journalism 1968–1973
Conservatism as Heresy: In Defence of Monarchy
Provence: An Inspired Anthology
The Florida Reader: Visions of Paradise
Spain: True Stories: The King Who Saved His Country
Why Bosnia?
Miami, the American Crossroad: A Centennial Journey
Busted: Stone Cowboys, Narco-Lords and Washington's
War on Drugs
These United States: Original Essays by Leading
American Writers
Killed: Great Journalism Too Hot to Print
Marguerite Yourcenar and the USA: From Prophecy to Protest

In French

Un Destin Ambigu
La Floride: Cœur révélateur des États-Unis

In Spanish

Miami: La Ciudad del Futuro
El Hombre Mas Peligroso del Mundo

In France Profound

The Long History
of a House, a Mountain Town,
and a People

T. D. ALLMAN

Atlantic Monthly Press
New York

FIRST EDITION

Published simultaneously in Canada
Printed in the United States of America

First Grove Atlantic hardcover edition: August 2024

Library of Congress Cataloging-in-Publication data is available for this title.

ISBN 978-0-8021-2784-6
eISBN 978-0-8021-6386-8

Atlantic Monthly Press
an imprint of Grove Atlantic
154 West 14th Street
New York, NY 10011

Distributed by Publishers Group West

groveatlantic.com

24 25 26 27   10 9 8 7 6 5 4 3 2 1

Profound Thanks

With respect and affection I dedicate this book to

My esteemed neighbor and Lauzerte civic heroine,
The Brave Widow Gandillonne,

My beloved friend Pierre Maury, Avatar of Human
Goodness and Shepherd of Montaillou,

and to

My colleague and mentor, Abbé Barthélemy Taillefer,
Historian of Lauzerte and Curé of Cazillac,

While offering profound thanks to the countless
others of my neighbors who have taught me so
much about Lauzerte, life, and humanity.

CONTENTS

Between stone and sky: My house in Lauzerte

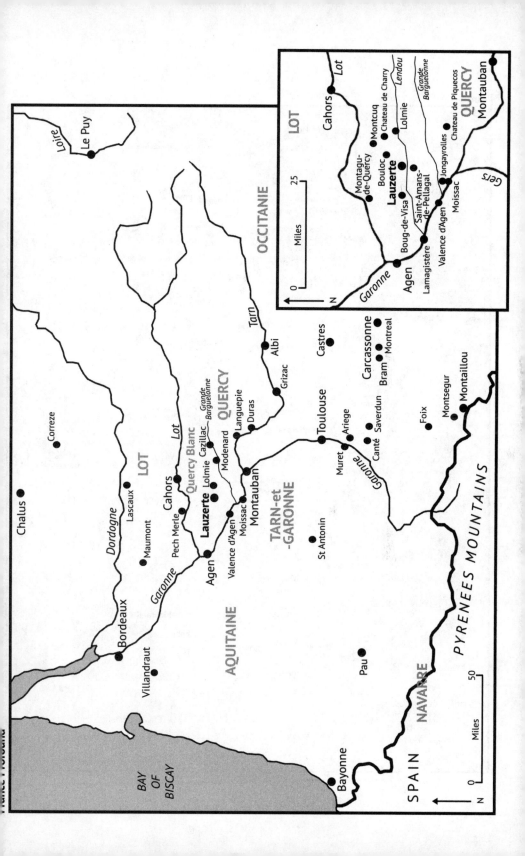

Inset map (top right):

LOT

Cahors · Lot · Lendou · Grande Barguelonne · **QUERCY** · Montauban

Montcuq · Chateau de Charry · Lolmie · Chateau de Piquecos

Montagu-de-Quercy · Bouloc · **Lauzerte** · Jongayrolles

Saint-Amans-de-Pellagal · Moissac

Boug-de-Visa · Valence d'Agen · Gers

Lamagistère · Garonne · Agen

Miles 0 25

N

Main map:

Loire · Le Puy

OCCITANIE

Tarn · Albi · Castres · **Carcassonne** · Montreal · Bram

Grizac

QUERCY

Languepie · Duras

Grande Barguelonne

Correze

LOT

Lascaux · Maumont

Quercy Blanc · Cazillac · Modenard · Montauban · Toulouse · Ariege · Saverdun · Foix · Montsegur · Montaillou

Chalus

Cahors · Lolmie · Muret · Canté · Garonne

Pech Merle · **Lauzerte**

Dordogne

Agen · Valence d'Agen · Moissac

TARN-et-GARONNE

St Antonin

Bordeaux

Garonne

AQUITAINE

Villandraut

Pau

PYRENEES MOUNTAINS

SPAIN · **NAVARRE**

Bayonne

BAY OF BISCAY

Miles 0 50

N

France

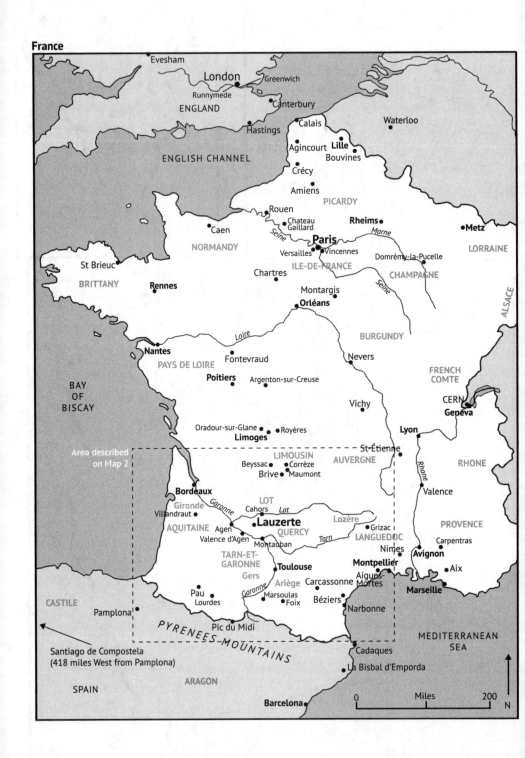

Evesham
London
Greenwich
Runnymede
ENGLAND
Canterbury
Hastings
Calais
Waterloo
Agincourt
Lille
Bouvines
Crécy
Amiens
PICARDY
Rouen
Chateau
Gaillard
Rheims
Metz
Caen
Seine
Paris
NORMANDY
Marne
LORRAINE
St Brieuc
Versailles
Vincennes
Domrémy-la-Pucelle
BRITTANY
ILE-DE-FRANCE
CHAMPAGNE
Chartres
ALSACE
Rennes
Montargis
Seine
Orléans
Loire
BURGUNDY
Nantes
Fontevraud
PAYS DE LOIRE
Nevers
FRENCH
COMTE
BAY
OF
BISCAY
Poitiers
Argenton-sur-Creuse
CERN
Vichy
Genéva
Oradour-sur-Glane
Royères
Lyon
Limoges
St-Étienne
Area described
on Map 2
LIMOUSIN
AUVERGNE
RHONE
Beyssac
Corrèze
Brive
Maumont
Bordeaux
LOT
Gironde
Garonne
Cahors
Lot
Lozère
Valence
Villandraut
AQUITAINE
Lauzerte
QUERCY
PROVENCE
Agen
Tarn
Carpentras
Valence d'Agen
Montauban
LANGUEDOC
Avignon
TARN-ET-
GARONNE
Nimes
Aix
Toulouse
Montpellier
Gers
Rhone
CASTILE
Ariège
Carcassonne
Aigues-
Mortes
Marseille
Pau
Marsoulas
Béziers
Lourdes
Foix
Pamplona
Narbonne
Pic du Midi
MEDITERRANEAN
SEA
PYRENEES-MOUNTAINS
Cadaques
Santiago de Compostela
(418 miles West from Pamplona)
La Bisbal d'Emporda
SPAIN
ARAGON
Miles
0
200
Barcelona
N

1

44°15'4" NORTH, 1°08'18" EAST

W HERE IS IT?

That's the first thing people ask when I tell them about my eight-hundred-year-old House in the French mountaintop town of Lauzerte. In New York, even in Paris, no one's heard of Lauzerte. I tell them that's because I live in a place that does not exist. I call it France Profound, as opposed to *France pro-fonde*, because Profound has the force needed to convey how special it is. As with Faulkner's Yoknapatawpha County, so it is with France Profound. Many strange truths lurk there. Many curious characters cavort across it on the way to fulfilling their destinies, for here Character Is Destiny. Search as you will, you won't find France Profound on any map. You can't get your electricity reconnected or your internet suspended there. You can locate all the mysteries of human existence in France Profound.

In France Profound people are always talking about nonexistent or, to put it more precisely, ex-existent places. They tell you they live in Gascony or come from the Auvergne, even though you can't sue someone in Gascony. You can't send a letter to the Auvergne. The historic provinces of France were abolished in 1789, yet nigh unto a quarter-millennium later they still define people's ideas of who they are, as well as of the places where they live. The ex-existent province enveloping Lauzerte is called Quercy. Most people also never have heard of Quercy. Unlike its vast and famous neighbors Aquitaine and Languedoc, Quercy conjures up no stereotypes. Even fewer know of its subset, *Quercy blanc,* of which Lauzerte, the place where I live, is both epicenter and paradigm.

There is no Black Quercy, so why a white one? Look to the creamy off-white limestone that gives my House its imposing and distinguished but also its light and elegant appearance. Immense as my House is, you find no ponderousness there; that's true of *Quercy blanc* also. Picture the landscapes Prince Galahad mythically traversed to get an idea of its coiling streams and picturesque crags, all seemingly surmounted by villages plucked from Jean Froissart's *Chronicles,* first published in 1369. Upon this dulcet stage set countless comedies unfold, but what fun would the pratfall provide, without the pride that precedes it? With my own eyes I've seen *denouements*—French for comeuppances—that would make Maupassant flinch.

The twentieth-century French historian Fernand Braudel once remarked that time is simultaneously different in different places. Lauzerte outdoes that esteemed savant, because here time is simultaneous all in one place. The Crusades are today, along with the latest vintage of the Cahors wine my neighbor Joel produces from grapes grown in his own vineyard. The Wars of Religion are coterminous with the foie gras from ducks my friend Fred the Foie Gras Guy force feeds, then strangles. Françoise, purple-haired Queen of Goats Cheese, is the contemporary of Eleanor of Aquitaine when it comes to all the complications the will of a powerful woman can generate in this world of ours.

Everyday life is full of pratfalls and now, as in the gory past, much worse can befall you when you least expect it. Everything can seem so idyllic until the Catholics and Protestants or the French and the English start massacring each other again, or—this happened only last week—my washing machine breaks. The dread of it! Not of washing my own clothes, but of all the diplomacy and persistence required to get a repair-man to come fix it. Even in a place as idiosyncratic as Lauzerte not all stereotypes are false, certainly not the one concerning French attitudes to work. For all too many, work is something they do for as few hours a week as possible, in order first to get their social benefits and then, as soon as possible, retire on a comfy state-subsidized pension. Benefits first. Work last. Try tinkering with that relationship, and you risk winding up like President Emmanuel Macron—berated, despised, contemned for daring to raise the nation's retirement age.

With broken washing machines, as with everything else in France Profound, the best solutions are always to be found closest to hand. The secret is to seek out the people around you who love what they do—and then make them love you. Would you leave someone you love without a functioning washing machine? There is a catch. To achieve this transfor-mation of humdrum toil into labors of love, you must love them too, and after all these years, there are more people I love in and around Lauzerte than any other place on earth. Foremost among them are my faithful friends and long-time collaborators, Dominique and Patricia Darnière: For more than thirty years, my House has been their labor of love. Every nook and cranny bears witness to their skill at restoration and their gift for preservation.

Whenever upon a pilgrimage you embark—in search of sal-vation or a SIM card—the perils are as numberless now as they ever were. Once upon a time it was highwaymen. These days you must be mindful of the menace posed by little red cars, though once arrived at your destination there is always a park-ing space in front of the cathedral. Along with Character Is Destiny, that is one of the governing revelations life in France Profound has conferred on me. Never settle for some parking spot hundreds of yards away because There Is Always a Parking Space in Front of the Cathedral. Something else they never tell you: Everything Is Closed Monday, including everything you were planning to see or do once the weekend ended.

Lauzerte's exact location is 44°15′4″ North, 1°08′18″ East. When people hear I live in the South of France, they think of palm trees and bikinis, but if Lauzerte were transported to North America, it would be located on the Vermont-Canada border. Thanks to the moderating influence of the Gulf Stream, it seldom freezes, but when it does, watch out! The time I went down to Barcelona to celebrate New Year's with a Catalan sculptor friend taught me what lies behind the old adage about keeping the home fires burning. When I returned, the temperature inside each of the House's four gigantic fireplaces was the same as the inside of an American refrigerator. The House in essence is a giant stone box. Its magnificent three-foot-thick Quercy stone walls keep out the heat in summer. They also protect the House in winter, but there must be some heat inside to protect! Lauzerte's latitude likewise explains why it has such long days in summer, and such short ones in winter. You may feel, on those stiflingly hot summer days, like you're in the tropics, but come November you rise in darkness, and by late afternoon you're in darkness again.

Lauzerte's longitude as opposed to its latitude shows how today, as it has for a thousand years, the perpetual English-French rivalry imbues and, in this instance, warps every aspect of life. Lauzerte's longitude is the exact same longitude as Canterbury, home to England's famous cathedral. It is actually closer to London in longitude than it is to Paris, yet as a result of what William the Conqueror began in 1066, and Brexit only made worse, Lauzerte time is perpetually askew. This is because no north-south line of longitude divides European Central Time from Greenwich Mean Time. As a legacy of centuries of English-French conflict, the English

Channel horizontally separates the two time zones. Unlike a proper line of longitude, the Channel runs east-west, not north-south. In consequence, Lauzerte is forever one hour off, and in the summer two hours off, what the planet's geography says it should be. For a long time, the chronology was even more discombobulated. England, ever insular, kept itself eleven days—not a mere hour—distant from the continent until 1752.

A mountain to those who live upon it, Lauzerte from a broader perspective is but a knobby, stubby protuberance 886 feet high, flanking the south side of the Massif Central, that almost-empty upland wilderness that dominates the center of France. Quercy, Lauzerte within it, is a realm of transitions—uplands to lowlands, Atlantic to Mediterranean. Lauzerte is located just on the Atlantic side of the watershed. Its streams, after flowing into the Rivers Tarn and Garonne, and then into the vast Gironde estuary, flow past Bordeaux before reaching the ocean. Hydrographically, Lauzerte is tributary to Aquitaine—from *aqua*, Latin for water. Its red-tiled roofs, along with the history of its civic melodramas, reveal its emotional as well as cultural kinship to Languedoc and its dependency on Toulouse, whose noble counts wrung Lauzerte into existence as part of their long struggle with the English, whose beachhead was Bordeaux.

A wise man wants to know a place's philosophical as well as its geographic location. Right from the start, that's why I started buying maps. According to my latest census, fifty framed antique maps now hang in my House. They are displayed in all the great rooms: the Red Room, the Green Room, the Studio, the Club Room, the Loft, the Atrium. Maps also line the entry corridor on the ground floor. Limits are essential when it comes to collecting. Simply collecting maps of France would have required me to buy a warehouse. Had I limited myself to regional maps, the scope still would have been too vast, so I narrowed my perspective to maps showing Lauzerte. These

maps are all the same in the sense they depict the same geographical location, yet every one of them is different because
each locates Lauzerte in a different temporal, cultural, and
spiritual situation.

Over the years I have come upon maps of Lauzerte in a
curiosity shop near the British Museum, and in a gift shop in
Franklin, Tennessee. I was in Egypt when I first successfully
established Lauzerte's exact location as a wise man would wish
to comprehend it. I was wandering through that part of down-
town Cairo that seems to have nothing but shops selling
women's high-heeled shoes when I noticed the little place selling secondhand books. I was digging through the dog-eared
Barbara Cartlands hoping to find something by Cavafy when,
thanks to my peripheral vision, I noticed the old maps stacked
up like last month's newspapers at the back of the store. Many
were very old; most of them were in unexpectedly good condition. Egypt's dry climate, I realized as I handled them,
preserved maps as well as mummies.

I didn't have to dig very far to find a pair of maps showing Lauzerte. One was civil: it showed the administrative departments of France. The other showed the country's military
districts. I could tell immediately the two maps had been
printed between 1790 and 1808 because, on those maps, Lauzerte was not located in the department of Tarn-et-Garonne,
as it is today. Tarn-et-Garonne, named for the two largest local rivers, was not created until 4 November 1808. Before
that, Lauzerte was part of the department of the Lot, which
was where these maps placed it, in the Lot. This meant the
maps in the Cairo shop dated back at least to 1808. How
much further I could reckon because the original French
departments, including the Lot, had been created in early
1790. That meant these two maps had been produced during
the eighteen years and eight months bracketed by those two
dates.

Those maps had wound up in a Cairo book shop for the same reason English and French time zones to this day are divided by the English Channel. They were English, not French maps, and there was an excellent reason for English military maps of France of that period to be found in Egypt. On 1 July 1798, Napoléon Bonaparte began his invasion of Egypt. Only a month later, the Royal Navy destroyed the French fleet in the Battle of the Nile. Little more than a year later, on 24 August 1799, Napoléon fled Egypt, abandoning his own army, in the first of the great disasters that marked the trajectory of his career. It was entirely likely, I realized as I purchased them, that these maps had been brought to Egypt by an officer of the Royal Navy around the time of Napoléon's great defeat, and had been there ever since. Today those two maps sit in gilt frames on the mantel of the red marble fireplace in the Red Room of my House in Lauzerte. They were red and so, like the Chinese scroll I found in a Beijing hutong, they migrated there.

Sometimes, when I'm trying to understand why history keeps repeating itself, I look at those maps, and remember how adamantly people refuse to learn from their mistakes. No one illustrated this better than Napoléon Bonaparte. Long before his enemies won the Battle of Waterloo, Napoléon had defeated himself. From Cairo to Moscow, the trajectory of his self-inflicted disasters was identical. Again and again, he proceeded from grandiloquent conception to magnificent advance to the utter undoing of his grand scheme, upon which Napoléon would abandon those who died for him and betray those who stood by him. In a tiny sloop he would escape from Egypt, or in a closed carriage he would rush across the Russian steppes, reaching Paris before the news of his defeat could. There he blamed others for his defeat. He confused his critics, and enhanced his own powers. This permitted him to unleash anew the same arc of catastrophe until, finally, he was undone definitively. Even then, Elba was not enough. He had to do it again and so, finally, destiny brought him, via Waterloo, to a windswept volcanic rock: Saint Helena.

At the time I found those maps, I had not yet discovered that the destinies of Cairo and Lauzerte have been intertwined for more than eight hundred years. From the first moment, though, I realized those maps pinpointed Lauzerte's exact position, and its role, in relation to the great flux of human events. Empires and religions rose and fell, but this town, this Square, my House—the mountain upon which it sat—were here then, and they are still here. Throughout its long history, as today, France Profound doesn't make history. History periodically remakes it, and then rolls on its way. Somehow what remains is revelatory. That is what finding English maps with Lauzerte on them in Cairo revealed. My House was what, in French, they call the *point de repair*—the reference point. By the time Napoléon lost Egypt, my *point de repair* had been surviving events for more than half a millennium.

The most Important map is the map in my mind. Rising like a ziggurat at the center of my mental map stands the Lauzerte mountain. Circling the mountain in a widening arc are Lauzerte's attendant villages, each with its funny, archaic-sounding ack-ending to their names—Cazillac, Bouloc, Montcuq, Montignac, Flaugnac, Brassac, Loubrassac, Vazerac. Also speckling this undulating terrain are the places whose names refer to mountains: Montagudet, Monpezat, Miramont, Montfermier, Monbarla, Montesquieu, Montagu, Montjoi, Montlauzun. The names of Sainte Juliette, Saint-Amans, Saint-Clare, Saint-Paul-d'Espis, Saint-Vincent take their names from the long-ago Christianization of these lands. Then there are place names whose provenance is unknown, or apocryphal: Tréjouls, Toufailles, Fauroux, Lauzerte itself. Certainly, the town's name does not refer to Lauzerte's many lizards, as some pretend. Others aver that Lauzerte is cognate to lantern. A lantern, for decades, is what Lauzerte has been for me—casting light on a panoply of events.

Extend the circle around Lauzerte twenty-five miles, and my mental map encompasses the neighborhood's three most sizable settlements: Cahors to the northeast, Montauban to the southeast, and Moissac due south. As viewed from Lauzerte, they form a semicircular field of vision. From its perch atop the mountain, Lauzerte scans its surroundings cautiously, and with good reason. For nearly eight hundred years outsiders have been unleashing their inquisitors, their recruitment dragoons, their tax assessors, their demands for free labor, their administrative "reforms," and their regional planning edicts on Lauzerte.

Beyond Moissac, Cahors, and Montauban, my mental map acquires tentacles. One tentacle runs south to Toulouse and then, passing the famous walled city of Carcassonne, extends itself to the Mediterranean Sea. There, one branch, avoiding the Pyrénées, follows the coast south toward Spain and the closest global metropolis, Barcelona. It's to Barcelona, not Paris, I flee when I need a big-city break. The other branch slinks east along the Mediterranean, leading directly or indirectly to places like Montpellier, Marseilles, Lyons, Avignon, and, eventually, Rome. Another tentacle swings west, via Bordeaux, to the Atlantic Ocean and the planet full of possibilities that lies beyond it.

One of the most consequential of these overland traceries links Lauzerte with Poitou, capital of Aquitaine and redoubt of the troubadours, as well as the royal abbey of Fontevrault. There the corpses of three of the gaudiest personalities to engender Lauzerte—Eleanor of Aquitaine, Richard the Lionheart, and Joan Plantagenet, Queen of Sicily and Countess of Toulouse—were interred until wrathful revolutionaries tore open their tombs, and cast their desecrated remains to the wind. By far the most consequential tentacle is the one that links Lauzerte to Paris—monopolizer of power, inciter of dreams! Lauzerte shows what the whole of French history shows: Events Inevitably, Ultimately, and Ineluctably Tend to the Benefit of Paris.

Every place has sounds as well as sights that lock it in your sensibility forever. Such are the recurring sounds that rhythmically fill the Square in front of my House, which is called the Place des Cornières. Monday through Friday I hear the quondam sounds of the postman, the delivery trucks, the school kids with their backpacks, and the sound of my front door bell ringing. In France Profound there is no escaping politeness. Joining the line at the post office, you must never say *Bonjour*. No, you must say: *Bonjour, mesdames. Bonjour, messieurs.* On Saturday mornings comes the welcome babble of the weekly market. Then, some Sundays I awake, startled. Where's the noise? I luxuriate in the absence of noise until the Sunday kinds of sounds commence. Sometimes it's a wedding party—the shy brides in their frilly machine-made lace; the grooms in their shiny suits that will hang unworn in their armoires until there's another wedding, or a funeral. Sometimes French horns herald the arrival of a hunting party. I also hear the clack-clack of people setting up tables for Lauzerte's communal dinners. Other times it's the clip-clop of promenading equestriennes, students from the dressage academy located on one of Lauzerte's attendant hills. Do the horses have any idea how soon these young females will transfer their fascination with them to boys?

The definitive Lauzerte sound comes from the bells in the church tower opposite my House. For a long time, they sounded each hour twice, with a pause between the double tolling. At noon and at midnight the bells would ring twenty-four times, in two phases of twelve. This went back to the days when people didn't have clocks in their houses, let alone watches to put in their pockets or, later, on their wrists. The housewife pumping water, the baker kneading dough would hear the bells, but had they heard the first ring of the bells? That repetition, they knew, was coming. That second time the bells sounded, they were expecting it, so they could count the hours, exactly.

For me, the most moving part of this tintinnabulation has always been the gap of silence between the two ringings of the bells. My head cupped in my hands, lost in the contemplation of some long-passed crime, gallantry, or absurdity—or while half-dozing over my *Dictionnaire des pièges et difficultés de la langue française* in one of the armchairs in the Club Room—a lifetime of sensations would seem to unfold within that interstice. Then, the second steady, stately tolling of the bells would begin, sometimes after I had forgotten there had been a first one. I would realize this eternity within me had lasted but thirty seconds at most.

2

DISCERNING THE FACE
OF THE SKY

HOW OLD IS YOUR HOUSE?

That is the other question people keep asking. Before answering, I ask them to understand it is not really my House. One of the many things my House has taught me is that we are all renters on this planet. I like the French word for renter: *locataire.* I value the combined sense of legitimacy and impermanence it conveys. You have certain rights here, but don't imagine you own the place.

As you approach it from the Place des Cornières, my House presents a noble facade of handsome tall windows and gracious cream-colored Quercy stone; this is but one of the many faces it has presented to the world in the course of Lauzerte's, and Europe's, historical transformations. While restoring the passageway leading down to the House's vaulted wine cellar, I uncovered a patch of half-timbering, dating back some seven hundred years. This last remaining trace of its original half-timbering revealed how the House looked before it was girt in its current imposing facade. Actually, Dominique and Patricia uncovered it. I was in New York, but they knew, in those pre-internet days, that there was no need to indulge in the luxury of an overseas telephone call. They understood I would want to preserve that vestige, to honor it, not cover it.

Previous occupants of my House have included French conquerors, English conquerors, papists, and Protestants. Following the epochal struggles of the cross and the sword came the victories of the manipulators of symbols—lawyers, postal clerks, tax collectors, curates, royal administrators, and judges. This elite lived where I live, in the fine houses facing the Place des Cornières. Farther down the mountain, the butchers, bakers, vintners, millers, and milliners practiced their trades, along with the purveyors of poultry, pastry, and many sorts of cheese. Much as the world changes, in every epoch, goat's cheese as opposed to cow's cheese takes pride of place.

In due course, epitomizing the universalization of personal technology, an American moves into the House. He believes this imposing edifice, so eminently positioned on Lauzerte's town square, will change his life. It will, though not for the reasons he supposed, nor in ways he envisioned. The sales contract he signs, after thinking it over for an entire ten minutes, is called, marvelously in French, the *compromis de vente*. In the course of his life in this House his faith in humanity's moral progress is among the many things that will be compromised. As, sitting there in the Café Central on the same side of the square as what now became his House, he lifted the ballpoint pen of destiny, and signed many little spaces with an *x* next to them, it was Easter 1990. If ever modern times provided an excuse to hope, this was it! Only months earlier the Berlin Wall had fallen; the most vicious of the dictators, in Romania, has been devoured by his people. With his own eyes, over but a year or two, he has seen the Filipinos and the Nepalis seize their destiny with their own hands. Using a rented sledgehammer, he has taken his own piece out of the Berlin Wall, and he was in Tiananmen Square too! In the face of such marvels, who could doubt that the future was going to be better than the past?

More than thirty years later, sitting in this same house, he will look up from his desk, and realize: Just while I have been living here, that Age of Optimism has become like the Age of Enlightenment, a vanished moment of false hope followed by events that destroyed those hopes. The shock is that something he breathed, and held in his own hands, could simply vanish, that is, become History.

In my House I cohabit with magic and madness, joy, folly, good food and good wine, along with every one of the petty vices and a fair number of the civic virtues inherent when human life is constricted to one specific space, in this case the slopes and top of a mountain. The melodramas of many epochs lurk in its ancient beams and period parquetry. From my House you also can perceive the structure of the universe, but in order to get to that vista, you must climb and climb, all the way to the Top of the House. On your way up the Great Staircase, you'll be enveloped by jungle foliage. My House breathes. It teaches. It speaks. You can hear its wooden beams shifting in the night, and when there's a storm, the House moves like a ship. It is a ramifying echo chamber. Scents—of lavender, of cheese, of a woman's perfume—infuse it too. It has microclimates. In time it revealed to me the nature of God. I was poaching foie gras when it happened.

So how old is it? As Fernand Braudel would have explained, that depends on where, exactly, you position yourself. On the ground floor you are standing where previous inhabitants set out their sun-seeking geoglyphs tens of thousands of years ago. That makeshift celestial chronometer empowered them to foresee when it was time to sow, to hunt, and to seek shelter, hence caves. The mountain's summit provided perspective; its limestone caverns provided protection. Having made their mountaintop observations, they went deep inside the mountains. There in lightless caverns these paleolithic humans painted the animals they revered and hunted to extinction. The torque of the rhinoceros horns they painted is at one with the spiral structure of our home galaxy, just as all the history that has unfolded within my House, and in view of it, is at one with life as it continues to be lived today. If you leave out the people who for thousands of years came and went here, you could say work on my House began about 1175. It has not stopped yet.

My House sits on the summit of the Lauzerte mountain. Its topmost crag protrudes into the back of my Cave, as wine cellars are called in France Profound, behind racks and racks of our local oenological pride and joy, Cahors wine. Cahors wine reaches its perfection after eight years. You should never drink it before then, but thanks to my Cave's constant temperature and gentle air circulation, wines drunk after twenty, even thirty years have the elegance of a stylish dowager. The crag behind the wine racks explains why this House and the town around it exist.

From a mountaintop like this one you can scan the heavens. You also can keep watch on the surrounding countryside. Provided its summit is broad enough, you can construct a town atop it. Century after century, its inhabitants will personify, and at times, epitomize the age.

Chronologically, the history of my House begins at the bottom, but in order to appreciate where and why my House came to be where it is, you must start at the top. The narrow ground floor entry hall leads you to its first astonishment. Halfway up that first dark flight of stairs you enter a realm flooded by light. I cannot forget the moment I first started climbing that staircase, my own private Jacob's Ladder. At that moment I understood: My life has taken me here.

Keep climbing that staircase. Don't stop until you cannot climb any more. Slide open the thermopane rolling glass doors, and go outside. You first will notice the large, red-tiled turret on a neighboring house. The soldiery of the Plantagenet kings of England occupied that turret in 1291. It held German POWs in 1945. Beyond, dulcet France spreads on and on, until it isn't France anymore. On a brilliant afternoon, with that high Watteau sky speckled with those Fragonard clouds that make the skies of France so engrossing, the view extends all the way to Spain. The peaks of the Pyrénées Mountains, one hundred miles to the south, stretch along the far horizon like the jagged teeth of an old, long saw, the kind used to fell the gigantic timbers that hold aloft my House.

Each mountain has its own profile, individualistic as the profiles of the old peasants who, every Saturday at the market, provide me with the finest plums, the most succulent pears, the most irresistible apricots, all depending on the season, of course. Some of those mountains, like Pic du Midi, I know by name. Others, even though I don't know their names, are as familiar to me as the faces of people I see every week at the Saturday market. I'd be disconcerted if one day I looked, and they weren't there. On exceptionally clear days you can see where Andorra is, cupped between France and Spain, though most of the time that great mountain range is only an indistinct smudge. Even when the sky is cloudless, the Pyrénées hide behind a vaporous curtain of air that, having circulated across the North Atlantic, piles up against that immense, long wall of rock. Then the wind shifts. Not expecting it, I look up from my desk. The mountains shimmer in plain view. Local wisdom states that the day after you see the Pyrénées it will rain, so when I do see the Pyrénées I know I don't need to water the herbs, plants, and flowering trees flourishing there at the Top of the House, leaning on their ledges toward the Sun.

Many lessons are to be gleaned from studying that beautiful view. One revelation is that nothing is ever perfect. Whatever the weather, most days a pair of clouds billows on the horizon, only they're not clouds. They're funnels of steam ascending from the two nuclear towers which, rising above the intervening mountain ridges like gigantic milk bottles, intrude smack-dab into the middle of the idyllic vista I just described. The electricity those reactors generate lights my house and runs my computers. It keeps me connected with the farthest places on this globe. Those same reactors, twenty-seven kilometers distant, also could kill me, and but for two kilometers, no one would bother to help. "Twenty-seven kilometers! Good for you!" an amiable French physicist remarked, upon hearing how far my House was from those reactors. "In case of melt-down," he explained, "we assume everyone less than twenty-five kilometers away will be dead."

My view of the Pyrénées demonstrates how persistently geographical determinism, whatever the passing fads of historicism, shapes our lives. The Pyrénées are not dramatic. They do not assail the heavens as the Alps do. Long and regular, they form a high wall stretching from the Atlantic to the Mediterranean. The existence of that natural barrier helps explain why, when tourists from Spain show up in the Square in front of my House, French people ask me to translate for them. Because of those mountains, the vulgates of the same Latin they both once spoke diverged into different languages. Comparing those European mountain ranges demonstrates how the shape as well as the size of geographical features counts when it comes to human organization. Unlike the Pyrénées, the Alps are a jumble of mountains, hence the cultural-linguistic jumble you find there, epitomized by Switzerland. The regularity of the Pyrénées has helped to produce two separate states, France and Spain, on their separate sides of that mountain wall. As the afternoon fades, and then the sunset shrinks to a vivid red band tracing the hilltops, I can see individual branches on each tree on each distant ridge—or rather I see the shapes of those branches, backlit by the last of the red sunset. "Red sky at night, shepherd's delight," I remind

myself, anticipating another meteorologically glorious to-
morrow. I first heard about that handy forecasting tool from
my father, though being a master mariner he said, "Red sky at
night, sailor's delight." The paleolithic humans who roamed
this area some 20,000 years ago, creating the marvelous cave
art that stuns the world today knew what my father knew. So
did Jesus. "When it is evening you say, 'It will be fair weather,
for the sky is red'; and in the morning, 'It will be foul weather
today, for the sky is red and threatening,'" He observed. Addressing the Pharisees, He then added (in Matthew 16:2–4):
"Hypocrites! You know how to discern the face of the sky, but
you cannot discern the signs of the times."

From the kitchen four flights below ascends the aroma of
guinea fowl simmering in homemade stock, so I turn to grab
some tarragon. This causes me to glance over my shoulder, up
and to the left. I discover anew that the Milky Way does not
flow. It surges across the sky! Tonight there is no need to focus
my giant brass telescope, dating back to Jules Verne's time, on
that distant wonder. The Milky Way is so perfectly in focus I
can see with my own eyes its differently colored dots and
smears of light.

The guinea fowl can wait a moment or two. After all, now
that you have climbed all the way to the Top of the House,
you will want to inspect the rest of it, starting with the Loft.
Big as a floor-through New York loft, its sloping ceiling soars
thirty feet high before swooping back down almost to floor
level on the front side of the House, the side overlooking the
Square. When I first started living here, sunlight streamed
right through the roof tiles, yet so artfully arranged were they
in the time-tested master artisan manner that not one rain-
drop could penetrate them, though heat and cold sure could.
Dust-encrusted walls concealed this old attic from the rest of
the House, and blocked the view, but even then, the might of
those ancient beams stunned me.

It was quite a production, tearing up that rough plank floor and dismantling those walls. Hardest of all was getting those giant slabs of thermopane glass, the cumulative size of a tennis court, up all those stairs. "In France," my master mason Dominique Darnière explained, "you buy insurance by the day for jobs like this one." The House would teach me the folly of seeking perfection. The House early on also taught me that everything you do produces unintended consequences. When I insulated the roof, a tremendous undertaking, I thought it would keep the Loft warm in winter, but its main benefit has turned out to be keeping it habitable in summer. Traditionally, people simply abandon their top floors during heat waves. Today that grungy grange is my sleek Loft, and I use it year-round. Where holes in the roof once were, light now streams through modern skylights. Blond wood flooring has replaced those old grey planks. You'll find a modern bathroom here, as you do now on all the four main floors of the House, a feature my French neighbors consider idiosyncratically American.

Should you someday entertain the dream of turning some ruin in France Profound into your dream house, keep in mind that Everything Costs Twice as Much and Takes Three Times as Long as initially estimated, unless you insist on rushing things. In that case it will cost you three times as much, and take twice as long. As the work progresses, take lots and lots of Before pictures. They will make your After pictures all the more gratifying. When—ooh and aahing—visitors say things like, "I never knew you were a designer," I tell them they've got it backwards. Over the decades the House has redesigned me.

I had no plans to turn all those ancient stone niches into bookshelves, but at our local junk sales—called *vide-greniers*, as in empty-your-attics—I found the great masterpieces of French literature were cheaper by the kilogram than onions. Mme de Lafayette and Mme de Sévigné? Georges Sand, Victor Hugo? Yours for pennies! Most of these cast-off volumes

I buy intending to read them someday. Others I bring home like ugly orphans. No one wants you? Okay, kid, come with me. There are books up and down the Great Staircase. Books also line the funny little staircase within the Staircase, which looks like Maurits Cornelis Escher installed it. It leads up to the Sleeping Cage, which perches atop a thirty-foot precipice. A careless dreamer could roll right off it but for the wooden slats that keep you safe from falling.

Right beneath the Sleeping Cage is my Philosophical Reflection Nook. There a plush red armchair awaits of the kind upon which royal courtesans repose in old Technicolor movies, so if upon the Great Staircase I espy some "quaint and curious volume of forgotten lore," I can stop there, and meditate upon its contents. After midnight, with the moon beyond the great Pyrénées-facing window skimming the tiled rooftops, it might be Edgar Allen Poe lost in thought there, but Poe never could have written "The Raven" here. He would have had to write "The Pigeons," a poem about a writer who keeps missing his deadlines because of their infernal clucking.

The Sleeping Cage and Philosophical Reflection Nook are but subsidiary features of the House's most dramatic space. The Atrium soars all the way up from the Green Room, so called because of its vivid green floor, to the Loft. Enveloped by this extraordinary indoor space you feel as though the sky came for a visit, and decided to stay. Among the paintings hanging in the Atrium is a mural-sized seascape I got in Moscow for five dollars in the frenzied final days of the Soviet Union. It depicts ships riding at anchor during a storm. Its splotchy waves, slashing rain, and streaky clouds turn this exercise in socialist realism, samizdat-style, into a clandestine tribute to Jackson Pollack.

In another triumph of unintended consequences, the Atrium over the decades has transformed itself into a Jungle. I've returned, on one occasion after an absence of more than two years, to find my unintended Jungle thriving because all forests have dry seasons, don't they? Today dozens of plants hang from rafters. Others perch on terracotta pedestals. Their tendrils reach down into giant old hand-blown repurposed wine vials. There their roots form fascinating subaqueous filigrees.

For centuries, this most special of all my House's special places wasn't part of the house at all. The Great Staircase started out as an outside ladderlike affair. What now is my atrium-art gallery-jungle was the rear courtyard leading to the village cloaca where the House's animal, vegetal, and human refuse was thrown. Then, during a spate of prosperity, its inhabitants extended the roof to cover what, until then, had been a courtyard.

The Red Salon of my House is located on what the French call the *premier étage*, Americans call the second story, and Italians call the *piano nobile*. The most formal room of the House, it is what my Boston grandmother would have called the front parlor. It offers the best views, in the same sense that orchestra seats at a Broadway or West End play do, of the human comedy constantly on display in the Place des Cornières. Sitting with a few select friends on the brocaded Louis XIII high-backed chairs we have drawn up to the windows of the Red Salon, one can imagine oneself to be a rich merchant, a powerful magistrate, or a scion of the regional nobility. We are gathered to watch a play being performed for our amusement below, in the Square, by wandering performers.

Back in Lauzerte's heyday, which ended with the French Revolution, rich merchants, powerful magistrates, and members of the local gentry did sit, on similar chairs, in this same room. Then, too, the rough-hewn ribaldry of the groundlings, jostling just beneath us, could have been heard as one and all waited for the performance to begin. The same plays are still being performed. Watching *The Miser*, or *Le Bourgeois Gentilhomme*, from the intimate vantage point of my own windows,

I experienced firsthand how the fun in the play comes from the way the quatrains let the audience know in advance what witticism is coming next. As soon as the first half of a couplet is declaimed, people start chuckling because they can see the next rhyme coming. They know what the exact word will be.

There is no better place to watch an opera than from the windows of my House. I have seen *Tosca* performed in New York, Miami, and London, but my favorite performance of Puccini's opera took place right beneath my windows in the Place des Cornières. The public toilet stood in for Scarpia's torture chamber. When Cavaradossi screamed, the terror echoed off the arcades. At the climax of the opera, Tosca jumped to her death from the funny upturned sculpture at the other side of the Square, the one my neighbors and friends, Jacques and Marielle Buchholtz, left as their legacy. Another time, an itinerant English theater company performed *Henry V* right where the English soldiery, back in 1291, slaughtered real-life people.

In French they call the ground floor the *rez de chaussée*— the place where you change your boots. I call it the Studio because, in the course of refurbishing the House, I turned the ground floor into a studio apartment. Initially it was meant to be used by guests. It still sometimes is, but it also serves as a refuge within a refuge, my place to get away from it all without leaving the house. During the most stifling nights of the worst heatwaves, it is still comfortable to sleep down there, where the old hardwood floor lies just above the cool stone of the mountain.

Sometimes I read there, or think there, motionless in the semidarkness. Then muffled sounds intervene. It is like listening to radio. The sounds speak so eloquently because down here in the *rez de chaussée* I cannot see the Square, even though it is just outside. The ground floor does have a set of large windows running the width of the House: I keep them boarded shut for the same reason I never have done anything with the dull paintwork on the exterior of the House. I like the idea of people walking past, never suspecting that inside this near-featureless exterior there might lurk situations different from what they suppose. Of course, that's an illusion, as privacy always is an illusion in a village like Lauzerte. *"L'américain habite ici,"* or some variant of it, is the phrase I hear most often as people walk past the house unaware of me listening, nearby. "Here is where the American lives."

Five levels down from the Loft we are back in the Cave, the very oldest part of the House. The practical artisans who built it, wasting nothing, used the stone they excavated to construct the upper parts of the House. That first phase of my House's structural evolution occurred some three hundred years before Columbus crossed the Atlantic, around the time Kublai Khan was emperor of China. The Cave's barrel-vaulted brick ceiling was installed by masons whose lord, Raymond VII, Count of Toulouse, played a crucial role certifying Lauzerte as a city. The great lintel of the kitchen fireplace was shouldered into place by soldiers of the Plantagenet kings of England. The Red Room's wannabe elegant décor was installed by yokel administrators of the Bourbon kings as they aped the fashions of faraway Versailles. The entry hall, with its Second Empire parquetry and Beaubourg-style exposed plumbing, combines Napoléon III floor boards with Pompidou Center pipes. Those exposed pipes, I explain to mystified French friends, are meant to be seen.

The Cinerama-sized looking glass in the Spa dates to the epoch of Louis Philippe, France's last king, who was overthrown in 1848. Its purple Las Vegas–style bathtub, the size of a sailboat, looks American. It actually came from a French bricolage store. *Bricolage* means Do It Yourself. It is one of those counter-stereotypical instances in which the French language is more, not less concise than English. The crystal chandelier in the Spa, though it looks French, is American. I got it from a street vendor holding it up for sale on lower Broadway, then disassembled it and transported it here in my hand baggage. In the Club Room the wrought iron chandelier, the size of a wagon wheel, is also American, which brings us to another helpful hint. Table lamps get smashed in transit, but once you disassemble a chandelier, you can fit its components safely inside a suitcase or two, then reassemble it when you get there, so go for chandeliers!

Rising every morning, I survey the Square in front of my House through Restoration windows. The old front door lock is Third Republic, which lasted from France's defeat by Germany in 1870 until its defeat by Germany in 1940. Some of my plumbing dates from the post–World War Two Fourth Republic. The electrical wiring chiefly belongs to the Fifth Republic De Gaulle-onward epoch, which began in 1958. In every waking moment, all the more so when I dream, the eternal themes of the universe and the latest local gossip are recombinant. History is today as well as yesterday, so up in the Loft I—not some long-gone noble—have been the historical agent of change. If, five hundred years from now, archaeologists take a look, they will discover that this House, which bore witness to the Crusades and to the French Revolution, was also shaped by the digital revolution.

The onward march of history, my House keeps demonstrating, never takes a rest. Just since I've been there, history has overtaken my fax machine. A historical milestone in its own right, it was one of the first three such devices in Lauzerte. The notary public, the bon vivant-restaurateur living catty-corner to my House, and I treasured our rolls of fax paper as though they were gilt-edge bonds. Today the fax machine is in the dust bin of history, which in my House is located under the table in the ground floor entry hall. An antique linen bed sheet hides the technological debris underneath it. This, according to my latest census, includes seven defunct computers. One of them is the shape and size of a portable sewing machine. Another has a holder for a telephone receiver. Someday, I periodically promise myself, there will be a market for computer antiques, and all that techno-junk will make me rich.

In the process of doing this and that around the House, twelve truckloads of debris were removed, not including the tons of muck excavated from the Cave. The unintended consequence of all this physical and historical disruption is a profound harmony, both of the whole and within the different elements that comprise it. Every special place within the House complements the others, making it seem—quite falsely—that these different spaces are timeless, that they never have changed and never will change. The secret of this harmony is that I always let the underlying structure of the House call the tune. Then I let each space sing.

Marveling at all my House has been, and has become, I more than once have found myself saying what Hamlet did: "I could be bounded in a nut shell and count myself a king of infinite space." My House all these years has been, to paraphrase the opening of *Moby Dick*, my university, the spaces within it its different faculties. The kitchen—guests gathered there around my six-foot-long Quercy farm table—has taught me more about human nature than any degree course in behavioral psychology. The Green Room with the Atrium soaring above it provided me with a case study in the nature of climate change. Another day as I climbed it, gasping for breath, the Great Staircase taught me a lesson those health warnings on the packets never had. I was killing myself with every cigarette I smoked.

Debris goes. Debris comes. One time I set out to take a census of the chairs in my House. There turned out to be sixty of them, including a monk's chair, a milk stool, and a bright-green tractor seat. Another time I composed a list of the countries of origin of all the stuff I've carted back here. I identified objects from some forty countries. In addition to that piece of the Berlin Wall I'd hammered off it in 1989, and some cluster bombs, defused, which I picked up on the Plain of Jars in Laos, was the Big Bird abstract sculpture I'd found while researching Jimi Hendrix's erstwhile haunts in Morocco. I was flying straight back to New York, so how to get my Big Bird, the size of a spinet piano, to Lauzerte? A resourceful and kindly French vacationer who was returning to France in his camping car dropped it off at the café on the same side of the Square as my House.

Months passed before little Mathew, the café's kid proprietor, figured out it was for me. Though I tried and tried, I never was able to contact the Frenchman, and thank him. All that remains of his *beau geste* is the constant, amiable, and vigilant presence of the bird itself. With the passage of the decades I have come to believe, almost, what everyone else seems to believe—that the bird, like everything else in my House, got here all by itself.

3

THE CONSTANT PROSCENIUM

My House is bifocal. Stand at the Top of the House, facing away from the Place des Cornières. Look to the Pyrénées. The immensity of history and the vastness of the universe display themselves. Then go inside. Stand at one of the windows facing in the opposite direction, onto the Square. You will find that the vista of the cosmos has been replaced by a microcosmic view of all the quondam, nutshell dramas that comprise the human condition. Maybe that helps explain why my inquiries concerning my House and the town around it shift ceaselessly from the infinite to the intimate, and back again.

The Place des Cornières is a stage, and all the men and women traversing it players—these bikers and acrobats, members of royalty and champion barbecuers, all and each of them having their exits and their entrances. The Square is also the turnstile of Lauzerte's festival cycle, so across the seasons my windows have provided front row seats for melon competitions, cabbage championships, firemen's reunions, dog shows, wine shows, junk sales, conventions of ceramicists, and black-robed Goths spitting fire. With the Place des Cornières my constant proscenium, I also have observed the unfolding feuds, infatuations, deceptions, lonelinesses, and snubs, the acts of generosity and joy as well as of pathos and spite that make up what Honoré de Balzac called the *Comédie Humaine*. Three times, the world's most famous bicycle race, the Tour de France, has zoomed through Lauzerte. The last time, on Thursday, 22 July 2022, the cyclists raced right up and over the mountain. There were so many of them, yet they pedaled so fast it was over in minutes, whereupon my phone started ringing. Excited friends were telephoning from America, My House was on TV!

One Sunday afternoon a family circus showed up in the Square: father, mother, two children, three donkeys. "Come one! Come all!" the paterfamilias implored through his megaphone. He wore a scraggly wig and a grubby tailcoat. As the highlight of the show, one of the donkeys stood atop a step stool, then stepped down. Those donkeys were portraits of patience as they waited for the scraggly-wigged man to give them the signal to go through their paces. Once finished, they stood there again, silent and still. Like shaggy statues they stood. Not one hair on their tall ears twitched.

The Lauzerte circus guy treated each donkey courteously. The woman with him was calm and cooperative as they reloaded their van, which was as dented as the props it carried. This French family did not at all resemble the somber circus families of Picasso's Blue Period, let alone the brutalized characters in Fellini's *La Strada*. With no notable signs of sadness, an apparently well-adjusted family traversed the French countryside, determined to put on a circus. The Place des Cornières was ready to provide them the needed proscenium, just as it has and does for all sorts of ironic, tragic, funny, and quotidian events.

The beautifully atmospheric Place des Cornières that I see from my windows is like the harmony and authenticity inside my House. The Square as it exists today is a recent concoction, reflecting the present's insistence on the past conforming to what it wants to imagine it was. Were that medieval-looking view from my House historically authentic, not a recent invention, I would be peering out at a graveyard or a dance hall, a place where chickens were slaughtered or at a gambling den, as well as the public pump. Before houses here got plumbing, this was where the women of the village, for two hours in the morning and two hours in the afternoon, were permitted to pump water from the municipal cistern.

The Square's most imposing edifice, the Church of St. Barthélémy, looks impervious to change. Its architecture demonstrates the opposite. At the time of the Saint Bartholomew's Day Massacre—beginning, but far from ending on Wednesday, 23 August 1572—a very different church stood there. If you know where to look, you can still detect its presence. A squat, much smaller Romanesque affair dating back to approximately 1250, the original church corresponds more or less to the transept of the church as it exists today. The great nave of the church dates only to 1654. Work on that seemingly ancient facade was not completed until 1815.

This superimposition of a neoclassical facade, an imposing bell tower and Notre Dame–style flying buttresses atop the original church provided a textbook case study of the present subsuming as opposed to obliterating the past. The church's incarnations help date my House's incarnations. That underlying half-timbering Dominique restored dates back to the House's first major refurbishment, around the time the old, smaller church was built some eight hundred years ago. The addition of the House's imposing Quercy stone facade was synchronous with the much later upgrading of the church and other houses around the square. That happened from 1650 onward, as Lauzerte gradually recovered from France's ruinous Wars of Religion and their aftermath.

The harmony of the Place des Cornières derives from its lack of uniformity. The house right next to mine is still half-timbered. It never got its Quercy stone facelift, so it gives an idea of how my House looked before it got its upgrade. This remarkable vestige of an earlier phase of Lauzerte's civic evolution provides the perfect rhythmic counterpoint to its neighbors. Especially when its window boxes burst full of the bright red geraniums my friend and neighbor Pierre Dessarts would display there every year, it is also the house where the tourists most love to have their selfies taken.

Life in medieval times was dreadful, an amalgam of disease, filth, ignorance, and violence. In the decades leading up to the year 1200, when local nobles first launched their scheme to turn the Lauzerte mountain into a town, humans lived better in China, in Persia, and in Mesoamerica. Civic brutality, regional butchery, religious massacre, and recurrent pandemics were rife, yet one by-product of the Industrial Revolution was nostalgia for a time that never existed. This was the idyllic pre-mechanical Europe of which, one way or another, Sir Walter Scott, Richard Wagner, Alexandre Dumas, and Walt Disney were coinventors. The Place des Cornières' "medieval" ambiance is but one manifestation of this much vaster reinvention. Its modern cobblestones, unweathered by time, were installed in 1986. The "medieval" streets leading up the mountain are a twenty-first-century addition.

The Square's very name is a recent invention. Until the Place des Cornières got its medieval-sounding name, everyone called it, simply, the Place du Marché: Market Square. Today Lauzerte's twin towers, rising just opposite my House, command the mountaintop like ancient sentries. Neither tower is medieval. America already was independent by the time the church tower was built. The other tower dates all the way back to 1955. It was built after World War Two in order to conceal the water tower installed here when Fourth Republic France began making it possible for people in places like Lauzerte to have flush toilets in their homes. Until then, people used the public toilets you still see around town.

Uncamouflaged, the new water tower would have looked just like the ugly water towers dominating townscapes from Saskatchewan to Madya Pradesh. Compounding the civic ungainliness was the old covered market that gave the Place du Marché its name. Meant like the water tower to update the place, it had, also like the water tower, a repulsive effect. For its real estate to be marketable, Lauzerte's civic authorities realized, they had to edit reality to create a pulchritudinous and inoffensive version of the past. Thanks to this process of prettification, the water tower was sheathed in that medieval-looking tower. Then the covered market was demolished, its concrete surface eventually replaced by those ancient-looking, brand new paving stones. Lauzerte's leaders announced that the Place du Marché was now the Place des Cornières, in reference to the arcades flanking the Square.

Back in the twelfth century, the town's promoters had proclaimed Lauzerte the perfect place to build a new life, yet ever since the Revolution, Lauzerte had been in decline. Now, with the twenty-first century beckoning, its notables launched a campaign to give the town a new lease on life by making it seem old. A notable success in this rebranding campaign came in 1988, when the town was classified as "One of the Most Beautiful Villages" in France. More than a slogan, it was an official classification. In France everything is officially classified, not just wine. The acquisition of this coveted status unleashed a process of permanent medievalization. In medieval times Lauzerte made do with mud tracks and gravel paths. When I first got there, Lauzerte still had perfectly serviceable blacktop streets, but competition is stiff. To hang on to your classification as one of France's Most Beautiful Villages, you need medieval-looking streets, and more of them! Among its most recent manifestations are those medieval-looking streets running up the mountain to the Square.

In addition to its status as one of France's Most Beautiful Villages, Lauzerte even more recently has acquired official recognition as a historic stop on the Pilgrimage Route to Santiago de Compostela, hundreds of miles distant, in Spain. On Lauzerte's websites the official logo of the Pilgrimage Route shares pride of place with the logo of the Most Beautiful Villages. At the town's public viewpoint, also recently reconstructed, citations from poems pilgrims supposedly composed have been cast in ceramic tile, and affixed to the adjacent walls. Nearby is "The Garden of the Pilgrims."

No pilgrims ever rested in that garden. It was created at the end of the twentieth century as a result of a local catastrophe. It was already starting to get dark on the winter afternoon of 13 February 1994 when, as Jean-Claude Martinez, president of the local historical society, later reported, "A huge noise disturbed the tranquility of the *Lauzertins* on this Sunday around 4:00 P.M." The broad plaza connecting the steep mountain path called the Barbacane with the entrance to the upper part of town, known as the Pont de Gandhillonne, collapsed. Tons of concrete and rock, as well as trees and benches, cascaded down the mountainside. Two giant boulders, the size of church altars, careened into my hillside garden, but just as Character Is Destiny, and There Is Always a Parking Space in Front of the Cathedral, in France Profound Things Do Not Necessarily, Inevitably Turn Out for the Worst. No one was injured or killed.

The collapse of this popular vantage point, offering by day magnificent views of the Lendou valley, and by night providing the venue for generations of romantic flirtations, was not so much as mentioned in the town's annual compendium of inevitably pleasant events. Four years later the scene of the most destructive avalanche in Lauzerte's history was front page news, though not even then was the avalanche mentioned.

The festivities instead celebrated Lauzerte's brand-new status as an ancient landmark on the Campostela pilgrimage route. Until that moment, no one had referred to pilgrims in connection with the place. It had simply not occurred to anyone, before then, to make such a claim.

In the course of examining documentary evidence going back to the eleventh century, the oldest references I found to Lauzerte being a stop on any pilgrimage route dated to 1985. That year only 690 people in the whole of Europe made the pilgrimage. One reason the custom had fallen so far out of favor for so long is that in the real as opposed to the imaginary past, walking all the way to Santiago was considered both arduous and a disgrace. Ecclesiastical tribunals imposed the trek as an act of penance. Lauzerte, Europe, and the world might be different today had not, in 1137, one of those penitents died in the course of his pilgrimage of atonement. This was William X, duke of Aquitaine, whose death made his fourteen-year-old daughter ruler of one of Europe's most pivotal realms. She would be in turn Queen of France and Queen of England, but everyone remembers her as Eleanor of Aquitaine. Lauzerte might not exist but for her.

The pilgrimage route to Campostela as it currently exists was invented by Generalissimo Francisco Franco's economic advisers. Following World War Two his regime set out to turn one of Europe's last fascist dictatorships into a holiday destination. In the new consumer age of packaged vacations, Spain's Mediterranean beaches were a natural sell, but what about the interior of the country? As one study notes, Franco "was raised in Galicia. To Franco," it adds, "St. James [Santiago] was a Spanish Nationalist," so resurrecting the pilgrimage route served the caudillo's ideological as well as economic objectives. Thanks to astute marketing and the emergence of the modern fitness craze, trekking to Campostela was transformed from something sinners had been made to do in the distant past into something the fit and the philosophical aspired to do on their next vacation.

When extended to the country's northern border, the pilgrimage route Franco's tourism authorities had reinvented allowed aspiring municipalities all over neighboring France, and then across Europe, to claim that, once upon a time, devout pilgrim throngs had passed through their towns en route to Spain, ergo today's pilgrims—whether jugglers, fitness freaks, camping enthusiasts, or sincere communicants—should come spend their money there too! This being France, the newly invented status must be regulated and registered, so Lauzerte sought and won confirmation of its official status as a halting place on the pilgrimage route, just as earlier it had in the Most Beautiful Villages program.

This falsification of the historical reality revealed a truth. In Lauzerte, as everywhere else, things are connected in ways that seem invisible until you take the trouble to look. Franco wanted to change. Lauzerte wanted to change. Europe was changing, so, much as in the age of the Crusades, a unifying myth was constructed that encompassed many different actions undertaken for a wide variety of motives. No book published before 1980 so much as mentioned the pilgrimage in connection with Lauzerte, nor did any town in France claim such an honor, yet today hundreds of thousands of trekkers believe they are continuing an unbroken tradition going back more than one thousand years.

This effort to recast Lauzerte in the image of the popular idea, as opposed to the historical reality of a medieval town, achieved apotheosis that afternoon in 2022 when the Tour de France swept through town. Thanks to the newly introduced use of drones, the television coverage was stunningly evocative. As the racers pumped their way to the top of Lauzerte, viewers were provided a strong sense of the topographical reality of the place. There on TV, a global audience was informed, correctly, that Lauzerte's charter had been issued in 1241 by the Count of Toulouse. Its twin towers were praised, only half-correctly, for their grace and authenticity. The enduring antiquity of the Place des Cornières was noted appreciatively and incorrectly. This *tour d'horizon* culminated in the fictional revelation that Lauzerte was not merely one of the most beautiful villages in France, it was an "important stop on the pilgrimage route to Campostela." Hundreds of millions of people around the world—forty million in France alone—now knew it for sure: Lauzerte was not just any stop. It was an important stop on the mythical pilgrimage route even though, even now, dozens of other towns were traversed by more or less the same number of backpackers every summer.

Not everything in Lauzerte is of such recent refabrication. Our genuine original Louis XIII parking lot does date back to the reign of that seventeenth-century monarch. The parking area's name—the Place du Château—hints at the reason for its existence. The fortification was the focus of Lauzerte's existence until 1614, when Louis XIII ordained that the Lauzerte château, along with all other such redoubts, "be razed and demolished; even ancient walls shall be destroyed," he ordained. Louis XIII had especial reason to crush resistance in the Lauzerte area. Nearby Montauban would humiliate the young king when its Protestant defenders successfully defied his siege of that city in 1621. He had better luck the following year in Lauzerte. In June 1622 some seven thousand royal troops, backed by five cannons and four artillery pieces, seized control of Lauzerte, and drove out its Protestants. The unintended consequence of Montauban's successful resistance was that eight years later Louis XIII, this time opting for guile as opposed to violence, would eradicate Protestant power in Montauban as well as Lauzerte.

The debris of a demolished castle might not suffice to fill up the Cave of the Sénéchaussées, so called because, starting some seven hundred years ago, it became the headquarters of Lauzerte's *seneschals*. That word usually is translated as bailiffs, but these were not the kind of bailiffs who repossess cars or eject rowdies from court rooms. Local lords and notables, they had good reason for locating the town's administrative headquarters, constructed around 1350, atop Lauzerte's most capacious cavern. Back then, when most taxes were paid in kind, the cave afforded safe storage for the grains and wines the taxpayers provided. The cave had another use. The notables of the town secreted themselves down there when, periodically and variously, they needed to hide from brigands, looters, killers, Englishmen, and religious fanatics.

One authentic item in the Place des Cornières goes back far beyond medieval times, to the earliest presence of humans on the mountain. It antedates money, monotheism, and any suspicion that someday such a thing as France might exist. It is so enduring because it is not a physical object. It is an intellectual concept, though in every epoch, for tens of thousands of years, it has taken physical form. I am referring to the human understanding that the movements of the stars, including those of the sun, are predictable so long as you have some sort of yardstick—anything from a line of stones to a computer chip—to plot their progress. The space in front of my front door has served that purpose for millennia, and so also played its role in the ongoing saga of mankind's efforts to turn the universe to its own purposes by understanding it.

Long before Ptolemy tried to make sense of the heavens, people understood the importance of the links binding their own lives to the sun and the stars. Many thousands of years would pass before Einstein propounded the unity of space-time, but their life experiences already had taught them that if you don't heed the stars, both winter and summer can trick you and, if given the chance, kill you. They understood that they needed to navigate through time as well as grazing lands if they and their beasts and, later, their crops were not to perish in a world of false springs and deceptive autumns.

These primordial humans also knew that, having found the information they needed in the great almanac of the skies, they needed to mark it for future reference, so people used specific vantage points to align themselves with certain specific stars, including the sun. Like computer passcodes, these vantage points could take many forms. They could be the mouths of caves, or the junctions of rivers, or a gap between hilltops, such as the one opposite Lauzerte where the sun sets every summer solstice.

The lines paleolithic humans traced across the Lauzerte mountaintop in order to track the sun's annual progress vanished countless thousands of years ago, but the sun never stops tracing that line, nor have humans ever stopped inventing ways to track it. Lauzerte's current astral tracking device, located right outside my front door, takes the form of the arcades that give the Place des Cornières its name. To see what paleolithic people saw, all you need do is stand just outside my House, under the arcade, facing the square. Now look up at the arch to your right. Find the keystone in that arch. Next, look to your left. Run an imaginary line from the keystone of the arch on your right through the keystones of the arches to your left. Next, extend that line in the direction of the afternoon sun. Prolonged to the horizon, that line runs straight across the valley to the exact spot on the mountain ridge where every year, right on schedule, the sun sets when it's the longest day, the summer solstice.

I call it my year-dial. Eons ago, people used megaliths as well as natural features to locate themselves in the cosmos as the Earth, with them on it, rotated through the seasons of the year. Knowing that, they knew when it was necessary to reap, safe to sow. Today I use my Lauzerte year-dial to decide when it's time to plant basil on the Top of the House. Thanks to that enduring line the sun began tracing across the Lauzerte mountaintop long before history began, I don't need an almanac or a search engine. Every June, positioning myself beneath the vaulted arcade, using those keystones as the cross hairs, I track the sun as it glides unerringly, sunset after sunset, toward the solstice line. Finally, the sun sets exactly in line with the keystones.

This precision is all the more impressive because, with this one exception, all shapes are so irregular in Lauzerte. The solstice alignment, in contrast, is so precise that, weather permitting, this is the one and only sunset that casts no shadows inside the arcade in front of my House. The entire passage glows as the solar orb centers itself in the exact middle of those arches. It is very beautiful to see the cream-colored Quercy stone turning rose-colored as it absorbs the radiance of the sun. It is also intellectually fulfilling to watch the sun trace its celestial arc, drawing nearer and nearer, until finally it touches that imaginary line on the year-dial.

The next day the shadows will start to return. Almost imperceptibly at first, the days will keep getting shorter, yet in the depth of the winter dreariness my year-dial consoles me. The time will come again, it pledges, when the fields of flowering colza will cascade down the hillsides like bright yellow waterfalls, to be followed, when the heat arrives, by undulating oceans of yellow sunflowers that blaze so bright you want to put on sunglasses.

"Look! Look!" I call to the people in the square as, each solstice, the sun slides into its socket at the end of the line traced by the keystones. "Look to the Sun!" Some look. Most don't bother. The people at the cafés eye me tolerantly, then turn back to their lives. The American is always carrying on about something, isn't he? Like all the other anachronistic enhancements to the Place des Cornières, I have become part of the decor.

4

OF WASPS AND WOMBS

The best figs in life are free. At least they are for me. All summer long they ripen on the giant fig tree growing beside the swimming pool belonging to my friend Mme Nicole de Renzy, who lives on the Saint-Amans-de-Pellagal mountain across the Lendou valley from Lauzerte. By September the figs, initially pale green, have become brown on the outside, pink on the inside. They reach maximum succulence when the sexual similes become inescapable—pendulous and crinkly as a scrotum on the outside, rosy and smooth as a vagina inside the fruit. On hot early autumn afternoons, dripping wet from my swim, I devour them by the fistful. Tastiest are the ones so ripe they fall onto the brick walkway leading to Mme de Renzy's swimming pool. There they bake on the warm brick until I grab them and eat them.

Wasps swarm around me as they, too, feast on the figs. Naked, I brush them away. They never sting. We both know there is enough for us all. The figs I am enjoying are pollinated exclusively by these particular wasps. The wasps then feed exclusively on the figs they pollinate. Their symbiosis is an extreme example of what biologists call obligate mutualism. Each specific species of fig tree, including this one, is obligated to live with its own specific species of wasp, and vice versa. Otherwise, both die. In this evolutionary dance of death, the female blossoms of the fig tree emit an aroma so enticing it compels female wasps to burrow, suicidally, inside the emerging fruit. There the wasp both pollinates and lays the eggs inside the fruit that later will nourish a new generation of wasps—and delight my taste buds too. In the course of doing this, she also tears herself apart. It is a process, I gradually came to discover, that has its resonances with the historical melodramas, self-destructive and generative alike, that created Lauzerte.

They say past is prologue, but once my life in France Profound got underway, experience taught me that present and past run both ways. Spend one winter in Lauzerte and you will understand how, during the Wars of Religion, neighbor denounced neighbor. They were cold. They were angry. They were hungry. They had nothing else to do. Strip off the ex post facto prettified window dressing of Europe's past; it becomes clear Europe was a horrible place to live until not long ago. Only after World War Two, really, did the northwestern portion of the continent become a safe, healthy, and prosperous place for great numbers of people to live for more than a generation or two. My dear friend Nicole de Renzy—she of the wasps, figs, and swimming pool—exemplifies how very contingent life in Europe was until recently.

One hot summer day, while sipping fizzy water on her back porch, Nicole told me the story of how death crept up on her when she was so young she scarcely knew what a kiss was. Then, after coming so close she could feel its breath upon her, death turned away, to embrace another girl. It happened during Europe's last great general bloodletting, World War Two. "I was seventeen," she remembered, "when they took her, not me." In the village where she'd been sent for safety's sake after the fall of France in June 1940, some partisans heard the newcomer speaking with a funny accent. They decided to kill her. The town's mayor pleaded with them to understand that Nicole belonged to a local family in spite of her Paris accent. She only glimpsed once the girl they killed instead of her. She was riding a bicycle. "She was the prettiest thing you ever saw," Nicole remembered. "They grabbed her and killed her just like that." Partisans, not Nazi collaborators, killed her. "I think she was Jewish. She had fled the Germans and now she was killed by their enemies. They said she had an accent, so that made her a spy."

It was gray and November when Nicole described the story of how she and one of her daughters traversed Europe and most of the Middle East in the family's Volvo station wagon. Following the routes the Crusaders took, they drove from Kent almost to Dubai. Some four thousand miles they drove—across Belgium, Germany, Austria, as well as the now-defunct Czechoslovakia and the now-sundered Yugoslavia, into Bulgaria. Next, they traversed the entirety of Turkey. Then, diagonally, they crossed the immensity of Iran, which is the size of the United States east of the Mississippi minus New England. The two women traveled unescorted all that way, but when they reached the port of Bandar Abbas, they were forbidden to accompany their car on the dhow carrying it across the Persian Gulf. "It was fascinating watching them maneuver the car onto that little boat," Nicole recalled. "They said it was bad luck to sail with females on board." She and her daughter had to fly to Dubai, and meet their car there.

My friend Nicole, as she serenely approached her one-hundredth year, personified the defining philosophy of her native twentieth century, that is to say, existentialism, the modern incarnation of stoicism. In a world where the reasons some live and others die are equally absurd, reasoned existentialism's propounder Jean-Paul Sartre, what else are we the living to do, except go on living—as ethically, as honestly, as decently as we can, while we can? Certainly, that's what Nicole did, raising her family in places as far-flung as Sumatra and the Trucial States, in the process becoming the dowager regnant of a veritable dynasty, with some fourteen grandchildren and ten great-grandchildren at last count. One day, discussing reproduction, Mme de Renzy referred to her uterus using the third person. "It served its function," she remarked, as though judging a flower show.

The Lauzerte link to another notable female, who could have made the exact same remark, had occurred to me earlier, as Nicole first related her firsthand experience of the absurdities of war, and then again as she described her Volvo *hegira*. Now her latest comment once again turned my thoughts to the *grande dame* whose womb was the font of dynasties, and to this day still cuts quite a figure in these parts. I am referring to Eleanor of Aquitaine, who lived from 1122 to 1204. You'd think you could explore the origins of a town like Lauzerte without digging into what Eleanor of Aquitaine was up to more than eight hundred years ago. But, no, in order to understand how and why Lauzerte came into being, and how and why my House got to be there, one must trace the footsteps of that notorious lady nigh unto the Holy Sepulchre in Jerusalem, then back again to a dinky French town called Châlus.

Heiress to the vast Duchy of Aquitaine, which covered the southwest quadrant of France, Eleanor first married King Louis VII of France in 1137; she was only fourteen. Then, in 1154, she divorced him and married King Henry II of England, taking her immense inheritance with her. In her lifetime Eleanor was the most powerful, the wealthiest, and most famous woman on Earth. From puberty into her eighties, she was also an implacable historical protagonist, molding the present to her purposes and, yet more important, shaping the future. The dynastic complications she bequeathed provoked a Four Hundred Years War. Involving most of Europe at times, it pitted England and France against each other in a struggle that, on many levels, continues to this day.

The fatal die was cast in the summer of 1147 when Eleanor and her first husband, the French king, embarked on a journey covering much of the same territory Mme de Renzy traversed in her station wagon. It was the equivalent of traveling from Washington to Los Angeles by horse, mule, and oxcart through territory infested by brigands, assassins, conspirators, zealots, and disease. Their destination was fabled Jerusalem, seized by the Franks and other Western Christians in 1099, at the climax of the First Crusade. Long before they reached the Holy Land, the royal couple witnessed massacre, plague, and starvation. They barely eluded death.

Their horrific excursion poisoned, then doomed, this first of Eleanor's royal marriages. "They both hid their wrath as much as possible," the French monk and bibliographer Guillaume de Nangis later observed, "but at heart they had ever this outrage." At Antioch, today located in Turkey between Syria and the northeast cleft of the Mediterranean Sea, Eleanor announced the decision that would have baleful military, dynastic, and humanitarian consequences for the whole of Europe, while leading, inter alia, to the foundation of my French home town, Lauzerte, and the construction of the House where I now sit, writing this sentence.

She was leaving him, Eleanor informed the king of France. Eight days after their divorce, she married the French king's archenemy, the soon-to-become king of England, Henry Plantagenet. According to the Roman Catholic Church, divorce was a ticket to damnation, yet Eleanor terminated her marriage with no more inconvenience than, in a later time, American housewives undertook the long train ride to Reno, Nevada. The pope freed Eleanor from her French marriage on the genetically absurd grounds that her marriage was incestuous. To use a politer term, the pope ruled that her marriage was consanguineous, therefore invalid. While ruling their union never had been valid, the pope simultaneously proclaimed the two daughters born of this illegitimate union to be legitimate. Eleanor and Louis VII were third cousins, once removed. She was more closely related to her second husband, Henry II. Far from being avoided as dangerous and sinful, nominally incestuous marriage was popular when it came to royal match-making because consanguineous marriages made divorce so convenient when they failed to yield the required dynastic fruit. That consisted, as the posh idiom has it, of an heir and a spare, though in those days of recurring pestilence and constant sepsis, many spares were usually needed to secure dynastic continuity.

Eleanor's inheritance of the Duchy of Aquitaine illuminated another anomaly that would complicate European history right into the twenty-first century. This was the gratuitous illogicality and capricious inconsistency of Europe's dynastic inheritance laws. In Aquitaine, agnatic primogeniture prevailed. This meant that, absent a direct male heir, a female could inherit the duchy, as Eleanor did. In England, female inheritance of the throne was also possible, but dreaded. When William the Conqueror's granddaughter Matilda inherited the throne in 1141, the result was civil war and the emergence of a usurper king. This eighteen-year breakdown of civil authority, later known as The Anarchy, deepened the belief that a woman on the throne meant disaster, a notion that history would prove decidedly wrong. Three of England's longest-reigned and most successful sovereigns—Elizabeth I, Victoria, and Elizabeth II—would be women, yet not until 2015 was the British and Commonwealth law of succession changed so that the first-born inherited the crown, whether or not the infant had a penis.

When she married her second husband, Eleanor was almost thirty. In those times, by that age, many women's lives, along with their childbearing years, were ended. Eleanor's uterus was just beginning its extraordinary career. Having failed to produce the requisite male heir for Louis VII of France, she now bore Henry II of England five sons, also three daughters. Given the violence of the times, and above all the lack of sanitation, she needed those numbers. All but two of those eight, including four of her five sons, would be dead before she was. Her first-born son died in infancy. Next, Eleanor lost her second son, today remembered as Henry the Young King, even though his father outlived him, and he never reigned. This junior Henry was busy pillaging monasteries in order to get gold to finance the latest incestuous bloodletting when diarrhea overtook him.

"He cost me much, but I wish he had lived to cost me more," his father is reputed to have said. His mother tried to get the son who had been stealing gold chalices made a saint. Eleanor's third son was the vastly famous Richard the Lionheart, born in 1157 in Beaumont Palace, outside the north gate of Oxford. In an age that idealized warfare, Richard was the only son to actually die in or, rather, as a result of combat and, then, only under the most absurd of circumstances. Her fourth son Geoffrey II, Duke of Brittany, was playing at war when he was trampled to death while jousting, age twenty-seven, in 1186. Eleanor's fifth and last son, the only one to survive her, was John Lackland, more infamously remembered as King John.

Richard, later known as the Lionheart, refused absolutely to wed the first princess chosen to be his bride. This was Alys of France, daughter of none other than his mother's ex-husband, Louis VII, by a different wife. Explaining his refusal, Richard told a tale that might have made Oedipus blind himself. His own father, King Henry II, had ravaged the child Alys, Richard claimed, turning the son's prospective bride into his father's whore. Whether fact or fiction, Richard's story told a truth about one of history's most dysfunctional and influential dynasties. Eleanor, Henry, and their sons were caught in a psychodrama in which every kind of betrayal was possible, no boundaries respected. They were a family, Richard himself acknowledged, "which came from the devil and will return to the devil."

With their crimes and cruelties, they foreshadowed Europe's future. They also unleashed the tumult that would wring Lauzerte into existence.

5

FRYING PAN BOY

The Crusades launched in 1096 and 1145 were supposed to protect Christendom; instead they facilitated Islam's advance into Europe. Their assaults on their fellow Christians hastened the decline and eventually the fall to Muslim forces of Christian Byzantium. They did nothing to save Jerusalem for its Frankish overlords. By 1187 Jerusalem and its holy places had reverted to Muslim rule.

In 1190, forty-five years after his mother's fateful journey to the Holy Land, Richard set out on his own, even more catastrophic, Crusade. Imagining he could undo his predecessors' disasters, Richard aimed to retake Jerusalem from the fabled Muslim statesman, Saladin. Once the Christian cross replaced the Islamic crescent atop Jerusalem's Dome of the Rock, he intended to make himself master of Egypt and Syria. This misadventure turned out the same way Napoléon's later expedition to the pyramids would—ruinous and prophetic.

Eleanor had traveled overland. Richard embarked by sea for the Holy Land. It turned into quite an excursion. In one of her many forays into royal matchmaking, Eleanor had married her daughter Joan—Richard's sister—to the Norman king William II of Sicily. When he died, leaving Joan a childless widow, Tancred of Hauteville usurped the throne, imprisoned Joan, and confiscated her immense fortune, so in September 1190 Richard invaded Christian Sicily, then pillaged and burned Tancred's capital, the city of Messina. Finally, in March 1191, Tancred agreed to transfer nearly two-thirds of a ton of gold to the Plantagenet coffers in order to get rid of Richard. He allowed Joan to leave with him.

Devastating Sicily provided Richard no respite from his mother's attempts to get him married. Eleanor of Aquitaine had last visited Sicily more than forty years earlier, in 1149, when—presumed dead—she was cast ashore there returning from the Holy Land. In 1191 she arrived from the opposite direction, intent on orchestrating the equivalent of what today is called an intervention. Eager that Richard produce an heir before embarking on warfare in the Holy Land, Eleanor once again pressed on her son the necessity of marrying, though not to Alys. Richard's bride, instead, was to be an Iberian princess, Bérengère of Navarre.

The better to hem in her son, Eleanor had brought Bérengère with her on her months-long journey. Confronted with an offer he could not refuse, Richard equivocated. It was Lent, he argued, when marriage, like killing people, was forbidden. Boarding his males-only flagship, Richard took to the high seas. Chaperoned by Joan Plantagenet, Bérengère of Navarre followed in a different ship. Some seven months had passed since Richard set out on his Crusade. All he had done so far was kill Christians. More killing of Christians ensued at Cyprus. After ransacking the island and overthrowing its Byzantine ruler, Richard finally tied the knot with Bérengère in Limassol in May 1191, whereupon she was again placed aboard her now sister-in-law Joan's ship. Richard sailed separately.

Once Richard finally got to the Holy Land, the fighting unfolded at places familiar today as the Gaza Strip and the West Bank. Back then the Crusaders gave them names like the County of Tripoli, the Principality of Antioch, and, most redolent of the European-style destiny they imagined they could impose on such places, the Kingdom of Jerusalem.

Whatever the labels, these places and their inhabitants had been stymieing invaders and occupiers long before Richard got there, just as they would go on doing for ages to come.

As usual at the onset of such misadventures, victory at first seemed to glimmer just within reach, a mere matter of running up the body counts. After one of his assaults, Richard force-marched three thousand prisoners to a hill outside the port city of Acre. He chose that location so that Saladin and his troops, encamped nearby, would see everything. "On reaching the middle of the plain," one of Saladin's nobles reported, Richard "ordered all the Musulman prisoners, whose martyrdom God had decreed for this day, to be brought before him. They numbered more than three thousand and were all bound with ropes. The Franks then flung themselves upon them all at once and massacred them with sword and lance in cold blood." It took a long time; many prisoners were forced to watch others being killed for hours until their turns came. The mutilated bodies were left for Saladin's men to recover. "We were all wounded, either in our bodies or in our hearts," recalled the Kurdish jurist Bahā' ad-Dīn Yusuf ibn Rafi ibn Shaddād, who is remembered to this day for his richly detailed biography of Saladin.

Then as now, terrorism strengthened the adversary's will to resist as Richard's grand enterprise ground itself into dust, and pestilence, desertion, and, on occasion, actual combat took their toll. Twice he and his troops got within twelve miles of Jerusalem. Twice they turned back, lacking the strength to seize the city. Even if they could, how would they hold it? Another time, Richard the Lionheart got close enough to see with his own eyes Jerusalem's ramparts. He covered his face with his shield, so as to avoid the view that taunted all his pretensions.

Within months the warrior who had subdued Christian Sicily and broken Byzantine rule in Cyprus was pleading with

Saladin. Both sides "are bleeding to death, the country is utterly ruined and goods and lives have been sacrificed on both sides," Richard now admitted. "The time has come to stop this" but, he added, not until he got his hands on Jerusalem. "Jerusalem," Richard declared, "is for us an object of worship that we could not give up if there were only one of us left," not that Jerusalem was his to give or take. "Jerusalem," Saladin replied, "is even more sacred to us, for it is the place where our Prophet made his ascent into heaven." Saladin added an observation that eight and a half centuries later would gnaw at the heart of every Palestinian: "The land also was originally ours whereas you are recent arrivals and were able to take it over only as a result of the weakness of Muslims living there at the time."

In his eagerness to find any way out, Richard made one of the most bizarre proposals in the history of Middle East diplomacy. If Saladin's brother would marry his sister Joan, Richard suggested, they all could live happily ever after. In his desperation, the king of England had proposed the solution that still eludes peacemakers in the Middle East: the solution of love. In this case, it was the literal marriage of the opposing camps. What the pope, arbiter of all royal marriages and later, the Inquisition, would have made of this interfaith alliance, there is no way of knowing. We do know how Richard's sister Joan Plantagenet, the widowed queen of Sicily, reacted. She flew "into a towering rage," as one account puts it, "swearing she would never consent to being an infidel's wife."

At least, Richard pleaded, could Saladin please give him a splinter from the One True Cross? Saladin refused, though, as consolation, he informed Richard he was welcome to visit Jerusalem as a tourist, so long as he checked his sword at the gate. There was nothing notable about the offer, other than the humiliation accepting it would have inflicted on the Christian king. Visiting Jerusalem was a privilege its Muslim rulers regularly accorded to pilgrims of all religions. Many of

Richard's own soldiers took advantage of Saladin's invitation and visited Jerusalem before leaving the Holy Land.

By then Richard had become notorious for risking his life unnecessarily. In one battle, when Richard's horse was killed under him, Saladin sent him a replacement mount, and a spare. A king should not have to fight on foot, he remarked. Some 286 years before another English king named Richard, in Shakespeare's words, offered his kingdom for a horse, Richard I, unlike Richard III, got two horses, thanks to the chivalry of a Muslim. On 9 October 1192 Richard the Lionheart did what Napoléon would on 23 August 1799. Having lured thousands of his subjects to their deaths, and mired his allies in an unwinnable war, as well as inflicting enormous suffering on people who never harmed him, he abandoned his army, forsook his allies, and fled by boat across the Mediterranean.

Richard's Muslim adversaries had treated him with tact and respect. It was different with his fellow Christians. Shipwrecked at the head of the Adriatic, the king of England was first kidnapped by the duke of Austria, then handed over to the Holy Roman Emperor, who held him for ransom—a king's ransom. A pack train was needed to transport the treasure in silver coinage, amounting to more than twice England's annual revenues, which his mother extracted from Richard's English subjects in order to secure his release in 1194. By then, both friend and foe knew firsthand the havoc Richard unleashed wherever he ventured. "The devil is loose," the king of France warned John Lackland when he heard the news.

From his captivity in Germany dates the tale of Richard and Blondel de Nesle. This long-tressed troubadour was said to have followed his beloved captive king from castle to castle, singing love songs. Surviving accounts, as well as a modern sculpture erected near Dürnstein Castle where Richard was imprisoned, reflect the idea that Blondel had flowing locks so blonde and beautiful a Hollywood starlet might have envied them. Even after King Richard safely reached England, he refused to let his wife near him. Bérengère of Navarre remains the only queen regnant of England never to set foot in England.

The Plantagenets, one French scholar later remarked, were "a dreadful blood line, celebrated for its violence, its love of women, its inveterate betrayals of sons by fathers, fathers by sons, brothers by brothers." Richard was the embodiment of all his tumultuous family's traditions, except one. He did not share "its love of women." In 1191 and again in 1195 Richard was publicly condemned for what one analyst described as the "sin of sodomy." A hermit, it is recorded, rebuked Richard as follows: "Be thou mindful of the destruction of Sodom, and abstain from what is unlawful." Implicitly acknowledging the truth of the allegation, Richard now begged forgiveness; "receiving absolution, [he] took back his wife, whom for a long time he had not known, and putting away all illicit intercourse, he remained constant to his wife and the two became one flesh." No children issued from their cohabitation, though thereafter, at Richard's court in France, it was one of the local entertainments to watch them attending Sunday Mass together.

Less exalted families had feuds. The Plantagenets fought wars with each other as fate and circumstance picked them off, one by one. Abetted by his mother, Eleanor, Richard took up arms against his father, King Richard II, for the first time in 1173, at age fifteen. The Plantagenets' culminating family squabble erupted sixteen years later, in 1189. It centered on France Profound, including Lauzerte. This vast area, comprising Aquitaine and several important adjacent territories, including Quercy, was bigger and richer than England itself, yet the Plantagenets had no sovereign rights there. Only thanks to Henry marrying Eleanor, not through legitimate royal inheritance, had it fallen under their control. Meting out his French domains among his sons, Henry II had allotted Aquitaine along with Quercy to Richard, but following John Lackland's bitter complaints about his lack of land, the king changed his mind. He decided to take the region away from Richard, and give it to his youngest son.

Outraged at the prospect of losing a domain far dearer to him than England, Richard launched another war against his own father. Things went so disastrously for Henry that, forced to plead for a cease-fire, he was obliged to give his traitorous son the kiss of peace. "God grant that I die not until I have avenged myself on thee," Henry is said to have whispered into Richard's ear. His wish was not granted. Two days later, on 6 July 1189, Henry II, aged fifty-six, died while revising the Enemies List composed of those who had betrayed him. At the top of the list, now, was John Lackland, on whose behalf King Henry had suffered this final, most humiliating defeat. At the last moment, Henry's youngest and most treacherous son, switching sides, had betrayed his father too.

His two older brothers already being dead, and with his father now dead too, Richard inherited the crown of England, just as he would have had he not raised his sword against his own father. The vast lands that came with this inheritance stretched from the Netherlands to Spain, and from the Atlantic almost to Paris and Switzerland. The king of England's realm encompassed nearly half the entire kingdom of France.

There are destinies fated to unfold, also accidents waiting to happen. Both converged in Châlus, a town where, neither before nor since, has occurred an event as consequential as Richard's death turned out to be. By the time he was ransomed, Richard had been king for nearly five years. His Crusade had ended in catastrophe. England had been bankrupted, yet he was still in the prime of life, thirty-six years old. Experience urged him to beware, yet so careless was Richard of his own life that he wore no mail or armor that day he was fatally wounded. He was equally reckless with his soul. Ever short of money, Richard attacked Châlus castle because rumor had it, falsely, that a cache of Roman gold was secreted there. By attacking Châlus, Richard was committing a mortal sin—not by killing people, but because it was Lent, when such attacks, like marriage, were forbidden.

Had this danger-addicted monarch respected the Church's ban on killing people until the Resurrection had come and gone, the king of England would not have suffered such a silly death. Instead, as the chronicler Ralph of Coggeshall observed, he violated the same Lenten precept he had used to avoid marriage in Malta; "he devastated the . . . land with fire and sword, as though he did not know that arms should be laid aside during Lent, until at last he came to Châlus." Voltaire may have been wrong when he claimed history never repeats itself, but as events at Châlus proved, he had Richard right when he added, "Man always does."

The first time I saw Châlus I was returning to Lauzerte from Poitiers, storied capital of Eleanor's great realm, the Duchy of Aquitaine. Of all the tentacles connecting Lauzerte to history's greatest events and its most famous protagonists, none was more consequential when it came to Lauzerte's founding than the squiggle of tracks, fords, and mountain passes connecting it, via Poitiers, to the Royal Abbey of Fontevrault. Avoiding freeways, and even the highways, eager to see the land as Eleanor and Richard had seen it, I zigzagged on country lanes up and down the same mountain passes they had traversed. Where they saw sheep grazing on hillsides, I saw sheep grazing; where they crossed streams, I did too. Traversing such a landscape, you see with your own eyes how arduous it was making history back then. The journey that took me a full day on those twisty back lanes would have taken Richard the

Lionheart a week. A royal progress like those Eleanor of
Aquitaine undertook could take a month.

The death of Richard *Coeur de Lion*, as he is known in
French, was one of the emblematic events of a vicious and col-
orful epoch. To see Châlus castle up close is, as a result, to
experience major visual anticlimax, that is to say, to make you
burst out laughing. You find no portcullis there, only a cheap
metal gate with the kind of lock-and-key padlock available at
any hardware store. The mythically unbounded Richard the
Lionheart was felled while besieging fortifications that would
barely pass muster in a medieval theme park in the American
Sunbelt.

On 26 March 1199, the day Richard played Goliath, the
role of David was performed by a country boy with no military experience, aged twelve or so. Irony called the shots. The
king would die from a wound inflicted by one of his own arrows. Having none of his own, the boy collected and shot back
the spent arrows the king's archers rained down on the place.
One of them plunged deep into Richard's left shoulder. Trying to extract the projectile, his doctors shredded the king's
flesh like home cooks in Lauzerte making duck *rillettes*, which
consist of the shredded meat left on the carcass once the duck's
thighs and breasts are removed. As would be the case with such
other notables as Juan Ponce de León in Florida and President James Garfield, the wound did not kill Richard the Lionheart. Sepsis did.

For reasons that long had been the subject of dynastic
tittle-tattle, the Lionheart had produced no cubs. Eleanor's
fourth son, Geoffrey II, Duke of Brittany, would have succeeded Richard had he not been trampled to death while
jousting. At the time of Geoffrey's misadventure on horseback,
his wife Constance was newly with child. For seven months
and ten days—from 19 August 1186, the date of Geoffrey's
death, to 29 March 1187—Europe waited. Then, to the joy of

some and the resentment of others, a healthy son was born. They also had an older daughter. The better to ensure the legitimate succession—and to spite John Lackland and his ceaseless plotting—Richard had explicitly invested his nephew Arthur as his legal and rightful successor.

The most consequential event to unfold at Châlus was not Richard the Lionheart's death. It was what his mother, Eleanor of Aquitaine, did there just after he died. At age seventy-five, Queen Eleanor covered nearly one hundred fifty miles as she rushed to be by her wounded son's side. Earlier, she had rescued Richard from captivity in Germany, personally delivering the king's ransom. This time all she could do was watch him die, which after eleven days he did. Had Richard reigned another five or fifty years, that would not have changed the legitimate line of succession to the English crown. By explicit royal proclamation, as well as law and tradition, King Richard's nephew Prince Arthur was now, at age twelve, England's king. At least he should have been, had in this instance, as in so many others, Eleanor of Aquitaine not placed herself above the law, both the law of God and the dynastic laws of succession.

Determined that her sole remaining son, John Lackland, not her grandson Arthur, be the new king, Eleanor announced that with his last breath King Richard had named Lackland, the brother he hated most, as his successor. In blatant violation of the laws of primogeniture, she set aside the legitimate heir. She caused to be named king of England, and ruler of half of France, a vicious conspirator who remains England's most detested king. Even Shakespeare's vile hunchback, Richard III, has his apologists, not so King John. To this day there never has been another King John of England, so poisonous is the legacy of that name.

"A lion by an ant was slain," as one metaphor aptly had it. Having no knightly accouterments, Richard's killer, according to eye-witness accounts, used as a shield one of those iron casseroles you see in subterranean kitchens during guided tours of French châteaux. Richard the Lionheart was killed by a little boy with a frying pan! Eleanor left her son's entrails in Châlus. His corpse she carried back to her royal seat at Fontevrault. In a separate casket she carried her son's heart. Modern pathologists later examined the Lionheart's heart. The centuries, they found, had reduced it to a powder the color and consistency of instant coffee. Chemical analysis dispelled the myth that he had been poisoned, leaving intact the kid archer's status as the historical protagonist who changed the course of history.

Richard in reality was one of history's big losers. This poses the question of why the Lionheart is so lionized. As that *ne plus ultra* propagator of the English sense of superiority, *The Telegraph*, noted in 2015: "Richard the Lionheart remains a shining national hero, with a unique place in popular culture, a name every schoolchild repeats with conviction when asked for a great medieval English king. Richard inspires a misty reverence," yet his mother tongue, learned from Eleanor, was the *langue d'oc*, the language of southern France today called Occitan, as opposed to the *langue d'oïl*, the idiom of northern France. While a prisoner in Germany, Richard wrote poems in *langue d'oc*. His letters to his mother, pleading with her to hurry up with the money, he wrote in *langue d'oïl*. There is no record of this most "English" of kings speaking, let alone writing or conducting his kingly business, in English.

The myth of the Lionheart as the paradigm of the valorous English gentleman is, like many of Merrie Olde England's heroes and traditions, a by-product of the Victorian Era. Shakespeare, note well, never applied his literary burnishing brush to Richard. Poets like Spenser, Milton, Pope, Byron, Keats, and Tennyson never gave the Lionheart much shrift. Chaucer, writing much closer in time, did not so much as allude to him.

More than six hundred years after the Lionheart's self-annihilating assault at Châlus, Sir Walter Scott let loose upon the world his utterly romanticized fictional account of Richard's exploits, *The Talisman*. Published in 1825, the book's immense popularity would inspire generations of novels, plays, and Errol Flynn-genre movies.

This gallant, heroic, and imaginary version of Richard was also cast in bronze. Installed in 1867, a life-size statue of Richard on horseback, wielding a mighty sword, stands guard in front of Parliament to this day. Casting Richard, literally, as the protector of English liberty was doubly antihistorical. Parliament did not come into existence until long after Richard was dead. Had it existed, we know from how he approached the statecraft of his time, Richard would have striven to crush, not defend, Parliament's privileges. In other ways, the statue of Richard in front of Parliament turned out to be unintentionally revealing. Inspired by the fictionalizations of a Scotsman, the heroic statue of a king who spoke no English was created by an Italian, Count Pietro Carlo Giovanni Battista Marochetti. The day after the statue was first exhibited, at the behest of Prince Albert, a German, the tail fell off Richard's horse.

The bizarrest aspect of Richard's emergence as the perfect English patriot is that he hated England. "I would have sold London if I could find a buyer," he remarked, in order to replenish his perpetually emptying coffers. The stereotypical Anglophobe, he complained it rained too much there. Of his entire reign of nine years and nine months, Richard the Lionheart spent less than six months in England. This was less time than he spent in the Holy Land, or as a captive in Germany. Certainly not English, he also was in no sense "a thoroughbred Frenchman," as some in England have irritably complained.

Richard the Lionheart was like the colza blossoms and the sunflowers that, as the seasons pass, bedeck the hillsides I see from the Top of my House. He was the showy flower of a land the English never permanently conquered, but that the French ultimately would subdue. Had he not thrown away his life, Richard the Lionheart might have visited Lauzerte. Like so many English people today, he had close relations in the neighborhood by the time his character turned into his destiny at Châlus. The closest of these relations was his sister Joan. As an unintended consequence of the tumult the Plantagenets unleashed from Messina and Limassol to Acre and Châlus, the ex-queen of Sicily and proposed sister-in-law of Saladin turned out to have a very special relationship with Quercy, Lauzerte included. These borderlands between Aquitaine and Languedoc became part of her dowry when Eleanor of Aquitaine, whose intrigues never rested, married off this English princess for a second time, to the reigning Count of Toulouse.

In fulfillment of her dynastic reproductive responsibilities, Joan in 1197 literally gave birth to the ruler who figuratively would give birth to Lauzerte. By then Lauzerte already had begun transforming itself from a mountaintop into a human settlement resonating, as it still does, with the transformations and idiosyncrasies of its time.

6

IN BOUVINE'S UNSEEN WAKE

My excursion to Châlus introduced me to Frying Pan Boy. Seeking to understand how and why Lauzerte came into existence led me to encounter another remarkable personage. King Philip II of France was one of the most consequential protagonists in the history of England, yet like most people educated in the English language, I was ignorant of his importance until I started tracing the threads linking Lauzerte to the great events of European history. This time I had to go almost to Belgium to find out why this forgotten king was so important.

Having had only daughters by Eleanor, Louis VII had only daughters by his second wife. Like Henry Tudor later, he was third try lucky, in his case with Adela of Champagne. With the birth of a son in 1165, the French royal succession at long last was stabilized in the male line. Louis VII called his long-desired heir Philippe *Dieudonné*, the god-given. From birth, the boy bore the burden of redeeming his father's failures. Of them, Louis VII's greatest was his failure as a judge of character. Failing to judge Eleanor's character correctly, Louis VII had fooled himself into believing she would never remarry. Eleanor's surprise marriage to Henry of England, not her divorce from him, was the catastrophe that undid King Louis VII's kingship. By combining her lands in southwest France and his lands in northwest France, Eleanor and Henry created a network of territories so extensive that nineteenth-century historians fabricated an ex post facto name for it. They called it the Angevin Empire, though no one did at the time.

Redeeming the losses of his reign, and then transforming the kings of France into actual rulers of the kingdom of France, would be the epochal work of Louis VII's successors. He did not wait for biological inevitability for that struggle to begin. More than nine months before he died in 1180, in keeping with the old Frankish tradition, he had his son, by then fourteen, crowned co-king. The scene was set for a stupendous clash of wills and wits, in which Philip would vanquish every one of those much more famous English royals. Richard, John, along with the Plantagenet don, King Henry II, all would be bent to the young French king's will. His relationship to Eleanor of Aquitaine was the most fraught of them all. Unlike any of her sons, he would be a great king.

One curious aspect of power politics back then was how very little power French kings often had. Our idea of kingship is epitomized by an autocrat like Louis XIV, but that was hundreds of years into the future. At the time Philip II was crowned, he barely could call the surrounding fifty leagues his own. This powerlessness was demonstrated when Eleanor left Louis VII, taking her vast domain with her. At a stroke, the royal writ again was reduced to a squiggle of lands connecting parts of the Seine valley with parts of the Loire valley. Eleanor's marriage to Henry of England meant that the king of England, not the king of France, was now the most powerful sovereign in France.

The overarching objective of France's new boy-king was to undo the failures of his father, and then unite all the lands within the kingdom of France under the rule of the king of France. With the exception of lands in the east, today abutting Germany and Italy, the territory of the kingdom encompassed more or less what France does today, but by then the French kings' power over their kingdom had shriveled. As a result of the disintegration of royal power under feudalism, the king in Paris controlled less of the kingdom than many regional notables did. For even the most powerful of these potentates, that did not change the juridical reality. Both Eleanor's possessions as duchess of Aquitaine and Henry's possessions—in his capacity as duke of Normandy—indisputably lay within the kingdom of France, therefore were legally subject to the king. In political and military reality, they were for the moment defiantly independent, but under the kingship of Philippe *Dieudonné* that changed. Within fifteen years of John Lackland succeeding Richard as king of England, the Plantagenets were on the retreat, and France's young king was on the high road to achieving all he desired in both Normandy and Aquitaine. His key to success was his understanding that legality was not enough. To be successful, he understood, the king's authority must also rest on the force of arms and the power of money.

The progenitor of the modern nation-state, Philip II was the first French king to build a serious navy, the first to establish an elite corps of administrators. While other kings jousted, he restructured the royal administration. While other kings occupied themselves with stately progressions, Philip centered himself in Paris. With him, France started to become a web with Paris at its center. From boyhood into old age Philip was guided by a clear idea of what he aimed to accomplish. We know that from what he called himself as well as from what he did. Every one of his predecessors had called himself king of the Franks. Philip styled himself king of France. With that change of title, the ideology as well as the function of kingship changed, from a kind of tribal chieftainship, into a supreme civil office involving sovereignty over a specific, designated territory.

When he assumed the throne in 1180, Philip could summon no more than 250 knights, 250 horse sergeants, a hundred mounted crossbowmen, 133 crossbowmen, 2,000 foot sergeants, and 300 mercenaries. By 1214, he commanded 3,000 knights, 9,000 sergeants, 6,000 militiamen, and tens of thousands of foot soldiers. These forces were the manifestations of the underlying administrative and economic power he had built. Philip understood accountants win wars, because he understood no wars are won without money. He knew one well-placed spy could win more battles than a host of knights in shining armor. Centuries before Shakespeare wrote *Othello*, Philip II also understood what Iago did: The best way to destroy a man is to befriend him.

So adroit was his command of human nature that after less than ten years on the throne, Philip had enticed all of Henry II's sons to pledge fealty to him, the king of France. As his own flesh and blood tore away at his French domains, Henry himself was obliged to pay court, in person, to the French king. Though the 1188 parley at Tours was supposed to be a peace conference, it quickly assumed the appearance of a honeymoon—the two love birds being Richard, then thirty-one and soon to be king of England, and King Philip II of France, still only twenty-three. According to the *Annals* of Roger de Hoveden, Richard "remained with Philip, the King of France, who so honored him for so long that they ate every day at the same table and from the same dish, and at night their beds did not separate them." Hoveden added an observation concerning Richard's soon-to-be-vanquished father, Henry II, who was an eye witness to his son's relations with the enemy king. "They loved each other so much," he writes, "that the king of England was absolutely astonished at the passionate love between them."

When Eleanor caused John Lackland to be crowned following Richard's death, Philip found himself in the enviable position of being able to choose his principal enemy. Did he want as his rival on the throne of England the rightful Prince Arthur, an apparently healthy and intelligent twelve-year-old who, just as he had, would assume the throne on the cusp of manhood, with a lifetime of kingship before him? Or did he prefer his Enemy Number One to be a middle-aged incompetent whose weaknesses and venalities he already knew well? Philip bestowed his blessing on John Lackland, the usurper, not young Arthur. As one French historian points out, Philip understood John's "undulating nature, his native treachery and his falseness, and how those traits would work ceaselessly to the king of France's own advantage."

Philip did not have to wait long for John to blunder. In 1202, less than three years after succeeding Richard, King John ensnared himself in another of those recurring dynastic melodramas involving sex and seigneury. This one flowed from John's renunciation of his lawful wife, Countess Isabella of Gloucester, the better to marry the fifteen-year-old Countess Isabella of Angoulême. John's renunciation of his first wife was ecclesiastically dubious. His second bride had been pledged to another. Outraged, the jilted suitor appealed to the king of France. Springing his trap, the king of France summoned the king of England to present himself, in his capacity as his French vassal, so that he could adjudicate the dispute. John defied the summons.

In response, Philip used this act of insubordination as the pretext for audaciously declaring all the English king's French lands forfeit. Divvying up these vast territories, Philip claimed Normandy for himself, and reassigned John's other French lands to the rightful heir to the English throne, young Arthur. This act of largess ensured Arthur's doom. If allowed to take possession of such vast terrains, the boy would pose a mortal threat to John's kingship, so he caused his nephew Arthur, by then aged fifteen, to be imprisoned, then killed, apparently strangled to death.

Philip had gotten one of his two great English rivals in France to eliminate the other; within two years he had recaptured the whole of Normandy, first step in France's four-hundred-year struggle to rid itself of English usurpations. The future was visible in Philip's siege of the supposedly impregnable fortress of Château Gaillard, the gateway to Normandy, strategic nexus of the Plantagenet kings' holdings in northern France. It also was a monument to how Richard the Lionheart had squandered his talents as well as his life. Even had he never been king, he would have been renowned for the fortifications he designed. A masterpiece of military architecture, the Gaillard castle had been declared unbreachable, but every human adversary, as Philip well knew, has his fatal flaw. Every castle, he also knew, had its Achilles Heel.

Château Gaillard's turned out to be the cloaca of the fortress. Excrement could be seen oozing out of it. Follow those feces to their place of origin, Philip reasoned, and you could impale the Plantagenet soldiery where least expected. The significance was metaphorical as well as tactical. What greater counterpoint could there be to the supposed purity of medieval knighthood than *merde*-encrusted killers emerging from cesspits? The cloaca led to a chapel, whence Philip's sappers rushed Trojan Horse-style to throw open the castle gates to the French forces. In March 1204, less than two years after King John had defied King Philip's summons, Château Gaillard surrendered. By the end of the year, the whole of Normandy was lost. From Fontevrault Abbey, Eleanor watched as the wayward son she had placed on the throne of England lost the French lands he had inherited from his father.

Ten years after that overture victory, on Sunday, 27 July 1214, John's incompetence and Philip's relentlessness converged definitively near a village in extreme northern France called Bouvines. Philip owed his victory there to the same stamina and organization, tactical expertise and strategic insight that guided his peaceful endeavors. King John's cowardice and incompetence were also the French king's allies at

Bouvines. Ten years earlier John had left it to his underlings to lose Château Gaillard. This time too, he sequestered himself hundreds of miles away from the fighting.

Bouvines was a sign of the future, in which men marched to their deaths for king and country, rather than out of obligation to a feudal superior, or for religious reasons. Disregarding every dictum of chivalry, Philip summoned up forces that depended neither on the sword nor the cross for their power and legitimacy. At Bouvines, Philip's enemies outnumbered him by three-to-one, but knights and nobles were not the only ones to fight that day. Cobblers, carders, blacksmiths, and stone masons fought for Philip too. "On the French side," notes one historian, "this was undoubtedly the first time that the people's soldiers, and not just those of the military caste, participated in a pitched battle."

Unlike the royal troops, these forces drawn from the emerging bourgeoisie provided their own weapons. Unlike mercenaries, they fought for free. Also, these townsmen were far more numerous than members of the feudal aristocracy were. Some two thousand men from the Abbeville region joined the fight; a thousand came from Arras. The cities sent troops because, thanks to his revolutionary stewardship of the French state, Philip's cause had become the cause of modernity. As the outcome at Bouvines showed, a dynastic struggle between the Plantagenets and Capetians was starting to become a nationalist struggle, between England and France, more than a hundred years before the so-called Hundred Years' War began. Cities, harbingers and incubators of the future, were nationalism's natural allies.

For England, not just France, Bouvines was the most consequential military engagement since the Battle of Hastings, 138 years earlier. As a result of the French king's victory, according to one English academician, in 1215 "King John was forced by his barons to sign the Magna Carta." After fifteen years of John's brutality, incompetence, and demands for more money for more wars in France, "Bouvines was the last straw," according to another historian, "If John had won the battle, Magna Carta could have been avoided." "Without Bouvines there is no Magna Carta," added another expert on the epoch, "and all the British and American law that stems from that. It's a muddy field, the armies are small, but everything depends on the struggle. [Bouvines was] one of the climactic moments of European history."

That debt English liberty owes to a French king helps explains why Bouvines was "the most important battle in English history that no one has ever heard of," as the BBC conceded in 2014, on the nine-hundredth anniversary of the battle. It was equally important for France, as one English blogger acknowledged after replaying the battle at a convention of war gamers. "Not only are we looking at . . . a massive expansion of the authority of the King of France," he observed, "we are looking at the geographical realization of what we can call modern France."

The English ignore his victories; the French gloss over the crimes Philip II committed. At the time of his accession, the royal revenues were less than half those the king of England received. He redressed this imbalance by seizing the wealth of the Jews. When women, children, and old people tried to flee his siege of Château Gaillard, he refused to let them escape. They starved while, heedless of their cries for succor, Philip pursued his attack, meticulously, right nearby. None endured the king's wrath longer than Philip's second wife Ingoborg, France's only Danish-born queen. By all accounts, Ingoborg was beautiful, willing, and virginal when, in 1193, she reached France following her arduous journey from the northern reaches of civilized Europe. Their marriage rites unfolded with the requisite pomp and solemnity. As the royal couple took leave, their courtiers' bawdy laughter provided an earthy counterpoint to the holy *Te Deums* chanted to bless the impending carnal fulfillment of their marriage contract.

No one was snickering the next morning, when the king proclaimed the marriage void. This Scandinavian maiden had provoked a rage-filled eruption of disgust, panic, and fear in her new husband, the king. Never again would he let her within reach of his person. For the rest of her life Ingoborg averred that, on that night which scarred them both so deeply, the marriage had been consummated, but what did an eighteen-year-old virgin know of such things? Some speculated she was deformed or diseased, but had there been some physical impediment, Philip would have included that in his claim that the marriage was invalid. He never made any such claim. He made it clear that his own sexual dysfunction was the problem.

Whatever the nature of his relations with Richard the Lionheart, Philip had no aversion to women. By his first wife, Isabella of Hainaut, who died in 1190 after giving birth to twin sons, who also died, Philip had a surviving son, the future King Louis VIII. While still legally married to Ingoborg, he bigamously wed Agnes of Merania. Before Agnes too died in childbirth, she bore the king another son as well as his only daughter.

It was the king's horror at the prospect of coitus with one particular woman that engendered his emotional venom. From the night of his marriage in 1193 to the time of his death thirty years later, the king of France swore he had been unable to consummate the marriage due to impotence caused by Ingoborg of Denmark because she was a witch. The allegation seems risible today, but in order to understand its plausibility, one must place this hysterical reaction in context. Since Philip, like most everybody back then, believed in witches, and since Philip, in his own eyes as well as those of his courtiers, could do no wrong, the explanation had to be that Ingoborg, like the

Jews, was a servant of the Devil. In order to avoid starvation, Ingoborg was obliged to sell her wedding trousseau.

Bested and beset by Philip of France, the kings of England lost Brittany as well as Normandy, bailiwick of William the Conqueror, font of Plantagenet legitimacy, wealth, and power. The northern half, approximately, of Eleanor's dower lands also was lost. One sizable chunk of France did remain under the control of England's kings. Centered on the port city of Bordeaux and adjacent to Spain, it was the part of Eleanor's realms farthest from England. Legally, linguistically, geographically, and culturally, this territory had absolutely nothing to do with England. The kings of England ruled there only through matrilineal descent from a French woman, yet it would remain "English" from the time of the Crusades almost until the time America was discovered. Though everyone called it Aquitaine, by then it no longer included the whole of Aquitaine as Eleanor inherited it. It did include Gascony, parts of Navarre, and what today we call the Basque Country.

It also included the fiefdom known as Quercy, including the subregion called Quercy blanc. The pleasing paleness of its building stone already giving the place a distinctive air, Lauzerte by then was all set to play its walk-on role in history. In the coming centuries, the great figures of the age would become implicated, one way or another, in the founding, then the havoc-strewn growth of Lauzerte as an actual city. In addition to the kings of France and the kings of England, the popes in faraway Rome would sow mayhem there too.

7

THE SLEEP OF REASON
PRODUCES MONSTERS

Today many people, the English especially, think of the French as a southern people. "The jungle begins at Calais," they tell each other, propagating a cultural as well as a climatic illusion. As it existed in the time of Philip II, in honor of his successes remembered today as Philippe-Auguste, France was a northern country. The Franks, like the Angles and Saxons, were Germans. Before the southern half of what today is France became French, the English would have to be expelled from Bordeaux and the rest of Aquitaine. Before that could happen, a second melodrama would unfold in the other great southern region—the one centered on Toulouse, as opposed to Bordeaux, facing the Mediterranean as opposed to the Atlantic. Here the main font of travails was not the king of England. It was the pope in Rome.

Philippe-Auguste bent kings and emperors to his will. He never managed to subdue the pope. This was because the pope in Rome wielded powers no merely political or military rival possessed. Only the pope had the power to save, and not save, souls from the dark forces infesting every venue of human life from the peasant's hovel to the king's bed chamber. The pope's spiritual power was enhanced by the fact that no consistent temporal counterbalance to his earthly power as yet existed.

The empires of Rome and Charlemagne were gone. The nation-state had not yet become the fundamental unit of geopolitics. Like pieces of an unfinished jigsaw puzzle, a menagerie of political and ecclesiastical entities—some big, many very small—covered the continent of Europe. On rare occasions those various pieces coalesced. More often, they splintered. It was as though history, bored with the play, periodically overturned the puzzle, once again scattering Europe's kingdoms, principalities, duchies, counties, republics, and bishoprics across the table.

Theoretically, Christian Europe mirrored the hierarchy of Heaven, with the pope in Rome the terrestrial equivalent of God on his heavenly throne. In actuality, Christian Europe had remade Heaven in the image and likeness of its own power politics. Ostensibly Christ's vicar on Earth, the pope was, as he remains to this day in the postage-stamp state of Vatican City, a terrestrial monarch, the papal lands waxing and waning with the times. As late as 1861, the Papal States covered much of central Italy. At other times, the pope's territorial domain shriveled. Realpolitik, not the state of the penitent's soul, decided who, according to papal decree, was sinner or saint. That explains why in one century the pope, at that time allied with France, granted the annulment of Louis VII's marriage to Eleanor. It also was why, centuries later, the pope refused to annul the marriage of Henry VIII in England. The papacy, strategically speaking, was in bed with Catherine of Aragon's Hapsburg kinsmen, both Spanish and Austrian, at the time.

Sometimes a puppet, always a player, the pope could cause kings to beg forgiveness with the mere threat of interdiction. Originally a spiritual sanction imposed on unrepentant sinners, the interdict—like the papacy itself—had become a political bludgeon. Though sinfulness is an individual matter, specific to each human soul, towns, principalities, whole kingdoms that displeased the pope were placed under interdict. Until the pope relented, infants were denied baptism. The dead were denied burial. Even more feared was the pope's power of excommunication. It condemned the faithful to eternal damnation in the afterlife, but its this-life consequences terrified kings and princes the most. They trembled because, by excommunicating a monarch or prince, the pope revoked their legitimacy. As a papal legate informed Count Raymond VI of Toulouse in 1208, "He who dispossesses you will be counted virtuous; he who strikes you dead will earn a blessing."

In January 1076 the pope excommunicated Henry IV, Holy Roman Emperor. This potentate was also king of the Germans, king of Italy, king of Burgundy, yet just one year later, in January 1077, the emperor stood barefoot in the snow in Canossa in northern Italy, where the pope then was residing. There he stood for three days, until at last the pope acknowledged his repentance. Some 860 years before Josef Stalin posed it, Canossa answered the question the Soviet dictator asked the future French Nazi collaborator, Pierre Laval, when they met in Moscow in 1935. How many divisions has the pope? With the submission of the Holy Roman emperor, a new metaphor for the mighty being brought low entered the power lexicon. So distasteful would Adolf Hitler find his encounters with the *duce* that the *führer* described his meetings with Benito Mussolini as his Canossa.

Among the pope's most perplexing powers was his power to perform—and refuse to perform—juridical miracles. Whatever the carnal ins and outs of it, Philip's marriage to Ingoborg was a nullity. The pope had annulled the marriage of Philip's own father, Louis VII, to Eleanor of Aquitaine. Even so, Pope Innocent III refused to annul Philip's marriage to the Danish bride whose physical presence so disgusted him. In the eyes of the Church, the king's true love, Agnes of Merania, died in sin, hence was doomed to eternal hell fire. It also meant that Philip's two children by Agnes were bastards—until the pope consented to work an especially intricate miracle. Over-turning the laws of logic as well as those of God, Innocent III legitimized Philip's children with Agnes, while still refusing to annul his marriage to Ingoborg.

Philip II, king of France, reigned from 1180 until 1223. Pope Innocent III reigned from 1198 to 1216, so during the prime of Philip's life, throughout the most crucial years of his kingship, this exigent pope was the French king's tormentor-in-chief. A ceaseless meddler in dynastic politics, Innocent III was also the instigator and doctrinal commander of the most infamous of all the Crusades. This was the brutal, foolish, and failed Fourth Crusade, launched in 1202. This time the Cru-saders did not bother to go to the Holy Land, preferring to devastate Christian Constantinople. This attack upon the seat of the pope's archrival, the Patriarch of Constantinople, Inno-cent III declared, was a simple matter of meting out divine justice. The Greeks merited the devastation visited upon them, he explained, because they had failed to support his crusade enthusiastically enough.

Christian crosses still on their chests, the pope's legions raped Christian nuns; they tore tombs open and altars apart in order to get at the gold and silver. The great lions at St. Mark's in Venice are among the booty seized during the Sack of Con-stantinople. "The spoils were so great that no one could tell you what the amount was in gold, silver, tableware, precious stones, samite, silk cloth, garments of vair, grey fur and er-mine," testified Geoffrey of Villehardouin, in his eyewitness account of *La Conquête de Constantinople*, which today is the oldest historical account in French prose (as opposed to verse) still in existence. This literary transformation from poetry into prose mirrored a moral as well as a cultural transforma-tion. Barbarism, viciousness, and greed had triumphed in the name of Christ. So had self-illusion. This "imperious multi-tude," as Edward Gibbon later observed, "mistook their rage for valor, their numbers for strength, and their fanaticism for the support and inspiration of Heaven."

How and why Christendom had come to turn upon itself so viciously was clarified nearly six hundred years after the Crusaders ransacked Constantinople, by America's John Quincy Adams. In "An Address . . . Celebrating the Anniversary of Independence, at the City of Washington on the Fourth of July 1821," he explained retroactively why the Crusades inflicted so much harm, first on the Holy Land, then on Byzantium, finally on Europe itself. Once America succumbed to the temptation, the future president foresaw, to go "abroad in search of monsters to destroy, she would involve herself, beyond the power of extrication, in all the wars of interest and intrigue, of individual avarice, envy, and ambition, which assume the colors and usurp the standard of freedom. The frontlet upon her brow would no longer beam with the ineffable splendor of freedom," Adams warned, "but in its stead would soon be substituted an imperial diadem, flashing in false and tarnished lustre the murky radiance of dominion and power."

Following that orotund preface, Adams hurled down his prescient warning, as valid for popes as it would be for presidents: "She might become the dictatress of the world: she would be no longer the ruler of her own spirit." As the Christian brutalities at Constantinople demonstrated, the Church no longer was the ruler of her own spirit. No one personified this better than Pope Innocent III himself. The spectacle of Christians slaughtering other Christians, far from dismaying this pontiff, opened up to him new horizons for propagating religious brutality. If Crusaders could kill Christians in Constantinople, he realized, they could be unleashed on victims much closer to home. The objects of the pope's ire thus became not the Muslims of Jerusalem nor the Byzantines of Constantinople. The simple folk of France Profound, he now decided, were "heretics."

In 1207 Innocent III wrote an uncharacteristically friendly letter to Philip II. "Let the strength of the crown and the misery of war bring them back to the truth," the pope urged. The king's reply provided early documentation of the continuing crucial role of irony in French bureaucratic discourse. "Let the Lord Pope find sufficient money and soldiers, and above all oblige the English to lay down their arms," the king replied, "and we'll see." Innocent III was trying to drag the king of France into a campaign of religious butchery because he had failed to get the local rulers, most notably the Counts of Toulouse, to impose papal supremacy on the people there.

The County of Toulouse at that time was to France and its future what Lombardy was to Italy, and Catalonia was to Spain. It was one of those considerable realms whose independence would not survive Europe's transformation into a continent of nation-states. The Counts of Toulouse—almost every one of them named Raymond—dispensed their own justice and imposed their own tariffs. They fought their own wars when and where they decided. Even more vexing to popes and kings alike, they refused to fight other people's wars for them. Lauzerte is one of many enduring marks these almost-forgotten protagonists left on history.

Count Raymond VI of Toulouse, one of his time's revelatory figures, was the France Profound figure who most excited the papal ire. His tolerant and productive policies, above all else his disinclination to kill his own people, evoked paroxysms of papal rage. A mere spark sufficed to set ablaze the pope's pent-up frustration. In both the Julian and Gregorian calendars, 14 January 1208 fell on a Sunday. Instead of devoting himself to prayerful introspection as custom required, the count spent that day being berated by Pope Innocent III's legates for his failure to persecute his own people. As mindful of his own weakness as he was of his enemies' strengths, the count's constant policy was to agree to whatever happened to be the latest demand thrust upon him, and then hope the problem would go away. As a modern historian would put it, "He would promise anything, but he would do nothing." The remonstrances that Sunday reached such a peak of vituperation that the pope's emissary, a Cistercian monk named Peter of Castelnau, took it upon himself to excommunicate the count right there and then.

The next morning Peter departed on muleback for Rome, intent on informing the pope of the count's continuing failure to do what he was told. That Monday, 15 January 1208, was the Feast of the Ass, a spin-off of the Feast of Fools earlier in the month. The pope's enforcer was seated upon his ass when parties unknown lanced him through the back. When news of the assassination of this troublesome cleric finally reached Rome, Innocent III happily and at long last had the pretext for the massacre of the innocents he craved. Surely now, he thought, the king of France would heed the pope's call to arms, yet as Philippe-Auguste evaluated the pope's message, the political and territorial implications of the papal summons to war riveted the king's attention.

Consequent to Raymond VI's supposed excommunication, the pope averred that the County of Toulouse was, dynastically, a no-man's land. This, according to the pope, opened it to seizure by such princes as would take it upon themselves to drive the count from power, and then enforce obedience to the pope's edicts. The king of France was having none of that. He recognized that the pope, by claiming the right to decide who was and was not the legitimate ruler in the County of Toulouse, was usurping his own rights there. "As to the matter of your declaring the count's territory open to seizure," the king replied, "I must tell you that I have been advised by learned and eminent men that you cannot legally do this until he is condemned for heresy." He added: "So far you have not told us that the count has been condemned." The king of France knew the assassinated Peter of Castelnau's excommunication of the Count of Toulouse was invalid; so did the pope. Even should the count be condemned officially as a heretic, Philip added, that still would give no one the right to seize Raymond's lands on the pope's say-so. "When he is so condemned," the king informed the pontiff, "you should clearly indicate it and request me to declare the territory open to seizure, since it belongs to my domain."

To the pope's vexations with the Count of Toulouse now was added the irony-tinctured disobedience of the king of France, but kings and counts were not the only ones the pope could summon to the slaughter. Freelance killers abounded at that time in Europe's castle-speckled countryside. Violence was so pervasive because, beneath its supposedly rigid hierarchical order, it was a time abounding with angry men eager to kill. Crusading was the most desirable form of violence because it fulfilled "the desire to show one's skill and courage in armed combat, [and] the desire to gain fame among one's peers. Every young man of good family . . . felt the urge to go on a crusade." Not only the high born were so driven. Whenever they could, whatever the pretext, people of all stations threw down their plows, abandoned their families, and escaped their debts by thronging off to some new "crusade."

Like the Sack of Constantinople, these "crusades" had little and often nothing to do with their stated theocratical goals. The main achievement of the Paupers' Crusade, launched in 1096 was the massacre of some ten thousand Jews in the Rhineland. No one got beyond the future French Riviera in the course of the Children's Crusade, begun in 1212. His followers believed that Young Stephen, as the crusade's adolescent leader was called, carried a letter to King Philip from Jesus. Adept as always at crisis management, the king again made a show of consulting "learned and eminent men." Then, without arresting anyone, he sent the lad and his followers on to their doom. A short time later Stephen vanished from history after he tried, and failed, to part the sea at Marseilles.

In such times mythology synthesizes the real-life dreads stalking humanity. That happened around 1284, when these recurring spates of gratuitous mass violence gave rise to the story of the Pied Piper. Linking the factual and the apocryphal in all these instances was the belief that great evil had been done, and that the normal mechanisms of Church and State failed to correct it. Ergo, it was up to special individuals to right what was wrong. Jerusalem has been stolen! The Holy Cross was in infidel hands. The evil burghers of Hamelin have refused to pay Peter for ridding their town of rats! The solution was the same in both instances. The Pied Piper, like the popes, sent his children on a Mad Hatter's pilgrimage. In both history and myth, they marched joyously to their doom.

As clerics and killers responded to the pope's new appeal to join his crusade against heresy, this time inside Europe itself, an inconvenient question reasserted itself. What constituted heresy? Who was a heretic? Thousands of books have been written about what only centuries later came to be called the "Albigensian Heresy" and its supposed adherents, today remembered as "Cathars." One thing is for sure. Not a single one of these souls whose lives were taken in the name of combating heresy ever heard of such a thing as the Albigensian Heresy. These people never thought of themselves as Cathars. The Albigensian Heresy, like the Angevin Empire, was a term invented long after both "heretics" and those who persecuted them were gone. As even many of their persecutors acknowledged, the pope's latest victims thought of themselves as good Christians who in their poverty and piety were imitating Christ Himself.

According to the currently prevailing version of the past, these "heretics" were followers of the ancient Persian mystic

Mani, but Mani's vast influence, like the medieval paving stones in front of my House, is a modern construction. The "heretics" of France Profound did agree the world was an evil place, but there was no need to travel to Persia to find the origins of such convictions. A jaunt to Rome, philosophically speaking, would suffice. *De Miseria Condicionis Humane*, a Latin text of the time, expressed the disgust at material existence ascribed to the Cathars. *On the Wretchedness of the Human Condition* started by picking and poking at the human body—examining with gleeful horror its frailties, its lusts, its copulations, and excretions. Next, the book dealt with the absurdity of worldly pleasure, and the pointlessness of material ambition. The final panel of this dark triptych depicted what happened to the human corpse as it rots. No heretical preacher composed that exegesis of existential futility. *De Miseria Condicionis Humane* was written by Pope Innocent himself.

It also is true, as their persecutors claimed, that these "heretics" loathed and disrespected the Church hierarchy. In one contemporary statement typical of the beliefs attributed to the Albigensian Heresy, the bishops and priests of the Roman Catholic Church were derided as men "who will do anything for money. All of them, from the greatest to the least are zealous in avarice, lovers of gifts, seekers of rewards. [Because of] such men," it concluded, "the name of the Lord is blasphemed among the people." Although any "heretic" would have vouched for that statement, this too was written by Innocent III as he railed against the corruption infesting his own hierarchy.

As Innocent's own actions demonstrated, heresy is defined by its repressors, not by violation of any particular tenet or dogma. In 1209, even as Innocent III was launching his crusade, a passionate young cleric thrust himself into the pope's presence. Like the "heretics," this young idealist preached humility and self-abnegation. Like them, he scorned wealth and self-preferment, but before founding a religious order whose members would practice the same life of poverty and abnegation the heretical "perfects," or holy men did, this young cleric begged for Innocent III's permission. Since this ascetic had knelt to the pontiff, the pope agreed to his request. Since he vowed to obey the pope, the cleric today remembered as Saint Francis of Assisi was not labeled a "heretic." Neither the corrupt clerics he denounced nor the saintly founder of the Franciscans whose efforts he blessed were heretics, in Innocent's eyes, because they accepted his authority. They obeyed him.

Two representations of Innocent III, both made during his lifetime, show him to have had reddish hair with blond highlights, and dark blue eyes. These early depictions, as if acknowledging his crimes, show no halo. When, shortly after his death, Innocent III appeared in a vision to St. Lutgardis of Aywières, he was writhing in flames. "Alas!" he exclaimed to the Flemish nun. "It is terrible; and will last for centuries if you do not come to my assistance." The best-known version of this tale was related centuries later by Saint Robert Bellarmine, the Jesuit who bullied Galileo into recanting his discovery that the Earth revolves around the Sun. Innocent had explicitly proclaimed himself more powerful than the planets. Centuries later his successors were still pretending that they were masters of the stars as well as all things on Earth, no matter what Galileo saw through his telescope.

Across the centuries artists have striven to portray the papacy's murky obsession with dominion and power. Raphael's portrait of Pope Julius II, painted around 1512, Giorgio Vasari observed, "was so lifelike and true it frightened everyone who saw it," "*È troppo vero!* It's too true," Pope Innocent X is said to have exclaimed a century later, when the portrait Diego Velázquez painted of him was unveiled. For nearly two hundred years, this depiction of autocracy incarnate was kept hidden from public view.

Not even the masters of the Renaissance better depicted the stomach-churning spiritual consequences of the Roman Catholic Church proclaiming itself dictatress of the universe than the irreligious, Ireland-born, postmodernist painter, Francis Bacon. The title of one of Goya's most disturbing works, "The Sleep of Reason Produces Monsters" created circa 1798, aptly describes the "Screaming Popes" series of paintings that Bacon created a century and a half later. Transforming the painterly conventions of religious piety into an idiom of depravity, Bacon did to art what Innocent III had done to religion. Step by step, these papal visages reveal the stages through which Pope Innocent III's monomania progressed: impatience, annoyance, vexation, hostility, frustration, hatred. Finally, he rages!

Each age reveals itself in the uses it puts to the past. Thanks to that knack kitsch has for exposing the empty dark essence of things, Innocent III in our own twenty-first century has resurfaced as a killer action toy. "Armed with his formidable power of excommunication and an intimidating scroll inscribed with Latin text, this . . . Pope will soon have all of your other action figures lining up for confession," read the online ad for a "6-inch tall, hard plastic model" of Innocent III. "Comes with removable Pope hat!" added the website Entertainment Earth. Priced at "$11.99"—the first full year of his papacy—the item sold out quickly.

8

CAEDITE EOS

Like Jerusalem and Constantinople, France Profound now fell
victim to the prevailing spiritual corruption, as the brutality
and moral poison that propelled the Crusades circulated back
into the body politic that spawned them.

In the summer heat of 1209, the horde gathered for the
kill. "From near and far they come," wrote the geomancer William of Tudela, "there be men from Auvergne and Burgundy,
France and Limousin; there be Germans, Poitevines, Gascons,
Rouergats, and Saintongese. Never did God make a scribe
who, whatsoever his pains, could set them all down in writing."
Eager to kill in the name of God, even more eager to loot and
rape on behalf of the pope, the legions of this latest and most
depraved of the Crusades mustered at Lyons. There the killers awaited the pope's order: "Forward then, Soldiers of
Christ!"

As it coursed down the gorges of the narrow Rhône valley, the defile of men eager to kill fellow Christians stretched
ten miles long. So twisty was the route that today it takes the
French high-speed train some two hours to traverse the 189
miles south from Lyons to the Mediterranean city of Montpellier. The TGV, which normally flies along at two hundred
miles an hour, must cut its speed by more than half. Back then,
the journey south took weeks—time enough for Count Raymond VI of Toulouse to undo the pope's crusade before it

began. The pope had wanted the king of France to command his invasion. By refusing, Philippe-Auguste created a power vacuum. Who would fill it? Real-life events constantly take twists and turns no fiction writer would dare put in a novel. This was one such moment. Raymond VI, Count of Toulouse, would be the real-life Pied Piper leading the pope's invaders astray. Singlehandedly this erstwhile heretic would transform the papal crusade, launched to destroy him, into a secular war that served his own interests.

In the vast tapestry we are currently contemplating, some figures may seem more sympathetic than they deserve. Remember the massacre at Acre when tempted to identify with Richard the Lionheart's gallantry. Think of the peaceable Jews Philippe-Auguste victimized. Morally and ethically, Count Raymond VI of Toulouse is a special case, truly worthy of our respect and sympathy. Historians deride him because he strove to avoid bloodshed, and when he could not prevent bloodshed, he deflected it. His motives, as conventionally portrayed, are made to seem mysterious as well as pusillanimous. "Raymond was one of those undecided and feeble characters," declared one nineteenth-century French historian. As if resolving a paradox, he added: "He wished to live in peace with the Church without behaving cruelly to a large number of his subjects."

A twentieth-century French historian bestowed on the same Count Raymond VI the epithet "anti-hero." According to the chronicler Peter of Vaux-de-Cernay, who despised him, Raymond VI was "the count of cunning." Though his enemies accused him of every depravity, there is one deadly sin of which the Count of the Toulouse must be acquitted: Pride. This prince reveled in humiliation's embrace, the better to achieve his purposes. Beyond avoiding the crushing blow this very force was sent to inflict on him, his great strategic objective was no more or less than survival. He aimed to save his own life, the lives of his heirs, and of as many of his subjects as he could. The best way to achieve this, he understood, was not to stop the killers, but to deflect them, so Count Raymond rushed to orchestrate his own Canossa.

His ritual humiliation was staged on Thursday, 18 June 1209, in the Abbey of Saint-Gilles. This was in the same town, right near the Rhône River, where the count and Peter of Castelnau had their final stormy, confrontation. There the cleric had been interred after being lanced through the back. In another manifestation of the pervasive role of irony, the ceremony of ritual humiliation the Count of Toulouse underwent was called "Reconciliation." Peter of Vaux-de-Cernay, a young cleric violently opposed to "heresy" and all who condoned it, described the scene with evident delight. First, the Count of Toulouse was "led naked to the doors of the church. There in the presence of the legate and the archbishops and bishops (of whom more than twenty had gathered for the ceremony), he swore on the Body of Christ and on numerous relics of the Saints . . . that he would obey the commands of the Holy Roman Church in all matters." Next, so far as Peter of Vaux-de-Cernay was concerned, came the best part, as the papal legate raised his whip and "gave him absolution by scourging him."

More delights were to come; "after the count was scourged," the chronicler added, "he had to go down through the Crypt and pass, naked, by the tomb of the Blessed martyr, Brother Peter of Castelnau. How just a judgment of God!" rejoiced Peter of Vaux-de-Cernay. "The count was compelled to show reverence to the dead body of the man he had used so spitefully." Never a narrator to leave well enough alone, Vaux-de-Cernay added that the body of the blessed brother had shown itself impervious to material as well as spiritual corruption. "A marvelous perfume arose from his body," he informed the reader, as the Count of Toulouse—naked, flagellated, humiliated—was forced to pay reverence to his tormentor's cadaver. He made it seem the dead cleric's piety explained why his corpse smelled so sweet. In actuality, the "marvelous perfume" consisted of the same kinds of aromatics and chemicals also used to preserve the different parts of Richard the Lionheart's corpse.

Those lashes of the papal legate's whip, the documentation makes clear, served chiefly to stimulate the Count of Toulouse's circulation. "Lords, from now on there's vigor in my song!" Raymond VI declared following his naked romp. Having submitted to the papal legate's every demand, the Count of Toulouse asked one favor. Now that he once again was an obedient son of Holy Father the Pope, could he please join the Crusade too? Peter of Vaux-de-Cernay wasn't fooled: "After all these events, the count, displaying his usual cunning and fearful of the arrival of the Crusaders, asked the legate to bestow the Cross on him." To the chronicler's dismay, the legate agreed.

"Taking the cross," as it was called, turned every erstwhile apostate into a pope-authorized holy crusader. Whether one was an aristocrat with a Crusader's Cross that was made of silk, or a rustic knight with a Crusader's Cross made of home-spun wool, one of the many benefits accruing to this status was that other Crusaders were forbidden to loot your cities and pillage your lands. Peter of Vaux-de-Cernay could not believe that the pope's own legate could be so gullible. If his superiors would not tell the truth, then this passionate junior cleric would. "I declare the count a false and faithless Crusader," he thundered, "he took the Cross not to avenge the wrong done to the Crucifix, but to conceal and cover his wickedness."

Pride he may have lacked, but Raymond VI was no stranger to audacity. There was no time to lose! On 18 June 1209, the count underwent "Reconciliation." Only days later, right at the summer solstice, he was permitted to take the Cross. All day long, and into those summer nights when it seems the last sliver of daylight will never disappear, Raymond VI rushed north on horseback. The advancing throng was nearly halfway to the Mediterranean before the count intercepted the Crusaders at the old river town of Valence. There, Raymond VI, without resorting to violence, stopped in its tracks an advancing army bent on his own destruction.

Three-quarters of a millennium earlier, Pope Leo I had dissuaded Attila the Hun from sacking Rome. Not even he had assumed command of the invading army, as Raymond VI now did. With his habitual tact, he informed his brother Crusaders he was only there to help—to show them the best routes, to help them acquire suitable supplies and find convenient encampments. Thanks to this audacious maneuver, the count was able to deflect the vast throng assembled to destroy Toulouse, but to where and upon whom? At Montpellier the count's design became evident when his young kinsman and rival, Raymond-Roger Trencavel, Viscount of Beziers, rode posthaste into camp, alarmed that his spies might be right in telling him the pope's throng now intended to attack him and his citadels.

This was indeed true, for two reasons. First, Raymond-Roger of Beziers, young and proud, had spurned "Reconciliation." The much more important reason why, before long, the Viscount of Beziers would die in an underground dungeon, and even sooner, his proud namesake city would be the scene of Christian-on-Christian violence surpassing the horrors at Constantinople, was that the Crusaders had to pillage someplace. They had to massacre people somewhere. As Raymond VI well understood, if the Crusaders' bloodlust were not expended on some other victim, it surely would turn, once again, on him.

With Raymond-Roger of Beziers now the designated victim, the viscount's two main cities, Beziers and Carcassonne, replaced Toulouse as the targets of the Crusaders' rage and avarice. Beziers, the Crusaders' first objective, was five hundred years older than Paris. It had been a center of trade, learning, worship, and administration going back through Roman and Greek to Celtic times. For just as long it had been a thriving example of diversity, with Christians as well as non-Christians embracing a variety of philosophical regimes. No one thought of these freethinkers, ascetics, and reformers as "heretics" until the pope in faraway Rome started categorizing them as such.

Having forewarned the *Biterois*, as the townsfolk of Beziers were called, the young viscount dashed off to Carcassonne, promising to return as soon as he could raise a rescuing army. He took the entire Jewish community of Beziers with him. The viscount's good deed served his own interests; these people were far too valuable to his treasury to let them be slain by gangs of Christian killers, as Jews had been during other Crusades. The viscount's good deed also contextualizes the pope's rage at the failure of local rulers to persecute Christian "heretics." In an age of religious viciousness, a deep spirit of human toleration, extending beyond Christianity, was a characteristic of this region famed for its troubadours and courts of love. This spirit of tolerance and humanism, more than any specific belief or deed, doomed such people to papal persecution.

No Christians left Beziers with the viscount. It did not occur to them that the pope's killers would massacre fellow Christians, yet on the morning of Wednesday, 22 July 1209, the people of Beziers, looking down from their ramparts, saw that a mass of killers surrounded them. Relying on the libels and lies his spies were paid to manufacture, the new papal legate, Arnaud-Amaury, Abbot of Cîteaux, had prepared his Beziers enemies list. Exactly 222 names were on it. The Roman Catholic Abbot of Cîteaux then presented the Roman Catholic Bishop of Beziers with an ultimatum. Hand over these 222 "heretics," or the assault would begin. When the townsfolk refused to hand over their neighbors, the bishop abandoned his flock. He joined the killers as the people of the town, gathering inside their churches, prayed for their city's patron saint, Mary Magdalene, to save them.

Along with drought and pestilence, siege warfare was a familiar feature of life in those times. Provided your redoubt had stout walls, ample stores of food and, most important, sufficient sources of fresh water, the besieged often held the advantage. The time-tested strategy was to sit tight, letting disease, infighting, homesickness, and hunger defeat the besiegers. Such sieges best ended, so far as the besieged were concerned, not in some glorious battlefield triumph, but with the happy sight, one morning, of the rubbish left behind when the siege army gave up, and went home. The immensity of the force besieging Beziers made this approach all the more logical. The more mouths there were to feed, the sooner the besiegers would exhaust their own supplies, and those they looted in the surrounding countryside, allowing hunger to defeat them.

There was another reason for optimism. The papal legate delivered his ultimatum on the feast day of Beziers' patron saint, Mary Magdalene. Surely, she would protect them. That auspicious circumstance—along with the role testosterone plays at such sociobiologically pivotal moments—helps explain why, after rejecting the papal legate's ultimatum, some impetuous young men of the town went on the attack. At dawn they surged out of the town's eastern gate, waving banners and shouting imprecations. They killed one Crusader, captured another, threw him off a bridge, and then tore him apart. In their inexperience and enthusiasm, these youths imagined they could scare away the besiegers. Instead, as a contemporary account put it, "this unexpected attack . . . awoke the whole camp as a frightened swarm. The marauders, full of rage, shirt- or rag-clothed, without shoes but armed with pike, lever, mace," went on the attack. In their inexperience, the *Biterois* had not thought to close the eastern gate behind them. Resistance was fierce as the killers, counterattacking, pushed into the city, though not for long. As the citizens were forced back, the fight became a stampede and the stampede a slaughter; they "cut the throat of anyone, women, children, old men and even priests," according to one account. Mass looting ensued until finally the papal killers, like curs snarling over a cadaver, turned on each other as they fought over the loot.

As at Constantinople, the killers truly had done the pope's work. "Attack the followers of heresy even more fearlessly than the Saracens," Innocent III exhorted, "since they are even more evil." Proud of the carnage, the papal legate hastened to send Innocent III the good news. "Our men spared no one," he boasted, "irrespective of rank, sex or age, and put to the sword almost 20,000 people. After this great slaughter the whole city was despoiled and burnt." It was the victims' own fault, Peter of Vaux-de-Cernay explained. By rejecting the papal legate's ultimatum, the people of Beziers "chose to die as heretics rather than live as Christians." Some three hundred years would pass before the city of Beziers was completely restored. Repair work on the cathedral, within which a multitude of faithful Catholics were slain, would continue until 1932.

From the massacre at Beziers dates the papal motto, *Caedite eos. Novit enim Dominus qui sunt eius.* That dictum— "Kill them all: God will know His own"—was uttered by the pope's own legate, in answer to the great question Beziers posed. These "Crusaders" were there to kill heretics, but how to tell who was a heretic? It was natural to assume that those gathered in prayer inside the pope's own churches were faithful Christians, but the pope's legate was having none of that. When asked for theological guidance on whom to kill and whom to spare, the Abbot replied: "Kill them all: God will sort them out," as another translation has it. This use of violence for religious purposes, contrary to what we imagine today, was a recent development. Scholars have established that in the six hundred years from 600 to 1200 A.D., no more than six people, on average one a century, had been burned for heresy. What accounted for this newfound normalization of violence, the Count of Toulouse would have agreed, was the delusion that if violence did God's work thousands of miles away in the Holy Land, then violence could achieve God's purposes in Europe too.

Never one to learn from his mistakes, Pope Innocent III was in northern Italy, churning up yet another Crusade when death overtook him. The state of his corpse revealed how deep ran the hatred he had provoked. When the French theologian Jacques de Vitry went to look at the body, he found looters had stripped the pope's corpse of its jewels and costly garments. No one had bothered to embalm the body. Innocent's near-naked cadaver, Vitry related, stank. What shank and hair remained of him was not returned to the Vatican until 1891, as the papal "prisoners of the Vatican" cultivated a cult of papal infallibility to compensate for their vanished temporal powers.

Innocent III and his many imitators did their greatest harm to the future. As a result of the wanton mayhem he unleashed upon Christian Byzantium, the schism with Eastern Christianity, bred of Rome's pretension to spiritual hegemony and baptized in blood with the Sack of Constantinople, would permanently divide Europe, with echoes extending down to Cold War times. The blood feud with Islam he pursued continues to traumatize the Middle East and Europe. Just as the word "heretic" expressed and justified the Church's newly asserted right to kill whomever it chose, the word "crusade" epitomized and legitimated the belief that white, Western, Christian males were entitled to do whatever they deemed best to the whole Earth, regardless of the harm they did to others, or to the planet.

Pope Innocent III also did enormous harm to the Church itself. As the nineteenth-century French Protestant historian and statesman, François Guizot, would observe, the pope's attack on France Profound "did more than as much evil to the Catholics as to the heretics, and to the papacy as to freedom." This was, he explained, because the pope and his henchmen had been guided by "two principles equally false and fatal." These were "the denial of religious liberty to conscience, and of political independence to States." The slaughter at Beziers answered the questions of what a heretic is, and what is to be done with them, more than six hundred years before Fyodor Dostoevsky wrote "The Grand Inquisitor." As the pope's legate defined it, everyone and anyone—including, as Dostoevsky noted, Christ Himself—was a heretic if the bureaucrats of the soul decided so. The papal legate's line of reasoning was the same one Robespierre and Stalin and Hitler and Pol Pot among others would follow.

Everywhere you go in the former realms of the Counts of Toulouse, the landscape is so pleasant; people like to imagine only pleasant things could happen there. Because life in places like Lauzerte seems so disconnected from the world's travails, people also imagine nothing of transcendent historical import could happen there—certainly nothing of dire import for the whole human race. That too is myth. The papal massacre in France Profound was "one of the great pivotal moments in world history," observes the historian Mark Gregory Pegg. It was so pivotal because *Caedite Eos* set Europe on the road that would lead from Beziers to Auschwitz. The campaign to eradicate the "distinct Christian culture in the lands of the counts of Toulouse," Pegg explains, "led to an irrevocable moral obligation for mass murder;" it "ushered genocide into the West, changing forever what it meant to be Christian."

9

VULGARIUM NUMERUS INFINITUS

Beziers provided the paradigm with avarice moderating the mayhem. As the town of Castres was being looted, Peter of Vaux-de-Cernay related, two men were dragged into the commander's presence, "one a 'perfected' heretic and the other a sort of 'novice.' The second heretic—the disciple—was seized with heartfelt grief; he began to show contrition and promised that he would freely forswear heresy." In the course of "a heated discussion . . . amongst our people," Vaux-de-Cernay added, "some said that now that he was prepared to do what we had told him to do, he ought not to be condemned to die."

In response, the commander demonstrated how far down the chain of command the *Caedite Eos* dictum ran. He ordered that both men "should be burnt, taking the view that if his contrition was genuine, the fire would serve to expiate his sins; if he was lying, he would receive a just reward for his perfidy. Both heretics," the chronicler related, "were then tied with strong chains round their legs, middle and neck, and their hands were fastened behind them. A fire was lit around the stake, and burned vigorously." Vaux-de-Cernay gave this gruesome spectacle a happy ending by introducing what he called "a miracle." "The 'perfected' heretic was consumed by the flames instantly," he informed the reader, "but the other quickly broke the strong chains that bound him and escaped from the fire so unharmed that he showed no sign of injury except that the tips of his fingers were slightly scorched." The two revelatory phrases here are "what we had told him to do," and "the tips of his fingers." Even when the disciple did "what we had told him to do," there was no reprieve from torture, mutilation, and death. The detail about "the tips of his fingers" explains why, all these centuries later, this obscure cleric's account still makes good reading. Peter of Vaux-de-Cernay was ever eager to insert a telling detail, even if he needed to invent it. These embellishments only enhanced the value of his work, for the more he fictionalized the more he laid bare the truth about the barbarism he was celebrating.

Thanks to Carcassonne's crenelations, so reminiscent of Jerusalem's fabled walls, the young viscount, Raymond-Roger Trencavel, held out for nearly a month. Finally, in return for his surrender, the papal forces agreed to spare the lives of Carcassonne's people, though the conditions were harsh; "all the inhabitants were to walk out of one gate, wearing only their shirts and breeches, and leaving all their possessions behind them." No religious test had been applied at Beziers, where all had been killed. No religious test was applied at Carcassonne, where all lives were spared.

Once again Peter of Vaux-de-Cernay revealed more than he intended. "If matters turned out the way they had at Beziers," he explained, "all the goods in it would be ruined." Whatever their beliefs were, Carcassonne's people were "allowed to go free [so that] all the contents of the city would be kept for the designated future lord of the territory." "And it was so," the chronicler rejoiced. "All the inhabitants came out of the city bearing nothing but their sins." The textual key unlocking the meaning in this instance is the phrase "designated future lord of the territory." Another important reason why theological disquisitions on the supposed beliefs of the "heretics" are so largely irrelevant is that they ignore the papal war's terrestrial objectives. As the king of France astutely recognized, the pope had launched a territorial power grab whose purpose was to overthrow the established aristocracy, and replace it with a client nobility obedient to Rome, not Paris, hence the reference to the "future lord."

The same papal legate who had said to kill them all at Beziers promised the viscount safe passage, but "no sooner had the terms been agreed than Raymond-Roger was seized and taken away in chains in flagrant breach of his safe-conduct." So young and fit that he had galloped through the night to warn the people of Beziers, then been the picture of strength and agility as he prepared the defenses at Carcassonne, the viscount, cast at age twenty-five into the citadel's dungeon, was soon dead. To replace him, "the Abbot of Cîteaux, legate of the Apostolic See and the father and master of this sacred business," named one of his most vicious warlords to be the new Viscount of Beziers. This latest legate had no more authority to do that than the earlier legate had to excommunicate the Count of Toulouse but, as this incident demonstrated, Christian realms and rulers were now subject to the same violent and capricious usurpations as the lands and powers of Muslim nobles were.

Heir to an obscure fiefdom in northern France, the usurper viscount, Simon de Montfort, was one of those petty nobles whose title conferred no power and whose land generated no wealth. He had established his reputation for brutality as a result of participating in the infamous Fourth Crusade. When Innocent III proclaimed his crusade against the peaceful Christians of France Profound, Montfort was ready to epitomize how totally the depravity of the Crusades against the Muslims had corrupted the ideals of chivalry in Christian Europe. Now, in violation of the king of France's rights, and exceeding the pope's instructions, the Abbot of Cîteaux conferred on Simon de Montfort "the government of the territory for the glory of God, the honor of the Church and"—lastly—"the suppression of heresy."

Simon de Montfort ordered both heretic and repenter burned at Castres. When the lord of Montréal, a town some sixty miles east by southeast of Lauzerte, was captured, Montfort ordered that this noble, along with eighty of his knights, "all be hanged from forked-shaped gibbets," our chronicler reports. Montfort's desire to kill them all, and quickly, led to a mishap. While "the most distinguished" lord was being "hanged, the gallows-pole started to fall down." As a result of Montfort's "great haste" to kill, the gibbet had "not been firmly fixed in the ground." "Perceiving how great was the delay" involved in constructing a new gallows, Simon "ordered the rest to be slain" immediately. "The pilgrims therefore fell upon them right eagerly and slew them on the spot." Out of consideration for her sex and respect for her status, the Dame of Lavaur was spared the indignity of being killed in male company. After having "caused stones to be heaped upon the lady of the castle," he ordered her thrown down a well.

At Bram, west of Carcassonne, Montfort ordered his troops to "put out the eyes of the defenders, over a hundred in number, and cut off their noses. One man was spared one eye [so] that, as demonstration of our contempt for our enemies, he should lead the others" about the countryside, relating what had happened. The chronicler William of Puylaurens, himself a Roman Catholic parish priest in the region, was not taken in by the talk of fighting heresy. Montfort only "sought to govern unwilling subjects and gave no thought to purging the land of heresy," he complained. Montfort's terror campaign, he added, proved that, far from doing God's work, he "had departed from His way." As in the Holy Land, so it proved to be in France Profound. The invasion, which began with some seemingly decisive victories, degenerated into a guerrilla war of constant attrition.

Unable to consolidate his control in richer, more strategic areas, from May into September 1212 Montfort ravaged the remote marsh lands where Languedoc and Aquitaine, Gascony and Quercy rub up against each other, sinking deeper and deeper into a quagmire of asymmetric warfare. The venerable towns of Laguépie, Saint-Antonin, Caylus, Montcuq, Agen, Biron, Marmande, Penne d'Agenais, and Moissac all fell within the gyre of Montfort's mayhem. Connect the dots and you find Lauzerte is in the rough center of this zig-zagging spiral of death and mayhem, yet Lauzerte is never mentioned. According to some accounts the settlement, still in its infancy, was spared because the Bishop of Cahors placed it under his protection, but the essential reason Montfort never pillaged the place, as a local priest and historian later observed, was that Lauzerte in 1212 had the good fortune to be "only a little place without importance," though that was soon to change.

Montfort's impending victims tried to reason with him. From Laguépie they "sent messengers begging him to make peace and offering to submit." In response, Montfort accused those he had chosen to attack of "crimes and exceptional depravity [and decreed] he was in no way prepared to treat with them." Today Laguépie looks much as Montfort found it. Not a human seems to stir there. The reason for the current somnolence is demographic. These atmospheric towns have long been losing population as people forsake the countryside for the cities. The place was so empty back then because the entire population had fled; "finding it empty he ordered it to be pulled down and burnt."

Saint Antonin, patron and namesake of the next village Montfort ravaged, was himself murdered, grotesquely, in 506 on the grounds he was a "heretic." A canonized saint of the

Roman Catholic Church, Antonin was the missionary who introduced Christianity to this part of the world. In the town that bore his name, Antonin was revered as a human dowser, adept at finding miraculous springs whose waters cured all kinds of diseases. When thrown into the Garonne River with a millstone round his neck, it was furthermore recounted, Saint Antonin floated to the surface. Saint Antonin's buoyancy proved impervious to death itself when he returned to his native Pamiers, where in his absence a rival evangelist, Métope by name, had gained ascendancy. Lest Antonin's return cost him congregants and revenue, the rival preacher accused the evangelist who had converted thousands to the Roman faith of "heresy," and had him sentenced to asymmetrical bisection. When the swordsman's work was finished, Antonin's head and right arm formed one piece, his left arm and the rest of his body the other. In the 706 years separating Saint Antonin's martyrdom from the martyrdom Simon de Montfort inflicted on his namesake town, "heresy" remained the pretext, but Métope, like Montfort, killed for power and to get rich, though there was a variation in nomenclature. Saint Antonin was denounced as an Arian, as opposed to a Cathar.

Simon de Montfort's brutalizations unfolded within a landscape so beautiful that the Romans had used the words *nobilis vallis* to describe the Saint-Antonin area. Under the Sun King Louis XIV, "Noble-Val" was officially appended to the name. During the Revolution, radicals renamed it Saint-Antonin-Libre-Val—Saint Antonin of the Free Valley! After that it once again relapsed to plain old Saint Antonin. Then, in 1962 local boosters restored that attractive and accurate epithet, Noble-Val. The Romans, the Sun King, and the town council were right. The valley Montfort ravaged, town by town, is noble! Even the place names cannot help but pay tribute to the area's beauty. The River Bonnette runs through

Saint-Antonin-Noble-Val like a pretty girl. The stately Roc d'Anglars commands the intriguing and magnificent Gorges of the Tarn. If unicorns truly did inhabit this earth, they surely would roam the Forest of Grésigne.

By the time Montfort attacked Saint-Antonin-Noble-Val in early 1212, the ten-mile throng that three years earlier had followed the papal legate down the Rhône to Beziers, had been reduced to a bitter trickle. Montfort's "army" boasted maybe a dozen swordsmen on horseback. Clerics as well as soldiers rode with him. Among them was William, Bishop of Albi, the town that much later, anachronistically, would give the Albigensian Crusade its name. As on chess boards, these knights and bishops were grossly outnumbered by the pawns. Escaping debt, vengeful wives, penal mutilation, or worse, these real-life peons trudged along in the dust kicked up by the horses their betters rode. *Vulgarium numerus infinitus*, the chroniclers called them, using a Latin phrase needing no translation. At each village they plundered, they hoped to grab a meal or snatch a ring off some dead or living finger. Too often, in the conduct of "Christ's business," they found every larder empty, making them all the more hungry for plunder and thirsty for violence.

As he terrorized the countryside, Montfort presented people with a fight or flight dilemma. The Knight of Saint-Antonin chose to fight. "A crowd of Stick Carriers will never take my castrum," he declared, referring to the staves the mob of lowlifes who trailed behind Montfort brandished. Saint Antonin's defenders made the same mistake the defenders at Beziers had. Instead of sitting tight, they went on the offensive. "Our adversaries," continued Vaux-de-Cernay, "came out of the castrum and harassed our men all day long. As evening began, the enemy [again] attacked us." This time, too, the defenders' courage, instead of dissuading them, provoked the ire of the *Vulgarium*. "A great clamor arose in our army [as]

unarmed crusaders of low rank ran to join the fray," this eyewitness account continued; "they set about the enemy with
such incredible and unheard of courage that they reduced them
to fear and stupefaction by a continuous heavy bombardment
of stones." Put in chains, the Knight of Saint-Antonin was
dispatched to the same dungeon in Carcassonne where the
young Viscount of Beziers' life had been extinguished. Inspecting the damage that the "Stick Carriers" had wrought, Peter
of Vaux-de-Cernay found the entire town ravaged, its entire
population killed, captured, or set to flight.

"A fight without swords, a glorious victory!" the monk ex-
ulted, unmindful of the implications underlying this show of
force by the *Vulgarium numerus infinitus*. Beneath the endless
dynastic and doctrinal vyings among kings, popes, and emperors, there lived and breathed the great mass of humanity.
These were the people who, regardless of whomever the history books claim won or lost, and for whatever reasons, went
on tilling fields, procreating, and, before they died, perpetuat-
ing their mothers' superstitions and their fathers' hatreds, generation unto generation.

A dozen generations would have to unfurl before
philosophers and politicians started attributing the magical
omnipotence of popular sovereignty to such people. For those
who "made" history, as well as those who wrote it, the people
were like domestic animals—to be ridden or herded, then
fleeced. The Church still calls them its "flock." This metaphor
disregards the fact that the Good Shepherd, after taking such
good care of them, sends his lambs to the slaughterhouse. The
difference is is that humans sometimes can unify into a single
beast with a will of its own. By the hundreds and, on occasion,
by the millions they can trample, or be made to trample across
history. Beziers had shown that. So, now, had the charming
postcard town today known as Saint-Antonin-Noble-Val, as
would also, eventually, the Bastille.

10

SECRET ROUTES

No matter how many he murdered, the enemy Simon de Montfort most wanted to destroy eluded him. This was the very personage who first provoked the pope's Crusade, and then deflected it: Count Raymond VI of Toulouse. Unsatisfied with usurping the Viscount of Beziers' lands and titles, Montfort and the papal legate conspired to get Raymond VI, yet again, condemned as a "heretic." Once again Raymond VI deflected catastrophe, this time through diplomacy. On a series of lengthy missions, he pleaded his case with Philippe-Auguste in Paris, then journeyed to England as well as Spain to argue the legitimacy of his cause. In his most spectacular démarche he went face-to-face with the pope himself. Condemned twice for "heresy," Raymond VI traveled twice to Rome. There he begged the Holy Father to understand that he was the true Christian. The Count of Toulouse also warned of the dangers of letting a usurper use the Church to seize power from a land's rightful ruler.

Raymond VI carried generations of dynastic legitimacy in his saddle bags. Like a badge of honor, the loyalty of his people embellished every costume he wore. Then, on his second trip, in 1215, Raymond VI brought with him the most resplendent adornment of his legitimacy, his charming young son. In a Church where clerics were banned from engaging in legitimate sexual activity, Innocent III was neither the first nor last to delight in the sight of a beautiful boy. Few, if any, have expressed those feelings so fulsomely. "Never was a more attractive young man born," marveled Innocent III, "he has good sense, he is wise and well mannered," the pope added. He then made a comment that bore directly on the future of Montfort and his usurpations, and on Lauzerte's future too. This beauteous youth, the pope emphasized, was "the offshoot of the best lineage there is."

So taken was Innocent III with this resplendent young man that, while refusing to reinstate his father's rights as Count of Toulouse, the pope bestowed on his son and heir the Marquisat of Provence. Thereafter, both Montfort and the papal legate detected a diminution in the pope's ardor for killing "heretics" in France Profound. At one point the pope actually acknowledged the reality behind the wanton bloodshed he had authorized. There were remarkably few heretics in Quercy, the pontiff observed. Translation: Remarkably few of the *Quercenois* had aroused his ire.

Only by eliminating "the best lineage"—by killing both the Count of Toulouse and his son and heir—could Montfort make his cause prevail, yet time after time he failed to land the killer blow. A notable fool's-gold triumph transpired at the redoubt of Caylus, located like Lauzerte in the modern-day department of Tarn-et-Garonne. Like a knight in dusty armor, the Caylus fortress commanded the rough lands where the sinuous valleys feeding the Tarn and Garonne gave way to the harsh landscape of France's *massif central*. Montfort's initial "victory" at Caylus was the paradigm of the dilemma that spited all his successes. He could seize any fort or village, but as soon as he charged off to his next massacre, his supposed subjects reaffirmed their allegiance to their original ruler.

As Peter of Vaux-de-Cernay acknowledged, referring to Caylus, Montfort "had once held the place," but as soon as he left "the inhabitants had ... handed it over to the Count of

Toulouse," whereupon Raymond VI entrusted the defense of Caylus to his younger brother, Baldwin of Toulouse. When Montfort besieged Caylus a second time, Baldwin neither bared his teeth, nor turned tail. He simpered, rolled over, and waved his paws in the air. Betraying his brother and his dynasty, he pledged his loyalty to the usurper. Such a spineless nullity could not be entrusted with a redoubt as important as Caylus, so Montfort put Baldwin in charge at "Montcuq, a castrum belonging to the Count of Toulouse," located just under seven miles from Lauzerte. As always, success seemed preordained. "Hearing of our approach," Vaux-de-Cerny explained, "the defenders of Montcuq all fled," but just as no castle can protect its defender from his own incompetence, no pedigree can compensate for cowardice.

Fearful for his life in Montcuq, Baldwin sealed himself inside a squat stone structure at an even more unprepossessing place called Lolmie, only five miles from my House. Insignificant then, nondescript today, Lolmie is one of those places where, counterintuitively, history keeps happening. Long before Baldwin installed himself there, Roman soldiers bivouacked at Lolmie. Later the fabled Black Prince assaulted it. Smaller even than the castle where Richard the Lionheart got himself killed, the Lolmie fortress resembles an upended cinder block. In front of it, a closed-up auto repair shop and a weed-infested passel of rusted used cars give this spot, where some of history's gaudiest figures once strode, an Appalachian look.

"Baldwin of Toulouse was sleeping in his own castle of Lolmie in Quercy," relates one historian, when "his bedroom was quietly locked from the outside." Meanwhile "traitors opened the castle gates to a force of mercenaries gathered beneath the walls under the command of a local lady. Baldwin, who was sound asleep in bed, was seized and carried off in triumph to Montauban." According to another version, Baldwin was apprehended "as he slept naked in a house at Lolmie—complaisantly, confidently—[when] some village nobles and mercenaries (first having obtained the key to the room) kidnapped him. He was taken to Montcuq, where he was starved, beaten, and humiliated and then carried (limp, half-dead) to Montauban."

His captors locked him inside his bedroom, according to one account. His captors unlocked the door to his room, another assures us, even though very few doors had locks back then, as opposed to bars and bolts. Mercenaries and traitors apprehended Baldwin. A local lady assured his comeuppance. He was taken directly to Montauban. He was taken first to Montcuq. Some say Count Raymond, "more resigned than vengeful, acquiesced to the execution." Others claim the Count of Toulouse, vengeful, watched as his brother was killed. All agree that Baldwin of Toulouse, once in Montauban, was strung up on a tree, not hanged from a scaffold, and that it was "a walnut tree." Whatever the details, Montfort's attempt to turn the "best lineage" against itself had produced another success for the legitimate Count of Toulouse, while prompting an outburst of popular rejoicing.

In keeping with its fundamental depravity, the papal Crusade's highest-ranking victim was a Christian monarch renowned for his valor in defense of the Roman Catholic faith. So faithful was King Peter II of Aragon that Innocent III, personally crowning him king, added the honorific "Catholic" to the king's title. To this day Spain's monarchs style themselves Catholic Majesties. These tokens of papal esteem were well merited. While Simon de Montfort was irrelevantly ransacking places like Saint-Antonin, Peter the Catholic's victory in the Battle of Las Navas de Tolosa in southern Spain, remembered by Muslims as the Battle of Al-Uqab, marked the beginning of the Christian Reconquest of the Iberian Peninsula. This would lead, among much else, to the voyages of Columbus to the New World.

Many of the nobles whose lands Montfort was now pillaging owed allegiance to neighboring Aragon. When called upon for help, Peter the Catholic—protégé of the pope, valorous incarnation of the Church Militant—decided to put down Simon de Montfort's usurpations through a full-frontal assault. The Count of Toulouse, sensing the danger in such gallantry, urged the king of Aragon to adopt his own strategy of passive aggression. When Peter the Catholic, like Richard the Lionheart, opted instead for personal heroics, Raymond VI distanced himself from the battlefield. Taking his son, the future Raymond VII, with him, he fell back to Toulouse. It was another wise evasion. During the Battle of Muret, fought on Thursday, 12 September 1213, Peter the Catholic was butchered by fellow Christians. Montfort's *Vulgarium* had picked the body clean by the time the royal corpse was recovered. They called it Montfort's greatest victory, yet killing a Catholic king proved no more effective than cutting off "heretic" noses. After so much killing, Montfort's "writ only ran where he stood armed from head to toe, his men behind him; not an inch further."

After sowing havoc up and down Quercy, Simon de Montfort "decided to lay siege to a castrum named Moissac," a town I know well. Along with Cahors and Montauban, Moissac is one of Lauzerte's three attendant cities. A physicist might ask you to envision a trio of smallish suns orbiting a pint-sized black hole. I prefer to imagine three juicy figs orbiting a succulent plum; I won't need a map, let alone GPS, for today's trip. Moissac is part of the practicalities of my everyday life. A dental cleaning costing hundreds in the United States costs forty-five euros there, twenty-one euros for the upper jaw, twenty-four for the lower. In Moissac, my Moroccan barber gives me a haircut as good as any I ever got at the Astor Place barbershop in New York City, for only ten euros.

I have my own secret way to get to Moissac. It is a local version of the back-country route of discovery that led me to Richard the Lionheart's death place. One of my secret route's satisfactions consists of the names of the hamlets it traverses: La Moler, La Tuque, Montesquieu, La Comtesse, Misere, La Feyne, Las Roques, Claval, Jongayrolles, and Calvary. Someday, I've promised myself, I'm going to take those place names, and produce a France Profound alternative to Marcel Proust. In my fascinating, fast-paced Proust-improvement opus, Moler, the dyslexic playwright who couldn't spell his name right, will be a principal protagonist, along with the epigrammist Montesquieu, who could. Jongayrolles will be the composer scorned by the human piano-rolls of the musical establishment. Only much later will he be revered as Jelly Roll Morton's precursor. In the plot I have devised, their passions and intrigues revolve around the amber diamond that is the Countess of Misere. Will the cynical Claval never recognize that Misere's main rival, Madame de La Feyne, is a virtuous woman in spite of her name?

Such musings are integral to my back-road wanderings. Sometimes, while upon them, I recall a tale by Gustave Flaubert. Entitled *A Simple Soul*, it encapsulates my modus operandi as I wander France Profound in search of facts, and once enough facts and the interconnections among them have accumulated, the truth. The physical, geographic journey Flaubert described matches to a tee my intellectual and emotional wanderings.

"The road was so bad it took two hours to cover the eight miles," Flaubert wrote. "The two horses sank knee-deep into the mud and stumbled into ditches. In certain places, Liébard's mare stopped abruptly. He waited patiently till she started again, and talked of the people whose estates bordered the road, adding his own moral reflections on the outline of their histories. Thus, when they came to some windows draped with nasturtiums, he said: 'There's a woman, Madame Lehoussais, who, instead of taking a young man—' Félicité could not catch what followed; the horses began to trot, the donkey to gallop, and they turned into a lane; then a gate swung open, two farm-hands appeared and they all dismounted at the very threshold of the farm-house."

In the course of my explorations, I too would get stuck in the metaphorical mud as some distraction or diversion led me away from what I imagined was the main point of the tale. Then, often when least expected, the donkey galloped, the gate would swing open, and *voila*! I would find myself, as Balzac put it, "at the very threshold" of the latest discovery of a situation or person or group of people to widen and deepen my "own moral reflections on the outline of their histories"— whether those histories unfolded eighteen thousand or eight hundred years ago, or yesterday.

One time on my way to Moissac, in the course of these "moral reflections" on how seemingly disparate people, events, and conditions are interconnected, I found myself pondering the structural similarity of sunflowers and the Milky Way. The connection came to mind when I stopped to admire, and then using the clippers I keep in the car for that purpose, take for myself some of the magnificent sunflowers currently abounding on the hillsides overlooking Lauzerte. Their yellowness astounds the eye and enriches my life when I take them home and display them, for maximum contrast, in the Green Room. No farmer's crop is diminished. I only help myself to maverick sunflowers, the ones that crop up outside the margins of the farmers' fields.

Mme de Renzy mentioning her uterus brought to mind Eleanor of Aquitaine. The spiral arrangement of the seeds in the sunflowers I collected that day turned my thoughts to the polymath Fibonacci, whose birth around 1170 corresponded with Lauzerte's birth as a polity. Fibonacci never killed a heretic or went on Crusade, but no pope or king changed life more in Lauzerte and across the European world than he did when, in 1202, he published *Liber Abaci*, his book of calculations. "The nine Indian figures," he informed Europe, are: "9 8 7 6 5 4 3 2 1." He then made the announcement that changed the world, though not human nature. "With these nine figures, and with the sign 0, any number may be written."

Children today learn their decimals in preschool, so it's easy to forget that Eleanor of Aquitaine and Pope Innocent III never learned to count to ten. Prior to Fibonacci, Western civilization was innumerate. Geometry—the science that needed no numbers—sufficed to build Europe's great cathedrals, as well as the Parthenon and the pyramids, but as his *Book of Calculation* revealed, only mathematics could empower the human mind to probe exoplanets and explore the subatomic universe. His famed sequence of Fibonacci numbers remains one of the most elegant examples of how mathematics can express realities other forms of expression cannot, at least not without enormous difficulty. The formula $Fn = Fn - 1 + Fn - 2$ describes the way sunflower seeds and spiral galaxies are structured. It shows how pine cones and pineapples form. It links the spiral nature of the nautilus seashell with hurricanes, and them both with DNA molecules, as well as the structure of cauliflower and the way your hair organizes itself on the top of your head.

Before those Indian numerals, via the Arabs, reached Europe, science—epitomized by Claudius Ptolemy and his Ptolemaic system—consisted of what the eye could see. Plato had propounded the maxim that misguided human knowledge for thousands of years. "Science is nothing but perception," he ordained, and as our perceptions showed us quite clearly, the Earth was flat, and the Sun revolved around it. Before science could transcend the limitations of what the eye could perceive, it had to have mathematics, and all the practical calculations and epistemological revelations mathematics made possible. Without Fibonacci's revelation, Copernicus never could have verified that the Earth was not the center of the universe. Isaac Newton never could have uncovered the laws of motion guiding the planets, and Einstein would never have done the mathematics yielding the most fateful of all equations: $E = mc^2$. Knowledge of the unseeable separates medieval civilization as well as classical antiquity from the world we inhabit today.

Meaning—and meaninglessness—cannot be understood out of context. The context of Montfort's rampage was that his exertions amounted to a game of blind man's bluff, nothing more, in the context of a world on the cusp of being transformed unimaginably first by numbers, then by the printed word.

My sunflower route to Moissac is secret only because no one wants to know about it. That's because everyone has their own competitor route that they claim is better than mine. Everyone, as I see it, is wrong about that. My route, in addition to being shorter, is also more picturesque. Avoiding the exurban sludge on the outskirts of the little canal-side city, whence Balzac wrote letters to his mother while on his way to Egypt, my secret route runs right down the mountainside to the town's great treasure, Moissac Abbey. It already was over five hundred years old by the time Montfort commenced his siege there, in 1212.

11

THE REMEMBERED MONTFORT

Montfort's Moissac siege was the final fiasco of his disastrous Quercy campaign. His problem there, as everywhere else, was a crisis of legitimacy: No one wanted Montfort as their ruler. "On hearing of our approach," explained Vaux-de-Cernay, Moissac's residents did not flee or surrender. They "summoned mercenaries and a large force of people from Toulouse, hoping to rely on their aid to withstand our soldiers." Self-defense was not the only crime the "evil and perverted" people of Moissac committed; "to show their contempt for God and our army, they rang the bells of the church . . . every hour of every day as if celebrating a festival."

Only outsiders would fight for Montfort, and only for the forty days required by papal sanction to achieve remission of their sins. "Since there were too few Crusaders for us to surround Moissac completely, our opponents came out each day . . . and attacked us arrogantly," Vaux-de-Cernay related. Montfort himself was wounded "in the foot with an arrow. They [also] captured a young soldier from our side, the nephew of the Archbishop of Rheims, and dragged him off. They slew him and shamefully dismembered him." The good folk of Moissac then fired various pieces of the archbishop's nephew back at Montfort's forces.

When Montfort's men did get close to the walls, the *Mossaguais*, as Moissac's residents call themselves, counterattacked, "bringing fire, dry wood, straw, tar, salted meat, fat, oil and other combustible materials," which they used to set fire to Montfort's siege engines. "The flames leapt higher; the enemy kept on throwing the inflammable material, whilst our men, without a pause and with great effort, threw wine, water and earth onto the flames [and] others tried to pull the lumps of meat and vessels of oil from the fire with iron hooks." Stymied by these gastronomic tactics, Montfort agreed to abandon the siege "on condition that they hand over the mercenaries and the soldiers who had come from Toulouse." Betraying those who had saved them was a small price for the *Mossaguais* to pay to rid themselves of Montfort, the *Vulgarium*, and his chattering clerics. "The agreement was duly concluded, the mercenaries and the men from Toulouse were handed over," whereupon Montfort's men "killed them with great enthusiasm."

He lived by the sword, but Simon de Montfort did not die by the sword. His character turned into his destiny in 1218 as yet another redoubt, this time Toulouse itself, resisted Montfort's claims he was its rightful ruler. Hearing that Montfort himself had appeared beneath the walls, a crowd of volunteers lugged a heavy petrary to within striking distance. "The catapult was loaded, fired and reloaded," recounts *The Song of the Albigensian Crusade*, then fired again and again "by little girls and men's wives, and now a stone arrived just where it was needed and struck Count Simon on his steel helmet, shattering his eyes, brains, back teeth, forehead and jaw. Bleeding and black, the count dropped dead on the ground. Such was the joy," this account continues, "that all over the town they ran to the churches and lit candles in all the candlesticks and cried out, 'Rejoice!' Trumpets, horns and universal joy, chimes and peals and clamoring bells in belfries, drums, tambors and slender clarions rang through the town until every pavingstone re-echoed."

When that block of masonry beaned him at Toulouse, Montfort yet again was besieging the home of poets, freethinkers, and troubadours or, as Henry of Marcy, the Cistercian abbot of Clairvaux, had described it, the "cess pit of evil with all the scum of heresy flowing into it." He died beneath the walls of Toulouse on 25 June 1218, nine years almost to the day since Raymond VI, intercepting the papal killers, had turned them away from Toulouse. Deflecting their fury onto the hapless young Viscount of Beziers was only a delaying tactic, but the delay had sufficed. The Crusade to seize Toulouse, loot its riches, and overthrow its rulers never again gained the cohesion, strength, and fury expended at Beziers.

Across the centuries our great chroniclers and subtle theorists, our esteemed philosophers and careful pedants, are always quick to perceive in the unfolding of events the guiding hand of God (or the class struggle, or Manifest Destiny, or Nemesis). Does that explain why they so seldom pay homage to the "little girls and men's wives" and their block of masonry, or to the kid archer and his frying pan? Few protagonists are more closely linked to the cult of chivalry than Richard the Lionheart and Simon de Montfort, yet the commonest of the common people, not some knight in shining armor, were the ones who undid them both. As William of Puylaurens put it, "The man who inspired terror from the Mediterranean to the British Sea fell by a blow from a single stone."

In their joy and rage, the people of Toulouse mutilated Simon de Montfort's body before allowing his family to retrieve his various parts. Observing those who, at his obsequies, avowed that Simon de Montfort was a saint and martyr, a local troubadour heaped higher the irony of the denouement: "If one may seek Christ Jesus in this world by killing men and shedding blood, and by the destruction of human souls; by compounding murder; by setting the torch to great fires; by winning lands through violence, and working for the triumph of vain pride; by fostering evil and snuffing out good; by slaughtering women and slitting children's throats—why, then he must needs wear a crown, and shine resplendent in Heaven!"

In his futile forty-three years, Simon de Montfort had shaken the earth and achieved nothing, but thanks to the youngest of his three sons, Simon de Montfort, Jr., that name would be remembered for centuries. Every one of the three Montfort boys, like their father, died grotesquely. The middle son, first to perish, was bludgeoned to death in the flatlands town of Castelnaudary, today famous for its *cassoulets*, located between Toulouse and Carcassonne. It happened when some locals he tried to command resorted to an early version of fragging. Instead of killing "heretics," they killed him. Simon de Montfort's eldest son, Amaury, acted out his father's melodrama in reverse. The elder Simon de Montfort first ravaged the Holy Land, then perished while savaging France Profound. His eldest son, having savaged France Profound, died as a result of ravaging the Holy Land. Captured in the future Gaza Strip, he was transported in chains across the Sinai Peninsula, held for ransom in Cairo, only to perish, once freed, on the shores of Otranto.

Since Simon de Montfort, Jr., was the youngest son of his namesake father, his prospects at first seemed as dim as John Lackland's, but unlike his father and brothers, he understood geopolitics. While they were throwing away their lives at points south and east, he recognized that a curiosity in the family's matrilineal descent offered dynastic possibilities not to be found in Toulouse or Jerusalem, but in England. The mother of the elder Simon's father happened to be the daughter of a French nobleman named Robert de Beaumont. That Frenchman, thanks to the Norman Conquest, held an English title, Earl of Leicester. This meant little until Simon's mother's father died, and then her brother, heir to the earldom, also died, childless. Through this unanticipated female link, the ambitious Montforts now had claim to one of England's grandest titles, except that succession through the female line, especially at such a distance, seldom ran smoothly, and often did not run at all.

Arriving in England friendless and penniless, the younger Simon de Montfort got himself recognized as Earl of Leicester, then seduced the king of England's sister. He also stole money from the king. When Henry III reproached him, Simon turned on his royal benefactor. At the Battle of Lewes on 14 May 1264, the younger Simon de Montfort gained the kind of victory over the king of England that his namesake father never won over the Count of Toulouse. Routing the royal forces, Simon made the king as well as the crown prince his prisoners. The youngest son of a France Profound loser was now master of England, though not for long. At the Battle of Evesham on 4 August 1265, squads of assassins stalked the junior Simon de Montfort, then fell upon him. His head, according to the *Chronicles of the Mayors and Sheriffs of London*, "was severed from his body, and his testicles cut off and hung on either side of his nose." His son and heir also was killed that same day. The Montforts' ambitions, which had spanned the known world from the English Midlands past the crenelations of Carcassonne, to Jerusalem's remarkably similar ramparts, died that day with them.

Though the younger Simon ruled England for less than fifteen months, what he did during his brief tenure assured his name would be remembered as long as people retell the tale of how England's most cherished institutions came to be created. Desirous to base his power on some foundation other than the coerced consent of a captive king, this usurper—more than a quarter-millennium after Richard the Lionheart's death—convoked England's first true parliament. In addition to two knights from each shire, two burgesses from each borough were included. This threat to the privileges of the religious and military elites could not go unavenged. After they chopped off his head and testicles, Simon de Montfort's "hands and feet were also cut off and sent to diverse places to enemies of his as a great mark of dishonor to the deceased."

Desecrating a usurper's corpse did not reverse the course of history. More and more, the growing power of money made in towns and cities—as opposed to swords wielded on battlefields, and prayers incanted in churches—propelled events. This gave the people who knew how to make money a power that lay outside the traditional structures of hierarchical obligation. How was the king to get ahold of such money? By including the burgesses, that first parliament that Montfort convoked at the City of Westminster in 1265 established a monetary as well as a political precedent. Thirty years later, King Edward I, better known as Edward Longshanks, needed money. Like his father Henry III, and his grandfather King John, he also wanted a counterweight to the feudal barons, so in 1295 he summoned his "Model Parliament." It was modeled on the Montfort parliament, and not by accident. As Crown Prince, Longshanks was Montfort's prisoner and then, after escaping, the architect of his murder.

As it still does today, Parliament thus innovated consisted of the king-in-parliament, the parliamentary lords and, Montfort's great legacy, it also included the "communes." The future political history of England, and much of the rest of the world, would tell the tale of how a conclave representing the towns, the burgs, the nascent bourgeoisie, became the supreme repository of popular sovereignty—the House of Commons.

The English already had a French king to thank for Magna Carta. Now they owed the birth of that most "English" of their institutions, the Westminster Parliament, to a francophone usurper who, not content to seduce the king's sister, or involve the king in financial fraud, treasonously made war against him, and then held both him and the royal heir captive. Should an epoch of sculptural justice ever dawn in which public monuments reflect historical truth, that statue of Richard the Lionheart will be removed. Monuments to two Frenchmen will stand guard outside the London Parliament. Sharing a place of honor with King Philippe-Auguste, godfather of Magna Carta, Simon de Montfort, Jr., his severed parts reconstituted, will hold aloft his proclamation of the Model Parliament, as if in benediction to the politicians scurrying thither about their business.

12

EVERYTHING THAT RISES

That chunk of stone killed Simon de Montfort, but the Count of Toulouse defeated him. A watcher who knew how to wait, he understood that being valiant can kill you, so the cautious Raymond VI had won the only way winning mattered. He was left standing. His son, the one the pope found so toothsome, lived too.

To this day chroniclers deride his achievement; "remarkably clumsy in warfare" is how one savant described him. If, going back to Homer and Achilles, our civilization did not so universally empathize with those who kill, Raymond VI of Toulouse today might be revered as an example for our children to follow. One memorial does give this equivocating master of compromise his due, though it is far from France Profound. When I set out to piece together this mosaic, in which both the lives of long-vanished people and the lives of my neighbors in Lauzerte, France, would be integral units, I never imagined the search would lead to St. Paul, Minnesota. There, a work of art unlocks the meaning of Raymond VI's great achievement, without which Lauzerte might never have come into existence.

Like Raymond VI himself, this masterpiece has not gotten the attention it deserves, in part because you must crane your neck in order to see it. It is located on the ceiling of the Supreme Court of the State of Minnesota. There a series of

four lunettes—semicircular paintings—depicts four protagonists in the struggle to base human organization on the Rule
of Law. The first so honored is Moses. Next come Confucius
and Socrates. In the fourth of these panels the Count of Toulouse occupies his coequal place with those incomparably more
famous sages in humanity's long, never entirely successful effort to govern itself through recourse to reason.

We have the painter and sculptor John La Farge to thank
for this remarkable tribute to an otherwise almost forgotten
figure. La Farge's forebears came from France, but that does
not explain why he chose Raymond VI. Had the artist wished
merely to honor his French heritage, the obvious choice would
have been Napoléon Bonaparte, promulgator of the Code Napoléon. La Farge chose the Count of Toulouse, the artist himself explained in a monograph he wrote on his lunettes, because
Raymond VI personified a crucial aspect of the law that is of
utmost importance, yet too often ignored. La Farge titled his
portrait "The Adjustment of Conflicting Interests." Why did
Raymond VI seek compromise with the papal killers? Why
did he abase himself so willingly while showing so little interest in battlefield glory? La Farge, an American artist living
seven centuries later, understood that "The Adjustment of
Conflicting Interests" was the goal that shaped Raymond VI's
life, as well as the life of his and Joan Plantagenet's son, the
future Raymond VII. He also understood that his efforts to
reconcile conflicting interests, not push them to the conflict
point, made him worthy of being celebrated on the ceiling of
a courtroom in the American Midwest, in the company of Moses, Confucius, and Socrates.

Rather than creating some stereotypical scene "of fierce
Medieval war," La Farge explained, he chose to depict the
count as the glamorous avatar of nonviolence. The Count of
Toulouse was sixty-one when Simon de Montfort met his
end beneath the walls of Toulouse. In far-off Minnesota, La

Farge presented Raymond VI—or, rather, the principles he personified—as a lithe hero in the prime of life. His gilded sword might be Excalibur, but instead of the sword, he brandishes his powers of reason. By casting his protagonist in such a triumphant light, La Farge revealed Raymond's long struggle to have been a refutation, not some mere evasion, of the prevailing ethos of violence.

A deep understanding of his struggle, and of its cultural and psychological context, enabled La Farge to depict Raymond with such insight. "This line of sovereign lords," he explained, "had to struggle with the demands of the Church, formulated more distinctly then than before." It also had "to meet the opposing claims of their vassals," while at the same time coping with assaults on "their rights as regarding their own interior claims of sovereignty." Then there was the crucial matter of "their relations to the King whose power, gradually increasing, devoured theirs." Beyond all that was the necessity to deal with "the ferocious attacks of other lords anxious to dispossess them of their properties and rights of sovereignty." La Farge's comment concerning "the demands of the Church" refers to Innocent III. The "ferocious attacks of other lords" describes Simon de Montfort. The "King whose power, gradually increasing, devoured theirs," was Philippe-Auguste.

Had the Count of Toulouse not been as conscientious in pursuit of his procreative responsibilities as he was when it came to the territorial preservation of his realm, Lauzerte and its liberties might never have come into existence. He was the sixth Raymond of Toulouse. Not to produce a seventh would have been a defeat exceeding any humiliation inflicted by whip-wielding clerics. With his wives, as in warfare, it was a long slog to success. Raymond VI's first wife died childless within three years of their nuptials. His second marriage, to the sister of his ill-fated rival, the Viscount of Beziers, did produce a daughter. Still lacking a male heir, the Count of Toulouse took for his third wife a daughter of the king of Jerusalem. It was not third time lucky, so he procured another annulment. Then, in 1196, the Count of Toulouse took a fourth wife, whereupon all the heteroclite events so far described in this narrative converged in a successful act of sexual union. This fourth wife was the one who finally produced the much-desired son and heir, the one the count took with him to Rome. By giving birth to a healthy son, the latest Countess of Toulouse assured the independent survival of the County of Toulouse and its dynasty for another generation. This in turn helped shape political, military, and ecclesiastical relations all over Europe.

This real-life denouement once again involved plot twists no writer of fiction would have dared to invent. The uninventable detail in this instance is that Raymond VI's new wife turned out to be Eleanor of Aquitaine's daughter and Richard the Lionheart's sister: the same Joan Plantagenet her brother had tried to marry to Saladin's brother. Zero degrees of separation now stood between the farthest-flung melodramas and most famous historical celebrities of the epoch and the Quercy hilltops of France Profound.

Behind her daughter Joan's marriage to the Count of Toulouse craftily moved, as always, the deft diplomatic hand of Eleanor of Aquitaine. Romance in this supposedly romantic epoch counted for nothing as Eleanor, seeding her progeny across Europe, constructed a dynastic web that in the end encompassed the forebears of every occidental king, queen, empress, and emperor. The success of such efforts relied on the oldest, deepest, and most reliable human urge: the sexual urge. Negotiate a treaty with the prospective spouse. Have a bishop mutter the requisite Latin over them, then lock them inside a royal bed chamber, and await the dynastically desired result. Not all these arrangements produced optimum results. Initially Joan's betrothal, at age twelve, to the king of Sicily seemed like an astute maneuver. Her widowhood in 1189, following the failure of the union to produce any heirs, was a strategic reversal, but Eleanor was ever adept at transforming disadvantage into opportunity. In Sicily, in Malta, in Cyprus, then in the Holy Land, Joan had survived tumults that had cost the lives and consumed the life possibilities of countless souls, yet upon her return to Europe she was still in her twenties.

In this situation Eleanor perceived a new dynastic opportunity, to transform her daughter from a widowed queen into the countess regnant of one of Europe's choicest domains, so in 1196 Joan Plantagenet, the former Queen of Sicily, became Countess of Toulouse. Today such a title seems like a comedown; back then it connoted immense domains. All by itself the County of Toulouse was richer and more populous than many kingdoms. The Count of Toulouse was additionally Marquis of Provence. What were the parched tablelands of Sicily, or the sere mountains of Judea, in comparison to the realm of which Richard the Lionheart's sister now was chatelaine.

Raymond VI's marriage to Joan Plantagenet was the crucial event that made the foundation of the city of Lauzerte a practical possibility. As part of her dowry, Joan added to her husband's realm the lordship of Quercy, named for the Cadurci, one of the Celtic tribes Caesar subdued. Right in the middle of this dower land, wedged between Aquitaine and Languedoc, the Lauzerte mountain stood like a sentinel commanding the valleys linking the highlands to the north with the plains to the south. These valleys, in turn, led to Paris, northern France, and the English Channel and, in the opposite direction, to the great southern cities, including Toulouse, as well as to the Atlantic and the Mediterranean, and to Spain.

For generations, passers-by had been remarking on the strategic potential of this "isolated flat-topped mountain at the entrance of the valleys of the Barguelonne and the Lendou," to cite a nineteenth-century description as accurate today as it was in Joan Plantagenet's time. Before Raymond's marriage to Joan, according to undated documents of the period, a local noble named "Arnaud-Gasbert de Castanher and his sons [deeded] to their lord, the Count of Toulouse, Marquis of Provence, the entire plateau of Puy-de-Lauzerte, in order to build there a château . . . in return for a commitment to grant to its inhabitants rights and privileges as profitable to them as to the Count himself."

Under the count's protection they aimed to launch what today would be called a real estate development scheme consisting, initially, of "two hundred houses," but there was an impediment. The Lauzerte mountain was part of Quercy. Quercy owed homage to the Dukes of Aquitaine, not the Counts of Toulouse. Only thanks to his marriage to Joan Plantagenet in 1196 did the "plateau of Puy-de-Lauzerte" fall under the rule of the Count of Toulouse. As Peter of Vaux-de-Cernay noted less than twenty years later, these "territories had long been held by the King of England, but when King Richard gave his sister Joan in marriage to Count Raymond of Toulouse, they were ceded to the count as a dowry."

Her mother's daughter when it came to dynastic alliances, Joan was her brother's sister when it came to waging war. Having expeditiously given birth to the requisite male heir, and now pregnant for a second time, in 1199 she, like her brother, was besieging a rebellious redoubt of no import when fate turned against her. Guillaume de Puylaurens described Joan Plantagenet in his *Chronicle*: "She was an able woman of great spirit, and after she had recovered from child bed, she was determined to counter the injuries being inflicted upon her husband at the hands of numerous magnates and knights. She therefore . . . laid siege to a castrum belonging to them known as Les Cassés." In comparison to this petty outpost, Châlus where her brother perished was a metropolis.

"Her efforts," Puylaurens continues, "were of little avail; some of those with her treacherously and secretly provided arms and supplies to the besieged enemy. Greatly aggrieved, she abandoned the siege, and was almost prevented from leaving her camp by a fire started by the traitors. Much affected by this injury, she hastened to see her brother King Richard." She hoped Richard would rescue her, as he had rescued her in Sicily, "but found that he had died." Dynastic ambition, filial affection, and happenstance had intertwined the lives of Richard the Lionheart and his favorite sister in places as far-flung as Oxford, Messina, Limassol, and Jaffa. Now death, stalking and then striking them in these French realms, became symmetrical too.

Her first birthing saved a realm. Her second killed her. Joan Plantagenet died hemorrhaging placental gore less than five months after her brother died of his puss-filled shoulder wound. Before joining that host of queens, princesses, duchesses, and countesses to perish attempting to fulfill their dynastic reproductive responsibilities, Joan Plantagenet, Princess of England, Queen of Sicily, Countess of Toulouse, as well as putative sister-in-law of Islam's most famous statesman, had lived a life full of unforgettable events—except that for all practical purposes she would be forgotten. Dead at thirty-three, she was far from the last to demonstrate that childbirth in those times could be to women, no matter how exalted their rank, what warfare was to men, a field of blood.

13

OF ALL HER ILK

Like Count Raymond VI, King Philippe-Auguste had one and only one male heir, so in Paris, as in Toulouse, dynastic anxiety was a constant feature of statecraft. The king's strategy was to seize hold of biological possibility as soon as puberty permitted, but who should the future king's bride be? Eleanor of Aquitaine, dowager queen of England, not the king of France, would be the decider. More than fifty years after she betrayed his father, Louis VII's divorced ex-wife would decide via what womb King Philippe-Auguste's DNA would spin itself into the kings and queens, rogues, magnates, winners, losers, criminals, and mediocrities, as well as the occasional genius and prince of good will, who would dominate Europe in the future.

Eleanor's hegira to the Holy Land, more than half a century earlier, had reshaped the history of Europe by poisoning her marriage to the French king, and engendering her marriage to the king of England. In 1191 she had made the arduous journey to Sicily, where she finally had ambushed her son into agreeing to marry. In 1194 she personally accompanied the king's ransom all the way to Germany. Then in March 1199 she had rushed to Richard's death bed at Châlus, the better to disinherit the rightful heir and place the runt of her litter, John Lackland, on England's throne. In September 1199 she had witnessed the latest unraveling of her dynastic web, with the death of her daughter Joan Plantagenet.

Undeterred, at the end of this *annus horribilis*, Eleanor at age seventy-seven set out on the last of her immensely consequential journeys. In an expedition that would have daunted Odysseus, she traversed France, the Pyrénées, and Castile in order to execute a dynastic coup with consequences stretching right up to today. On the way she was kidnapped by a rebellious noble, but intrigued her way to freedom, and continued on to Spain.

A Spanish princess named Urraca had been chosen to marry Philippe-Auguste's only son, the future Louis VIII, ergo be the next queen of France. Urraca's mother, Queen Eleanor of Castile was Eleanor of Aquitaine's namesake and, following Joan Plantagenet's death, her sole surviving daughter. Betrothed at age nine to the king of Castile, this younger Eleanor had produced four daughters of her own. That made her granddaughter Urraca the presumptive queen of France, a circumstance allowing Eleanor of Aquitaine yet again to seize control of the destiny of Europe. Upon arriving at the court of Castile, the most powerful grandmother on earth ordained that Urraca was not going to be queen of France after all. Her younger sister, Blanca, would. When asked why Urraca had been discarded, Eleanor blandly replied that Blanca translated better into French. Urraca was consoled by being made queen of Portugal.

Whether whim or clairvoyance guided her choice, Philippe-Auguste—the French son Eleanor never had—soon had every reason to be satisfied with the daughter-in-law she procured for him. Only twelve when they were betrothed in 1200, the future King Louis VIII and his bride expeditiously achieved what other dynasts often failed to achieve in the course of their lifetimes. With the birth in 1214 of a healthy grandson, the future Louis IX, the kingship of France was assured for two reigns to come. That was only the beginning of her importance. Little Blanca of Castille, as Queen Blanche of

France, would be Philippe-Auguste's true successor when it came to consolidating and expanding royal power. This left his son and grandson—Louis VIII and Louis IX—free to fritter away their life possibilities in suicidal Richard the Lionheart–style vendettas of no consequence.

From childhood, Philippe-Auguste had grasped the great truth about successful statecraft, which the German philosopher of violence, Carl von Clausewitz, would enunciate some six hundred years later. "War is the continuation of politics by other means," Clausewitz proclaimed. By that he meant war ought to be the tool of statecraft, as opposed to a mindless process of butchering people. Philippe-Auguste's victory in the Battle of Bouvines exemplified the expedient use of warfare as a political tool. The king's refusal to abet the papal bloodletting in France Profound bespoke his understanding that, just as often, avoiding war was the better tool for achieving political objectives. As Philippe-Auguste astutely foresaw, love, not war, in due course would get him what he wanted. When, sooner or later, the Counts of Toulouse failed to produce a male heir, their lands would revert automatically to the king, or if the sole heir were female, she could be co-opted through marriage. Either way, there was no need to kill people to get what he wanted, provided he was willing to wait.

Philippe-Auguste's ability to do nothing adroitly was one of the foundation stones of his greatness, yet for neither the first nor last time the lessons of an illustrious father were lost on an impatient son when Louis VIII succeeded him as king in 1223. Disinterested in the drudgery of civil administration and thirsty for battlefield glory, Louis VIII wanted a war. Following a failed expedition against the English, his eye settled on the County of Toulouse. The new king had no pretext for war. Never once had the Counts of Toulouse denied their fealty to the crown of France, so the Montforts' ruination was twisted to provide the pretext; "hopeless for his personal cause," the one surviving Montfort son "ceded his rights in his father's conquests" to the king in Paris in return for support for yet another suicidal Crusade in the Holy Land. No matter that those "rights" had been usurped, that those conquests were now nonexistent, this meaningless gesture provided the new king the pretext he wanted.

Abandoning his father's nonintervention policy, the new king instead took Simon de Montfort as his exemplar and so wound up as he had. The difference was how much time it took. Simon de Montfort needed nine years to get himself killed trying to subdue France Profound; Louis VIII managed it in less than five months. The fatal blow that smashed Montfort's skull, according to eye witnesses, turned into splattering bloody goo the brain that never stopped conspiring. Louis VIII died of dysentery, as his bowels expelled the viscous bile and gassy humors that, according to the medical science of the time, were the sources of violent impetuousness.

With her husband Louis VIII dead, and her son, Louis IX, inheriting the throne at age twelve, the little princess Eleanor had spirited out of Spain was now, at age thirty-eight, ruler of France. Her husband had tried war, and it had killed him, so, adjusting tactics, Blanche's "love of influence and domination put on the appearance of religious strictness." Until the yet-again "heretical" Count of Toulouse repented, Queen Blanche decreed, her wrath would remain unappeasable. History repeated itself as Raymond VII, like his father before him, seized with both hands the opportunity to save his dynasty through a dramatic act of self-abasement. This time the ritual humiliation was orchestrated in Paris, in front of Notre Dame cathedral.

The gawkers were out in force on Thursday, 12 April 1229, when Raymond VII underwent his own "Reconciliation." As part of the deal, Blanche got the pope yet again to abandon all outstanding charges of "heresy" against him. In return, the count assured Queen Blanche he henceforth would forever and faithfully "remain in the service of . . . the queen-mother, my cousin." In Paris, words spoke louder than deeds. Safely back in Toulouse, Raymond VII, still only thirty-two, for the next twenty years would be a player, not a pawn, in European power politics. Balancing and counterbalancing the conflicting interests of England, the Iberian monarchies, and the papacy as well as of France, the Count of Toulouse continued to act as a sovereign lord, not the servile liege he had promised to be. The two biggest promises Raymond VII had made were to suppress heresy vigorously, and then join Blanche's son Louis IX on yet another Crusade. As Pope Gregory IX later complained, Raymond VII "did not keep a single one of the commitments" he had made.

Raymond VII, like his father, was happily immune to the great hysteria that for centuries gripped Western Europe's princes, along with countless numbers of their subjects. The mania to go on Crusade erupted in the decades leading up to the launch of the First Crusade in 1095. Variously directed outward and inward, it continued right up to 1492, and the first violent European incursion into the Americas. The subsequent subjugation of the western hemisphere, followed by the imposition of European rule across Africa and Asia, lasting into the twentieth century, constituted a universalization of the original notion that prompted the Crusades. This was the pretense that Europe enjoyed the right to impose its will anywhere it wanted, for any reason it wanted. The conquest of Jerusalem, the usurpation of the Aztec and Incan empires, to say nothing of the future colonization the Indian subcontinent, were all of a piece.

While other rulers squandered the wealth of their realms, their life opportunities, and, very often, their own lives, Raymond VII, like his father, avoided the Crusades entirely. This freed him to concentrate on preserving and edifying his home realm. His canny survival instincts also matched those of his father, Raymond VI. By avoiding overseas misadventures, eschewing pridefulness, and tacking with the geopolitical winds, they both achieved through suppleness what force of arms could not ensure. This was the preservation of their dynasty and its territories into the next generation.

The successes of the two Raymonds mirrored each other. The same in reverse was true when it came to the father-son suicidal disasters first Louis VIII and then his son Louis IX inflicted on themselves. In the so-called Seventh Crusade, which the Count of Toulouse adroitly avoided joining, Louis IX and his army landed in Egypt in June 1249. By April 1250 the king was the captive of those he planned to conquer. "The King of France was put in chains," related the chronicler Abū Shāma. "The eunuch Sabih Almoaddhami was put in charge of watching over him." The eunuch's first job was to keep the king alive. A Muslim physician was summoned; he cured Louis IX of dysentery, ensuring that a king's ransom could be paid.

His mother manipulated Louis IX while he was in France. Now, in Egypt, another redoubtable female bent him to her will. This was Sultana al-Malika 'Aṣmat ad-Dīn Umm-Khalīl Shajar ad-Durr. Like Eleanor, Shajar al-Durr married two kings in sequence, growing richer and more powerful at each step. Unlike Eleanor, the sultana had been born a slave, an advantage when it came to discerning men's weaknesses, and putting them to use. After Queen Blanche paid the sultana a ransom equivalent to one-third of France's annual revenues, Louis IX did not return to France. Betraying his Crusader's Oath, he and what survived of his contingent served as the sultana's border guards, shielding her from her dynastic rivals in Damascus. Outraged Christians protested that the turncoat king had become the Muslims' cat's-paw. Only when his mother's money ran out did he come home.

Having shirked his kingly duties for six years, Louis IX returned to a realm more peaceful and prosperous than the one he had deserted. England had thrived during King Richard's absence thanks to Eleanor's regency; France prospered during Louis IX's absence thanks to Blanche's regency. Like Richard earlier, Louis IX still had the chance to make something worthwhile of his kingship, and of his life, but that was not his character. He had not learned from his father's disasters nor, he now demonstrated, was he capable of learning from his mother's successes. Having already once brought disaster upon himself, he launched what was called the Eighth and turned out to be the Last Crusade.

Death, inglorious and futile, finally smote Louis IX in Tunis, a march of some 2,170 miles across North Africa from Jerusalem. It all was part of his latest grand design. This time, Louis IX ordained, the flower of European knighthood would fall first upon the Tunisians, forcibly converting them to Christianity. Thus enhanced, the hordes of Christendom would conquer Egypt. After gloriously subduing the country where he earlier had been so abjectly defeated, Louis IX reasoned, taking Jerusalem would be easy.

They never got a day's march beyond their beachhead near Carthage. Not needing to draw his sword, the Caliph of Tunis, Abu Abd Allah Muhammad al-Mustansir ibn Yahya, let the diseases spread by the Europeans' squalid personal habits defeat the intruders for him. This time no eunuch summoned a doctor as Louis IX perished of "flux in the stomach." Lest the body of a Christian king be laid to rest in Muslim soil, his corpse was boiled down to the bones. For three hundred years his remaining remains reposed at the royal sanctuary at Saint-Denis, near Paris. Then, during the sixteenth-century Wars of Religion, looters stole the magnificent repository that served as Louis IX's ossuary. A single finger is said to have survived.

Like Richard the Lionheart, Louis IX was a pathetic loser. Also like Richard, he was transmogrified into a national hero and, going Richard one better, canonized as a saint. El Greco portrayed "Saint" Louis as a dreamy spiritualist, his skin so pale that the desert sun seems never to have touched it. Louis himself bequeathed us a more accurate moral portrait of who he was. For him the Holy Land was not the paradise of piety, charity, chivalry, and curious relics he supposedly sought to redeem. It was another Beziers, his policy *Caedite eos*. Even "if you go to Christian priests and monks and if you carry candles before my eyes as a sign of obeying the Cross, all these will not persuade me from reaching you and killing you," this future saint of the Roman Catholic Church proclaimed as he set out on his final futile foray.

His own soldiers understood how vain and foolish such threats were. "Anyone who wishes to fight the Turks is mad," lamented one of his knights, "for Jesus Christ does not fight them anymore. God, who was awake, sleeps now, and Muhammad waxes powerful." Among those he vowed to subdue, Louis IX evoked ribald scorn. "Greetings Frenchie," one bit of doggerel began: "May God reward you for having gotten so many Jesus worshipers killed!" It then offered some advice for those "thinking about coming back for revenge or in pursuit of some grand design. The house where your king was held still exists," it warned them. "The chains are still there, and so is the eunuch."

That France survived, indeed prospered, in spite of the folly of men like Louis VIII and Louis IX bore witness to Queen Blanche's competence. It was an age of great women, as all epochs are, but also, as in most epochs, most women never got their due. Eleanor of Aquitaine is unforgettable because every major event of her life was a font of calamity, from her divorce from the king of France through her interference with the succession to the English throne, with one great exception: her choice of Blanca of Castile to become Queen Blanche of France. Blanche managed crises, instead of provoking them. She preferred collecting taxes to waging war, yet Blanche is forgotten because, like the Counts of Toulouse, she devoted herself to "The Adjustment of Conflicting Interests" rather than pursuing policies of mayhem and illusion. Of all her ilk, not excluding Eleanor, Blanche was the most adept at statecraft.

The triumphs of Blanche's uterus were no less spectacular, as a comparison with the reproductive career of her sister demonstrates. As Queen of Portugal, Blanche's sister Urraca bore Alfonso II three sons and one daughter, but by 1385 her royal line had expired. Blanche bore thirteen or, by some counts fourteen children, five of whom lived reproductively fruitful lives. Their numerous progenies provided the genetic core of the Valois and Bourbon dynasties that, in various permutations, would rule France until 1848. The current king of Spain, among countless others, is here today because Eleanor of Aquitaine chose Blanche. In addition to Blanche, Eleanor's regnant grandchildren included the kings of Castile and England, and the Holy Roman Emperor.

Along with future kings and queens of countries like Denmark, Belgium, Italy, Greece, and Romania, Eleanor's descendants would include Byzantine emperors, an empress of India, two emperors of Brazil, and a Russian tsar. Every current European monarch is her descendant. One of Eleanor's American descendants via Blanche was clerk of the US Senate. Another was a Mississippi river boat captain. Her Hollywood contingent, in addition to Maggie and Jake Gyllenhaal, includes Brooke Shields, Ellen DeGeneres, Paris Hilton, and the Duke of Sussex. Thanks to Prince Harry's

American wife, Meghan Markle, Eleanor of Aquitaine now has descendants whose progenitors were African slaves.

Within a few generations most of Europe's kings and queens had become family—descendants, via Blanche and others, of Eleanor of Aquitaine. In this family, son had made war on son. Sons made war on their father. The grandmother engendered the murder of one of her grandsons by one of her sons. In Europe's "family of nations," Plantagenet family values would prevail, its members—like Richard the Lionheart and "Saint" Louis—propelling their peoples, and themselves, to needless destruction. The closer the degree of consanguinity, the more horrendous the consequences often were. In the famous Willy-Nicky telegrams of 1914, the German kaiser and the Russian tsar vainly pleaded with each other to halt the war in which tens of millions would kill and wound each other in their names. Like Blanche and Raymond VII, Wilhelm II and Nicolas II were first cousins, as well as Eleanor's descendants.

14

SWEARING ON THE ALTAR

Look out the windows of my House long enough and you will witness the rise and decay of cultures, the formation and disintegration of economic systems. You will witness the abandonment of some forms of legitimacy and the embrace of other notions of what constitutes worthwhile human organization. That is what happened in February 1241 when Count Raymond VII of Toulouse, paying obeisance to the town's burgesses by pledging to respect and defend Lauzerte's Charter of Rights amplified and codified the work of his father by issuing the edict that transformed Lauzerte into the full-fledged city it is today. The title of La Farge's painting—"The Adjustment of Conflicting Interests"—summed up Raymond VI's life work. Its subtitle, "Swearing on the Altar to Respect the Liberties of the City," encapsulated his son's.

In his exegesis of the struggles the Counts of Toulouse faced with the king in Paris, the pope in Rome, and Simon de Montfort, the artist had introduced a new protagonist—the towns, the cities, and those who were enriched and empowered by them. The time, La Farge's painting showed, had come when both church and state faced the choice, as the artist himself put it, of being "either friendly or antagonistic to the temporal ruler of the city. The representatives of the city," La Farge emphasized, owed allegiance neither to lord nor to the Lord, but had the "freedom of the city at heart, the rights of the citizens easily trenched upon by both war-lord and ec-clesiastic." Here, too, a more astute summary of the emerging complexities of what already was on its way to becoming the modern world would be difficult to find. Although the artist does not mention a specific name, there is no doubt La Farge had Count Raymond in mind. A sketch for the painting, in the possession of the Metropolitan Museum of Art in New York, though not currently on display, is described as follows: "The Adjustment of Conflicting Interests: Count Raymond of Tou-louse Swears at the Altar to Observe the Liberties of the City; Color Study for Mural, Supreme Court Room, Minnesota State Capitol, Saint Paul."

In this new situation, the natural allies of the Counts of Toulouse were the same ones who fought for Philippe-Auguste at Bouvines—the same ones the younger Simon de Montfort hoped would help stabilize his rule when he convoked his Model Parliament. Raymond VI had fused his own interests with those of the towns so successfully that, in the end, the "little girls and men's wives" of Toulouse, not the warrior caste on the battlefield, rid him of his bitterest enemy. Raymond VII in turn formalized and expanded this alliance through his pol-icy of chartering new towns called *bastides*.

After marrying twice more, for a total of six times, "the Count of Cunning" had died in 1222, age fifty-six, having never again begat a son, or a daughter, so in a ceremony of the kind La Farge glamorized in his painting, his son and successor Ray-mond VII "proclaimed, confirmed and swore" in writing, before Jesus Christ and "all the saints of Paradise" to "grant, keep, maintain and uphold, everlastingly," the rights and privileges specified in the Lauzerte Charter. This pledge, he swore, ap-plied "to all the inhabitants who were now there, as well as to all those who will come and live there in the future, in perpetuity."

By the time Lauzerte's charter was promulgated in 1241, twelve years had passed since Raymond VII promised Queen

Blanche to devote his reign to persecuting heretics and prosecuting the war to reconquer Holy Jerusalem. Avoiding the first and evading the second of these commitments, he dedicated himself to the transformation of his domain into a new kind of polity based neither on the traditional nobility, whose power derived from agricultural serfdom, nor on the papal hierarchy. Raymond VII, instead, set out to make himself chief magistrate of a realm of free, prosperous, and loyal cities. He was acting in his own self-interest. By chartering new towns like Lauzerte, Raymond VII was creating new sources of wealth and power for himself. In the nearly forty-five years since Joan Plantagenet's marriage had transferred seigneury over Lauzerte to the Counts of Toulouse, it had evolved into a thriving town, with a hospital, a municipal council, and its own standards of weights and measures. Every November, on All Saints Day, Lauzerte hosted a regional fair. Municipal fees were doubled on such important occasions, but only for outsiders; residents were exempt. Now, half a century and more after local notables requested "a commitment to grant to its inhabitants rights and privileges as profitable to them as to the Count himself," Raymond VII fulfilled that commitment by confirming Lauzerte's legal status as an independent, full-fledged *bastide*.

Bastide in the sense of a human settlement was a term newly in use back then. Originally it simply meant any structure built of stone. Under Raymond VII *bastide* acquired a larger meaning—of a planned, chartered polity inhabited by free citizens that in very many cases, notably Lauzerte's, was built of stone. The following definition described Lauzerte in 1241. With certain alterations, it describes it today: "A bastide [was] a new walled city of county, or royal and ecclesiastical foundation built in the Middle Ages on the basis of a subdivision whose regular plan includes a central square surrounded by a covered passage opening by arcades, and a municipal charter allowing the inhabitants to administer themselves with an elected council."

With Raymond VII's proclamation, Lauzerte became a community governed according to the rights and responsibilities defined in its charter. It also became part of world history. Henceforth the identities of Lauzerte's tradesmen and clerics, its merchants and connivers, its nobles and ne'er-do-wells would be officially recorded. So would its births, deaths, bankruptcies, homicides, and pious legacies. On the ensuing cadasters of the town also would be documented—historicized—all the property owners, including me. Safe inside my House, its thick stone walls and giant rustic beams sheltering me, I feel protected and also proud to be counted among "all those who will come and live there in the future, in perpetuity." For this policy of urbanization to succeed, the count understood, the measures he authorized had to be as beneficial to those he governed as they were "to the Count himself."

This strikingly modern approach—secular, nonviolent, practical, transactional, and consensual—marked a distinct departure from medieval norms. In terms of his personality, Raymond VII also broke the chivalric mold. He had no interest in seeking glory through slaughter in distant lands, but when an astute recourse to violence served a practical purpose, he did not shirk it. His prime military task, once Simon de Montfort was killed by the townswomen of Toulouse, was to dispossess his son and supposed heir, Amaury de Montfort. Exploiting the tactics of asymmetrical warfare—unpredictable feints and gnat-like sallies—he sent Amaury de Montfort scurrying off to his death in the Levant, a development which in turn lured Louis VIII to his death. With his two principal adversaries having eliminated themselves, Raymond VII, opting for a patient approach, "gradually reclaimed his inheritance with a strong, courageous hand."

Very much his father's son, Raymond VII was also Eleanor of Aquitaine's grandson when it came to turning crisis into opportunity. The papal invasion had devastated his realm as it previously existed, so Raymond VII set out to rebuild it as a commonwealth of cities, founded on the wealth they generated. Key to creating this new kind of polity, based on the encouragement of urbanization, was making the cities he chartered attractive to new settlement. The key to getting people to do that, Raymond VII understood, was to turn these new bastides into escape routes from feudalism.

In terms of human rights, the Lauzerte Charter of 1241 was a precursor, guaranteeing liberties we today associate with America's Declaration of Independence. The charter's rules and regulations numbered fifty-one. They dealt with matters ranging from the town's boundaries and the tolls the town fathers could collect, to the quality of cloth sold in the town's Thursday market, ancestor of the Saturday market I attend every week. The charter regulated the sale of fresh fish and dried fish as well as procedures for settling business debts and gambling debts, which were treated differently. To read the Lauzerte Charter is to step into the lives of people who, dozens of generations ago, were coping with the same messy matters of communal life that still vex those of us living on the same mountain today. To cite one pertinent example, what would life have been, then or now, without the social animation, the emotional turmoil, the physical gratification, and the civic complications adultery provides?

"Concerning Adultery" was the title of Article VI of the Lauzerte Charter. Its single paragraph offered deep insights into how people dealt with the civic consequences of their sexual urges back then, and how they still do today. The charter's regulations in regard to sex, more modern than medieval, concerned themselves with protecting individual rights, not punishing sin. Fornicators were presumed innocent until caught in the act, and not just by some tittle-tattle. "If the lord or bailiffs surprise in adultery a man who has a wife, or a woman who has a husband," Article VI begins, "their number must include three tribunes whose loyalty to Lauzerte they have sworn by oath, and who are not [members] of the family of the lord, or financially dependent on him for income. These tribunes," it goes on to stipulate, "must find the man, his pants lowered, atop and between the legs of the woman, and the woman undressed, her skirts bulging up over her stomach, or else find both while naked in bed. And it's in that manner," the article emphasizes, "that the perpetrators must be surprised."

For a crime to occur under these circumstances, mere fornication did not suffice. At least one of the protagonists had to be married to another person. Circumstantial evidence—soiled bedding, embarrassed faces—would not be enough. The sworn testimony of unofficial eyewitnesses, including neighbors and relatives, was also disallowed. The purpose in making proof of guilt so very nearly impossible to obtain was made clear in the final sentences of Article VI. "Only if found guilty," it provided, "will the goods and possessions of the guilty be available to the lord; however [even if found guilty] these perpetrators can neither be mutilated nor killed. Furthermore, if they succeed in escaping from prison, they will owe nothing to the lord as a result of their escape."

In this manner a provision ostensibly designed to punish sexual irregularity revealed its real purpose: to shield Lauzerte's citizens from the pretexts such transgressions might provide for an avaricious lord to seize their property, torture them, or kill them. Article VI also explicitly prohibited traditional public punishment of the adulteress, including branding and stoning—men being traditionally excused from punishment. Only under such highly unusual and specific circumstances could even habitual adulterers be convicted of adultery, and with its mention of the adulterers' "escaping from prison,"

Article VI codified what customarily happened, today as well
as then. Once the adulterous liaison became too scandalous to
ignore, the offending couple was free to flee the town without
having further punishment hanging over them while, to the
distress of the gossips, life slipped back to normal. Such scandals, the charter makes clear, were a feature of life in Lauzerte
in the thirteenth century, as they continue to be in the
twenty-first.

Article XXXVI of the Lauzerte Charter protected the
wives of convicted criminals after they were put to death. "If
any man whatsoever is executed for homicide, theft or any
other crime," it provided, "the wife cannot be held responsible for the mischief of her husband." While his share of their
property would be seized, "her interest in their property was
to be held in reserve." In this manner the woman's dowry
was protected, and the wife and children of the convicted
felon were saved from destitution.

Article XIV—"Concerning Homicide"—expanded that
protection to include the family relations and business associ-
ates of the guilty party. "The property and possessions of the
person who committed homicide," it stipulated, could be seized
only "when the homicide has been proven by reliable witnesses.
Creditors are then paid out of the murderer's property." Even
when the funds were insufficient, no one was required "to stand
surety for a murderer, [including] his father, his mother, his
wife, or any other person." Once a convicted murderer was executed, the charter provided, what remained of his wealth
after his creditors were satisfied "belongs to the lord," since he
and his agents were the ones obliged "to execute on the body
of the murderer the judgment delivered by the tribunal." In
this manner the convicted murderer paid his own hangman,
and also bore the costs of disposing of his corpse.

A humane and coherent conception of civilized secular
life, its provisions make clear, animated the Lauzerte Charter.

Its many interesting clauses posited a legal system that priori-
tized social harmony and sought to assure individual well-
being. The objective most definitely was not an eye for an
eye, as Article XXXII, "Of Rape," reveals: "If someone violates
a virgin, against her will, and if the offender belongs to a family
of a higher rank, more noble and richer than this woman, he
must take her in marriage, or give her in marriage, if it is so
agreed, to a husband of her choice." In this manner the degradation the raped woman suffered was assuaged by the possibility of upward mobility.

Downward mobility was explicitly precluded. "But if the
woman violated is of higher social rank, nobler than he who
raped her," this same article provided, she under no circumstances was to be married to the cobbler or plowman who took
advantage of her. Instead "the guilty party must, if he can, give
her in marriage to a man of her choosing, and if he cannot af-
ford that, all his property [is forfeit and] becomes the property
of the woman." Social humiliation for the high-born, penury
for the low-born rapist: Whether high- or low-born, "once his
guilt has been proven," the sexual offender was to be subjected
to public lashings, the precise number to be decided, according
to details of the rape, by the bailiffs.

The Lauzerte Charter depicted epochal change as it was
reshaping the lives of everyday people. It showed females being transformed from chattels into legal persons, and lords
being transformed from masters of all they surveyed into notaries and justices of the peace. Article XVIII, which banned
frivolous law suits, provided that neither "the lord nor the bailiffs can initiate any action against anybody in Lauzerte, man
or woman," unless an independent complaint had been made
against them. Anonymous denunciations were forbidden. The
accuser had to be publicly identified. Even then, legal action
could proceed only if proof existed that some actual wrong
has been committed. Judicial ambush was prohibited; "the

defendant, man or woman . . . is entitled to a delay of eight days" in order to prepare the defense.

Right from the start, the Lauzerte Charter was a human rights document; 532 years before the Boston Tea Party it banned taxation without representation. Article II established that, "now and forever," all men and women living there would be "free and exempt from all charges, fines, encumbrances and compulsory service if they have not consented to them." "Inviolability of Persons and Property" is the title of Article III. It guaranteed what today we call due process, habeas corpus, and freedom from cruel or unusual punishment. "No person, man or woman," it ruled, "can be killed or seized (by the lord or his agents); nor have them killed, nor have them made prisoners, nor confiscate their property or possessions" unless it be as a result of valid judicial process. Past brutalities provided no precedent. "Under no circumstance," Article III stated, could the lord or his agents "inflict violence on anyone, whether man or woman," by invoking "bad customs" which did not respect the inviolability of the people and their possessions as defined in the charter.

The Lauzerte Charter also protected its citizens after they died. "Every man and every woman" was entitled "to give, sell, alienate, commit or bequeath by will and testament, all their property, whether movable or real estate, whatever that property is, and wherever it may be located." This provision then expanded posthumous protection to the negligent, the illiterate, to those mentally or physically incapable of dealing with such matters, and to those without immediate family. "Should a man or a woman die intestate, all their property will go to their next of kin up to and including the fifth degree of familial separation."

In those days when a candle was a luxury, the charter drew a strong distinction between what happened by day and what went on at night. "And if a man or a woman takes vegetables from a garden, or grapes from a vine, or the germ of unripe wheat, or hay in a meadow, without the permission of the proprietor, and [then is] convicted, the lord will have five Cahors sous for rendering justice if the theft is committed by day," but if a theft "is committed by night," the perpetrator was punished four times more severely, with a fine of "twenty Cahors sous." A man's home was his castle, most especially after dark. Article XVI provided that when anyone entered a home without authorization "during the night, after the door has been shut, the fire put out, and the householder and his family have gone to bed, the householder is entitled to seize the intruder and place him in the hands of the law." What today is called Stand Your Ground in the United States was a defined right in Lauzerte nearly 800 years ago: "And if the householder in the course of defending himself and arresting the intruder kills him, he will owe nothing, by this act, to the lord."

The Count of Toulouse as well as the local notables knew that the freedoms the charter established would matter little if the people they wanted to attract there were not free men and free women. They also knew official protection of their freedoms was essential to transforming the Lauzerte mountain into a thriving generator of wealth and taxes. This the Lauzerte Charter did, Gordian-knot fashion, by abolishing serfdom within its borders. "And all those men and women who come . . . to live there, and who will come there, shall be free," Article XXVII, "Of the Right to Protection and Asylum," boldly announced. To sweeten the pitch, the charter offered the Lauzerte version of a money-back guarantee. Article XVII—"On Emigration"—promised every settler the right, if not satisfied with life there, to leave Lauzerte and "move to another place, no matter what the place." On moving day, "the lord must have [the departee] accompanied, and all the property he is taking with him, for an entire day no matter how far he is able to go that day."

This meant that no bounty hunters, lurking just outside Lauzerte's borders, could claim the departing people as serfs. Nor could roaming brigands seize their property because the lord's own men would protect both the departees and their possessions. The charter also offered an incentive to return. "The emigrants' lands, possessions and goods," it ordained, "must be protected the same as [those of the remaining] inhabitants are." Thanks to this agglomeration of incentives and safeguards, peasants could come to Lauzerte safely, transform their lives under official protection, and so revolutionize the possibilities of their progeny, while enriching the economy, and reshaping the society around them.

The Lauzerte Charter shows how historical change can bring meaningful improvement to actual people's lives, including the lives of poor people and of women. The charter also documented changes in the status of the nobility. No longer were the fish in the streams and the beasts of the fields, along with their serfs, the lord's property. He was transformed by the charter from a feudal seigneur into a civil custodian. In return for all this jurisdictional largesse, nobles like the Count of Toulouse got money. "Those who sell salmon must give the tail to the lord," Article XLVIII provided, "but if they sell the entire fish, they will pay to the lord two Cahors deniers." Article XL imposed a fee on the sale of every cow, pig, lamb, and goat. These provisions documented the transformation of a barter economy into a money economy. Theoretically, the lord was entitled to fish tails; what he really wanted was money. When it came to selling salmon, "two Cahors deniers" was the sales tax.

In Lauzerte's abolition of serfdom lurked inklings of the class conflict that, 548 years later, would culminate in the Storming of the Bastille. No longer serfs, the citizens of Lauzerte could sell their labor, and the fruits of their labor, in order to gain their daily bread. The lord, like capitalist barons of the future, remained in control of the means of production. Article XXXIX imposed a seigneural monopoly on forges, as well as bread baking. Since most crops were grown in adjacent valleys, not on the mountain slopes, the charter carefully defined the extent of farmland covered by the count's monopolies. This delineation followed roads I still follow, to villages I visit today. From the base of the mountain, the charter specified, Lauzerte's territory "extends along the main road that goes to Mondenard and from there it extends to the church of Saint-Urcisse and from there to the church of Sant-Fort and from there to Saint Hippolyte and from there to Beaucaire and thence to Lagarde."

"All those men and women" living within that area, it emphasized, "must sharpen their instruments at one of the [count's] four forges." Here, too, the emphasis was on generating revenue, not punishing people. "If someone has the sharpening done at some place other than the four aforementioned forges," the charter stipulated, "the Lord will have ten Cahors sous, and the sharpening will be treated as if . . . done in the four forges." With monopolies, the charter emphasized, came responsibilities. "The blacksmiths must perform their duties honestly, in good faith and, [as pledged] under oath, they must sharpen new plowshares and forge cattle prods" and other necessary implements "when so requested." The revelation here is that these payments were not treated as tribute, due by divine or hereditary right to the lord. Each fee was rationalized as a payment for services rendered.

The Lauzerte Charter that Raymond VII proclaimed resembles Lincoln's Emancipation Proclamation both in the importance of the freedoms it ordained, and the care with which it hedged its bets. In spite of its magnificent-sounding rhetoric, Lincoln's proclamation only "freed" slaves in Confederate territory. Slaves in areas controlled by the US Army remained slaves. The Lauzerte Charter's promises of emancipation were similarly circumscribed. Several lengthy paragraphs detailed how serfs seeking freedom in Lauzerte had first to settle their obligations to any lord with a claim on their labor or property. Only after one full year had passed, and no further claims had surfaced, were those who sought refuge there unconditionally free.

There were further exemptions. "All those men and women who have come to inhabit the castle of Lauzerte, and who will come there in the future, will be free," the charter grandly proclaimed before adding, "except those [subject to] Arnaud-Gasbert de Castanher, Ratier de Rouzet [and] Pons de Castanher and their successors." To his stirring proclamation that the people of Lauzerte "are and will be free and exempt from all charges, fines, encumbrances and compulsory service if they have not consented to them," the Count of Toulouse appended the following proviso: "however the right of *chevauchées* will be reserved to us and to our successors, according to what we have been accustomed to do in our other lands." Chevauchée involved the lord's right to raise armies—of laborers as well as fighters—in order to defend his lands against invaders, but also to build roads and dig canals, and erect fortifications. Thanks to the charter, the count could not seize people's money or property without their consent. He could command the entire male population to take up arms and follow him, as he subdued, edified, or merely inspected, his domains.

Freedom from the compulsion to go on crusade enabled Raymond VII to put into practice his understanding that the future belonged to the cities. He did this by empowering cities that already existed, and then creating more new cities wherever he could. Though similar, each of the charters he promulgated was customized to suit the idiosyncrasies of the town it protected. Mondenard, so close to Lauzerte I see its lights every night from the Top of my House, petitioned for a charter of its own precisely because of that proximity. Having its own council, public security force, and connection to the Count of Toulouse through a resident bailiff consolidated its independence from the larger town. The "knights of Mondenard and all the other inhabitants who are there" made sure that under their charter, issued five years after Lauzerte's in 1246, theft was much more severely punished than it was in Lauzerte. Compared to Lauzerte's five sous for daylight theft, twenty if the crime were committed under cover of darkness, in Mondenard, only five miles away, the fine for daylight theft was twenty sous in the first instance, sixty in more serious instances. If the theft occurred at night, everything the miscreant owned could be confiscated.

Raymond VII's ceaseless journeyings across his domains would tax the stamina and also the forbearance of any modern politician. It was on "one of these trips, where nothing escaped him," according to an early nineteenth-century account, that he first "saw in Quercy a locality which had the double advantage of providing both a defensive position in case of need, and a pleasant hunting rendezvous." It adds the claim that Raymond VII built a castle at Lauzerte in 1245.

Nearby Moissac was Raymond VII's frequent base of operations on such tours of inspection. Moissac also provided the template for many of the charters he issued, including Lauzerte's. Following Simon de Montfort's rampage there, clerical authorities had been obliged to acknowledge the rights of the abbey town's civil population. Implementing his seigneury over the town following his marriage to Joan Plantagenet, Raymond VI updated and secularized those rights. Forty-four years later, many provisions in the Lauzerte Charter issued by his son were "modeled and sometimes copied verbatim from those of Moissac." Even so, the Lauzerte petitioners, like those of Mondenard a little later, made important changes in order to ensure that their charter addressed their concerns. The "stand your ground" privilege, to cite one example, had been removed from the Moissac charter in 1197. In 1241 it was reinstated in the Lauzerte Charter.

The Count of Toulouse issued Lauzerte's charter in February 1241 as he was heading north for another encounter with Queen Blanche and her son, Louis IX. March 1241 found him at Montargis in the Loire valley, where the royal court was installed. There he yet again pledged to fight heresy and join the Crusades, while fulsomely renewing his protestation of absolute loyalty to the king and his mother. In July 1241, Raymond VII did stage a mock siege of the "heretic" redoubt of Montségur, then quickly withdrew his troops without mounting an assault. By that December he was conspiring with the English to foment a regional uprising against the same king of France he earlier that year had pledged in person to serve and love.

Under oath, the Counts of Foix, Comminges, Armagnac, and Rodez along with the Viscounts of Narbonne, Lomagne, and Lautrec joined the Count of Toulouse in pledging to support the English attack on the royal domain. When the English advance failed, the conspiracy collapsed, and the count did what he—and his father—always did; he redoubled his earnest pledges of fidelity to the king and his mother. Meanwhile, in a virtuoso feat of diplomatic legerdemain, the Count of Toulouse turned the pope in Rome from enemy into his enabler. This he accomplished by making himself the pope's indispensable interlocutor in his conflict with the Holy Roman Emperor. Whether Raymond VII was consorting with the English, or ingratiating himself with the pope, the strategic aim remained the same. It was to find some counterbalance—any counterbalance—to the inexorable advance of the power of the kings of France, centered on Paris.

Denounced as a "heretic" on multiple occasions, then embraced by the pope as a devoted and diplomatically useful son, and then denounced yet again, and again, Raymond VII's countless excommunications—as much as the charters he promulgated—were a sign of things to come. The "spectacle of such a wide abuse of excommunication in matters where religious and material interests were inextricably confused," as one French savant later explained, meant that, increasingly, "excommunication [was] not taken seriously by those who were struck by it, nor was it taken seriously by those who should have enforced it. Raymond VII understood this well," and exploited it to his own advantage. Meanwhile, he kept chartering bastides.

The "Reconciliation" Blanche devised in Paris for Raymond VII in 1229 had provided for a brilliant marriage for his daughter Jeanne. Raymond's father had married a princess of England. His grandfather had married a princess of France. Now intermarriage with royalty of the highest order would be carried into a new generation. One of Blanche's own sons, Alphonse of Poitou, it was stipulated, would wed the Count of Toulouse's only daughter. At the time, Raymond VII was thirty-one. His libido was in as fine fettle as his political instincts were. His father had produced a daughter by an early marriage, then a son later.

In the sexual domain too, Raymond set out to follow precedent. His latest intended, the legendarily beautiful Sanchia of Provence, was one of four star-crossed daughters of the regnant Countess of Provence. At the time Sanchia was promised to Raymond VII, one of her sisters, Eleanor, was already Queen of England, having been married in 1236 to King John's successor, Henry III. Another had wed Louis IX, and therefore was Queen of France. Now Sanchia was to become chatelaine of the realm where Joan Plantagenet had reigned.

Then came stunning news. The marriage, it was announced from Paris, was off. The count's prospective bride instead would be wed to the younger brother of the king of England. This was Richard of Cornwall, titular king of the Romans, famed for being one of the richest men in Europe. Behind this complot adroitly moved the hand of Queen Blanche. At a stroke she enhanced her influence in London, where Blanche's other daughter, the young Queen of England, was wont to do her mother's bidding, while dealing a body blow to the dynastic prospects of the Counts of Toulouse. Meanwhile in Paris, Blanche's "tyranny was remorselessly exercised toward [her son's] queen, Margaret of Provence."

Raymond VII had been checked, though not yet checkmated. That happened when, ever persistent, he sought to marry the fourth and youngest of Provence's queenly sisters. Yet again Blanche stymied him. Instead of the Count of Toulouse, she ordained that Beatrice of Provence would marry yet another of her sons, Charles of Anjou—provided he could get ahold of her before Raymond did. In late 1245 the usurper bridegroom, leading a force of five hundred knights and following the same route the papal Crusaders had thirty-six years earlier, rushed down the Rhône valley from Lyons. Back in 1209 Raymond VI had deflected the advancing throng. This time the opposite happened. Blanche's son turned aside Raymond VII's attempt to intercept him, then seized Beatrice for himself. Armed soldiers stood guard as the bride was delivered to the altar. All was not entirely lost. Upon Raymond VII's death, his daughter Jeanne of Toulouse would become countess regnant and her husband, Blanche's son, Count Alphonse II of Toulouse. Should Jeanne and Alphonse beget viable heirs, there might yet be a Raymond VIII.

Vacillating though his survival tactics made him seem, Raymond VII never wavered in his efforts to avoid going on crusade. His modus operandi, as his father's had been, was to agree to everything, then do nothing. In August 1248, he was summoned to meet Louis IX at the Mediterranean port of

Aigues-Mortes, whose atmospheric crenellations these days harbor armadas of tourists. The count, prodded by Queen Blanche, had pledged to accompany the future "Saint" Louis on the first of his disastrous crusades, the one that would make him the eunuch's prisoner, but when the king embarked, Raymond VII did not sail with him. He proceeded to Marseilles. There, he promised, he was going to take possession of the warship he had ordered specially outfitted in Brittany. Alas, the count presently announced, the ship somehow had failed to make the voyage from Brittany across the stormy Bay of Biscay, around Portugal and Spain, through the Straits of Gibraltar up the Mediterranean to Marseilles in time.

Offering no explanation as to why he had not ordered the ship outfitted at a near-by Mediterranean port, Raymond pledged that he would join the crusade next year. A year later, in August 1249, he did appear for the promised rendezvous at Aigues-Mortes—this time with his daughter Jeanne and Alphonse de Poitiers, his son-in-law. Once again, the Count of Toulouse found a pretext to slip away. He was needed to adjudicate some vital matters in Quercy, he explained. Thanks to this latest evasion, Raymond VII was thousands of miles away from the Holy Land, when suddenly he died as he had lived, in La Farge's phrase, engaged in "The Adjustment of Conflicting Interests."

The new Count and Countess of Toulouse were not even in the country when they succeeded Raymond VII. Like generation after generation of both grand and petty nobles, they had abandoned their administrative and dynastic responsibilities to pursue a Pied Piper fantasy. In their case they had done it twice. It was following their return from this first of Louis IX's disastrous crusades, the one to Egypt, that the first documented sojourn in Lauzerte by a reigning count— and countess—occurred. During this brief visit, which began on Monday, 12 June 1251, Raymond VII's successor and her royal spouse received pledges of loyalty from Lauzerte's notables, in return, as always, for reassurance that the new rulers would respect the town's traditional rights as codified in its charter. They would not survive Louis IX's second folly, the "crusade" that took them all to Tunis.

Queen Blanche could choose her sons' wives. She could pay their ransoms. She could not save them from the foolishnesses of the epoch. Of the four of her sons who survived to adulthood, all four died foolishly, as the result of unprovoked wars. These included the son she married to Raymond VII's daughter. Although taken prisoner and held hostage there, Alphonse of Toulouse managed to survive his brother's first futile adventure in Egypt. He almost made it back alive from the second fiasco, in Tunis, before dying in Italy, near Savona, in 1271. His wife Jeanne, Raymond VII's heiress, died too. Rather than tending to affairs in Toulouse, as Blanche did in Paris and Eleanor had in England, Countess Jeanne had accompanied her husband on both those ill-fated crusades. She died in Italy four days after her husband died, while taking a different route home. In the course of their journeyings, the couple had produced no offspring, male or female.

Raymond VII, as much as his father, had appreciated that the grave dangers of going on crusade went far beyond questions of personal survival. Evading participation in the Crusades was one of the great achievements of his reign. Even so, the mania for making war in the Holy Land had undone his dynasty, by luring his heiress to her doom. With the biological extinction of "this line of sovereign lords," King Philippe-Auguste's strategic patience was rewarded forty-eight years after his death. The caprices of human sexual reproduction, just as he had foreseen, gained for the crown of France what violence had failed to achieve. Without a single battle being fought, the great realm centered on Toulouse reverted to direct royal rule. Thanks to this magnificent addition, the squiggle of a royal domain Philippe-Auguste inherited in 1180 now extended, ninety-one years later, to the Pyrénées, to the Mediterranean, unto Italy and Spain.

Raymond's true heirs were the bastides he engendered. Between 1222, the year of his accession, and 1249 when he died, Raymond VII endowed dozens of bastides, each with its own charter, His strategy was to grant charters precisely in those areas where the devastation had been greatest, and where his writ was weakest. Under his daughter Jeanne, her husband, and their administrators, the total of bastides chartered in their lands exceeded 150. Once the territory reverted to royal rule, France's kings continued the policy of implanting bastides, the better to preempt English claims there. In less than a century, as many as five hundred bastides were chartered in France Profound.

In this instance as in others, Lauzerte's transformation epitomized the transformations of the times. Castles had to be defended, or besieged, while these peaceful bastides generated wealth instead of consuming it. There was no need to repress people whose loyalty was based on self-interest. Thanks to Raymond VII, bastides became to France Profound what châteaux are to the Loire valley. To this day, its craggy bastides—and their doughty townsmen—define the region's administrative and cultural as well as its physical landscape.

Some of the towns he chartered prospered; others withered. Raymond VII's efforts called to mind the Parable of the Sower in Matthew 13 of the King James Bible. Raymond VII "went forth to sow; And when he sowed, some seeds . . . fell among thorns; and the thorns sprung up, and choked them: But others fell into good ground, and brought forth fruit, some an hundredfold, some sixty-fold, some thirty-fold." In 1886 a self-described "Archivist Paleographer" named Émile Rébouis made a comparative study of the charters of Lauzerte and four other towns, and submitted his findings to the Archaeological Society of Tarn-et-Garonne. In addition to Lauzerte, the four others were the settlements of Fajolles, Angeville, Larrazet, and Valence d'Agen.

Three of those five settlements today are little more than the hamlets they were back then. One, Valence d'Agen, grew into the bustling unfashionable market town it remains to this day. At Valence d'Agen's weekly market, held every Tuesday, you still can buy horse steaks. Valence d'Agen was where I had to go for gas on weekends in the days before credit card machines—decades after it happened in America—were attached to gas pumps in Lauzerte. I still go there to get my insurance policies updated. The flowing waters of the Tarn and Garonne rivers, and the produce they carry, decided Valence d'Agen's destiny in the thirteenth century. They still do. Those rivers are the reason those two giant nuclear cooling towers I see from the Top of my House are located just across the river from Valence d'Agen.

Lauzerte was the other town that turned into a success, the exact outcome here too depending on the prevailing alloy of law and topography. Now that it had its charter, the advantages that its mountain-top position offered made Lauzerte a pivot, never more so than when the lands around it were convulsed in turmoil. In the generations to come, Lauzerte would survive military, economic, and dynastic turmoil. Most disruptive of all, it would be forced to endure the spiritual upheaval bred of humanity's insistence on spilling blood in disputes over what no eye has ever seen, or ever will see.

15

UNINVENTABLE
DENOUEMENTS

Pope Innocent III had set out to control France Profound. Instead, the exact opposite happened. The region around Lauzerte wrested control of the papacy away from Rome. This took less than one hundred years to accomplish. In 1209 the papal killers committed their first massacre in France Profound. In 1305 France Profound installed its first pope. Never again would the area and its people play such a consequential role in the affairs of the world. Petrarch, whose life was congruent with this extraordinary state of affairs, called it "The Babylonian Captivity of the Church." "Now I am living in France, in the Babylon of the West," he wrote to a friend. "The sun in its travels sees nothing more hideous than this place. Here reign the successors of the poor fishermen of Galilee; they have strangely forgotten their origin. I am astounded, as I recall their predecessors, to see these men loaded with gold and clad in purple, boasting of the spoils of princes and nations; to see luxurious palaces and heights crowned with fortifications, instead of a boat turned downward for shelter."

The source of this uninventable reversal of fortunes lay in the failure of the *Caedite eos* approach, as epitomized by Simon de Montfort. It was a perpetual mystery to such killers as to why the local people refused to abet their slaughter. They usually concluded it was because Satan had ensnared these "heretics." As a knight "full of sagacity" named Pons d'Adhemar explained well before the papal massacres began, the reason was much simpler. These "heretics" were human beings whose faces they knew, whose lives they respected. After attending a theological debate, he complimented one of the papal envoys on the fluency of his arguments. "Why, then," the envoy asked, "do you not expel them from your lands?" "We cannot," Pons answered. "We have been brought up with them; we have amongst them folk near and dear to us, and we see them living honestly."

As blunderers like Montfort made matters worse with every innocent they killed, others—no less fanatic themselves, but more sincere in their religious motivation—sought more cost-efficient ways to impose the Church's will. Domingo Félix de Guzmán, founder of the Dominican order, was a vegetarian with an interest in astrology who hated luxury. Displays of ecclesiastical privation, he came to believe, could prevail where *Caedite eos* had failed. Once the "heretics" saw that the pope's prelates were not corrupt, the future Saint Dominic imagined, killing people no longer would be needed. Awed by the resplendent piousness of the clergy, they would believe what they were told to believe. So, Dominic and his followers fasted instead of feasting, at the beginning. They abjured violence, for a while.

Surely, they thought, the "heretics" now would heed their preaching, but that did not happen. Even after having been patiently instructed as to the error of their ways, these sinners persisted in their contrarian beliefs, so to the sin of failing to heed the Church's teachings was added the grievous sin of disobedience. This happened for two reasons. In every age and place, a certain percentage of the population insists on deciding for itself what God's instructions are. The much greater reason was that the Church's definition of "heresy" never stopped changing.

Massacre and earnestness both having failed, terror turned out to be the Church's ticket to success. The townsfolk of Moissac had stymied Simon de Montfort's 1212 rampage. In 1235, just twenty-three years later, terror once again stalked the vales and villages of Quercy. This time squads of Church inquisitors launched the assault. They personified, and their tactics epitomized how enormously in the eighteen years since its founding, the Dominican Order had changed its nature. These inquisitors did not walk, as Saint Dominic had. They arrived on horseback, flanked by "an armed escort that . . . included, over and above men-at-arms, various jailers, notaries, assessors and counselors." The dead were not exempt from these inquisitors' wrath, nor were the dying. "At Cahors they held a series of posthumous trials, and exhumed and burnt numerous corpses as a result." On Saint Dominic's feast day, a woman in her eighties was ripped from her bed, and burned. In Moissac, "the Inquisitors found two hundred and ten [living] persons guilty of heresy, and burnt them too."

The mastermind of these travesties, a son of France Profound named Peter Seila, incarnated the Dominicans' dark transformation. He also foreshadowed an astonishing historical development that would see low-born sons of France Profound dominate Christendom. In 1215, in Seila's own house in Toulouse, the ascetic Dominic and his acolytes had founded their Order. Following Dominic's death six years later, Seila became the clerical Stalin to Saint Dominic's Lenin. Fanatical when it came to burning "heretics," Seila was also relentless when it came to pursuing the Dominicans' indoctrination programs. "Give me the child for the first seven years," the founder of the Jesuits, Ignatius of Loyola is said to have proclaimed, "and I will give you the man." More than three centuries earlier, Peter Seila was the Dominicans' archangel of wrath and hate. In the indoctrination centers he ran, the brightest and best of provincial youth were inculcated in the values of intolerance and schooled in the virtues of extremism. Contravening its founder's teachings, the Dominicans also offered these young men a life of comfort and privilege here on Earth. It started with room and board, access to books and mentors, and then a way up in the world that could, and often did, lead to immense riches and fearsome political power.

This fusion of privilege and fanaticism soon bore dark fruit. More than 150 years before the Spanish Inquisition was founded in 1478, France Profound wrote the book on inquisitions. It was entitled *Practica Inquisitionis Heretice Pravitatis*. Though he wrote in Latin, Bernard Gui, author of this *Practical Guide to the Conduct of the Inquisition into Heretical Wickedness*, was a true son of France Profound. To this day he remains the most notable son of Royères, a village located a hundred miles from Lauzerte, halfway between Poitiers, pivot of Eleanor's inheritance and all the turmoil it bred, and Carcassone where Gui, a fervent Dominican, was named Grand Inquisitor in 1307.

France Profound's literary lions range from the Troubadours to Montesquieu, but in the dark realms of history no book has been more influential than Gui's treatise on terror. Renowned while he lived for the effectiveness of his interrogations, the Grand Inquisitor of Toulouse was well-enough remembered five hundred years later to make a cameo appearance in Victor Hugo's five-volume 1862 epic, *Les Misérables*. Among the churchmen, his inquisitorial handbook remained so esteemed that in 1886 it was republished, with the Church's imprimatur, in the original Latin, then translated into French and other languages. His name recurs as late at 1986, in Umberto Eco's *The Name of the Rose*.

Gui's gleefulness makes the account of his inquisitorial methods chilling. The adept inquisitor started, as Gui himself boasted, by turning the victim into his own accuser: "I ask him why he has been brought before me. He replies, smiling and

courteous: 'Sir, I would be glad to learn the cause from you.'"
The smiles did not last long as, step by step, the inquisitor
deconstructed the accused's professions of faith, while dismantling his self-worth as a human being. The better to
convey his delight in his victims' growing panic, Gui added
parenthetical stage notes. The inquisitor could tell he was
well on his way to crushing his victim when the victim replied
as follows: "(Raising his eyes to heaven, with an air of the
greatest faith), Lord, thou knowest that I am innocent of this,
and that I never held any faith other than that of true Christianity." Quite soon the prisoner, led on by the inquisitor's
perverse version of the Socratic method, realized that whatever
his answer, it would be used to condemn him. "Ought I not to
believe this?" the victim asked when queried on some theological nuance. The inquisitor knows he has him now. "I do
not ask if you ought to believe, but if you do believe," he re-
joindered. "I know your tricks."

Soon Gui had the victim pleading: "I am a simple and ignorant man. Pray don't catch me in my words." Steadily, the
inquisitor edged his victim into the trap he had set. Would he
swear to God he is not a heretic? "Willingly," the victim would
answer and then: "(Growing pale) If I ought to swear, I will willingly swear." The Grand Inquisitor will have none of that; "a
vigorous Inquisitor must not allow himself to be worked upon
in this way," Gui counseled, "but proceed until he makes these
people confess their error, or at least publicly abjure heresy, so
that if they are subsequently found to have sworn falsely, he can
without further hearing abandon them to the secular arm."

As that final comment about having "sworn falsely" revealed, this interrogation had a hidden purpose. Perjury, in addition to being sinful, was a crime against the State. As one
scholar notes, "To 'abandon them to the secular arm' is a eu-
phemism for condemning the accused to be burned alive."

Gui's objective, now achieved, was to assemble a dossier so incriminating that the inquisitor—"without further hearing"—could condemn his victim when, if, and as it suited his purposes, to be burned alive, with no further possibility of extenuation or appeal. In George Orwell's *1984*, Room 101 would be an underground torture chamber located in the Ministry of Love. In Toulouse, the Grand Inquisitor's torture chamber was integral to the Church's ministry of love. "You believe that I believe it, which is not what I ask, but whether you believe it," Gui's Inquisitor states at one point. "Is it your opinion," the interrogator in *1984* asks, "that the past has real existence?" In both cases, any possibility of an independent reality has been excised. Big Brother, dystopian avatar of the power popes, is all-triumphant.

Digging up corpses, putting wormy cadavers on trial, like torturing bed-ridden old ladies, worked in the short run, but in order to achieve long-term cost-efficient results, a bureaucratization of the terror was required. That explains why Bernard Gui, who began his climb to power at one of the schools Seila himself had founded and ran, achieved such renown. Heavy-handed inquisitors like the notorious Dominican monk Robert le Bougre, remembered as *Malleus Haereticorum*, the "Hammer of Heretics," operating in different areas of France, killed thousands during the same years Gui was developing his quite different way of instilling doctrinal compliance. In his fifteen years as Grand Inquisitor in Carcassonne, Gui interrogated as many as twenty thousand suspects, yet returned only nine hundred guilty verdicts. Of these, forty-two were executed. His success lay not in how many he tortured or killed, but in infusing the whole of secular society with an aura of dread.

The lad from Royères had come up with the answer to questions that had bedeviled the hierarchs of the Roman curia until then. How to compel obedience without destroying civil society? How to eliminate "heresy" without provoking the kind of socioeconomic implosion that destroyed the Church's sources of wealth? Gui understood that a living "heretic" who survived his inquisition was a living warning to everyone around him for so long as he lived. No wonder the bishops so revered this low-born friar that they made him a bishop too.

Bernard Gui was far from being the highest-ranking of this new class of power players, composed of young men of modest origin exploiting the opportunities for upward mobility that the Dominicans provided. That distinction goes to a fellow son of France Profound named Bertrand de Got. He hailed from Villandraut, a tiny village eighty-eight miles west of Lauzerte, which I often pass on my way to the dunes of Arcachon. Previously, the papacy had been the plaything of great noble Italian families, yet in 1305 Bernard de Got, a rustic from France Profound, became Pope Clement V. The growing power of the French state was one reason outsiders were able to grab away the cloak of Saint Peter, but the main cause was to be found inside the Church itself. In more recent times, the American war in Vietnam Vietnamized America, its national life becoming ever more violent in the political and intellectual, as well as the ethical and spiritual sense long after Saigon was lost. It was the same with the Crusades. Long after Jerusalem was lost, the Crusades' malign effects continued to corrupt and deform Rome in matters of public order, as well as in religious affairs.

By 1305 the city of Saint Peter was so in thrall to factional violence, it was life-threatening for a new Bishop of Rome to be elected, let alone reside there. Fleeing Rome, the College of Cardinals convened in Perugia. While the curia squabbled over its morally rotten corpse like black-feathered vultures, the French snatched the papacy for themselves. Once de Got was crowned pope in Lyons, the question was where to put him.

In 1271, the popes had gained possession of the Comtat Venaissin, a band of territory nearly encircling the city of Avignon. First in the Comtat, then in Avignon itself, not far from where Francis Bacon would paint three of his earliest popes, seven popes would reside, from 1309 until 1377. Pope Clement V, as Bernard de Got was now styled, set up shop there exactly one hundred years after papal invaders in 1209 had surged down the Rhône valley, imagining that Toulouse would be theirs within weeks.

The failure of the Crusades, including the failure of the papal invasion of France Profound, had demonstrated the inability of the traditional warrior castes, both secular and religious, to control events. As the Inquisition, thanks to Gui and France Profound cohorts, replaced the Crusades as the organizing principle of papally condoned violence, the *noblesse de la robe* of the Church—the inquisitors and their institutional allies—replaced the *noblesse de l'epée*, just as in secular society the bureaucratic and judicial elites were supplanting the feudal lords, whose power had been based on violence rather than money.

With France Profound's Grand Inquisitor popes now on the papal throne, the definition of "heresy" did not change. The identity of the "heretics" necessarily did, since "heretics," definitionally, were those whom those in power wished to destroy. In every Crusade the Knights Templar had fought valiantly, but now that the Crusades had failed, the Templars and their ilk constituted a potential threat to the new popes in their new papal seat at Avignon, so these stalwarts of the church militant were now declared, themselves, to be "heretics." In return for confessing under torture to worshiping a bearded human head, spitting on the Cross, and engaging in public fellatio, Jacques de Molay, twenty-third and final Grand Master of the Knights Templar, was spared public incineration but then, in 1314, when he renounced his confession, this Knight

Templar who had fought for Christianity unto the gates of Jerusalem, now aged about seventy, was "without further hearing abandon[ed] to the secular arm." After he was burned at the stake, what morsels were left of him were put in a grinder, then extruded. As with King Peter the Catholic, the reward for loyalty to the popes was a gruesome death inflicted under the aegis of the Church itself.

Previously, popes had been born with names like Benedetto Caetani and Nicola Boccasini, who reigned as Boniface VIII and Benedict XI. Now, boys with names you still can find on the sports pages of *Depeche du Midi* grew up to become Vicars of Christ on Earth. The sudden preeminence of such a remote region when it came to controlling the most powerful institution mankind has ever invented may seem anomalous; actually, it was logical. Give one group or another power to suppress one's enemies; it is likewise given power over you. The papal crusade to crush heresy in France Profound had produced an inquisitorial elite drawn from the same stock as the "heretics" themselves. As a result, the tool seized control from the hand that held it, and France Profound took the papacy prisoner.

Seven popes in all, along with several anti-popes, would hail from that quadrant of the country which today corresponds to the 05 regional dialing code or, if you're calling France from overseas, the 335 prefix. Below are the reign names, the reign dates, the birth names, and, most revealing, the birthplaces of the Avignon popes, including the current departments of modern France where those popes were born. To grasp how transformational this was, draw a little triangle on a map of Europe with its apex just north of Limoges, its middle point a little west of Bordeaux, and its bottom point south of Toulouse. Six of those seven popes, as well as Gui, were born inside that triangle. Run a line eastward, toward the birthplace of the one remaining pope. You will see it forms a salient pointing straight at Avignon. In the middle of the triangle, only seemingly aloof from the world's travails and their uninventable consequences, sits Lauzerte.

The Avignon Popes	Reign	Name	Birth Place
Clement V	1305–1314	Raymond Bernard de Got	Villandraut, Gironde
John XXII	1316–1334	Jacques Duèze	Cahors, Lot
Benedict XII	1334–1342	Jacques Fournier	Canté, Ariège
Clement VI	1342–1352	Pierre Roger	Maumont, Corrèze
Innocent VI	1352–1362	Étienne Aubert	Beyssac, Corrèze
Urban V	1362–1370	Guillaume de Grimoard	Grizac, Lozère
Gregory XI	1370–1378	Pierre Roger de Beaufort	Maumont, Corrèze

16

OUR QUERCY POPE

Of all the Avignon popes, the wickedest was the one born closest to Lauzerte. Jacques Duèze, the eventual Pope John XXII, hailed from nearby Cahors. Only twenty-two miles away, it is, along with Montauban and Moissac, Lauzerte's third attendant city. According to the Roman Catholic theologian Bernard McGinn, among the 266 pontiffs gong all the way back to Saint Peter, John XXII "bears the distinction of being the most popular candidate for the role of Papal Antichrist."

Preaching Crusades, then using the Crusaders' money to enrich himself and his family, Pope Clement V had pioneered a new dimension of depravity when it came to papal corruption. Evidently de Got so tried God's patience He could not wait to plunge him into hellfire. As if in a fit of divine pique, lightning set ablaze the church where de Got's body lay following his death in 1314. De Got's body, it was remarked, resembled badly cooked pig, charred in some parts, bloody raw in others. Following Bertrand de Got's lightening-induced semi-cremation, it took the College of Cardinals more than two years to choose Jacques of Cahors as the second France Profound pope.

The prelates might have gone on drinking the papal wine and helping themselves to the papal treasury indefinitely had not two nephews of the dead pope, on Tuesday, 24 July 1314, launched a military assault on the cardinals' conclave being held at Carpentras, a pleasant Provencal town hundreds of miles distant from their traditional meeting place in Rome. As the princes of the Church fled for their lives, the dead pope's relations, having first pillaged the town and set it ablaze, made off with a papal treasure amounting to more than one million gold florins. Thanks to this timely attack, that immense sum, supposedly destined to support the latest Crusade, remained in the hands and under the control of the dead pope's kinsmen.

Appalled at their brush with martyrdom, the cardinals refused to reconvene. Finally, two years later, King Philip V lured the cardinals inside a church in Lyons, ostensibly for a memorial service in honor of his brother, the recently defunct King Louis X. He then surrounded the church with armed guards, and bricked up the entrances and exits. Forced to act, the cardinals compromised on Jacques Duèze of Cahors, aged seventy-two, because of the anticipated brevity of his reign. Pope John XXII—never to be confused with the saintly twentieth-century Pope John XXIII—spited his many rivals by living to age ninety, and ruling for eighteen years.

Ruthlessly consolidating his power base, the new pope had the Bishop of Cahors, Hugues Géraud, burned at the stake. After personally interrogating his hometown rival, he decreed the bishop guilty, in addition to murder, sorcery, and sacrilege, of plotting to poison no less a personage than the pope, that is, himself. This juridical murder opened the diocese of Cahors to infestation by the pope's family and cronies. It also provided the template for a papacy based on torture and murder, and propelled by greed. The nineteenth-century historian Ferdinand Gregorovius called him the "Midas of Avignon," and rightly so. Pope John XXII worshiped money the way others venerated fragments of the One True Cross. Considering his origins, that was unsurprising. He came from a family of wealthy bankers. By the time Jacques Duèze began his ecclesiastical ascent, Cahors long had been Europe's usury capital. Its remoteness was part of its success. Operating the way bankers in today's off-shore tax havens do, the *Caursines*, as its money lenders were known, built an empire of usury stretching from Muscovy to the Tagus, though then, as now, the biggest money was to be made in the City of London.

Yet again, France Profound was leading the way. More than one hundred years before the city of Florence and the Borgias became by-words for financial corruption, using their immense wealth to install two popes, Callixtus III and Alexander VI, Cahors already had its pope. Nothing better illustrated the state of the times than the new pope's attitude toward lending money, and collecting interest from debtors. According to long-established Christian articles of faith, to loot and pillage was permissible, provided you had the proper papal dispensation, but lending money for profit was beyond the pale. "Lay not up for yourselves treasures upon Earth," Jesus had urged, yet when the devout whispered that the new pope's love of money was un-Christ-like, the Caursine pope reminded the faithful that Judas, too, had possessed a purse, in which he kept money. Baby Jesus Himself, he furthermore reminded them, had accepted without demur the mythical Gifts of the Magi, including the horde of gold they brought with them. Ergo he, Christ's vicar, was entitled to do the same.

To buttress his theologically baseless assertion that greed was good, the pope instructed an English philosopher resident at the papal court to confirm that Christ and the Apostles had loved property. His name was William. He hailed from Ockham, a village today engulfed by the southwestern exurbs of London. He's the one we have to thank for Ockham's—or Occam's—Razor, which propounds that the simplest explanation is usually the best. Admired for its intellectual rigor, Ockham's thought over the centuries has inspired Copernicus, Galileo, Isaac Newton, Bertrand Russell, and the physicist Ernst Mach, among many others. After William of Ockham made the mistake of informing Jacques of Cahors, straight and simply, that Christ had abjured property, which is why He had driven the money lenders from the Temple, the pope threw William of Ockham into prison. He escaped, and set to work proving that Jacques of Cahors was the true heretic. His weapon of choice in this instance was the bludgeon, not the razor. William of Ockham's 1335 *Tractatus contra Johannem* ran to thirteen volumes.

The enemies whom Jacques of Cahors chose to persecute provided the measure of his character. His greatest grudge match was against the gentlest followers of Saint Francis, the pacifist apostle of song birds and lilies of the field. The Franciscans incurred the pope's wrath for the same reason William of Ockham had. The Rule of Saint Francis prohibited ownership of property. It required members of the order, in the manner of Buddhist monks today, to beg for their food, but like the election of a Caursine pope, the spiritual evolution of the Franciscans by then had become symptomatic of the times. Lust for money, like an STD, had infected even the saintliest of realms.

When pious "Spiritual Franciscans" expelled corrupt abbots from their monasteries, the Caursine pope "summoned them to Avignon within ten days, on pain of excommunication." "About the Feast of the Pentecost," recounted the contemporary chronicler Angelo da Clarino, "sixty-four brothers from the convents of Narbonne and Beziers . . . marched directly to the papal palace." Once the pope appeared, these devoted churchmen learned why they had been summoned. The delegation's interlocutor, "Gaufridus de Cornone," this chronicler continues, "was the victim of an especially shameless piece of bullying by the pope." Their dialogue unfolded as follows:

THE POPE: Brother Gaufridus, I wonder that you clamor for the strict observance of the Rule [of St. Francis], when you own five gowns yourself.

GAUFRIDUS: Holy Father, you are deceived; it is not true that I own five gowns.

JOHN XXII: Then we lie, do we?

GAUFRIDUS: Holy Father, I did not say, nor would I say that you lie; but I did and do say that I do not own five gowns.

JOHN XXII: We order you to be arrested, until we see whether it be true or not that you own five gowns.

"No wonder," observed the American scholar, David S. Muzzey, in his 1907 reconstruction of the pope's persecution of *The Spiritual Franciscans*, "that the rest of the deputation despaired of further audience and fell on their knees before the pontiff crying, 'Justice, Holy Father, justice!' Their cry fell on deaf ears." The leaders were cast into prison, all the others interrogated in close confinement. Under torture, four of the Spiritual Franciscans persisted in their contention that Christ had loved the poor, and that He had lived in poverty, so "they were burned at the stake in Marseilles, on the seventh of May 1318." These martyrs' names, truly worthy of remembrance, were Jean Barrani, Dieudonné Michaelis, Guillaume Souton, and Pons Rocha. In return for repudiating what Christ taught, a fifth Franciscan, Bernard d'Asla, was allowed to live, though he was "condemned to wear, for the rest of his life, two yellow crosses, one in front on his chest, the second in back between his shoulders." Much of the twentieth-century paraphernalia of the Holocaust would be adapted from the Holy Inquisition. John XXII's inquisitors also burned books.

As the martyrdom of these monks "of Narbonne and Beziers" demonstrated, *Caedite eos*, far from exterminating "heresy," had sowed the seeds of renewed spiritual resistance in the very places where it had been most ruthlessly repressed. As before, the persecution fed upon itself. Following the executions at Marseilles, there were "burnings at Narbonne, Montpelier, Toulouse, Lunel, Carcassonne, Beziers, Montréal,"

among other places. John XXII himself frankly acknowledged
the reason for this latest terror campaign. "Great is poverty,"
he allowed, "But perfect obedience is the greatest good." Disobedience remained the unforgivable heresy, and so these latest "heretics" suffered the familiar retribution. First, their robes
and rosaries were taken from them. Then these pious monks'
heads were shaven, to deprive them of their tonsures, their
last bodily link with their Order and their Church. As the
Archbishop of Marseilles later explained, "The four . . . maintained with obstinacy that Pope John XXII never had, and
still did not have any authority to make the declarations and
propound the precepts he had."

A posthumous portrait showed how devout Christians
like the martyred Franciscans and respected theologians like
William of Ockham regarded John XXII. It depicts Jacques of
Cahors greedily ravaging the Sacred Lamb. Monster-tailed
and bat-winged, the pope's bosom buddy Satan, voyeur-like,
witnesses the defilement approvingly. Satan was not the only
one to approve. Just as Gui and his *Practica Inquisitionis Heretice
Pravitatis* remained revered among churchmen unto the nineteenth century, Jacques of Cahors would be reverenced into
the twenty-first century, no more so than in Lauzerte, where
a shrine lauding him, and celebrating the tactics of his reign,
would be installed in the church right across from my House.
There the Midas Pope, the pope who averred that he, no less
than Judas, had the right to love money would be lauded as a
model for our times, as a Reformer Pope, as Our Quercy Pope.

This I would see, one hot Saturday morning, with my own
eyes.

17

LOVING THE SHEPHERD

No rogue fails to do someone some good. Were it not for Jacques of Cahors, I might never have found one of the true heroes of my life. His name was Pierre Maury. Even though 750 years separated us, only three degrees of separation were needed for us to connect. It started with the Caursine apostate's successor as Avignon pope. Jacques Fournier, the future Pope Benedict XII, was born eighty miles south of Lauzerte, in 1285, in a hamlet, current population 203, called Canté.

Though rustic, his birthplace was not remote. In an age when neither peasants nor popes could travel faster than their feet, carts, or mules could carry them, the village of Canté was a day's journey from Toulouse. Heading south, toward the Pyrénées, a healthy lad with a pair of good strong legs under him could reach the fabled redoubt of Foix before sunset. When the surrounding orchards are in bloom, Foix, with the snow-clad Pyrénées providing the backdrop, looks like a living tourist poster. Back then it was a military, also a theological fulcrum. Kings and cardinals, popes and princes were either stymied or enabled by Foix, depending on whether friend or foe controlled that gorgeous redoubt. Like Lauzerte, Foix derived its destiny from a chunk of rock. Three great towers— one cylindrical, one rectangular, the third pyramidal—surmount the crag of Foix. Another long day's trek would bring the intrepid pilgrim to Montaillou, the village that, starting in 1294, became the focus of the future Pope Benedict XII's inquisitorial endeavors.

Canté was a propitious home town for an Avignon pope. Convenient to Carcassonne, headquarters of the Inquisition, as well as Toulouse and Foix, it was even closer to Pamiers, the city where Jacques Fournier took his first giant step toward the papacy by being named bishop there. Administratively as well as theologically, Pamiers provided a perfect fit. Adept at collecting money, Fournier was so talented as an inquisitor that those he interrogated compared him to an experienced midwife. "He knew," one survivor admitted, "how to bring forth the lambs." This consummate spiritual bureaucrat painstakingly recorded the confessions he extracted from the "lambs" he lured to the inquisitorial slaughter in the volume today known as the Fournier *Register*.

For 633 years following his death in 1342, Benedict XII was a nearly forgotten pontiff, neither sufficiently depraved nor anywhere near virtuous enough to be one of the famous popes. Then, in 1975, immortality was thrust upon him. That year, in France, a book was published entitled *Montaillou, Village Occitan de 1294 a 1324*, by a scholar named Emmanuel Le Roy Ladurie. In 1980, a considerably abridged version appeared in English. Already a bestseller in French, Montaillou sold more than two million copies worldwide. The appeal of Le Roy Ladurie's narrative derived from the richness of its human specificity. This in turn derived directly from Jacques Fournier's diligence, while Bishop of Pamiers, in suppressing "heresy." This grand inquisitor, his records reveal, was a Simenon of the Soul.

Real people, in their own voices, speak to us, thanks to Fournier and his *Register*. As so many priceless documents are, the *Register* might have been lost entirely had the Bishop of Pamiers not become pope. When Fournier relocated to Avignon in 1334, his documents traveled with him. After the papacy returned definitively to Rome in 1376, the Avignon archives were transferred to the Vatican. At each remove precious documents were lost, until all that survived of Fournier's records was a single folio of 325 pages. The contents of that single surviving volume sufficed to turn an obscure pope and a hitherto unknown scholar into cultural celebrities. The third protagonist bringing me and Pierre Maury together, after Jacques Fournier and Emmanuel Le Roy Ladurie, was Jean Duvernoy. He was the archivist who actually found and translated the *Register* from Latin into French, and then published it in Toulouse in 1965.

The worldwide praise heaped upon Le Roy Ladurie obscured the reality that his famous book was a brilliant synthesis of someone else's research. At the very beginning of *Montaillou*, its author quibbles with the quality of certain selected bits of Duvernoy's translation, then never mentions him again. In the highly influential English abridgment, Duvernoy once again is consigned to a footnote. Long after Montaillou, so far as the rest of the world was concerned, became the last word on the subject, Duvernoy kept burrowing through the archives, searching for new material, and finding it. "His search was humble, without seeking honors," observed one scholar, rather pointedly. It was left to a French Unitarian blog post to give him his due. "Inventor of Modern Historical Catharism," its obituary called him, identifying what, together, Duvernoy and Le Roy Ladurie had wrought.

Like the vast majority of the "heretics" killed during the papal invasion and, later, condemned by the Inquisition, the "Cathars," as they were now called, had believed themselves to be faithful Christians, and for good reason. As Fournier's own interrogations showed, the beliefs these "heretics" held were much closer to traditional Christian teachings than what Le Roy Ladurie describes as "the theological fantasies" of the churchmen who persecuted them. Many of those whom Fournier interrogated described themselves as adherents of the "old religion." For them, the popes' financial compulsions and control obsessions, along with the bizarre presence of the pontiffs in Avignon, constituted the emergence of a cult that traduced the traditional teachings of the Church of Rome, and of Jesus Christ Himself. Historically and theologically, they were right about that.

Fournier had the Gui gift—the capacity to limit physical violence against individuals while assuring terror pervaded society as a whole. Between 15 July 1318 and 9 October 1325, a period of more than seven years, Fournier put only 114 persons on trial. Even when found guilty, fewer than half were sent to prison. The rest, sixty-two in all, were either acquitted, or subjected to various noncustodial penalties. When two avowed atheists, both women, persisted in their irreligion, Fournier did not order them tortured or imprisoned. He set them free, though with the familiar proviso that they wear the yellow cross, front and back. One villager named Raimond de l'Aire avowed beliefs many guests at my Lauzerte dinner table no doubt share. "God never made the world," he declared. He also claimed "that the resurrection was a myth, that the Eucharist was nothing more than bread and wine." Scorning any notion of either an Immaculate Conception or a Virgin Birth, he added that Jesus had come into this world "just through screwing, like everybody else." There is no record of what if any punishment was inflicted on Raimond de l'Aire.

Sex certainly played a big part in making the long-dead people of Montaillou come alive. Thanks to the *Register*, we learn that for those interested in gay sex it was best to seek satisfaction in Pamiers, where a homosexual subculture, including Church clerics, flourished right under Bishop Fournier's nose. Thanks to our "ethnographer-detective," we learn that bestiality was not unknown, and incest not uncommon. The parish priest, Pierre Clergue, took the prize in the Montaillou sexual Olympics. A "certainly incomplete" census of his mistresses listed by name one dozen paramours, approximately one-fifth of Montaillou's sexually eligible female population. The free-love priest was aided in his conquests by a special herb he kept in a pair of necklaces resembling the devotional scapulars that, along with rosaries, the faithful keep about their persons to this day.

"I have a certain herb," the priest would tell the women and girls he seduced. "If a man wears it when he mingles his body with that of a woman, he cannot engender, nor she conceive." Father Clergue wore one of these devices during intercourse, while placing another around the neck of the woman. Afterwards the priest would compel his paramours to surrender their sex scapular, only returning it when he wished to copulate again. Using their fear of pregnancy to enforce his sexual monopoly, the village priest refused to reveal the provenance of his magic herb. Character turned into destiny when Clergue's enemies denounced him as a "heretic," and in spite of his long service as an informer, he was himself seized by the Inquisition.

Father Clergue's runner-up in the sexual endurance domain was a "heretic" who could match any parish priest when it came to sexual hypocrisy. Guillaume Bélibaste had fled to Spain after killing a man. There he ingratiated himself into a small community of spiritual exiles and then, the better to enhance his material fortunes, made himself its "perfect." When Bélibaste got a woman pregnant he looked for someone who could be conned into taking the fall. Pierre Maury, the Shepherd of Montaillou, wintered his flocks in Spain. There he fell under Guillaume Bélibaste's spell.

Earlier, this holy man tried to marry a six-year-old girl to the Shepherd. Now, presenting it as an act of generosity on his part, Bélibaste urged the Shepherd to take his pregnant mistress as his wife. The good-hearted Pierre Maury remained loyal to Bélibaste even when, just three days later, he took her back. Thanks to the Shepherd's kindheartedness, the murderer-turned-preacher now had plausible deniability when it came to his mistress's pregnancy. He also tricked the Shepherd out of some of his sheep. Even so, Pierre Maury continued to love Bélibaste, but then the Shepherd of Montaillou loved everybody—even as everybody took advantage of his nobility of spirit. Even his Aunt Guillemette cheated him in a sheep deal, he conceded.

"Three times I have been ruined," the Shepherd of Montaillou related, before adding with characteristic good will, "and yet now I am richer than I have ever been. I am rich," he explained, "because our custom, thus ordered by God, is as follows: if we have but one farthing, we must share it with our poor brothers." Pierre Maury understood that his character was his destiny. "A shepherd I have been. A shepherd I shall remain as long as I live," he explained. "What one has kneaded, that one must bake," he added, metaphorically. The Shepherd of Montaillou harmed no one and hated no one. He loved God and he loved his fellow humans.

Thanks to the Fournier *Register*, one can see this admirable human alone but never lonely in the mountain fastness, tending his flocks on a starry night, his mind full of thoughts more profound than those the quibbling scholastics disputed. Yet not even this gentle person could the inquisitors leave in peace. "Pierre, after a few further wanderings of little interest, was himself taken captive by the Inquisition," notes Le Roy Ladurie. "In 1324 he was sent to prison and thereafter disappears from the record." As I read those words, perhaps for the hundredth time, I grieve for Pierre Maury. Thanks to the Fournier *Register*, I know how horrible those prisons were. I also understand what it meant to be deprived of the freedom of those mountains, because I myself have followed in the Shepherd's path many a time.

Often, returning to Lauzerte from a getaway to Cadaques or Barcelona, I do as the Shepherd did. I head straight up into, then over the Pyrénées, rather than following the freeways around them. On a map, they look so symmetrical but the Pyrénées are a labyrinth. Traversing that chaos of abrupt climbs and steep descents in my tiny French sports car, I was scared only once. Realizing I was running out of gas, I tried to calculate if I had reached the point of no return. As my Michelin map revealed, I was right upon it—midway between the last town in Spain, and the first in France likely to have a gas station. It was midafternoon in early September. In Barcelona it was so hot you needed a siesta before commencing the evening's adventures along the Ramblas. At Cadaques people would be taking sunset swims. Up here I shivered with the cold, but also with apprehension. Could I survive a late summer overnight in this wilderness where Pierre Maury and his flocks every year spent months?

A thick fog had replaced the drizzle. At the top of one slope, the road entered a meadow, and there I was, in the middle of his flock. Hundreds of sheep stood there appearing then disappearing then reemerging in the fog. Instead of a shepherd, two Pyrénéan mastiffs bounded up to my tiny car. Everyone knows about the Alps and their Saint Bernards. Fewer know that the Pyrénées have produced their own ca- nine giant. These soul-eyed behemoths, bred to rescue lost lambs from snow banks, were black as the paint on my car, the better to make them recognizable in the snow. These giant dogs peered down at me in my ground-hugging little vehicle, one through the windshield, the other through the driver- side window.

Together, they were trying to herd me into their flock.
Where my human eyes saw a little black car, they saw the black
sheep of the flock. After several attempts, the windshield mastiff turned away, with the canine equivalent of a shrug. The
driver's side mastiff made strong and long eye contact. It was a
unique experience looking up into those big blurry black eyes.
As, finally, he trotted away, he glanced back at me, as if to say:
"Really, would you not be happier with us? Do you not know
of the dangers and evils lurking in the valleys beneath us?"

Maybe Pierre Maury was incarnated in the kind man who
let me buy half his gasoline. Just as it seemed certain the car
could go no farther, I came upon a gas pump—with no attendant. It refused to take my American credit card, so when the
car with Spanish license plates arrived, I pleaded with the
driver for help. I held out a twenty-euro note. "The problem,"
he explained, "is that this machine will only sell 20 euros at a
time, and only once on the same bank card. There is another
problem," he added. "If we attempt two sales at ten euros each
using the same card, there is the possibility the second sale will
be refused." He then inserted his credit card, and put ten of
the twenty euros of gas into his car. I held the nozzle while he
advanced his car. Then he held the nozzle while I advanced
my car, and we put the remaining ten euros of gas into it.

Only gradually did I comprehend how deeply I revered
Pierre Maury, who probably died some time in 1325 as a result of disease or starvation caused by his imprisonment. It was
his capacity not to be embittered that made me wish I could
be like him. The full force of how much I loved Pierre Maury
thrust itself upon me one stormy night in Lauzerte. I was up
in the Loft. The rain was the rain that washes away mountains,
the wind the wind that flicks away eight-hundred-year-old
stone houses.

Suddenly a blast multiple times fiercer than all the others
struck. I was sure those giant beams, weighing several tons

each, were about to crush me. If ever there were a moment for last words, this was it. "I will always love the Shepherd!" I shouted defiantly. As if in rebuke, something happened that I never could have invented. A Niagara of water slashed down through the main beam of the ceiling. "My roof is gone," I told myself. "My life is gone. It doesn't matter. I will always love the Shepherd." I realized in that moment what Pierre Maury always had known. Life is the prize! Life is the treasure! Whatever happens, it is always better to have lived.

It was another of those many moments in France Profound when things did not, always, necessarily, and inevitably turn out for the worst. Next morning dawned bright blue. A flock of cumulus clouds, fleecy as the lambs Pierre Maury shepherded, ambled across the clear blue sky. The great beam was undamaged. The ceiling was dry. Out on the terrace, a pigeon eyed me insolently. The flood next time would come from a faucet, not through the roof.

18

BRAVE WIDOW GANDILLONNE

Living in Lauzerte you come to appreciate the recurring re-
semblance of people to trees. I first verified the phenomenon
while studying the two chestnut trees in the Square in front
of my House. When I got my House, the René Tree and the
Yves Tree weren't there. I watched them being planted way
back at the end of the twentieth century. I knew them when
they were saplings. I watched as kids who now have children
of their own played around them.

   The two trees, supplied by the same nursery, were planted
at the same time by the same people, yet they have grown up
to be as different as a bartender is from a garbageman. The
tree closest to the Café du Commerce grew up to resemble
the café's proprietor, René Beziat. The René Tree is short
rather than tall, circular rather than vertical, like René himself. The Yves Tree—same species, planted at the same time in
the same earth—has grown up tall and rangy, just like Yves
Bouleaunoire, the town's spiky slender cleanup man. As I
would notice every time I saw this master artisan of spic-and-
span sweeping up around it, the Yves Tree's foliage is fluffy on
top, just as Yves' hair is.

"By their fruits ye shall know them," the Good Book explains.
That certainly is true of the Reine Claude plum, Lauzerte's
paradigmatic fruit. Bite into a Reine Claude. Suddenly your

taste buds sing with Lauzerte's *genius loci*. In an American supermarket you'd never buy a Reine Claude plum. You'd walk right past it. That's what happened the first time I encountered them at the Saturday market. I was busy filling my straw basket with brightly colored fruit when my philosopher-friend and poultry provider Mr. Martial Paris urged me to buy some Reine Claudes, but why ever would I want a dinky-looking fruit like that? Being American, I had judged this fruit by how it looked, not by how it tastes.

"In order to know a fruit," Mr. Paris propounded, "you must taste the fruit," so I did. OMG! A whole cartload of emojis could not do it justice. Lauzerte had taught me its latest lesson. Never judge a plum by the color of its skin. Experiencing the Reine Claude furthered my philological as well as horticultural education. What is a plum, what is a prune, and what difference does it make? An email dispatched from Mme de Renzy's mountain redoubt dispelled this linguistic confusion. A fresh plum in English is a *prune* in French. A dried plum is a prune in English, while a dried plum is a *pruneau* in French. As she explained, delphically and digitally: "French *prune* = English plum." Her email continued, Gertrude Stein-style: "Fresh plum *prune* dried plum *pruneau* OK? Cadiot"— Cadiot being the name of her estate.

The real-life Reine Claude, queen of France in the early sixteenth century, was the daughter of one king, Louis XII, and the consort of another, Francois I. During her twenty-four years on this earth, she managed in the course of her seven pregnancies to make herself the mother of a third king, Henri III, and of a queen as well, though not for long. A mayfly monarch, her daughter Madeleine of Valois, Queen of Scots, was just seventeen when she died in Edinburgh's dank Holyrood Castle after six months and six days on the throne. Like "Gothic" and "Hundred Years' War," "Reine Claude" is a misnomer. The victim, not the mistress, of events, that pitiable queen had nothing to do with the horticultural development of the scrumptious green fruit that, piled high in great green glass bowls in the Green Room of My House, infuses the casualest nibble with gustatory magnificence.

Far more appropriate would it be for the French Academy to rename it in honor of a true female force in history who lived right around the corner from me 733 years ago. Her name was Gandillonne. Like those plums I love so much, Gandillonne was of great character, yet so nondescript in appearance was this unprepossessing widow that the English soldiers occupying Lauzerte skulked right past her, never suspecting she was a spy. In our current twenty-first century, the English infesting Lauzerte and its environs, especially its sister village, Montcuq, act like an army of occupation. Back in 1291, when Gandillonne conducted her surveillance, they were a real-life army of occupation.

Louis IX was to blame for inaugurating this distressing state of affairs. Having first betrayed his Crusader's Oath in Egypt, he then betrayed the people of Lauzerte and the rest of Quercy, handing them over to the English without a fight. As part of this diplomatic deal, the English king acknowledged the French king's control of Normandy and the Loire valley, which Louis IX's grandfather, Philippe-Auguste had seized from Henry III's father, John Lackland. In comparison to those crucial northern fiefdoms, places like Quercy, Lauzerte included, were but bagatelles. The misfortunes of their peoples were beneath consideration—except for those loyal subjects whom Louis IX abandoned. Elsewhere in France, the king who got himself captured in Cairo and killed in Tunis would be venerated as a saint, but he was not reverenced in Lauzerte. To this day you won't find a church, chapel, or convent named for him.

Off and on from 1259 until 1390 the English lorded it over Lauzerte, using some of that time to install the two biggest fireplaces in my House. In 1271, as part of their latest cease-fire, the English swapped Lauzerte back to the French, only to return in 1289, and assault the town. The massacre was so pitiless that up to the beginning of the twentieth century road-paving crews were still unearthing human remains, along with military debris. In return for acknowledging French sovereignty over the lands they had attacked, the English demanded that the town pay them the immense sum of 3,000 *livres* per annum. English soldiers, it furthermore was provided, would occupy Lauzerte to ensure this tribute was collected. Famine had swept the land in 1285; now the English plague had struck again. This set the scene for Lauzerte's defining moment.

"The general wretchedness, combined with the constant obligation to pay taxes to the foreigners, succeeded in exasperating the inhabitants," notes one chronicler. Lauzerte yearned to "throw off the foreign yoke," as another chronicler put it. In 1291 the Brave Widow Gandillonne would show them how to "kick out the accursed English." Her secret weapon was an apronful of chestnuts. The English troops. spread thin, maintained hill-top contingents in both Lauzerte and Saint-Amans-de-Pellagal, just over three miles distant. Lacking sufficient troops to secure both positions, the English soldiery sneaked back and forth between them, seeking to fool the locals into believing they were more numerous than they actually were.

Ascending the Lauzerte mountain is a steep pathway called the Barbacane. In Gandillonne's time this incline was a principal means of access to the upper part of the town. Humans, beasts, and produce all had to toil up that slope in order to reach the markets, shops, craftsmen, and government offices clustered around the Place des Cornières. At the top of the mountain, the Barbacane debouches into a picturesque passageway today called the Pont de la Gandillonne— Gandillonne's Bridge. When Lauzerte was a walled city, this narrow stretch of pavement was the "bridge" connecting the inner and outer gates of the city.

Gandillonne's house overlooked that narrow passageway, providing her a close-up view of whomever was leaving or entering the city. It was a gossip's paradise, but one time she noticed something more noteworthy than an escaped gosling frantically flapping its wings as the poultry merchant's apprentice chased after it, or a dealer in human flesh escorting a new prostitute to the bawdy house behind the church. The English soldiers were sneaking out of Lauzerte. Gandillonne did not know how many of them had left because the revelations of Bonacci's *Liber Abaci*, percolating across Europe, had not yet reached people like her in places like Lauzerte. As all accounts testify, she could count only to five, but she had her chestnuts. Each time another soldier passed, she put another chestnut in her apron. On my desk are descriptions of the ensuing incident dating from 1768, 1789, 1808, 1905 and 1955, as well as from the late seventeenth, mid-nineteenth, and early twenty-first centuries. They are as one voice when it comes to the vital role Gandillonne's chestnuts played in Lauzerte's liberation.

Here is how my intellectual soulmate, Abbé Taillefer, told the tale in 1905: "A poor widow who lived in the narrow alley that separated the two gates of the Barbacane already had seen several groups of passing soldiers. Intrigued, yet knowing nothing of the reason for these successive outings, she had the idea of counting the number of warriors, using the chestnuts she had with her; and when she realized that none or almost none of that damnable host remained in the town, she in haste made her way to the home of the village's First Consul. She was an energetic soul," Abbé Taillefer at this point patriotically editorialized, "skillfully hiding her hatred of the detested conquerors while remaining faithful to her king."

"'The English are all gone,' she announced. 'As many of them have departed as I have chestnuts here in my apron. See.

Count them, my lord Consul! With God's blessing we will have time to close the gates before they return.'" Once the chestnuts were counted, "the entire population rose up in revolt. The two or three English soldiers who had remained were thrown over the walls. When the English soldiers tried to return, not a single one of them could get into the town." Afterwards, "in order to perpetuate the memory of this happy deliverance, the name of the widow was given to the gate near to her home," the Abbé explained "and this same tradition has been perpetuated up to our times."

In its pungent specificity, the Gandillonne episode is to Lauzerte's civic sense of itself what the Reine Claude plum is to its taste buds. Like the townsfolk who heeded her call to expel the English, she was brave—courageous as the English version of that word indicates, also brave in its many French senses, including valiant, stalwart, and reliable. To this day she continues to personify the resourcefulness of the France Profound rustic. She isn't rich. She isn't powerful. Lacking book learning, she had the same native wisdom and keen eye for the realities of the world, combined with a lively sense of its absurdities and saving graces that, all these centuries later, I encounter in everyone ranging from the café owner my neighbor, through the postman my neighbor, and the master craftsman my neighbor, to the vintner my neighbor, and my neighbor the purveyor of the world's freshest oysters. She shucks them for me, or her husband does, depending on which one is at the market that week.

Gandillonne's spirit still animates Lauzerte, but what about her chestnuts? One time it occurred to me that the Yves Tree and the René Tree might be descendants of Gandillonne's chestnuts: I quickly had to discard that hypothesis. The trees in the Place des Cornières, like their April-in-Paris counterparts, don't produce edible chestnuts. It is impossible to imagine Gandillonne having chestnuts in her apron she could not cook and eat, or grind into flour. She was the kind of resourceful self-starter whom the Lauzerte Charter, promulgated exactly fifty years earlier, was designed to attract to the town. Since local serfs could not settle in Lauzerte, her family would have had links to the wider world—places as far distant as Cahors and Montauban, if not Bordeaux and Toulouse.

Far from being a simple peasant, she was a city-dweller with an independent mind, a harbinger of modern times. So, it turns out, was Gandillonne's son. His mother had triumphed through use of her wits. Her son, likewise, valued mental acuity. He had no desire to pick up a sword or a stave—to become a chivalrous knight, let alone one of the *Vulgarium numerus infinitus*. When the town consuls awarded him an educational bourse, the boy used his scholarship, it was proudly recorded, to study *belles lettres*—secular French as opposed to Latin canonical literature. This reflected a cultural bent that still pervades life in Lauzerte. On a recent morning I saw the fruit vendor's sons, who play Bach and Brahms at our village concerts, unloading his produce immediately beneath my window.

Under French kings, under English kings, through famine, plague, bloodshed, and those stretches of human life when nothing much seems to be happening, Lauzerte evolved into an influential human community. The English might reduce the number of town councilors from twelve to ten, but the citizens of Lauzerte continued to choose their own leaders. As its orchards, granaries, and vineyards flourished, both sides sought to curry the town's favor. Even though it was under French rule at the time, in 1323 the English offered Lauzerte wine duty-free access to the port of Bordeaux. There was a moment when Lauzerte had both an English and a French governor. Both respected, more or less, the town's privileges as specified in its charter. Lauzerte's rights were confirmed by King Philippe VI in 1328, by Jean II in 1351, by Charles V in 1379, and by Louis XII in 1499.

Under both the French and the English, the dividing lines were more fluid than posterity liked to imagine. In Lauzerte, as elsewhere, the invaders encountered willing collaborators as well as implacable resistance. Many of the "English" soldiers were as French as those they oppressed. Saint-Amans-de-Pellagal paid few taxes; English soldiers were posted there to protect its turncoat seigneur. Like Raymond VI's younger brother eighty years earlier, he had thrown in his lot with the invaders. Some accounts suggest the English soldiers actually were sneaking off to drink white wine at Miramar, another hilltop town I see from the Top of my House, or to go dancing at Sauveterre, nine miles distant. When it came to its civic self-esteem, such details mattered little. Much as Lauzerte prides itself, today, on being "one of the most beautiful villages in France," the *Lauzertins* back then reveled in their status as "the first in France to kick out the accursed oppressor."

In the year 1200 the town had scarcely existed. By 1300, having been restored to the French crown thanks to Gandillonne and her chestnuts, Lauzerte was a place of consequence. "Its trade was well known and people came in droves to its fairs and markets. As a reward for its zeal and loyalty," a *seneschal* was appointed to serve there. These influential justices, named by the crown, presided over their courts of law wearing long robes, so they became known as the nobility of the robe, in contrast to the nobility of the sword. "Sheltered by its strong walls, Lauzerte had become both a royal city, the capital of an important bailiwick, and," Abbé Taillefer proudly recounted, "one of the great *châtellenies* of Quercy." *Châtellenie* in those times was a term used to designate the basic administrative unit in a country. Though the nomenclature has changed, Lauzerte maintains that distinction to his day, as headquarters of the commune encompassing the town and its surrounding villages and hamlets.

In the minds of people like "Saint" Louis, it was still the age of sword play, holy relics, and miracles. Up on the Lauzerte mountain, as the Gandillonne episode demonstrated, the *noblesse de l'epée* was giving way to the era when the *noblesse de la robe* took charge. None of those who liberated Lauzerte in 1291, including the consul, was a product of the chivalric tradition. Like Frying Pan Boy and the "little girls and men's wives" of Toulouse, the Brave Widow Gandillonne and the townsfolk who heeded her call unmasked the growing irrelevance of what supposedly passed for legitimacy. Right in front of my House, thanks to her, the top-down version of history was undone. The dawn of a new idea of human valor was heralded as the *Lauzertins* liberated Lauzerte all by themselves.

None of this would have happened had Lauzerte not become a bastide with its own charter and the sense of civic right and human rights it engendered. By changing the template for history, the Count of Toulouse had empowered Brave Widow Gandillonne and countless others to make history. They would call it people power later.

19

THE BLACK PRINCE
SYNDROME

When people in Lauzerte refer to "the war," they often don't mean World War One, in which more French boys died than in any other war, or the war in Algeria, though it still wounds the country deeply. They are referring to that epic struggle of which the people of Lauzerte right from the start were such stalwarts, the war to rid France of the English. Historians inaccurately and misleadingly call it the Hundred Years' War.

As ex post facto misdefined, the Hundred Years' War lasted 116 years, from 1337 to 1453. As the Brave Widow Gandillonne demonstrated in 1291, the struggle was well underway long before that. Not one war, it was a spate of recurring conflicts as kings, killers, brigands, terrorists, and looters from England episodically ravaged France and plundered it. One way or another the conflict lasted some 492 years. Pretending that this epochal struggle lasted a mere century or so disguises its physical destructiveness, its human savagery, and the scars it left. Nigh unto a thousand years later the legacy of that conflict deeply shapes both the English idea and the French idea of themselves. It infuses their understanding—and chronic misunderstandings—of each other. It also contextualizes contemporary events, including Brexit.

The physical destruction and loss of human life during this long struggle were almost unimaginable, even in our current age of world wars and thermonuclear weapons. The whole brutal affair was also, as Sartre and the Existentialists might have put it, a triumph of the absurd. The absurdity was that a single French invasion of England led to nearly half a millennium of English invasions of France. This counterintuitive triumph of the law of unintended consequences, wrought by the 1066 conquest that made a French duke, William of Normandy, king of England, had been compounded in 1152 by the royal marriage that made a French duchess, Eleanor of Aquitaine, queen of England.

No amount of English rapine could alter the juridical reality that the dukedoms of Normandy and Aquitaine incontestably were French. This meant that whatever titles they held in England, their dukes and duchesses owed fealty to the kings of France, yet as England's French rulers became more and more English, a metamorphosis occurred. Sovereign in England, they increasingly purported themselves to be sovereign in their French territories as well. The irresolvable problem for the English was that, legally speaking, this pretense was groundless. They could defeat the French in battle, but when it came to legalities, French law—and French lawyers—would always prevail. This meant in the long run that the *noblesse de la robe* would triumph over the *noblesse de l'epée.*

When French people look back on those centuries of killing and rapine, they find echoes of the present; they wonder what, century after century, motivates the English to disrespect them so. When the English look back, they recall the English victories at Crécy in 1346 and Agincourt in 1415. They forget that winning battles is different from winning wars. No one demonstrated this better than the Black Prince, one of English mythology's greatest paladins. To this day Edward of Woodstock is revered as the prodigy who covered himself with glory by winning the Battle of Crécy, aged only sixteen.

Myth was the victor at Crécy, the battle the prelude to that unfortunate prince's utter undoing. In the actual fighting, the impetuous teenager was quickly thrown from his horse. His standard-bearer saved the lad's life by beating back the prince's assailants. In this near escape the Black Prince's father, King Edward III, sensed the chance to cloak his adolescent heir in an aura of invincibility. Rather than rush to his side, the king let his son, now protected by battle-hardened troops, continue fighting.

A monarch of enormous ambition, Edward III grasped that letting his son take the glory at Crécy that day would serve his—and hence his dynasty's—ambitions. By then those ambitions had gone beyond purporting to be sovereign in certain parts of France. The Black Prince's father was the first but far from last king of England to purport he was entitled to rule the entirety of France, as king. In violation of its royal succession laws, he claimed he was entitled to the throne through the female line, via his mother. It was a nice permutation. Having first insisted they were sovereign in Eleanor's Aquitaine, the kings of England now pretended their writ encompassed the whole kingdom of France. Even after Louis XVI got his head sliced off in 1793, they persisted in this pretense. Nearly twenty years after he involuntarily stopped being king of America, George III finally stopped pretending to be king of France, in 1801.

The Black Prince was so called because of the reputed color of his armor, not his complexion. His ballyhooed victory at Crécy did not crush French resistance to the English. No battle ever would, so in 1355 the prince, still in his twenties, was given viceregal writ to subdue the French definitively. Aiming to terrorize the whole of the region's civil society into submission, from the Atlantic to the Mediterranean, he and his invasion force arrived aboard a flotilla of three hundred ships carrying some two thousand archers, a thousand knights, plus an army of foot soldiers. Like Simon de Montfort before him, the Black Prince pillaged Carcassonne and plundered Narbonne. He equally found time to lay waste to little Lolmie, where the Count of Toulouse's ingrate brother had come to grief 142 years earlier. Lauzerte once again seems to have been spared.

The familiar denouement ensued. Instead of subduing the population, the Black Prince's cruelties roused the peasants to revolt. The taxes he extracted transformed the local nobility into loyal lieges of the kings of France, not England. While France Profound was thwarting this early English attempt at overseas colonization, its killer bacilli were winning the war inside the Black Prince's gut, transforming into excretory drool the grand scheme to make the Black Prince the cross-Channel monarch of both England and France. Disabled by gastroenteritis, he was obliged to orchestrate his last massacre, at Limoges in 1370, from an invalid's litter. Back in England, his life dominated by the constant need for chamber pots and fresh linen, the Black Prince, predeceasing his father, died after years of physical agony without becoming king either of France or of England. His own eldest son and heir had died of disease in France too.

As this never-king's own epitaph conceded, he should have stayed in England:

> On Earth, I had great riches:
> Land, houses, great treasure, money and gold
> But now a wretched captive am I
> Deep in the ground, so here I lie.
> My beauty great, is all quite gone.
> My flesh is wasted to the bone.

What started with Richard the Lionheart and continued with the Black Prince became a recurring motif as, over and over again, English royalty came a cropper in France Profound. The most revered of all the Englishmen to ruin themselves ravaging France was Henry V—the gallant Prince Hal, famous for his revelries with his pal Falstaff, and his Saint Crispin's Day speech: "We few, we happy few, we band of brothers." The real Henry V never uttered those words. That blood-stirring oration spewed from the quill pen of William Shakespeare some 184 years after the battle. Falstaff is fictional too.

Richard the Lionheart had died ironically, absurdly in France after reigning over England for nine years, seven months, and three days. Henry V died ironically, absurdly in France after reigning for nine years, five months, and eleven days. By dying so foolishly in France, Richard brought England's vilest sovereign, King John, to the throne. By dying so foolishly in France, Henry V doomed his Plantagenet dynasty to extinction. Both the Plantagenets and their rival Lancastrians would lose the War of the Roses. It ended in 1485, dynastically speaking, with a usurper named Henry Tudor, today remembered as Henry VII, seizing the throne.

Long before Shakespeare transmogrified Henry V of England from a real-life loser, like Louis IX of France, into a mythical hero like Louis, a Fleming named Jean Froissart transmogrified this whole horrid epoch of mayhem and murder into what we still call the Age of Chivalry. You may never have read Froissart, but when you envision the Middle Ages, you likely are picturing in your mind's eye the illuminations populating his vast manuscript, which by the end comprised more than one million words. In those charming visual vignettes, which inspired the décor of countless Technicolor movies, gold and magenta pennants waft while silver swords glint. Valiant knights joust gallantly as virginal maidens pray piously. In this fantasy world blood flows crimson, yet you find no vomit green, nor yellow oozing pustules, in Froissart's *Chronicles*.

Like Shakespeare, Froissart had the great advantage of having no firsthand knowledge of the events he romanticized. The author of this fairy-tale version of the Middle Ages was a boy of nine in 1346 when the Battle of Crécy was fought. At the time of his death in 1405, the Battle of Agincourt lay ten years in the future. Having been born too late and dying too soon to witness those famous events proved immensely helpful to him when it came to chronicling the conflict that Froissart, too, never called the Hundred Years' War. Yet more helpful was that he never once in his life set foot on any battlefield anywhere. Also disdaining intercourse with the common folk who, in every war, suffer most, Froissart confined his researches to the self-glorifying tales knights and nobles told each other once they were safely away from the fighting.

Froissart bequeathed a false chronology as well as a false notion of how history happens. Anyone relying on his account, for example, would consider 1346, the year the Battle of Crécy was fought, a decisive date in human history. They would be unaware that a vastly more consequential event occurred just one year later. In 1347 the Black Death entered France, prelude to conquering England and the rest of northern Europe. Earlier in the century a great famine had scythed through the land, yet by the time the English triumphed at Crécy the population of France had reached the total, extraordinary for the times, of 20,500,000. In the whole world only China and India had more people. Just half a century later, by 1400, France was a depopulated land of dead villages and abandoned fields. In the course of one lifetime, Froissart's own, France's population had fallen to 16,600,000, a net loss of nearly four million souls. Froissart never mentioned this horrific event even though, unlike all those battles he described, he would have seen the Black Death with his own eyes. Every human alive then did.

Froissart set the standard historians have followed ever since then. A historicist omertà envelopes the Black Death and subsequent plagues while gallant knights, mighty kings, and fearless explorers—aka white males—quest across the jousting grounds of History. Onward and upward flows the testosterone until the mindlessness of a nonexistent chivalric past encounters in the form of millions of young male cadavers that paradigmatic product of the Industrial Revolution, the machine gun. In this new epoch of mass-manufactured death, as in Froissart's pre-mechanical times, the microbes continued killing more people than people did.

Just as the Black Death killed countless more people than the "Hundred" Years' War did, the flu following World War One caused more deaths than the Great War, yet the epidemic is barely a sidebar in all those books about the Marne, Gallipoli, and the war to end war by saving the world for democracy. This disinterest, a perpetual feature of historical accounts, is mirrored across the centuries in the literature of plague times. Shakespeare never mentions the Black Death as his "band of brothers" traverses a plague-ridden landscape more reminiscent of *The Seventh Seal* than *When Knighthood Was in Flower.* Like *The Decameron* by Giovanni Boccaccio, the diaries Samuel Pepys kept are nearly unique in giving microbiologically induced mass death its due. In America in the twentieth century as in France in the 1300s, glamorization of death in warfare, along with denial of death by microbe, reigned supreme. You don't find the flu in Hemingway, who paints as false a picture of war as Froissart did. About the only well-known work of American literature to center on the influenza epidemic was written by a Texas lady, and set some five thousand miles from the Western Front. That was *Pale Horse, Pale Rider*, by Katherine Anne Porter.

I was in my Thinking Nook when my thoughts turned to the view right in front of me. Why were there so many empty houses in Lauzerte? I checked. Some three thousand people lived here when France reached its peak population nearly seven hundred years ago; a little under fifteen hundred do now. The same was true in the surrounding towns and villages. Contemplating all those villages where, I constantly complained, the shops and restaurants were always shut, provided a sense of what the impact of the Black Death, and all the plagues that followed it, must have been. Once life returned to "normal," it would have been as difficult to find a carpenter or a plumber as it is today. In thirty years I've never been able to find anyone to tend my hillside enclosure, so *mauvaises herbes*—France Profound versions of kudzu—first invaded, then conquered it. Back then the fields went untilled—the agricultural underpinnings of feudalism were sundered—because the plague killed incomparably more peasants than war ever did. Today it is because they have moved to the cities, and few in France care to do physical labor anymore.

Curious, I sought to establish exactly how many died in the course of all those pestilences that History gives such short shrift. I was astonished. Three million dead during the Hundred Years' War, that is, between 1337 and 1453! As many as four million dead in the Wars of Religion, which lasted from 1562 to 1598. In 1715, under Louis XIV, the population of France remained smaller than it had been 360 years earlier. Not until 1740 did France enter the epoch of consistent demographic growth that by 1914 found it with a population of some forty million. More than enough to pack the trenches to overflowing, it was still less than double of what it had been nearly six hundred years earlier.

Not even a thousand battles of Crécy and a thousand more battles of Agincourt could inflict such a reduction in the population. Only microbes could, yet the problem with acknowledging plague's power, whatever the epoch, is that it renders so many of our human-invented narratives irrelevant.

The telescope refuted all notions that the Earth, with us on it, was the center of the universe. The microscope, and the advance of the Earth's microbial protagonists it unveiled, demonstrated that even on this tiny blue speck, we live among life forms that were flourishing long before we evolved, which continue to flourish in spite of all our attempts to subdue them, and which may well go on thriving long after we and all the other placental mammals have disappeared.

Denial safeguards the illusion that human protagonists direct and control events. It does this at the cost of blinding us to the meaning, and also the consequences, of our actions, so in Genesis Adam and Eve had no sense that, in consequence of their disobedience, they and their progeny would be plagued by invisible adversaries far more malign than the Serpent. Those generations of Crusaders did not suspect they were opening up Christendom to the Black Death. Thanks to the microbes Henry V's band of brothers carried home with them, many more Englishmen would die of disease than Frenchmen they killed in battle.

Persistent denial of the meaning of events helps explain how "heroes" like Henry V and "victories" like Agincourt became phenotypes essential to England's ongoing fictionalization of itself as a land whose people are self-evidently superior to "the French." It also helps explain why, to this day, events in France strike the English as so very odd. If one believes that Agincourt was a great English victory, one naturally will be surprised to discover that, after nearly five hundred years of English torment, France won the Hundred Years' War! Within thirty years of Henry V's death, of diarrhea in France in 1422, the whole of Aquitaine was gone, and all else that had fallen to the kings of England as a result of Eleanor's marriage to Henry II. Virtually all the territories, going back to 1066 and William the Conqueror, which they inherited in their capacity as Dukes of Normandy, also were lost.

The English efforts to master France had thrust into motion a dynastic and, ultimately, a nationalist negative feedback loop. With every English effort to divide France, to crush France, to turn France into a servile appendage of the English, France became more united, more resolute, more French. Frying Pan Boy and the Brave Widow Gandillonne previously personified the resistance English aggression engendered. Now Henry V's self-defeating rampage raised to historical stardom another low-born protagonist. This peasant child was just three years old when France recoiled at the massacres the English committed at Agincourt, ten when the countryside rejoiced at the news the English usurper was dead. As non-elite prepubescents destined to leave their imprint on history periodically do, this French godchild of English oppression started having visions. In 1425 the Voices told Joan of Arc, as we now remember her, to save France!

The lifetimes of Henry V and Joan of Arc overlapped. She was born, in the village Domrémy-la-Pucelle, just 167 miles from the château of Vincennes, where he died. The same war and the same pandemic shaped the world around them, and in each case what they did with their lives turned out to be emblematic. Richard the Lionheart excepted, no figure better personifies England's illusions about itself than the version of Henry V Shakespeare invented. Without exception, no figure better personifies France's understanding of itself than Joan of Arc. This is not because she was virginal and only nineteen when she was burned at the stake at the behest of the English; Charles de Gaulle was neither young nor female when he saved France from itself some five hundred years later. As so often in the history of France, it would take a humble person, an average person—in her case a female nobody—to save France from the blunders and evils and defeats its own leaders inflicted on the country.

The loss in 1558 of Calais, England's remnant outpost in France, was lamented as a royal tragedy as well as a national catastrophe. "When I am dead and opened, you shall find Calais lying in my heart," bemoaned Queen Mary Tudor, yet the English defeat at Calais, like the English victory at Agincourt, wound up vindicating the law of unintended consequences. The victory at Agincourt had prepared the way for England's defeat in its effort to subdue France. England's expulsion from France, culminating in the loss of Calais, opened the way to worldwide dominion for the island realm.

Thanks to its many centuries of abusing France, usurping other peoples' countries had become one of England's defining national endeavors. Now, freed of their French vendetta, that's what the English continued to do on a planetary scale. English pennants no longer fluttered over French battlefields. Around the world the sun never set on the Union Jack. The life cycle of England's pirate-circumnavigator, Sir Francis Drake, epitomized the switch. He was just old enough to have gotten killed fighting England's last battle in France, at Calais in 1558. Instead, he spent his life devastating the wider world, finally dying in 1586 of dysentery, at Panama, instead of dysentery in France, as he might have a generation earlier.

20

BRIDGE OF THE DEVIL

Just as I have my secret route to Moissac, I have my secret vista of Cahors, the charming riverine town that back in the days of the Avignon papacy gave Christendom its vilest pope. Like my Moissac itinerary, my vista atop Mount Saint Cyr, twenty-two miles from Lauzerte, is secret only because no one bothers to go there. At first it does appear there's nothing much to see except a communications tower, but walk past that tower. Look down.

Cahors smiles up at you as though history never happened. With the sun glinting off the town's turrets, and the shadows it casts bringing each facade into focus, Cahors looks like a living diorama, except no team of theme park imagineers could have created a scale model this exquisite. That river seems flat as a mirror, but listen. Hear the water on the spillway way down there. As you watch, a model train pulls out of the railroad station, only it's a real train on its way from Paris to Toulouse.

Paris has the Seine. Cahors has the River Lot, which a lot of foreigners, especially people from Paris, mispronounce. The T in Lot is not silent. It is pronounced, as is the Q in Lauzerte's sister village Montcuq, and the final C in Moissac. On my way to the TGV station in Agen, the final N also pronounced, I pass a town called Lafox, with the X pronounced, as in fox hunting. To speakers of Paris French, these seem like provincial mispronunciations. In reality they reveal how, across the centuries, standard French pronunciation has diverged from its original. The farther you get from Paris, the closer you come to the pronunciations Montesquieu would have used, though the *s* in Cahors is not sounded. French wouldn't be French if the exceptions were not illogical, perverse even.

Nearly encircling Cahors in a U-shaped arc, the River Lot turns the tongue of land on which the city stands into what in French is called a *presqu'île*, an almost-island. A peninsula protrudes into a body of water. A presqu'île is integrally entwined within a body of water just as Cahors itself has been entwined in the flow of European history for some two thousand years. Wrapping itself round almost all of Cahors, the river forms a natural moat, except for a narrow pinch of land at the top. There Cahors is protected by a wall. The Romans started that wall, which has been refurbished many times across the millennia.

The Romans called Cahors Divona, cognate to divinity. Ample fresh water being vital to a Roman outpost's success, the *divona* in this instance was the supposed goddess of a sacred spring. Caesar would have known Cahors as *Divona Cadurcorum*—Divona of the Cadurci. Today, residents of Cahors refer to themselves as Cadurcians. The nominative "Caursine," used in Pope John XXII's time, was dropped because of its connotations of financial corruption and spiritual depravity.

Back in the times of sacred springs, not even a spot as remote as Cahors was exempt from Romanization. Today, analogously, the whole world, including the United States, is being Americanized, albeit at different speeds. Cahors provided an example of that in the waning decades of the twentieth century when its boosters decided the city must have an underground parking garage. In the course of its construction, a Roman amphitheater was unearthed. Remains of ancient public toilets were also integrated into the design, so as you park your car you see through your windshield the squat toilets where people defecated around the time Christ was born. It took Cahors a long time to fill out its *presqu'île*. Not until the Industrial Revolution did human structures cover the whole of the thumb-shaped enclave the river creates. Down at the bottom, the lanes of the old town twist around themselves like the lines in a thumb print. For more than a thousand years that warren of alleys was Cahors. Then, just as New York climbed up the island of Manhattan, Cahors expanded upward too.

A *presqu'île* requires bridges. Cahors has five of them, each a revelation of its time and of the people who built it. The most anonymous-looking of these spans, located not far from the Roman Wall, honors Stéphane Hessel, a free-thinker of the kind the Caursine Anti-Christ would have had burned at the stake. Captured in his twenties by the Gestapo, Hessel escaped the Nazis and, once free, he never stopped raising hell. The title in English of Hessel's most famous manifesto was *Time for Outrage!* His *vie sentimentale* also made him a role model for the age of revolt and free love. He was one-third of the *menage-a-trois* depicted in the New Wave cult film, *Jules et Jim*. Hessel had something in common with Simone Signoret, the quintessential French film actress, and Jacques Offenbach, the quintessential French composer. Like them, this paradigm of what it means to be a French social activist was born in Germany.

The name of the bridge at the bottom of the Cahors *presqu'île* honors another Frenchman who knew firsthand the trauma of exile and the privations of war. It is named for Louis-Philippe, the Citizen King. Everyone knows about Louis XIV, the Sun King, but when it comes to understanding the France surrounding you every day, the lives of its lesser-known monarchs can be no less revealing. A consummate survivor, Louis-Philippe survived the French Revolution, in part because his father, a traitor to his class if there ever was one, voted to guillotine his cousin, King Louis XVI. After that, Louis-Philippe survived two more revolutions. First the July Revolution of 1830 threw his cousin Charles X off the throne, and tossed him up onto it. Then the February Revolution of 1848 tossed Louis-Philippe off the throne, ending the kingship in France once and for all.

In the midst of his tumultuous career, Louis-Philippe fathered eleven children. In a sign of the advancing bourgeoisification of public morals, ten were legitimate. He survived seven assassination attempts before, using the pseudonym "Mr. Smith," he fled to England, there ending his life as he had lived so much of it, as an exile. For good and ill, Louis-Philippe's reign was prophetic. The French intervention in Algeria, the self-made quagmire from which France would not extricate itself, and then far from completely, until 1962, began in 1830, the year he became king. Under the Citizen King, the right to vote was expanded. Tradesmen, not just nobles, could sit in Parliament. This led to an incident I enjoyed relating to Lauzerte's long-time mayor, Alain Chauve. A member of the aristocrats' clique peered sneeringly at one of the new Members of Parliament, elected under the wider franchise, and inquired: "Sir, is it true you are a veterinarian?" "Indeed I am, sir," the veterinarian-parliamentarian amiably replied. "Are you feeling ill?"

Mayor Chauve, in addition to being mayor of Lauzerte, was the town veterinarian. He delivered calves while anxious farmers fretted. He calmed distraught ladies when their terriers got upset tummies. One evening each week the mayor held court in his town hall office, an open bottle of whiskey at the ready. We came to him with all our little civic upsets and communal distempers. As all good doctors do, he treated the patient, not the disease. It took him three years, and many appeals to Paris, but finally he got the Gendarmerie to dismantle the old communications tower blocking my view of the Pyrénées. By getting this lopsided, jerrybuilt Eiffel Tower imitation removed, Mayor Chauve made me realize: I really did belong to Lauzerte now.

When the train chugs southward out of the Cahors station, it crosses another bridge of revelations. I call it the Napoléon III Tressel. Just as the Louis-Philippe Bridge epitomizes the early Industrial Revolution, this span reflects the technological advances that culminated in the erection of the Eiffel Tower. When Marx said history repeats itself as farce, he had in mind Louis Napoléon, nephew of the famous Emperor Napoléon. The nephew's version of his uncle's suicidal sub-Arctic foray into Russia was his farcical tropical adventure in Mexico. Napoléon III's Waterloo was his foolish and unjustified declaration of war on Prussia. He too wound up dying in exile on a British island, in his case Great Britain as opposed to Saint Helena.

Like his uncle, Napoléon III today is revered in France in spite of the catastrophes he brought upon the country. The original Napoléon gave France the Code Napoléon and the world the metric system, people like to remember, preferring to forget how he drenched Europe in French blood. The Paris of elegant boulevards, it is now fondly remembered, was Napoléon III's conception, part of an aesthetic transformation he imposed on the whole country. Today, from the tip of the Cahors *presqu'île* all the way up to the Roman Wall runs a tree-lined Paris-style boulevard where Proust might have promenaded. What the Cahors wall reveals about the Romans' strategic sense, their engineering, and their gift for conquest, this boulevard tells us about the France of formal gardens and natty boulevardiers.

Boulevard Napoléon III would have been an appropriate name, but in an ironic juxtaposition of nomenclature, this Napoléon III-style boulevard is named for the public figure who first led the opposition to his farcical Second Empire, and then overthrew it. Following its defeat in the 1870 Franco-Prussian war, Léon Gambetta was to France what De Gaulle would be after the Fall of France in 1940. He offered a defeated nation hope and resolve at its moment of greatest humiliation. With Napoléon III taken prisoner by the Prussians, Gambetta proclaimed a republic, and organized a government of national resistance. Frying Pan Boy had his casserole, the women of Toulouse their glorified slingshot: Léon Gambetta had his hot air balloon. As the Prussian noose around Paris tightened, Gambetta, the better to rally resistance nationwide, escaped Paris by balloon. It seems to have been the first time a figure of such consequence undertook a mission of such consequence by flying through the air.

Napoléon III epitomized the essential frivolity of France, a nation that prides itself on taking light things seriously. Like the Brave Widow Gandillonne, Gambetta personified the stalwart France. This is the France of blacksmiths and pharmacists and garage mechanics and corner grocers who, after the intellectual fops and preening aristocrats have gotten France into its latest big mess, save the day. While many a French town has its Rue, Avenue, or Place Gambetta, Cahors had special reason to name its main thoroughfare after him. Gambetta, a son of shopkeepers who lost one of his eyes in childhood while playing with acid, was born in Cahors 614 years after the future Pope John XXII, son of money lenders, first saw the light of day there. The Carducian statesman, Léon Gambetta, and the Caursine apostate Jacques Duèze are the two most important historical figures Cahors has given the world. Together they demonstrate how there are simply no limits, moral and otherwise, on what forms human destiny can take.

High above all the other bridges soars the greatest feat of civil engineering Cahors has witnessed in its two thousand years. Completed in 1987, it is called the Viaduc de Roquebillère, yet the feature that impresses me most would have been familiar to the inhabitants of Divona Cadurcorum. Positioned near the base of one of its three-hundred-foot-high towers, the viaduct's modern sun dial, more than six feet in diameter, demonstrates that while technology changes, the underlying principles never do. Just as the arcades in front of my House unfailingly track the solstice, this mighty solar chronometer never fails to get the time right, though it is necessary to adjust its readings for daylight savings time. I never wear a watch, but whenever I pass under the viaduct, I use that immense sundial to check if my cell phone is telling good time. So far it has failed the sundial test only once. I'd forgotten to recharge it that morning.

The little Cabessut bridge provides the most intimate entry into Cahors. You reach it by a narrow road wedged between mountain and river. For years a floating restaurant nestled just upstream from that bridge. A hard-working woman, perpetually harassed but civil, kept the restaurant afloat culinarily speaking. Her food was reliable and not overpriced, except for the plates served with truffles. France Profound is famous for its truffles, so over the decades I've learned a lot about these super-expensive fungi. This has come at a cost equivalent, I estimate, to one semester at an American Ivy League university.

Sumo wrestler–resembling pigs, guided by valiant peasant women of similarly porcine dimension and appearance traditionally roamed the forest hunting for truffles, but today many trufflers prefer to take a horticultural approach. My great friend Dr. Amr Sultan's great friend Natalie's father has planted a truffle orchard, which he showed me one day. The trees were aligned as neatly as though they were there to produce plums, but it was their roots, where truffles tend to nestle, that if all went well yielded a lucrative harvest. "Even this way," he told me, "you can't just dig them up out of the ground. You must find exactly where they are; otherwise you destroy the roots, hence the tree. We let the pig go some time back," he added, in answer to my previous question. "So the dogs help you?" I asked next, while fending off the two dogs, one named Fendi, the other Otto, who seemed to think I had truffles in my crotch, "Well, Otto does," he said. "Fendi refuses," he added with a frown. The first thing to understand before spending all that money is that truffles are about smell, not taste. At the pungent peak of their fecal unforgettableness they make a simple omelet smell like Hestia, goddess of the culinary arts, broke immortal wind onto it. Most of the time, though, the presence of truffles is chiefly remarkable for the many euros it adds to the cost of whatever you order. After much experimentation, I have found that my Truffle Oil Popcorn is a good, and less financially ruinous, way to experience what truffles add to the experience of putting stuff in your mouth. The secret is to add most of the oil after the corn starts popping.

The last time I ate at the floating restaurant in Cahors, a drama unfolded that might have been culled from the archives of an avian inquisition. It was my fault. Some ducks were paddling near the boat, so I tossed them some bread. I would not have been surprised had the ducks squabbled over the bread, but that did not happen. I counted them. There were eight ducks. All except the eighth duck were mottled-colored. It was white as a dove. Instead of going for the bread, the seven other ducks attacked the dove-white duck. They tried to drown it, surrounding it, trying to shove it under water. Hoping to promote peace, I did as the Good Book suggests. I threw more bread on those troubled waters. The seven ducks ignored the bread. They continued attacking the white duck. Finally, thrashing and flapping, it escaped. Only then did the mottled seven turn to the bread.

In places like El Salvador and Ethiopia I'd seen a lot, but never had I seen ducks trying to drown another duck. "Heretics," birds of a different feather: surely there was no need to kill them all. Lost in my meditation on the inhumanity of ducks

I had not noticed that the *patronne* had come to my table, to say hello. "Did you know," I said to her, "that sometimes, when people hereabouts talk about their resistance to the English, and later their attempts to resist the supremacy of Paris, they call it the war of the ducks against the chickens?" The next time I crossed the Cabessut bridge the floating restaurant had vanished. The white duck was gone too. No one knew where, but thoughts of the Owl and the Pussy Cat flickered through my mind.

It is but a hop and a skip from the Cabessut bridge to the commercial premises of my friend, Mr. Jean-Claude Marlas. Thanks to him, I found myself in another situation I never could have invented, that of the village foie gras celebrity. People in Lauzerte already knew that I wrote books and traveled to places they saw on TV, but these were regarded, like most things I did, as eccentricities. Then broke the news that The American was making his own foie gras! Not only that, by all accounts it was delicious, people marveled.

Making your own foie gras is easy provided you have a truly superb foie gras supplier. Mine is Mr. Marlas. His lair is the handsome covered market right near the hideous Cahors cathedral. There are two secrets to making home-poached foie gras. First, never let it cook! *Mi-cuit*—half-cooked—is what the creamiest, pinkest most luscious foie gras is called, and that is what you want your foie gras to be. Always stop before you think you're finished. That's the key thing to remember. So just when you're telling yourself your foie gras is going to need another five minutes, take it off the heat! Once it reaches room temperature, put it at the back of the lowest shelf in your refrigerator. That's so you won't be tempted to taste it before it's ready. Now comes the hardest part. Leave it there inside the refrigerator for a good long time. The recipe books tell you three days. I say a week at least. Let it return to room temperature before you consume it.

The pride and joy of Cahors bridges is the world-famous Pont Valentré. It is to Cahors what the Golden Gate Bridge is to San Francisco, Tower Bridge is to London, and the Ponte Vecchio is to Florence all rolled into one. The Valentré bridge is so beautiful because it reflects the great love that animated Cahors in its heyday: the love of money. For the Romans, Cahors had been a moated fortress. For Caursines of John XXII's ilk, it was a safety deposit box. The Valentré bridge was the combination lock. The bridge had three giant guard towers, one on each bank of the Lot River, and another in the middle. Only those who could get through all three could get their money and themselves in or out of this bank vault of a town.

The twelfth-century patron saint of bridge builders, Saint Bénézet, had a natural connection to Cahors. Bénézet was a shepherd boy when, like Joan of Arc in 1425, Bernadette of Lourdes in 1858, and the Portuguese peasant children of Fatima in 1917, he was blinded by a vision. He was watching a total eclipse of the sun, it is said, when the Voice told him to build the famous bridge across the Rhône River at Avignon, future papal seat of Jacques of Cahors. That bridge no longer traverses the river, but several graceful sections of the Saint Bénézet Bridge, as it is officially known, still stand. With the spired city behind them, and the river flowing in front of them, people love to party there. The song, *Sur le pont d'Avignon*, celebrates all the times people have danced—and still do dance—on that bridge at Avignon.

Bénézet, poor lad, had no time for frivolity. Like Joan of Arc and Bernadette of Lourdes, he died very young, though not before becoming to bridges what Divona was to fresh water springs. The revelation in his case, as in theirs, is how animist themes reemerge in the guise of Christian revelation. Amid the many myths about Bénézet that have arisen across the centuries, one fact is indisputable. He never saw an eclipse. According to the American space agency NASA, the Earth witnessed ten solar eclipses between 1172 and 1177, only two of them total. None was visible anywhere near Avignon.

Work on the Avignon bridge, begun in 1177, was completed in less than eight years. Work on the Pont Valentré in Cahors began in 1308, eight years before Jacques of Cahors became pope. It would continue for more than forty years after that. In 1331, the pope from Cahors brought Bénézet a step closer to full sainthood by promoting him to Venerable. By then, work on the Valentré bridge had been underway for some twenty years, yet the Caursines did not light candles and implore the now-Venerable Bénézet to work his miracles on their bridge's behalf. They preferred to put their faith in the Devil.

In this France Profound version of Faust, Satan strikes his usual bargain. You get your bridge: I get your soul. The bridge does get finished, but the wily chief engineer outwits the Devil. I have a last request, he tells the Devil. I want to drink some cool water before my soul is scorched in Hell. Will you kindly go fetch me some? The Devil eagerly complies, but he is never able to bring him the water because the clever Caursine has given him a sieve to fetch the water! The Devil has his revenge, every night sending one of his vampire-like minions to remove a stone from the bridge, which means it isn't finished. Every morning the engineer replaces the stone. He gets to have his bridge and keep his soul too.

Truths lurk in fables. The truth here is that not even Satan was safe from those crafty Caursine money lenders. Cahors still honors Satan. When the bridge was restored in 1879, the authorities took pains to give the Devil his due. High up on the central tower, you still can see a sculpture—half bloodsucking bat, half depraved human child—crouched there. This minion of Satan is still trying to dismantle the bridge. To this day you won't find any trace of the patron saint of bridges on this most magnificent of Europe's surviving medieval bridges.

21

EVEN ANCIENT WALLS SHALL
BE DESTROYED

Something very important is missing from that charming view Mount Saint Cyr provides. The ugliness is missing. Clenched within its *presqu'île*, Cahors looks so pretty because from that mountaintop you cannot see the countless franchise-type establishments clogging its approaches. Want to conform? Need to conform? Conforama is there for you: also, Promocash, JouéClub toys, Dafy Moto, TaquiPneu ("Tacky Tire"), along with dozens more whose names I've deleted from the list I accumulated entering and leaving Cahors. *Ça va sans dire*, McDonald's is there. In France, McDo's, as French kids call it, has rebranded itself in our posttruth epoch as an ecological activist, environment-protection organization. Its green-themed placards are everywhere.

An incomparably more horrid kind of ugliness is also hidden from view. From Mount Saint Cyr you cannot see the vicious things people have done to each other over the centuries. As well as any place in this world, Cahors illustrates that when it comes to killing each other, humans will always find a will and a way, as the departure of the English demonstrated. For most of five hundred years the French struggle against the English dominated events. Finally, in 1558, the last of the English were expelled. Less than four years later, the French began killing each other with an abandon that transcended the previous bloodletting.

Historians tell us France's Wars of Religion began in 1562. As usual, France Profound was ahead of the times. A contemporary engraving of the Cahors massacre of Sunday, 19 November 1561, shows Protestants trapped in a courtyard. Having set the premises ablaze, the Catholics butcher their victims as they try to escape. A bestselling etching, *The Massacre at Cahors*, provided the template for copycat killings all over France. This slaughter yet again vindicated the definition of "heresy"—that it exists solely in the eyes of the beholder. It also illustrated the whack-a-mole inevitability produced by attempts to force people to believe what they did not. Killing all those "Cathars" 350 years earlier had not extinguished "heresy" in France Profound, or anywhere else. It merely provided the prelude to more religious killing.

In 1320, the same year Bernard Gui published his Inquisition manual in Toulouse, John Wycliffe was born in Hispwell, in the North Riding of Yorkshire. Wycliffe, too, would produce a literary work of great religious influence. In stages from 1382 to 1385 he coordinated the first translation of the Bible into English. A man of high morals, Wycliffe was appalled by the same clerical corruptions that had appalled so many in France Profound earlier. His dream was to reform the Church by replacing orders like the Dominicans with "poor priests."

Subjecting the "heretics" in France Profound to spiritual genocide had not stopped this English priest, nearly a thousand miles and more than a month's journey away, from coming to believe what they had believed, and preaching what they preached. Nor did branding Wycliffe a heretic in England stop the Bohemian village of Husinec, a four-day walk south of Prague, from becoming the birthplace of Jan Hus, the John the Baptist of the Reformation. Like Wycliffe, like the "perfects" the Inquisitors prosecuted, like the Spiritual Franciscans the Quercy pope's henchmen killed, Hus proposed a Christlike cleansing of the temple. The response was also the same. In 1415, the same year the Church tore Wycliffe's corpse from its grave in England, and burned it along with his highly esteemed translation of the Bible, Jan Hus was burned alive in Bohemia.

A single line of causality connected the emergence and reemergence of such "heretics." With many a halt and detour, it ran from the Holy Land through France Profound to England, thence to Bohemia and Germany. There, in 1517, a theology professor at Wittenberg University composed a screed of position papers. Fittingly enough, the Dominicans played a key role, as catalyst, in prodding the most famous heretic of them all into protesting. The corrupt enterprises of the Dominican Johann Tetzel—Grand Commissioner for Indulgences in Germany—goaded Martin Luther into issuing his "Ninety-Five Theses."

The Church's claims of universal supremacy had made "heresy" itself universal, generating the most consequential religious upheaval since the Great Schism of 1054. Those it persecuted had to be labeled as unchristian, so the Church generated a special nomenclature for the "heretics" it created: Cathars, Lollards (as Wycliffe's disciples were called), Hussites, Lutherans, Calvinists. Finally, a portmanteau term emerged that explains why these protests never ceased. Etymologically as well as spiritually, Protestantism was a papal invention and a grand, encompassing moniker it turned out to be. What other term could have encompassed contemporaries so utterly unalike in their theology as Martin Luther and Henry VIII back then, or "born again" televangelists and genteel Episcopalians today?

By making Europe numerate, Fibonacci's *Book of Calculation* had propelled the growth of greed and science. The resultant quest for power and gold provided the context, inter alia, for the European devastation of the western hemisphere. Now the invention of the printing press, and the publication of the Gutenberg Bible, like the advent of the internet in our own time, accelerated beyond previous imagination the spread of "heresy" and efforts to crush it. Once again, Lauzerte found itself exemplifying the times. A German cleric affixed some screed to the door of a church some 285 hours by foot from the door of the church on the Place des Cornières, and sooner than seemed possible, people by the hundreds wound up hacked to death in front of my House.

As early as 1543, nearly twenty years before the Lauzerte massacre occurred, Protestant preachers carrying the printed texts of Luther and Calvin had begun retracing the steps of the vanished "perfects" all over Quercy. By 1560, Lauzerte, like almost every village and town, had its Protestant deacon and congregation. They were called Huguenots now, but nomenclature meant nothing. Lauzerte's deacon, as one observer of the carnage put it, "had switched, like his brother the bishop of Agen, from being a papist into a Huguenot, but he was ready to become a Turk" should that help save his skin, or profit his purse. As Catholics, Cahors-style, massacred Protestants wherever they could find them, one of Lauzerte's preachers, Dominique Cestat, escaped death "almost miraculously" as he fled to the Protestant stronghold of Montauban. It was only a matter of time until the Protestants retaliated.

Unspeakable horror had swept the region 350 years earlier, in the form of Simon de Montfort. This time another ambitious noble of low estate, the Lord of Duras, personified the horrors this latest religious holocaust unleashed. On Sunday, 15 August 1562, Symphorien de Duras and his Protestant henchmen murdered more people in Lauzerte than ever before or since then. Some were murdered inside my House. Many more were killed in front of the House, and in the alleys leading into the Place des Cornières. "This city," according to a record written in semi-archaic French, "situated in a high place, having only one way of access, and garnished with good walls, had served as refuge for all the priests of the country." His objective as a Protestant militant, Duras frankly averred, was to kill "the priests, source of every evil and misfortune." As at Beziers 353 years earlier, it would prove simpler to kill them all, whatever their status or faith.

Many lives, laic as well as clerical, might have been saved had Lauzerte's defenders not made the Beziers mistake. Instead of reinforcing their defenses, they taunted Duras, "saluting him with insults and bravado." Enraged, the attackers redoubled their search for chinks in Lauzerte's armor. Soon enough, they found a barred window whose grill they were able to dislodge. As Protestant killers surged through the Pont Gandillonne, "a great murder of priests" ensued, though, as always, the innocent suffered most. Lauzerte's one-day death toll, the town clerk later attested under seal, totaled "567, of which 97 were priests."

"The streets and squares were strewn with corpses for want of burial. The air was corrupted, to the point that the inhabitants, on their return, had to suffer from two [additional] horrors, no less murderous than the arms and the fury of their enemies: plague and famine. These details, which may appear to have been exaggerated," Abbé Taillefer assured his readers, "are taken from the official report of the investigation, conducted after their return from captivity, by Jean Vigneaux, Arnaud Dalard, Giraud Arnal and Arnaud Lagacherie." It is said," he added, "that plague and famine carried away [another] 800 inhabitants."

These body counts reveal how far Lauzerte had come since 1241, when Raymond VII granted the mountaintop its charter. In spite of war and plague, Lauzerte had a larger population than it has today. The value placed on the material losses—"80,000 gold ecus"—shows that Lauzerte had developed into an economic as well as a strategic pivot. Amid the slaughter, Duras and his men found time to sack the Lauzerte tax office—located directly across the Square, as it still was 428 years later, when I bought my House. The gold grabbed from the tax office indicated how prosperous Lauzerte had become. The looting also bore witness to how much its prosperity had come to be envied.

Lauzerte by then was officially ranked among the major towns and most strategic castles of the entire Quercy region. In order of importance, the cities royal documents listed were Cahors, Montauban, Figeac, and Moissac. Quercy's most important castle-towns, also numbering four, were Caylus, Lauzerte, Gourdon, and Montcuq. Nearly 350 years after Raymond VI's feckless brother surrendered it without a fight, Caylus remained one of Europe's great fortifications, so renowned that in 2005 a war game based on Caylus won the Trictrac d'Or, the game board version of the Cannes Film Festival's Palme d'Or. That Lauzerte should be considered second to Caylus indicates how well its inhabitants had exploited the possibilities its mountaintop position provided. The presence on that list of Lauzerte's neighbor village, Montcuq, is also a revelation. As the renegade Baldwin of Toulouse found to his misfortune, Montcuq had neither mountaintop nor *presqu'île* to provide security, so the people of Montcuq created their own defensive topography.

What the Pont Valentré is to Cahors, its imposing *donjon* is to Montcuq. The character of the place and its destiny are fused into one of the most impressive civil defense structures of its kind to be found anywhere. If that makes you imagine the Montcuq *donjon* was dank and subterranean, you've been taken in by yet another of those sneaky Anglo-French vocabularial False Friends. In the original French, a *donjon* is an above-ground secular sanctuary, not an underground torture chamber, yet their meanings remain related. Both a *donjon* and a dungeon are impenetrable spaces. It is, or should be, as impossible for an enemy to break into a *donjon* as it is for prisoners to escape a dungeon.

An immense vertical shaft as angular and as tall as a modern skyscraper, though composed of countless tons of Quercy stone, the *donjon* played a double role in Montcuq's defense. With its commanding view of the surrounding countryside, it provided early warning when hostile forces approached; the *donjon*'s stout walls provided a safe haven for its people when the town came under attack. Today, Montcuq's *donjon* is considered picturesque, but to understand the terrible realities that impelled people to pour so much labor and treasure into that gigantic, otherwise useless, structure is to realize how totally fear of annihilation dominated their lives.

Just as provisions of the Lauzerte Charter of 1241 provided glimpses of how people lived back then, references to Lauzerte in official documents showed how life was lived there during the decades leading up to the 1562 massacre. The most interesting revelations concern the underlying social and financial causes for the religious killings. So constant were the Church's trumped-up demands for tithes that the Lauzerte Charter included an article specifically designed to protect its citizens from clerical cupidity. By mandating that the priests must collect their tithes in person, it provided protection from summary demands for produce, or its equivalent in money. That did not stop religious tithes from being traded like commodities futures. In 1512, the Lauzerte town council approved a budget totaling 441 *livres*, a sum trivial in comparison to the wealth the Church extracted from the people of Lauzerte every year. On one occasion, according to an old record book, "Mr Martial Voysin was then arch-priest of Lauzerte. In this capacity he ceded the tithe income—the *fruits decimaux*, or decimal fruits—of his churches for three years, averaging 1500 *livres,* to Jean Marnac, Étienne Feyt, Barthelemy Peyaroles, priests of Lauzerte."

So long as fear of divine retribution dominated their lives, townsfolk and peasants alike could be expected to pay their tithes, but the latest advance of "heresy" threatened all that. When Protestants refused to pay their tithes, it amounted to an act of economic as well as theological revolt. Today it is hard to imagine how thoroughly the clergy penetrated people's lives in those times, how they preyed upon and profited from life's every aspect. It was as though every psychotherapist, modern equivalent of the father confessor, was also a tax collector, the neighborhood cop as well as the principal snoop on the block, and, in many cases, a sexual predator as well. Back then Lauzerte had two separate parishes—one atop the mountain; the other on its slopes. Each had several priests, as did the surrounding hamlets.

Forming, economically speaking, a powerful, privileged, parasitical class, the lesser clergy—friars, nuns, members of various religious orders—greatly outnumbered the priests. For some seven hundred years, well into the twenty-first century, members of the religious orders were a presence in Lauzerte. In full regalia, starched white wimple and all, the head nun would stride across the Square with the authority of an archangel. I thought of her as the generalissimo of the nuns, *"Bonjour, ma soeur,"* I would greet her, in a respectful tone of voice. Then, one day, she was gone. With her vanished the last of the thousands of abbesses, abbots, friars, and nuns, as well as priests, who once dominated life here. A sign of our postindustrial as well as postconfessional times, Lauzerte's last remaining convent was transformed into an amateur arts center, complete with the endless intrigues and complots over who would head which committees, and whose paintings would hang closest to the entry of the building where the vows of poverty, chastity, and obedience no longer held sway.

One scrap of parchment that survived the Wars of Religion provides the information that, in 1529, the Lauzerte office of Inquisitor was abolished. Was this a manifestation of growing hostility to the Church, or an act of ecclesiastical overconfidence, a case of bureaucratic retrenchment, or indifference? The documentation always asks more questions than it answers, but as the Wars of Religion would show, one thing remained manifest. After so many attempts to subdue it, the soul of Lauzerte, like the soul of France, was still up for grabs.

22

WORTH A MASS

Great protagonists normally personify one side of a great conflict: Lincoln versus slavery: Churchill versus Hitler. Elizabeth Tudor takes on the Spanish Armada, while Gandhi takes down the British Empire. Within his one person, Henry of Navarre, King Henry IV of France from 1589 to 1610, subsumed both sides of an epochal conflict. With the age of English invasions ended, France's conflicts turned inward. They centered on what the historian Fernand Braudel called *The Identity of France* itself. Would France be united, or would it splinter like Italy and Germany? Would the country be Catholic or Protestant?

Henry's personal contradictions encapsulated the contradictions gripping the country as a whole. The way he resolved them likewise mirrored the way those conflicts ultimately would be resolved on the national scale—thanks in very large part to his humanism, his love of his people, and, most crucially, his opportunism. A Protestant born in the decade before the Wars of Religion erupted, a regional noble noted for his rustic ways, he wound up epitomizing the consolidation of the unified nation-state dominated by Paris. He was the founding father of the nominally Catholic but practically irreligious modern France where people do attend Mass on Christmas Eve, or when a friend gets married, but, otherwise, religion plays little or no role in their lives. In an age of fanaticism, his lack of religious conviction pointed the way to peace.

Like Richard the Lionheart, Henry of Navarre was a true son of France Profound. He was born in 1553 in Pau, a lovely morning's drive south toward the Pyrénées from Lauzerte, provided you avoid the freeway. An astute military strategist, he was keenly aware of the importance Lauzerte had achieved. Referring to that list of cities and castles, he called Lauzerte "one of four keys of the said Quercy land." Cahors, still under Catholic control, remained the prize of prizes, so in 1580, eighteen years after the first massacre there, the town endured another spate of bloodshed. This time Protestants, under Henry's command, killed Catholics. There was another difference. In the course of three days of street fighting, Henry of Navarre successfully prevented looting and massacre. At age twenty-six, his courage and humanity as much as his victory won him great respect. His victory at Cahors was notable for another reason. In the midst of the Wars of Religion, Henry downplayed the role of religion. His assault on the city, his propagandists announced, was actually a romantic affair, the key to Henry's victory in the "Lovers War." Cahors was part of the dowry of Henry's wife, Marguerite of Valois. So when Cahors defied his authority, what else was this Protestant prince to do?

Love certainly had nothing to do with Henry's marriage on 18 August 1572 to Marguerite, daughter of one king of France and the sister of three others, each of these brother kings more incompetent than the other. Because he was Protestant, and she Catholic, Henry was not allowed inside Notre Dame in Paris. As a proxy recited his marriage vows for him, this future king of France, like the Count of Toulouse 343 years earlier, was forced to wait outside on the cathedral's great parvis where today, as back then, the crowds gathered to gawk— at the fire damage now, at the nobles' finery then.

Marguerite's Florentine and Catholic mother, Marie de Medici, hypothesized that the interfaith nuptials of Henry and Marguerite would reconcile Catholics and Protestants, but the arrival in Paris of so many Huguenots offered the queen an opportunity she could not resist. Following her failed attempt to assassinate the Protestant leader, Admiral Gaspard de Coligny, she had Henry's entire bridal party massacred, along with all other Protestants in Paris. Instead of spreading peace, the wedding had ignited a tinder box. The Saint Bartholomew's Day's Massacre, beginning two days after the wedding, unleashed the most horrendous spasm of religious killing France so far had seen.

The bridegroom himself barely escaped thanks to the bride's Pocahontas-like pleadings, whereupon Henry of Navarre announced a miracle. In the same manner Jesus had transformed water into wine at the Marriage of Cana, marriage in Paris had transformed this Protestant prince into a Catholic! Held prisoner gilded cage-style, he took Communion, mouth agape, tongue extended, from the same Catholic eminences who, given the chance, would have ripped that tongue out of his mouth. Then, as soon as he could, Henry of Navarre did what Raymond of Toulouse did earlier. After escaping Paris, he resumed command of the Protestant revolt that eventually brought him to the Pont Valentré, at Cahors.

He would not become King Henry IV of France for another seventeen years, but two months before his marriage in Paris, in June 1572, he had become King Henry III of Navarre, a rump of a realm straddling the Pyrénées Mountains. Originally centered on Pamplona, today famous for the running of the bulls, Navarre had lost its last Spanish territories by the time Henry was born. Many assumed this remnant realm, like Toulouse, would be absorbed by the expanding kingdom of France. Instead, thanks to Europe's bizarre and inconsistent royal succession laws, Navarre, dynastically speaking, would acquire France.

Henry's mother, Queen Jeanne III of Navarre, was another of those revelatory females whom history consigns to oblivion. On Christmas Day 1560, her seven-year-old son and heir at her knee, Queen Jeanne proclaimed Navarre to be a Protestant realm. In order to break the papal monopoly on Holy Scripture, she paid to have the Bible translated from Latin into Basque and Occitan so that her subjects would have direct personal access to the Word of God. Navarre was small and she was a woman. Neither the pope nor Navarre's powerful neighbor, King Philip II of Spain, was overly alarmed at first. Outrage replaced bemusement when the papal legate implored her "with tears to return to the true fold," and the queen replied: "Keep your tears for yourself."

"Although I am just a little Princess," this remarkable woman informed the king of Spain, "God has given me the government of this country, so I may rule it according to His Gospel and teach it His Laws. I rely on God, who is more powerful than the King of Spain," she pointedly added. Some twenty-eight years later Elizabeth of England would respond in like manner to the same king. "I know I have the body of a weak and feeble woman," she announced, "but I have the heart and stomach of a king . . . and think foul scorn that Spain or any Prince of Europe should dare to invade the borders of my realm." Elizabeth I of England and Jeanne III of Navarre were near contemporaries. The queen of Navarre sent many a treatise, as well as volumes of her poetry, to her fellow sovereigns. She was in direct communication with Elizabeth when, seeking loans to finance the Protestant resistance, she pledged her crown jewels as surety. The difference was that Jeanne of Navarre, unlike the indomitable Elizabeth, truly did "have the body of a weak and feeble woman." Only four years separated their births, only three years the commencement of their reigns, but while Jeanne of Navarre was dead by 1572, Elizabeth would rule England a full thirty-one years longer, until 1603.

Henry of Navarre got his religion from his mother; he got his opportunism from his father, Antoine de Bourbon, Duke of Vendôme in the Loire valley. This French prince, notes one account, "was ready to sacrifice anything to his political interests." When Catholics offered him a key command, he turned coat on his Protestant wife. His death in 1562, the same year all those people got killed at Lauzerte, replicated Richard the Lionheart's death 463 years earlier, with two differences. A bullet, not an arrow, inflicted the fatal wound, which then took the usual fortnight or so of excruciation to kill him. The second difference is that "this prince who lived without glory," as Voltaire described him, "died pissing." The bullet hit him when he left his bunker to answer the call of nature.

Bullets, not arrows; muskets, not crossbows: His father's death, like Henry's own victory at Cahors eighteen years later, was a triumph of gunpowder. For 210 years the Pont Valentré had served as the city's chastity belt. No malefactor, however ardent, could penetrate Cahors once the gates of the great bridge were clamped shut. That changed forever on the stormy night of Monday, 28 May 1580, as Henry's troops blasted open the gates on the fortified bridge, then surged into the city. The explosive device he used both reflected and accelerated immense changes in the way Europeans killed each other. This new weapon's name, *pétard*, was derived from the French verb *péter*. Today, when some eminent person breaks wind in public, an innocent child will be shushed quickly when, pointing to the offender, he exclaims, "*Il a pété!*" Thanks to these noxious new weapons, what once might have been a months-long siege turned into a victory Henry won in "three days and three nights."

The immensity of the killing the new use of fire power made possible raised a theological question. If it was okay by God to kill thousands with swords, stones, and arrows, was it equally okay to kill millions using explosives? For once, Catholic theologians and Protestant theologians found themselves in accord: Yes. Kill as many as you wish, with whatever weapons you can, they declared. God will bless you because you are fighting a just war, as all wars whoever fights them, for whatever reason, always are to those who wage them.

Before his victory at Cahors Henry had been considered rather a callow king, yet his deportment, that early, was a revelation of his character. His final attack was on a school, many of those fighting him mere boys. Once the last of those resisting him had fled, Henry III of Navarre, the future Henry IV of France, took a good look at himself. He found that he was covered "in blood and gunpowder." His feet were bleeding. He did not pretend killing was virtuous, those at his side noted, or that God authorized the barbarities he had committed. Unlike 'Saint" Louis and other crusader kings, he understood that war was a calamity that degrades both killer and killed.

He also understood that, in the face of such calamities, the best option most of the time was simply to make the best of it. Following his victory at Cahors, Henry of Navarre, the historical winner—charmer, propagandist, opportunist, and, also, events would prove, an idealist—took flight full-fledged. Just as Philippe-Auguste and Louis IX personified the transformation of France in their lifetimes, Henry was ready to play his role as the arc of his life transformed him from provincial king of Navarre into France's first modern monarch, but before modernity could be crowned, chivalry had to commit suicide. That, obligingly and appropriately, it did in the course of the jousting match that opened Henry's way to the kingship of France.

Going back to 1186, when Eleanor of Aquitaine's son Geoffrey was trampled to death while jousting, more kings and

heirs presumptive had been undone playing at war than in
actual warfare. The most calamitous of these royal playtime
deaths happened on the very last day of June 1559, a time of
year when the landscape of France is at its most delectable.
The Valois King Henri II of France had just turned forty, an
age at which male humans often reveal with cruel precision
how old they are by trying to demonstrate that they are still
young. The season of tourneys being in full swing, the king
insisted on jousting that day. In the course of this mock combat, a splinter from the lance of one of his guardsmen pierced
the monarch's left eye. It had taken twelve days of puss and excruciation for Richard the Lionheart to die from his wound.
Henry II of Valois took eleven days to die of septicemia. As the
king's veins and arteries became polluted, the infection attacked
his lungs, his urinary tract, and his brain. By then the monarch had lost use of his mental faculties as well as control of
his excretory functions.

All the Machiavellian sagacity of Henry's widow, Catherine de Medici, could not save the Valois dynasty from itself.
One by one these three brother kings, her sons—Francis II,
Charles IX, and Henry III—reigned and ruined, but it was the
death of the fourth son, Francis Duke of Anjou and Alençon,
which ensured the Valois dynasty's extinction. It happened after
the duke made a fool of himself trying to seize the city of Brussels by ruse. Forewarned by their spies, the Flemings ambushed him instead. Rather than die honorably in battle, the
duke deserted his troops, at which point nemesis took the form
of parasitic protozoans of the genus *plasmodium*, injected into
his bloodstream by a female Anopheles mosquito.

Had there been a horse (or so Shakespeare assures us)
Richard III might not have been the last Lancastrian king. Had
that Belgian mosquito bitten someone else, the House of Valois
might not have lost the throne of France. The royal infection
followed the familiar course, as the trembling, the sweats, and

chills and, finally, the hallucinations seized control of his body and took over his mind. The "ague," as malaria was called then, had killed the Valois dynasty's last chance to propagate its DNA into future generations via the direct male line. As his mother later remarked, his death would have been more honorable, as well as less painful, had he let the Belgians kill him.

One brother, Henri III, still lived, but as his own mother acknowledged, no fruit would be forthcoming from his loins. Like his distant relation, Richard the Lionheart, this last Valois king loved men and loved killing men. On the first of August 1589, he was encamped with his *mignons*, or "dainties," when his assassin, a Dominican friar, stabbed him in the stomach. Yet again, the wound did not appear fatal. Once again it was; he died the next day. Some 370 years after their Order was founded, the spiritual depravity of the Dominicans who had dragged "heretical" cadavers from their graves in Cahors once again was triumphant.

The king of France was dead, and in an age that abounded in strong women, including Catherine de Medici herself, no queen like Jeanne of Navarre or Elizabeth of England could succeed him. As fecund a survivor of the birthing bed as Blanca of Castile, Catherine de Medici had produced, in addition to her four failed sons, five competent daughters. One of those royal daughters was Henry of Navarre's own wife, Marguerite, yet thanks to a double paradox, neither she, nor any of her sisters or their sons, would inherit the throne of France. Henry had gotten to be king of Navarre because the crown of Navarre could be inherited through the female line, in this case from his mother, Queen Jeanne III. He now became king of France because the crown of France never under any circumstances could be inherited through the female line.

Within France itself, as Eleanor of Aquitaine had shown, women could inherit veritable kingdoms, so long as they were counties or duchies, but when it came to the crown of France, the ban was absolute. You could be the royal son of a royal son of a royal son of a royal son, and still be excluded from the succession if, somewhere back there, you were royal thanks to a female. To get an idea of the complications this phallocratic approach engendered, try rolling only even dice (male), and see how many generations (rolls of the dice) it takes before you roll female (odd) and, in this dynastic version of craps, crap out. Upon the assassination of the last Valois king in 1589, genealogists had to go back 333 years to find the founding father of a direct male-to-male-to-male line of succession.

Once again, Eleanor of Aquitaine called the shots. Robert of Clermont was a grandson of the same Blanca of Castile whom Eleanor had made Queen of France. In his own lifetime Clermont was never closer than sixth in line to the throne, but following his uninterrupted male line down through the centuries reveals how the king of little Navarre became one of the greatest kings of France:

- Robert of Clermont [1256–1317], Son of King Louis IX
- Louis I [1279–1341], Duke of Bourbon aka Louis the Lame
- James I of Bourbon [1319–1362], Count of La Marche
- John of Bourbon [1344–1393], Count of La Marche and Vendôme
- Louis I [1376–1446], Count of Vendôme
- John VIII of Bourbon [1425–1477], Count of Vendôme
- Francois of Bourbon [1470–1495], Count of Vendôme
- Charles of Bourbon, [1489–1537], Duke of Vendôme
- Antoine of Bourbon [1518–1562], King Consort of Navarre, and finally, in the tenth generation, his son
- Henry of Navarre [1553–1610], King of Navarre, also King of France!

Considering how democratically royalty disseminated its semen in those times, it is likely that thousands of people descended from more recent kings than he did, yet Henry of Navarre possessed that one vital qualification all others lacked. He could trace an unbroken line of legitimate male descent from a previous king, Louis IX, who had reigned more than three centuries earlier. On 2 August 1589 the Protestant king of Navarre became to France what Scotland's Catholic kings would be to England, thirteen years later, when Elizabeth I died childless. With the accession of this quasi-foreign prince, the country had a monarch whose religion guaranteed that immense numbers of his new subjects would rise up against him, which in Henry's case, they immediately did. Four years and eight months of bloodshed roiled the country before Henry IV could be crowned king of France. Even then the proceedings were not quite kosher. Since his enemies of the Catholic League still held Rheims, where French kings traditionally were crowned, his coronation was held at the Chartres Cathedral, the scene illuminated by its stunning stained-glass windows, on Sunday 27 February 1594.

Yet again, political expediency produced a miracle: Henry of Navarre, and of France now too, it was proclaimed, once more was Catholic! "Paris was worth a Mass," goes his famous explanation for this latest theological flip-flop. In return for his Mass, Henry got something else that proved to be very important. His wife had helped save his life, but Marguerite had born him no children. Henry wanted a divorce, and one great advantage of turning Catholic again was that Catholics, provided the pope approved, could get rid of their wives. Henry had done the pope a good turn by returning himself, and therefore France, to the papist fold. Reciprocally, twenty-seven years after their wedding ignited the Saint Bartholomew's Day Massacre, the pope declared that Henry of Navarre never really had been married to Marguerite of Valois. The king was now free to marry anyone he wanted.

The Age of Chivalry was dead. The Age of Money was in full flood. Florence had long since outstripped Cahors as Europe's usury capital, so for the second time in fifty-three years a Medici heiress of nonroyal lineage became queen of France. Sixth cousins once removed, Marie de Medici and Catherine de Medici were only distantly related, but in both cases the golden M embroidered on the silks and brocades of their bridal trousseaux might have stood for Money. The Catholic Medicis imposed no religious test when it came to making money. Henry had borrowed Catholic gold to sustain the Protestant cause as well as finance his own royal ambitions; he owed Marie's family millions. Upon their betrothal, Navarre's war debt disappeared from the Medici books.

A gift more precious than gold was the Medici fecundity. Queen Marie de Medici produced fewer children for Henry than Queen Catherine de Medici had for the Valois—nine for Catherine as opposed to six from Marie—but the quality of her output set her apart. Envious courtesans called her the "fat banker's daughter," but winners came into the world when Marie de Medici gave birth. Her eldest son would become Louis XIII, first of the legendary Bourbon Kings Louis of France. Her grandson would be none other than the Sun King himself, Louis XIV.

Henry's greatest triumph as king of France, the Edict of Nantes, established freedom of religion for all his subjects. With that bravura decree, promulgated in 1598, Henry managed, as one account put it, "to reassure the Protestants and to grant them privileges in the state while at the same time promoting the Roman Catholic Counter-Reformation, protecting the monastic orders, and improving the recruitment of the Roman Catholic clergy in France." Everybody remembers his remark about Paris being worth a Mass, but once Paris was his, Henry of Navarre, now undisputed King Henry IV of France, said something else just as memorable. "So long as God spares me, I will make sure that not one yeoman in my kingdom lacks the means to have a chicken in his pot each Sunday," he promised.

Not since Philippe-Auguste had a great French king been such a practical king. In his person as well as in his politics, Henry rebutted the belief that any one religion or, for that matter, any religion, has something so special to impart that killing those who reject its revelations is virtuous in the eye of God. Henry of Navarre was marvelously antichivalric in his appearance as well. As his portraits show, he was ugly—Jean-Paul Belmondo ugly, the kind of ugly that projects a charm of its own.

Unique in many ways, Henry had one thing in common with his predecessor: God had no more interest in sparing this first Bourbon king than He had in sparing the last Valois king from the assassin's blade. He too was stabbed to death. The prosperity he brought to France got him killed. Had the country still been as poor as Henry of Navarre found it when he ascended the throne in 1589, he might not have died in a traffic jam in 1610. The royal carriage, wide open, was a mobile throne room. The king sat on an elevated dais at the rear, his courtiers lower, in front. This rolling audience chamber was halted in the narrow Rue de la Ferronnerie, the Dealey Plaza of French history, when first a hay cart and then a wagon carrying kegs of wine blocked the way.

Seizing the chance, yet another religious fanatic, using its spokes like rungs on a ladder, vaulted up the carriage's big rear wheel. He thrust his dagger into the right side of the king's chest, between his second and third ribs. Etchings of the assassin would portray the killer as a debonair figure, a feather in his cap, his dagger held jauntily erect, albeit with a scary gleam in his eyes. "The Assassination of Henry IV," an engraving by Gaspar Bouttats, would be as popular, and profitable, as "The Massacre of the Huguenots in Cahors."

In Cahors the valiant King Henry IV, like the venal Pope John XXII and the stalwart republican Leon Gambetta, remains a presence. In the airy, tranquil, and efficient departmental Archives of the Lot, I have seen with my own eyes documents he read. A pleasant twelve-minute stroll from the archives gets you to the Place Henri IV. That big house facing the river was Henry of Navarre's headquarters. One day, having traversed the town, I reached the section of the river where the floating restaurant no longer was. I was remembering the civil war among the ducks when I realized that, if meanders had names, the Cahors bend in the River Lot would be named Destiny.

Another afternoon I came upon a Punch-and-Judy show. The children squealed with delight when Punch punched Judy, and she hit back. Like the Brothers Grimm, Punch and Judy tell children truths their parents do not want them to know. That is why children love them so much. Three hundred years ago at this same spot I could have come upon the same scene. As I observed the children's guiltless delight in violence, it occurred to me that maybe so much history is so fake because it is written by grown-ups. Adults feel obliged to try to impart direction on history, to impose meaning on events. From egoism and murder they confect happy endings. They like to pretend humans are essentially benign.

Children know better.

23

JERRY-BUILT BY BONAPARTE

I have my secret route to Moissac. I have my secret vista of Cahors. I also have my secret castle overlooking Montauban, capital of our hydrographically denominated department of Tarn-et-Garonne.

Only twenty-three miles separate Lauzerte and Montauban, yet in that short distance the hue and texture of history change because the geology, hence the building material, changes. In Lauzerte the pale limestone that gives Quercy blanc its name gives the Place des Cornières its bright and sturdy ambiance. In Montauban, the traditional building material is made from river mud which, once baked into bricks, turns a deep rose color. Across the centuries Montauban constantly has been a stickler in somebody's craw. After being stymied at Moissac, Simon de Montfort dared not besiege Montauban. Later, following Lauzerte's example, the people of Montauban did not wait to be liberated. They kicked out the English all by themselves. Protestants found refuge in Montauban during the Wars of Religion. It was one of the major centers of Huguenot free thinking. During World War Two, Jews found refuge in Montauban's caves and caverns. So did the *Mona Lisa*.

To attack Montauban is to court disaster. Such was the lesson it taught Henry of Navarre's teen-aged son and successor, King Louis XIII, beginning on Monday, 24 August 1621.

Just as his attack on Cahors was a revelation of Henry of Navarre's character, so his son's attempt to seize Montauban revealed the kind of king he would be. Cahors, city of money lenders and launderers, had produced the corruptest of popes. Montauban, anticlerical and thrifty, was the most resolutely Protestant outpost in the whole country. If Louis XIII, in violation of his father's Edict of Nantes, could crush the Protestants at Montauban, he could crush them everywhere.

Like many a royal son, Louis XIII aimed to undo what his father had done, but before traducing Henry IV's pledges of religious tolerance, Louis XIII had to vanquish his mother, the domineering Queen Marie de Medici. In yet another notable triumph for the Law of Unintended Consequences, the absolute insistence that a woman never, under any circumstances, could succeed to the throne of France once again delivered control of the kingdom into the hands of a woman. Since her son was underage at the time he succeeded his father as king, Marie de Medici would be regent of France for seven tumultuous years. In 1618, at age seventeen, Louis took his first step out of boyhood by having his mother's principal favorite murdered, whereupon Marie set an army upon her son. The rebellious teenager's army defeated his mother's army. That was just the start. By the time Louis XIII was finished with her, one of the most powerful women in French history would be reduced to a powerless, penniless, and pathetic exile. Having murdered his mother politically, would he have married his father? Eyewitnesses described the time, when having made one of his male courtiers cross-dress as a bride, the king ordered: "To bed! To bed!" After years of spurning her, Louis XIII only consummated his marriage to Anne of Austria when warned that further conjugal negligence risked forfeiture of her immense dowry.

The Bourbon dynasty's reproductive prospects seemed to be shriveling until lightning struck, also slashing rain and the kind of flooding that sweeps away kingdoms. The storm ravishing Paris that night was so remorseless it obliged the king to seek shelter with his wife. After twenty-three years of childlessness, this led nine months later, on Sunday, 5 September 1638, to what the French press, freer than one might expect, described as "a marvel when least expected." This first son was none other than the future Louis XIV, the Sun King. Having produced an heir, Louis begat a spare. This second son founded the cadet, or junior branch of the Bourbons. France's very last king, Louis-Philippe, the one for whom that bridge in Cahors is named, belonged to the cadet branch.

Access to my secret château with its commanding view of Montauban provided another example of how everything, sooner or later, converges on Lauzerte. When I first got my House, I imagined that members of the nobility would grace my "At Homes," when maybe a hundred people, a good third of them uninvited, surge up and down the Great Staircase devouring my food and consuming my wine. There were plenty of wannabees, but the only certified member of the *noblesse de l'epée* who consistently graced these soirées was the cook. His specialty was paella; it was so good because he prepared it on the premises. Along with coolers containing all the ingredients, he always arrived with his immense smoke-black paella pan, heated by his container of liquefied natural gas. When he lighted the gas, it sounded like an acetylene torch. Over the years, Pavlov-like, I came to associate the sound of that acetylene hiss with the yummy taste of that gummy, gooey saffron rice after it has absorbed all that chicken fat and clam juice.

A large gelatinous fellow, my paella man resembled the late actor Zero Mostel, so I initially called him Monsieur Zero. He loved the nickname, but found my mastery of etiquette wanting. "Monsieur *de* Zero," he informed me with the emphasis on the aristocratic particle. The first time I asked him to use my Art Deco silverware instead of the plastic knives and

forks he provided, Monsieur de Zero sniffed: "Plated, not ster-
ling." He also corrected my Art Deco attribution. "Art Nouveau," he informed me, holding up one of the forks for
inspection. Monsieur de Zero had a strong sense of noblesse
oblige. When, periodically, truck drivers engaged in one of
their ritual blockades of the freeways, he provided the strikers
complimentary paella, an example of the nobility and prole-
tariat uniting to discomfit their joint enemy, the gas-guzzling
bourgeoisie.

Another neighbor, I eventually discovered, also genuinely
belonged to the ancient, for-real, sword-waving *noblesse de
l'epée*. I made the discovery in Bangkok. My colleague and
friend Charlie de Nerciat, at that time a reporter for AFP,
and I were drinking Mekhong whiskey when I mentioned that,
getting to and from Lauzerte, I often caught the train at Montauban. "Ah, Montauban!" exclaimed Good Old Charlie. "One
of my family's principal ancestral seats, Château Picquecos,
overlooks Montauban." This led me to ask Charlie if he knew
anything about Louis XIII's 1621 siege of the city. "They ate
us out of house and home," lamented Charlie. "Every day the
king would go up on our ramparts," he continued, "and wait
for word that Montauban had submitted. Then he and his
courtiers would resume eating our food and drinking our
wine."

"How long did the siege last?" I asked. "Months and
months," Charlie answered—two months and sixteen days, to
be exact, and I thought I was cursed with house guests! The
siege began in August, at the height of summer. It was November, cold and rainy, before it ended. "Did he kill them all?" I
asked, remembering the horrors of Beziers, 412 years earlier.
"He never got the chance. Montauban refused to yield," Charlie replied. "Louis XIII was forced to turn tail and ride back to
Paris." Of the twenty-five thousand king's men besieging Montauban, some sixteen thousand died, mostly of fever, while

Louis XIII, who turned twenty during the siege, looked on from Charlie's ancestral ramparts. Charlie then said something of fundamental importance: "Of course that wasn't the end of it," he remarked. "Paris always wins in the end."

Louis XIII's father had taken Cahors in a few days with a few petards. The young king had lugged four hundred cannons to Montauban. They fired more than fifteen thousand volleys into the city, approximately three cannonballs per resident. By expending so much firepower so futilely, Louis XIII bequeathed an idiom still current in the French language. *Les Quatre Cents Coups de Montauban* refers to an immense effort that achieves nothing. It later provided the title for *The Four Hundred Blows*, the film heralding the French New Wave's emergence as a world force in cinematic aesthetics.

His victory at Cahors in 1562 revealed Henry of Navarre's character, ergo his destiny. The same was true of Louis XIII's defeat at Montauban in 1621. His father had fought in the thick of it at Cahors. At Montauban his son watched his troops die from a distance. Henry IV knew how to live and let live. Louis XIII knew how to hold a grudge. Eight years after his siege failed, Louis XIII showed up again at Château de Pique- cos. This time the royal sojourn was less ruinous for the wine cellar because the king's cagey vizier, Cardinal Richelieu, made the *Montalbanais* an offer they could not refuse. Their lives and their prosperous enterprises would be spared, this Catholic prelate promised. The Protestants' freedom of religion would be respected too, provided they submitted to the king with- out a fight.

As it had been with Louis XIII's mother, so it was with Montauban's Protestants. Bit by bit every promise was be- trayed; humiliation was piled upon humiliation. In the final denouement, royal horsemen savaged the Huguenots' homes, ransacked their enterprises, and desecrated their temples. Louis XIII, grandson of a fervently Protestant queen, son of the agnostic king who had proclaimed religious liberty, had made it his mission to crush Protestantism in France.

Realpolitik, not religious fervor, propelled the killing. By the time Louis XIII took Montauban, on his second try in 1629, the conflict over religion had been transformed into a test of secular authority. A unified state, Louis XIII propounded, must have a unified religion, just as its armed forces and its bureaucracy must be unified. This irreligious argument had nothing to do with theological doctrine. The Protestant princes in Germany used the identical argument when they obliged their subjects to abandon the pope and follow Luther. "I am the State," his son Louis XIV would proclaim. "I am the Church," in essence was what Louis XIII (and, across the Channel, Henry VIII in England) announced.

Louis XIII died on 14 May 1643 in Paris, thirty-three years to the day after his father was killed there. He was not assassinated, though by then he might have welcomed a knife thrust. "His intestines were inflamed and ulcerated," notes one medical report. "Tuberculosis had spread to his lungs. His doctors' remedies—enemas and bleedings—made his end all the more gruesome." Wedged between the endearing figure of his father, Henry of Navarre, and the imposing figure of his son, Louis XIV, Louis XIII seldom gets his due, yet thanks to him his Bourbon dynasty would rule France for more than two hundred years.

A smooth order of succession, vital for all dynasties, was crucially important for the Bourbons because for long stretches of time France's kings were children. It started with the last of the Valois. Catherine de Medici's three sons ascended the throne at the ages of fifteen, ten, and twenty-three. Louis XIII came to the throne at age eight. Louis XV, like Louis XIV, was just five years old, and Louis XVI twenty, when they inherited the kingdom. For two hundred years, with the sole exception of Henry IV, France's kings became kings when they were children or very young men. This produced redounding triumphs of the Law of Unintended Consequences as, again and again, France's misogynistic royal succession laws guaranteed that women, whether mothers or mistresses, acquired power and wealth, while attracting envy and hate.

Not including their lesser liaisons, Henry IV, Louis XIV, and Louis XV had a recorded total of sixty-five acknowledged mistresses. Many of these women wielded more influence than the king's ministers did. The result was a feminization of France's males-only monarchy and, more broadly, of French culture with its enduring preference for the busy over the simplistic in design, and its insistence on the use of substances like gold leaf or ormolu as opposed to plain wood or metal in domestic as well as official decoration. Thanks to figures like Mmes de Maintenon, Montespan, Pompadour, and du Barry, never forgetting Marie Antoinette, rouge-cheeked shepherd boys still steal kisses from ceramic shepherdesses on top of *petit-bourgeois* TV sets. Festering across the centuries, the resentful hatred of the Medici queens would culminate in the suppurating loathing of the "Austrian Woman," as Marie Antoinette, Louis XVI's queen, was called. It did not end with her, as Montauban in due course demonstrated.

For generations the history of Montauban had been the history of Paris demeaning that city. The Revolution added insult to injury in 1789. Three days before Christmas, which the Revolution soon would outlaw, even before Louis XVI was deposed, the constituent assembly in Paris in one fell swoop abolished France's historic provinces. Many, like Burgundy, traced their origins back to Charlemagne. Others, like Aquitaine, dated back to the Romans. All were replaced by departments. Just as the royal ministries had their administrative departments, now the whole country would be run from the top down.

Montauban was not made headquarters of a department. Though its population was more than double, Montauban was

placed under the administrative tutelage of Cahors, as was
Lauzerte. Then, at the first stirrings of counterrevolution,
Montauban's wealthy and powerful placed their bets on an up-
and-coming conspirator who spoke even funnier French than
they did. Delegation after delegation made the pilgrimage to
Paris to renew their assurances of heartfelt loyalty to Napoléon
Bonaparte before, and then after he crowned himself emperor.
As one account put it, Montauban's "notables of all political
dispensations dispensed treasures of ingenuity flattering the
sovereign."

   It worked. On Thursday, 28 July 1808, during his first and
last official visit there, Napoléon proclaimed himself "satisfied
with the love shown to me by my faithful subjects in my good
city of Montauban." He then announced what the throng
yearned to hear: "You now can look on her as the chief town
of the department." Creating Tarn-et-Garonne did not alter
Napoléon's character, nor did it change his destiny. He passed
through Montauban en route to yet another grand adventure,
leading to yet another catastrophe for France and for himself,
as well as for those he attacked. It wasn't Egypt this time, or
Moscow, but Spain, where he would rescue, though only temporarily, his hapless big brother Joseph, whom he had placed
on Spain's teetering throne. The Peninsular Wars ended as all
Napoléon's grand enterprises would end, all the way to
Waterloo—his great scheme shredded by history, then thrown
to the wind where the forgotten proclamations and betrayed
promises tumbled like candy wrappers among the dead bodies, across the blood-stained earth.

   For one glorious day, though, Montauban basked in the
glow of Napoléon's glory and, more touching than that, the
emperor's unfeigned affection. All over the town he rode on
his white horse, reciprocating their love with calls to glory—
which, soon enough, would deprive many a family there, and
everywhere else in France, of more sons, more husbands, more

brothers, more lovers. As Napoléon made his triumphal progress across Montauban, a question percolated through the populace. Where was the empress? The well-born ladies of Montauban had spent days deciding which bonnets to wear. Many of the common women had risen before dawn in order to scrub their stoops and put on their Sunday best, but they would not see the empress that day.

Traveling all the way to Montauban, it was explained, had tired the empress. She would be sleeping in that day. Just as the *Lauzertins* would remember the wily heroism of the Brave Widow Gandillonne, the *Montalbanais* never would forget how that disdainful creature of the Paris salons, Marie-Josèphe-Rose Tascher de la Pagerie de Beauharnais, aka the Empress Joséphine Bonaparte, could not get out of bed to greet them.

To create the new department of Tarn-et-Garonne, the imperial cartographers took away a big chunk of territory from Cahors, including Lauzerte, and gave it to Montauban. Another chunk was taken from Toulouse, along with snippets from three other departments. On the map, France's newest department resembled the as yet undiscovered subterranean palm prints the paleolithic artists left, though in reverse. The legend quickly arose that Tarn-et-Garonne looked that way because Napoléon himself had placed his left hand on the map of France, palm-up, then traced the new department's boundaries around it.

This was another myth that told a truth. From the Top of my House, I survey bits and pieces of Tarn-et-Garonne which at various times belonged to the Lot, to Quercy, Aquitaine, Languedoc, Gascony, Gers, Haute Garonne, Toulouse, and Aveyron. Napoléon fused them together to make the new department just as, in his hubris, he imagined he could grab bits and pieces of Europe—provinces, principalities, duchies, counties, countries—and press them together to make the entire continent the product of his own hand.

Even within France many are barely aware of its existence, yet our funny little department can boast of a distinction no other can match. Napoléon's vaster creations—the Confederation of the Rhine, the Duchy of Warsaw, the Kingdom of Etruria, the Ligurian Republic, the Gozitan Nation, the Cisalpine Republic—vanished long ago. Of all the scratches and gashes Napoléon Bonaparte made on the map of Europe, only obscure, tiny Tarn-et-Garonne, our jerry-built department, endures.

24

PARIS IS THE PATTERN

Henri IV had killed Catholics at Cahors for the same reason his son killed Protestants at Montauban. "Paris was worth a Mass," and with every generation, whatever the theological labels, its value rose. Beneath all the turbulence one tide flowed in one direction, again and again vindicating the fact that in all wars and all revolts, as in all administrative refinements, Events Inevitably, Ultimately, and Ineluctably Tend to the Benefit of Paris.

In America, New York counterbalances Washington, as in Italy Milan counterbalances Rome. In Russia, Moscow has its Saint Petersburg. New Delhi has Bombay, Beijing Shanghai, but as the French Revolution demonstrated better than any other event, in France, Paris dominates all, even when the power structure centered on Paris collapses. Louis XVI wound up guillotined. Napoléon would die on a rock in the South Atlantic Ocean, but Paris never has its Waterloo. Before, during, and after the Revolution, Paris remained in the saddle, never more so than during the Reign of Terror, as it still is today.

Fernand Braudel in *The Identity of France* confirms that Paris is the Pattern. He goes on to present this triumph, as French cultural authorities generally do, as a happy ending. No matter all the wars and upheavals, the domination of Paris assures France's emergence as a land of "sheer delight." All

France's complexity, he is delighted to relate, in the end could not prevent Paris from dominating the rest of the country. For France, truly, to become France, he explains, "it would need to have at its service a large and powerful city, endowed with means and favored by circumstance. Paris, because of its size, became an urban monster very early on; but it did not immediately succeed in carrying the rest of France along with it. The motor might be more or less equal to the task: and the vehicle might follow a jolting course," he concedes, but in the end, whatever the struggle, whatever the epoch, whoever the protagonists, Paris wins: "Is this not perhaps a fair view of French history as a whole, infinitely repeating itself?" Or, as this latest of our great France Profound maxims pithily puts it: Events Inevitably, Ultimately, and Ineluctably Tend to the Benefit of Paris. The will and the caprice of Paris can neither be resisted successfully nor avoided. That is what makes it ineluctable. Events inevitably, ultimately, and ineluctably tend to the benefit of Paris. Keep that maxim in mind at all times, because this tendency of events to enhance the reach, and extend the control of Paris applies to everyone, not just counts and dukes. It explains why, however valid the complaint, dealings with the telephone company or with the EDF, the all-powerful electric monopoly, will always end up the same: Paris wins. Omnivorous in its appetite for control, Paris even dictates which way I am allowed to drive up the Lauzerte mountain.

When I first got my House, France Profound still had quaint country crossroads. That was before Paris ordained that they be replaced in every cranny of the land with traffic circles. You know an invader's will to conquest is insatiable if it bothers to conquer Lauzerte. That 1562 massacre, because it happened in Lauzerte, revealed how truly horrible the Wars of Religion would be. It is the same with traffic circles, or what the English expats call roundabouts. Today it is impossible to enter or leave the town without traversing one of them. Are you coming from Valence d'Agen? It is now forbidden to take the shorter, most direct route up the mountain. You must detour to the traffic circle. Another traffic circle monopolizes traffic coming from Cahors. Bespeaking the utter centrality of Paris in everything, not just its traffic patterns, every distance in France is measured from a specified point in Paris. Located in the parvis in front of Notre-Dame Cathedral, where traffic is forbidden, it is called "Point Zero." Zero itself takes the form of a big round bronze sun. This is in keeping with the self-assumed role Paris plays, radiating unto all others the correct way to do, appreciate, and understand everything.

Like a black hole, Paris, "City of Light," sucks talent and possibilities out of the hinterland, using them to increase its ever-increasing power over France's dreams as well as its waking hours. The result is what sociologists describe as the French Desert. A demographic wasteland of abandoned farms and ruined villages, it lurks like an empty heart in the heart of the country. One time I decided to make a straight-line journey back to Lauzerte instead of following the arc of the high-speed rail lines and auto-routes. I found myself traversing a sociological Chernobyl. Ten, thirty miles I drove, deeper and deeper into the void. A situation that at first seemed interesting, then disconcerting, became scary. What if I ran out of gas? Of course, I could go without eating. Even so, it was alarming to go thirty miles and not see one café. What would France be without cafés? A desert, I realized.

Panic bubbled to the surface when I reached a junction where five one-lane roads converged, then went their separate ways. There was no indication of which went where, so using the sun as a compass I picked the route most likely to take me in Lauzerte's direction. Finally, as the fuel gauge flashed Empty, I found a gas station. Things had not turned out for the worst, but that settled it. Soon as I could, I bought a GPS, and entered the following coordinates: 48.8534° North and

02.3488° East. Whatever the location, they lead quickly to a major highway, for those are the precise coordinates of Point Zero itself.

In addition to administering people's lives, Paris controls peoples' minds. It crowds out any sense there could be any alternative to Paris, as I discovered one time in Metz, in extreme northeast France. It was afternoon: I wanted to get straight back to Lauzerte. "No, monsieur," the ticket agent informed me. "You must go to Paris. In Paris you must spend the night. In the morning you may take the train to Montauban." Please, I asked him, please check your schedules again. He refused. Paris or nowhere: that was his decree. "Monsieur," I said to him. "Have you a train that goes to Barcelona?" Yes, he conceded. It departed in a few hours' time. "Does, perchance, it stop at Narbonne?" I inquired. referring to the old Roman capital, founded in 118 B.C., of Gallia Transalpina. The ticket agent conceded it did. "Ah," I continued. "By any chance do trains in France circulate between Narbonne and Montauban?" The glint in the ticket agent's eyes was no longer that of the self-satisfied Point Zero sun. He glared at me as he issued the Metz-Narbonne-Montauban ticket. Once again, things had not necessarily turned out for the worst. I got back to Lauzerte some eighteen hours sooner than if I'd gone via Paris. What I'd saved on a hotel room more than paid for a first-class sleeper.

On occasion even Paris recognizes it exercises too much control, so periodically Paris decrees that the entire country must be decentralized, under its micromanagement of course. What if Paris changes its mind? In January 2016 Paris snapped its fingers, and presto! Decades of decentralization disappeared. The entire region of Midi-Pyrénées, which included Lauzerte's Tarn-et-Garonne and seven other departments, vanished. Midi-Pyrénées had been the pride and paradigm of decentralization, Paris-style, until Paris decided it wasn't. No referendum was held. No popular assembly was convoked to rubber stamp this *anschluss*. Now that Paris's current preoccupation was *redecoupage*, as this disassembling and reassembling the country's administrative hinterland was called, Paris ordained that its brand-new mega-region would have a Euro Disney-style name: *Occitanie*.

Imposing such a name repudiated the system of official nomenclature going back to the French Revolution. When it abolished the traditional provinces of France, the National Assembly aimed to rationalize the nation's administration in much the same way the metric system would rationalize its weights and measures. The boundaries of the new administrative units were set so that every town and village in France was within a day's journey of the *chef-lieu de département*, as their administrative centers were called. The prefect of each department was directly responsible to Paris, not through some intermediary authority, feudal or ecclesiastical, as in the past.

The better to impose unitary control on the nation, the new administrative boundaries defied rather than reflected cultural, linguistic, political, and regional differences. The names chosen—in Paris, not locally—for the new administrative units also repudiated the past. Historical names were suppressed. Purely descriptive geographic terms replaced them, so the name given to the northernmost department of the country was *Nord*. The department between the Alps and the Mediterranean became *Alpes-Maritime*. What had been Quercy became the department of the *Lot* and, eventually, *Tarn-et-Garonne* after the local rivers.

For a counterintuitive demonstration of how the willfulness of Paris, also its fads and fancies, reign supreme over the most mundane aspects of life, consider the language on the signs you see entering towns like Lauzerte, Cahors, and Montauban. In addition to French, their names are displayed in the Occitan language, so Cahors is Caor. Lauzerte is Luzerta. Montauban is Montalban. Culminating in the creation of Occitanie, this imposition of a supposedly Occitan identity on every hamlet and town was anti-historical—a violation, not a reflection, of the local identity. Bit by bit, in the name of diminishing its monopoly on power, Paris had conjured up an entirely new province, beholden to Paris for its very existence, that would exist only so long as its existence suited its purposes.

The few remaining pockets of Occitan speakers had been eradicated more than one hundred years ago, a side effect of universal conscription during World War One. Here, as everywhere else in France, Arabic was the second language, but putting Arabic on the road signs would acknowledge the demographic and cultural reality that colonization overseas has been followed by recolonialization inside France. In every big town you see the scarved women in the supermarkets, the unemployed youths in the cafés. Your doctor may well be Arab (mine is), yet you'd never know from the official signage that France has the largest Muslim population in Europe.

We have, instead, the Paris-directed bureaucratization of cultural denial, in this case using the language Richard the Lionheart spoke in order to sustain belief in a whites-only illusory past of valiant troubadours and gallant chivalry. What about Dien Bien Phu and Suez? What about the million and more killed in Algeria? These depravities are remembered, when remembered at all, as evidence of the world's ingratitude. Big-hearted France blessed the heathen world with its *mission civilicatrice*. Why should France be blamed when its ingrate beneficiaries fail to be grateful that France civilized them?

25

INCUNABULA OF THE ATM

Traffic circles and road signs—along with cultural denialism and the way Paris micromanages everything—are much on my mind this morning, as I'm heading to Montauban's most revealing historical site. It dates back to 2012, and that's why it is so revealing. It dispels the illusion that History isn't now, that History is what happened to other people. No other place I know better illustrates the famous comment William Faulkner made in *Requiem for a Nun*. "The past is never dead," he observed. "It's not even past."

It is easy to find. First, get yourself to the Montauban insane asylum. Just as you won't find Ingres's most famous paintings in Montauban because Paris grabs all the best art, Paris foists all that it does not want on France Profound. In Montauban's case, that included the insane. The asylum, founded in 1838, is still in operation: I pass it on my way to the official archives of the department. Continue a little farther along the same street, and you pass the headquarters of the Seventeenth Parachute Regiment of the French armed forces. This elite strike force is the only one based inside Metropolitan—mainland—France. When the President of the Republic wishes to project French self-esteem into some distant hellhole, he sends in the Montauban Seventeenth. I first became acquainted with Montauban's role on the world stage back in 1995, following the first Gulf War, while rummaging around Iraq for an article I was writing about Saddam Hussein. Two of Saddam's spies, both named Mohamed, had been assigned to trace my every step, a marvelous convenience!

Mohamed One became my translator, Mohamed Two my chauffeur. We were heading up a gravel road north of Mosul when we ran into the French armored personnel carrier. "Montauban!" I exclaimed, when I asked the soldiers where they were based. "I know your headquarters. It's just up the road from the Archives." As we introduced ourselves, I noticed that not one of these French paratroopers was French in the fair-skinned sense. One was *antillais*, from the West Indies. Others were of North African origin. "Hey, I'm from Corsica," another said, "just like Napoléon." We were all enjoying this pleasantry when I glanced back at the two Mohameds. They did not look happy.

I walked back to the car. When they told me what the problem was, I said: "Let me fix it. We're not getting anyone killed today, okay?" Back at the APC I drew the commander aside. "You must turn around, and head up that road over there. You have wandered out of the U.N. zone," I explained. I gestured toward the two Mohameds. "*Ils sont des mecs de Saddam*," I informed him. "I'll keep them busy while you get away."

I remembered those good-natured paratroopers as I considered what happened at 2:05 P.M. on the Ides of March 2012, in Montauban, at the ATM located just up the street from the brigade headquarters. The paratroopers were lining up to get money when the fellow on the stolen Yamaha TMAX motor scooter shouted "*Alu Akbar*" and opened fire. The Montauban assassin was Mohamed Merah, twenty-three. One paratrooper was grievously wounded. The two he killed were Abel Chennouf, twenty-six, and Mohamed Legouad, twenty-eight. You read right. *Divide et impera* held sway in Montauban in 2012, just as it had some two thousand and fifty years earlier, in Caesar's time. Gauls or Arabs, the modus operandi was the same. Divide them in order to conquer them. Then get the conquered to fight, and die, for you. In a paradigmatical postimperial denouement, both killer and killed were progeny of the catastrophe France started inflicting on Algeria nearly two hundred years earlier.

I have to drive right past the ATM massacre site whenever I go to Montauban. Several times I stopped there. To see it up close was to see how this historical site, like Châlus castle and Beziers, was a revelation of its time, and also of how time changes everything. There was no way I could observe with my own eyes the changes overtaking the Place des Cornières following the Ides of August 1562 massacre in Lauzerte, but in our digital age it proved easy to zoom in on the historical metamorphoses of the Ides of March 2012 massacre site in Montauban.

Wanting to locate the precise spot where the Montauban paratroopers were killed, and also get an idea of how the scene would have looked from the assassin's perspective, I went to Google Maps and dragged that little yellow emoji-man to the site. I switched to the photo mode, and so activated a feature I had not known existed. It displayed various photos over the years that Google had taken of that particular spot. One photo, dating back to 2009, was taken shortly after the ATM was installed. The place was spotless. Some decorative shrubs had been planted against a low wall. In the second photo, taken a year later, cars were parked on the sidewalk in front of the money machine. People were littering the place with their ATM receipts. By February 2011, three large trash bins had been placed next to the money machine. One of them had litter spilling out of it—thousands of the little printed receipts you get when you use an ATM.

In a photo taken six months after the killings, the cars were still there, the garbage bins too, though the ATM was gone. The bank wanted out of there, but Paris had not yet decided what to do with the death site. Since nothing could be done without Paris ordaining it—certainly not something so significant as honoring some murdered paratroopers—nothing had been done. By May 2014, the photos showed, Paris finally had acted. A small red marble monument to the slain soldiers had replaced the garbage bins.

In a May 2016 photo, taken nearly four years after that gruesome event, the site honoring the massacre victims had resumed its role as a parking space. A commercial van was parked right up against the monument to the dead paratroopers, crushing the shrubbery. The garbage bins had returned. They were piled high with trash. The pavement around the monument to the dead paratroopers was littered with trash too. The earlier neglect of the place had resumed without reference to the famous event that happened there. An aura of quotidian banality had triumphed over History. When, flipping through these sequential photos of the murder scene, I speeded them up, it was like watching one of those moving pictures kindergarten kids make when they flip through a picture book. Unmindful of narrative convention, unneedful of dramatic resolution, my little show-and-tell demonstrated how heedless death is of décor. It also provided context. Others may have lived in the age of crossbows and jousting matches. These men-at-arms died in the age of parking lots and plastic refuse bins.

Not until I saw Châlus up close was I fully able to grasp the folly and futility of the mess Richard the Lionheart made of his life. It was the same with Montauban. These photos showed how—whatever the epoch and no matter how much the past is glamorized and fictionalized—time effaced the meaning of such deaths and, ultimately, any sense among the living that they ever had existed, even as the hatreds borne from the past that destroyed them were perpetuated into the future. After all, the living need places to park their cars. They need someplace to throw their trash.

Minutes after killing the paratroopers, Mohamed Merah was speeding toward Toulouse on his stolen motor scooter, traversing a landscape where you never will find an official sign in Arabic, even though several million people who speak Arabic live there. For most folks, it was all ancient History, but in the mind of the Montauban assassin, what began in 1099 with the Christian desecration of the Dome of the Rock in Jerusalem and continued with Richard the Lionheart's massacre at Acre in 1191 never had ended. It was all of a piece with the injustices infusing his own life. His sense of justification for what he was doing went beyond the legacy of colonization, to "Palestine / Dominion of the blood and sepulcher." So, citing mistreatment of the children of the Holy Land as his justification, he next used his Israeli-manufactured Uzi to kill a rabbi, the rabbi's two boys, and a little girl he grabbed by the hair as he killed her. Merah filmed his killings with a video camera strapped to his chest. A few hours later, it recorded his own death at the hands of the French security forces.

26

THE VOICE IN THE LOFT

He wore flowing white robes, a gold-braided burnoose. A falcon posed on one wrist. He might have been a time-traveler
from the Age of Saladin, except for the $50,000 gold Rolex on
his other wrist. We met in Bahrain. When I asked how you
train a falcon, he replied: "The bird trains you."

It was the same with my House. Even as I imagined it belonged to me, the House took control. At times my House
was like a resentful mistress. "Can't you see?" it would whine.
"I need new book shelves in the Club Room." Mostly, though,
the House was like a patient though exigent prefect. In addition to tuition in such sciences as psychology, sociology, engineering, and home economics, my House also educated me on
topics of planetary importance, including climate change.

Most of the time I think of My House the way most of us
think of the world. It is so strong, so enduring. Surely nothing
could destroy it. Then I remember my first winter there, how
desperately I needed wood for the bronze-footed, antique-tiled
wood-burning stove in the kitchen. At the time, it was the only
heatable room in the house. I had ordered lots of firewood, but
in my inexperience, I had forgotten to specify the size. All I had,
down there in the Cave, were logs way too big for the stove.

One morning, still in my bed, clinging to my hot water
bottle, I smelled something. In one of those neighborly acts
that define life in France Profound, the proprietor of the Café

Central had come into my house, which in those days was never locked. While I slept, he went down into the Cave. Using his chain saw, he cut up the firewood into pieces just right for my wood burning stove. The gasoline engine powering his chain saw was the source of the odor filling the House. Initially I supposed the smell would dissipate in a few hours, or days. It didn't. The stench penetrated armoires. It lurked under the Staircase. The stench did not vanish until the next spate of warm weather arrived, and I flung open every window to let it escape.

As the American physicist, Richard Feynman, loved to explain, there is a difference between knowing about something, and knowing something. It was like that time at a massacre site in El Salvador, I later told the neighbor who had been so generous with his chain saw, when I acquired direct personal knowledge that the Roman Empire truly had existed. To be sure, I'd known about the Roman Empire since first grade. Even before I could read, I was fascinated by the maps showing how the pink areas around the Mediterranean Sea expanded, then contracted as the Roman Empire rose and declined, but not until I stood as a journalist in a Central American forest, the stench of death clinging to me like greasy sweat, did I know in the Feynman sense that the Roman Empire had existed.

The spoken word provided the certainty. As the campesinos and I conversed using a degraded form of the Latin the Roman legions had brought to the Iberian Peninsula some two thousand years ago, and then the Spanish conquistadors had brought to the New World a millennium and a half after that, I realized Caesar himself could stride into this clearing and we would be able to communicate using variants of words he had used in his Gallic commentaries. In that same elemental way, as the benzene smell permeated my House, I now knew we humans truly do have the capacity to destroy life on Earth as we know it, but what about life as we do not know it?

Our origin myths thank God or some such other benign
Providence for making the Earth so hospitable to us, but biology and chemistry don't bear out those happy anthropo-
centric presuppositions. They show us that all we have, and
all we are, we owe, beginning some 3.5 billion years ago, to
the Earth's anaerobic organisms' flatulence. They ingested
methane-based compounds, and excreted oxygen-rich waste.
Those early life-forms created the oxygenated atmosphere
we breathe today. By doing so they committed suicide. They
had sucked in methane and excreted oxygen, which killed
them, and now my neighbor's chainsaw was sucking in oxygen,
and belching out carbon monoxide. Perhaps future living beings, I remarked as we sipped anisette in my friend's café, will
thank us for spewing out the chemicals that killed us.

Then came the time when my House explained the nature of God. I was preparing foie gras in the kitchen when I
heard the Voice:

> *If God is All-Powerful*
> *He is not All-Good.*
> *If God is All-Good,*
> *He is Not All-Powerful,*

it explained. On battlefields in Indochina, while dodging tanks
in Tienanmen Square, when I was kidnapped in Beirut, at
AA meetings in Brooklyn, I'd pondered monotheism's essential
conundrum, the mystery posed by the coexistence of good
and evil. Now my House, pithy as Pascal, rigorous as Kierkegaard, had spoken, but from where was it speaking?

The House, its own ecosystem, is also a resonating chamber. A book dropped in the Club Room echoes inside the
writing niche in the Studio on the ground floor. Whichever
CD is playing, wherever it is playing, the music sounds best
when you go outside, onto the terrace, at the Top of the House.

The whole House funnels, then focuses the music to the spot right beside the banana plant, where I have positioned my listening chair.

As if to make sure I got it, the House repeated itself: "If God is All-Powerful," it intoned, and then, following a pause, "He is not All-Good." Another pause: "If God is All-Good"—no pause this time—"He is not All-Powerful." So there had been a reason, after all, for buying this House! Speaking to me in voices as well as in other ways, my House, I now realized, sooner or later would define, if not resolve, the great paradoxes of existence, but whence came the Voice? As I listened, I was sure of it. The Voice was speaking to me from the Top of the House. I rushed upstairs. "The shipping news will be next," it said. Before going down to the kitchen, I'd forgotten to turn off the radio. That epistemological revelation had come from some BBC discussion show. The British Broadcasting Corporation had pointed out God's fatal flaw, one neither our France Profound popes in Avignon nor the "heretics" they persecuted, could ever resolve.

Not long after the Voice explained God, I found myself face-to-face with another discomfiting truth. It came in the form of the yellow blobs of viscous phlegm I expectorated each morning. To the tune of fifty cigarettes a day, I was doing to my body what that gasoline-propelled chain saw had done to the air. I'd started smoking, aged seventeen, during the Cuban Missile Crisis. Why worry about the long-term consequences, when the world was coming to an end next Tuesday? Over the decades, smoking became the writer's air I breathed, just as Scotch became the mother's milk of my every prose composition.

The first time I tried to stop, in New York, I quit for three days—three days more excruciating than any I'd experienced in El Salvador. Then I quit for three weeks, before failing a second time. The next time I lasted three months. The reason, as always, was that without cigarettes I could not write, therefore my existence would have no validity. Besides, smoking had saved my life. I was on my balcony overlooking Tienanmen Square when the bullet, grazing the left side of my neck, just missed the jugular vein. Many come back from China with knickknacks, I later joked, as I recounted my adventures to my neighbors in Lauzerte. I came back with a neck nick because I'd been leaning over to light a cigarette. That was why, I explained, the bullet only grazed my neck.

Smoking had saved my life, guaranteeing a more horrendous fate. I never would be able to stop smoking, I knew, because I couldn't face the humiliation of the addiction defeating me again. My House had different plans for me, and understandably so. For the first time since the French Revolution, when Lauzerte lost its status as a seat of justice, and its powerful judges, rich lawyers, and their free-spending hangers-on relocated to Moissac, my House had an occupant capable of providing the quality of upkeep its size and location demanded. To keep me pouring money into the House, it had to keep me healthy. When it came to my smoking, the Great Staircase would prevail where bullets had failed.

I have to climb sixty-three steps to get from my front door to my writing desk in the Loft. It's eighty-five steps if I'm bringing wine up from the Cave, plus one more step out onto the Top of the House. Five times sixty-three is 315 steps. That's close to my daily average, not counting trips to the cave. The number of steps to the top of the Statue of Liberty is 354. As gasping, gurgling, and expectorating, I made my way up those stairs, something counterintuitive happened. My breathing got better. My House had become my personal trainer. Although I kept smoking, I realized later, having no alternative but to climb those many steps many times every day had provoked intense internal debate. One sector of my brain remained adamant. I had to have all those cigarettes because, without cigarettes, I couldn't write. Other parts of the cerebral cortex, though, were asserting their right to live.

This internal dispute resolved itself when, once again, I returned to my House from the latest war zone, and found I had no cigarettes. The next morning, I discovered an open packet of cigarettes in the drawer of my kitchen table. The cigarettes were stale as old hay. I counted them. There were thirteen. I smoked every one of them. The next day, a Tuesday, was market day in the agricultural industrial town of Valence d'Agen. I went into a café and ordered my habitual breakfast consisting of coffee and cognac and, as always, my first cigarette of the day, except I didn't have a cigarette with me. Could the waitress spare one? She returned with two Gitanes cigarettes—the acrid filterless ones, with the picture of the gypsy on the blue packet.

If you are going to smoke one and only cigarette in your lifetime, it should be a Gitanes. If you are going to smoke your last cigarette, it should be two Gitanes, and that's what they were, I realized, as I drove back to Lauzerte. I had not planned it that way, but back at the House, as I climbed the staircase, it was so clear. I would never smoke again because stopping smoking finally had become the most important thing in my life. It didn't matter if I never wrote again! For one full year after that, the withdrawal symptoms tingled inside me, and every night I had The Dream. The Dream, that I was smoking again, was a nightmare. You're such a loser, The Dream kept telling me. Nicotine has defeated you again! Then I would awake, and it was wonderful! I had not started smoking again!

As the months of physical agony unfurled, I discovered the simplest way to give up smoking was to keep on not smoking, So, when the withdrawal symptoms tormented me, as they did approximately fifty times each day, I did not reach for a cigarette. I just sat there. That's how I discovered that the withdrawal symptoms lasted just about the same amount of time it takes to smoke a cigarette. The tingling torment initially concentrated itself inside my sinuses. Then, after many months, it migrated into my arms, then slowly moved down into my fingers. Then, one morning, I awoke. I wiggled my fingers. Nothing! My body was now free of the need for nicotine, but My House wasn't taking any chances. The Staircase still stood guard, lording it over me like a high-priced personal trainer.

My House was getting me in shape for one of the top ten most exhilarating moments in my life, this time in Cambodia. The epiphany took place at the summit of Phnom Bakheng, a mountain midway between Angkor Wat, the most gargantuan, and the Bayon, the most profoundly unsettling, of the Khmer temples. In colonial times the French rode elephants to the top of Phnom Bakheng. These days, starting at dawn, the mountain is besieged by thousands of tourists, but back then I had Phnom Bakheng almost to myself as I climbed straight up the mountain's great stone staircase, the same one the ancient Khmer had climbed. In places the steps were so steep it was like rock climbing.

Within five minutes, I was drenched with sweat. I was heaving great breaths of air in and out of me. The spectacle of this viscous pink blob of a person attracted a crowd of Khmer urchins. "Hot! Hot! Hot!" they cried, laughing and prancing up those steep steps as though they were on an escalator, all the while fanning me with palm leaves. "Hot!" Life was triumphing over death in Cambodia. Those laughing Khmer kids proved it. Their future would be shaped by globalization, not genocide, yet for that one moment, Phnom Bakheng was free of the future as well as the past, free of allusion too. Sartre would have called it the experience of the *en-soi*, the thing in itself. Feynman meant the same thing when he differentiated between knowing of as opposed to knowing something.

Once at the summit, I turned my back on Phnom Bakheng's famous view of Angkor Wat. I understood too well, by then, the dark line in the Khmer soul connecting these monstrous temples with the modern mass graves. I gazed west over the Baray Occidental, the great reservoir that nourished Angkor in its heyday. The sun was getting low in the sky, turning everything amber. My lungs were still heaving. I could feel the oxygen surging into the depths of my chest. As I looked out over the vast flood plain of the Tonle Sap, the great lake of Cambodia, I understood I too was an *en-soi*.

"This is your reward," the Voice announced. "This is your reward for not smoking." Then the House spoke: "You better get back here quick and bring that money you're getting for the Return to the Killing Fields story. How many times do I have to remind you? I need new shutters."

27

THE WISDOM OF OLD HOUSES

The House took care of me. It also knew how to take care of itself. I was in New York when a neighbor telephoned. "Water is flowing out your front door," he informed me.

In the course of one of those bone-chilling freezes that, like the winter drizzle and drear skies, are a feature of life in the sunny, balmy South of France, the pipes leading up to the Top of the House had frozen, then burst, so my neighbor Frédéric came to the rescue. Using the spare key I always leave with him, he entered the House, and disconnected the water. Following his phone call, I began dreading my return to Lauzerte, but this turned out to be another instance when things did not always, necessarily, turn out for the worst. Long before it happened, a house guest had explained why the House would slough off the Flood the way a playful dog shakes off the water when you turn the hose on her. As she informed me, "There is not a single straight line anywhere."

She was indeed right about that. The facade of my House creates an illusion of rectilinearity, but inside that facade the House warps toward the southwest. Not one of all those steps on the Great Staircase is even with another. None of the floors is precisely level. The ingrained structural irregularity of the House saved the day. Having overflowed the terrace, the Flood did not spread into the Loft. It cascaded down to the floor below. Then, avoiding the Club Room, it swept in one narrow path across the house to the slightly lower wall opposite. Then, avoiding the kitchen and the Red Salon, it plunged straight down that wall to the ground floor. There, instead of remaining inside the House, it flowed under the front door out into the Square.

Had all the ceilings and floors been perfectly horizontal, a general catastrophe would have ensued. Only where the House truly had been modernized was the damage catastrophic. That explained why the ground floor Studio—the part of the house farthest from the leakage—suffered the worst damage. I had installed an up-to-date fiberglass ceiling there, as precisely in plumb as in any American skyscraper. Only when the water reached that flat level fiberglass ceiling did it spread out, and stay there, though the ensuing damage did have an aesthetic silver lining. As the water seeped through the fiberglass, it made fascinating abstract patterns in the ceiling. As the ruined ceiling was being disassembled, I cut a particularly intriguing section of it into a rectangle, and had it framed. Today that framed extract from the blotchy, water-stained ceiling hangs in the entry hall of my House. Everyone thinks it is my very own Jackson Pollack.

Their structural rigor—all those perfectly straight lines— doomed the Twin Towers. The lack of them had saved my House. Fiscal catastrophe was avoided following the Flood because I got the stereotypical French insurance settlement. I feared a bureaucratic nightmare when I filed my claim. Instead, the ensuing, two-year marathon of protracted negotiations turned out to be instructive, constructive, and in the end gratifying though, as events never cease to demonstrate, France Profound wasn't built in a week. The scariest moment came when, finally, the insurance check arrived in New York. I nearly tore it up as, in the lobby of my apartment house, I was disposing of the junk mail. Fortuitously, I merely threw the unopened envelope into the trash bin. Then, even more fortuitously, I gave it a second look. The envelope was one of those serrated numbers, where you have to peel off the perforated edges in order to see what's inside it. It had, I now noticed, a very faint French postmark. Curious, I stripped off the edges. This erstwhile piece of junk mail was a big check made payable to me.

Nearly three years earlier, when I arrived for my first audition with the insurance agent, he had received me with notable affability, not the prosecutorial demeanor I had expected. Equally unanticipated was the way he kept making references to famous American basketball players. Finally, the penny dropped. This insurance agent and I had met years earlier, while he was working for a different company in a different town. I had given him my card, and so eventually received a request from him involving basketball in America. He and his son were coming to New York. The boy's dream was to see the NBA in action.

After considerable research, I discovered that (1) NBA tickets can cost more than trans-Atlantic airplane tickets and (2) you can attend local high school games for free. First, I assembled the relevant information, then translated it into French. I sent this dossier off to him, along with the suggestion that in addition to contacting the pro teams, they check out high school basketball in Queens and the Bronx. "You will get to know the city much better that way too," I advised.

Some ten years later, there he was, in a new office, and so glad to see me! "*Pas de souci,*" he assured me. No need to worry! After more than two years had passed, I informed him I was abandoning hope. "Your system is toying with me as well as torturing me," I confided, when yet another report had to be filed, and sent to Paris. "*Non!*" he replied. "We have only four more steps in the process." It was more like seven. Finally, he told me, all was done. "So when do I get the money?" I inquired. "After Paris approves," he replied. I groaned and left. Months passed. More months passed. No envelope with a check in it appeared—until that morning.

First rule of your French insurance settlement, when it finally does arrive: Pour every penny back into the house! Second rule, the face-lift rule. No one notices a truly successful renovation. They don't say: "Wow, what have you done to this kitchen!" They say: "I've always loved this kitchen," just as when a person has a successful face-lift, people don't say: "Who's your surgeon?" They say: "You look so rested." The subsidiary rule in this as with everything in France Profound is that, in the end, you must have everything done locally, by people you know who know you—by people who have a sense of responsibility for taking care of you.

My oriental carpets, the insurance adjuster informed me, only could be cleaned in Paris. To have them cleaned there, I was additionally informed, would cost more than the rugs themselves had. It was up to me to get them there and back, but I'd seen people washing their carpets on the sidewalks of Isfahan, so what was wrong with the fine cobblestones of Lauzerte? The insurance company, which also compensated me for the disruption of my creative processes caused by the inundation, sternly informed me that if we did the work ourselves there could be no reimbursement for value-added tax, a dictum I accepted without demur. Simultaneously my friend and master craftsman Dominique Darniere, ever faithful and effective, upgraded his skills in electricity and plumbing. In the hydraulic equivalent of bolting the barn door after the horse has fled, he installed a master water valve on the ground floor, right by the front door. It shuts off the water everywhere in the House—or it would, if ever I remembered to use it.

One Sunday afternoon, I noticed that a few details still needed attention. In the kitchen a line of shelves needed to be raised several inches. Sundays are sacred in France, but Dominique set to work. "I'm spending an entire Sunday afternoon fixing a few shelves," he grumbled. "I'll remember this afternoon." "Yes you will," I replied. "You'll remember this afternoon long after all the afternoons spent working on the shrubbery around your swimming pool, or cleaning your pet parrot's cage, or shampooing your Pyrénéan mastiff. You'll remember this as the afternoon you got everything perfect."

That's the real reason Dominique has stuck by me all these years. I let him get everything perfect. As a result, I have wound up living inside his masterpiece. The Flood had given Dominique the chance, one more time, to demonstrate what marvels a master craftsman can produce when his patron understands that the best work is never done for the money and never, ever finished on time. Dominique's reconstruction work following the Flood was so adept that the only evidence remaining of what happened was to be found in the guest book on the table in the entry hall. I had bought that guest book in Lucknow, India, for a few rupees. As soon as I saw it, I knew I had to bring it back to Lauzerte, to give it a home among the ancient stonework, the massive old timbers. What charmed me about it was that the cover was plastic—plastic!—so modern for India. Inside the plastic-covered guest book a number of the entries are ink-smeared, but the record of the House's most notable visitor, at least during my tenure there, stands out in big, bold letters, running across two full pages. "INONDATION," it reads. "FLOOD."

The Flood showed the logic and revealed the wisdom of the House. Only gradually did I come to appreciate how, in my researches, I had come to follow the House's example. Avoid the straight lines. As the House was built, construct your understanding of the terrain and people causing it to be there, and there's no limit to the fascinating people and situations you will discover—people and situations you never could have invented for yourself.

The nonlinear approach, which saved my House, had led me to Châlus, to the top of Mount Saint Cyr, to the Montauban ATM machine, though sometimes the greatest discoveries came when I returned to "the very threshold" of my House. Going inside, I would discover something new—something I'd never suspected about History, or the House, or me. There came the memorable moment, for instance, when sun, glass, light, shadow, House, combining as if in one soul, shone together. It was so stunning I had to photograph the shimmering green bowl. I'd come across that green glass bowl in a junk shop in La Bisbal d'Empordà, a Catalan town on the other side of the Pyrénées famed for its ceramics. People from all over went there to buy dinner plates and also planters, but no one was going to buy the green bowl I found in the back of that shop. Like so many of the events and personages I discovered, it had been lost for a long time, undervalued. It finally had been rediscovered, buried in sand. This gave that green glass an archaeological character I loved.

Now, today, it glowed—glowed!—as the sun glinting through the giant south-facing window shone on it, and in it. *Harmonices Mundi*—Harmony of the Worlds—Kepler had called it back in 1619, when my House was but four hundred or so years old.

Another time the House forced a revelation about me on me. Having used the toilet in the magenta bathroom, with its cut-crystal chandelier and polished mahogany toilet seat, I went into the Club Room. Through the glass wall I saw them— the scores and hundreds of my house plants. Their foliage, seeking the sun, stretched out over the balustrades. "Good morning," I called to them, aloud. Then I said to my plants: "I love you." I stood there stunned at the sentimentality I'd just heard spewing from my own lips. What was my House doing to me? Later, upon reflection, I decided it was okay. Lots of people talked to themselves. That didn't mean they were gaga, at least not yet. Besides, as the House had forced me to acknowledge, I did love my house plants. It was part of a larger revelation. Little by little, without realizing it or intending it, I was becoming a more loving person.

28

THE PIGEONS ARE CROWING

Lauzerte pigeons don't waggle their heads the way New York pigeons do. New York pigeons know they can make it anywhere if they can make it there, so their pigeon heads, with those beady little pigeon eyes, never stop darting this way and that, on the outlook for opportunity, but also danger. They know a speeding taxi as well as a stray morsel of pastrami can come rushing at them at any moment, from any direction. Lauzerte pigeons, in contrast, have a steady, stately gaze. They are so serene because they know they are the masters of Lauzerte. Strangers to stress, they reign philosophically over the medieval city by day. Then, as night falls, to borrow the American modernist Wallace Stephens' phraseology, Lauzerte's

> Casual flocks of pigeons make
> Ambiguous undulations as they sink,
> Downward to darkness, on extended wings.

They don't stay undulated for long. All night long they engage in the unambiguous pigeon-equivalents of snoring and breaking wind and—I've learned to differentiate their abominable, annoying squeaks and rustlings—fornication and, worse still, the courtship that precedes it.

In this instance, too, the past was not past. My struggle replicated the struggle of that moral monster, Simon de

Montfort. I, too, initially envisioned a quick, total victory. Instead, the pigeons vanquished me. In the course of losing my war against the pigeons I, like the Black Prince and Henry V, won many a battle, but those false victories proved to be as futile as Montfort's massacres. Life imitates literature when it comes to Lauzerte's pigeons. Stevens began his poem "Sunday Morning"—the one just quoted—as I began my life here, with an Edenic vision of horticultural perfection: the golden peaches of Samarkand in his case, the delectable Reine Claude plums of the Lendou in mine. Each winds up with pigeons.

One morning, I yet again was forced to face the naked truth. Actually, I was naked. Up in the Loft, seated at my plain-as-Amish Quercy farm table-desk. I was just about to tap out something profound about France Profound when I looked up from my computer screen. There, out on the Top of the House strutted the pigeon, maliciously blocking my view of the medieval turret of the former police headquarters, brazenly disrupting the asymmetry of the nearby dulcet hills and, beyond them, the evocative teal-grey smudge of the Pyrénées. "Get off my property, vile avian!" I shouted. With utter indifference the pigeon stared back at me, so I ran naked waving my arms at it. It merely hopped to a nearby spot, just beyond my reach. There it stared at me, as if to say: Why don't you go put on some clothes?

As with such banes as climate change and digital identity theft, we humans have ourselves to blame for the France Profound pigeon plague. They live in such intimacy with humans because we invited them into our lives. We wanted their feces. Gooey as unrefined petroleum, pigeon poop was the black gold of preindustrial France Profound. Adeptly applied in sufficient volumes, the pigeons' highly acidic excrement transformed the region's alkaline soil into PH-perfect earth.

Those wonderful Reine Claude plums wouldn't be wonderful without it, but how to keep the feces flowing? To make cheese, goats' milk—hence goats—are required. To make orchards flourish, an ample supply of pigeon feces—hence pigeons—is of the essence. As an unintended consequence of this demand for pigeon poop, France Profound acquired what the department of the Lot tourism website extols as the "unusual and major architectural elements of Quercy's rural heritage." This defining architectural icon is the *pigeonnier*, or dovecote, or pigeon coop. "Come Discover Our *Pigeonniers!*" the tourism authority exhorts. Some *pigeonniers* are square. Others are round. Some stand on pillars. Some are half-timbered. Others have classical pediments, looted from the manor houses of aristocrats during the French Revolution.

So heterodox in style and ubiquitous in location are these fascinating former sites of "columbine production," it seems like pigeon coops have speckled the landscape here forever, but not until the French Revolution did the *pigeonnier* start to become as emblematic of the region as windmills are of Holland. For most people Bastille Day—Tuesday, 14 July 1789—is the day to commemorate when it comes to the French Revolution. For *pigeonnier* aficionados, four Tuesdays later, 4 August 1789, is the moment to cherish. That night the National Constituent Assembly accorded everybody, not just a privileged few, the right to erect a *pigeonnier!* Previously, only aristocrats and a few others with a special claim to the privilege were permitted to have a *pigeonnier.* Used to flaunt the "agricultural opulence" of their proprietors, *pigeonniers* frequently became the cause of inheritance disputes. They also fostered envy, resentment, and, in due course, the revolutionary upheaval that shook first France, then the world. Only after producing pigeon poop had been proclaimed a human, not just a customary or aristocratic, right did these idiosyncratic structures proliferate.

Though chemical fertilizers now are used, discriminating aficionados still pay double for "Marvelous Pigeon Manure," as one fan lauds it. One time, upon returning to Lauzerte, I experienced firsthand pigeon poop's power. There were, I noticed, several stains on the green floor of the Green Room. When I tried to clean the stain, I found it wasn't a stain. It was a hole. The spilled substance had eaten right through the paint into the wood underneath it. It was as though battery acid had dripped on the floor.

My sagacious neighbor Libby Pratt, proprietress of the world-famous Camp Biche spa, resolved the mystery. "Don't you remember the pigeon that got into your House last summer?" she asked. How could I forget that drama, and Libby's starring role in it? Every day in Lauzerte is like one of Fontaine's fables—and, sometimes, like one of Aesop's fables too. Libby herself was the heroine of the fable I wrote in French, and later transposed into English in honor of that day's events. *La Dame et le Pigeon* was its title, though in English I called it *Libby and the Airborne Invader.*

"This morning," it began, "I awoke to the sound of breaking glass. Seeking refuge from the heat wave, a pigeon had sneaked into My House, and headed straight for the Green Room." There it had begun destroying my green glass collection. Chasing it away from the glass, I pursued the pigeon up the Staircase, into the Loft. Finally, under the lowest-hanging of the eaves, I apprehended the intruder, using my Tried-and-True Towel Technique. This I described as "*ambuscade par serviette*," ambush by napkin. You chase the pigeon into a corner. You throw a towel over it.

Through the big old-fashioned linen napkin, I could feel the pigeon's little heart throbbing. "As an experienced war correspondent, I knew better than to touch the pigeon. Who knows what maladies it might transmit?" At that point, as if written into the plot, the doorbell rang. "It was my friend the famous Libby Pratt," I related, "absolutist vegan curator of the world-renowned and super elegant Camp Biche Spa. What kindness! On this stifling day, Libby has come to invite me for a swim! 'Thanks, Libby,' I tell her, 'but what to do about the pigeon which I have here in this embroidered monogrammed antique linen *serviette*?'"

No problem for this courageous woman! Libby carefully carried the pigeon out onto the Place des Cornières. There she gently liberated it from the folds of the napkin. As she held the pigeon, I could see the reciprocity in their eyes: Libby loved life; the pigeon loved life. Then Libby did another of those things I never could have invented. Instead of tossing the pigeon into the air, she gently placed it on the cobblestones. Instantaneously the pigeon took flight. "It might have been injured," she explained. At that moment I realized this incident was a fable, which is to say it had a moral. "Count on the goodness of your neighbors," was the moral, "and not just when a pigeon gets into the House. Look to their inner moral sincerity, and you will seldom go wrong."

Another time my House, which had taught me so much about physics, gave me a biology lesson. It concerned the difference in cerebral evolution between placental mammals and the descendants of egg-laying dinosaurs, that is to say, birds. This latest encounter with an airborne intruder occurred while I was up in the Loft, late at night. I glanced toward the Staircase. The creature seemed suspended in midair but no, it was piloting its way up the Staircase step-by-step. I watched as, always in the exact center, it turned the corner at the topmost landing. It kept climbing step-pause-step-pause-step until it reached the top of the stairs. Then, with a squeak, the bat in a great arc soared up and across the Loft through the great open doors leading to the Top of the House out into the night, its home.

Thanks to the echolocation that the bat's mammalian brain had evolved, there was no broken glass this time, no need to capture the creature in order to save it. Unlike a bird, this flying mammal had a quality of intelligence that enabled it to find its own way out of the House. This combination of flight and brainpower helps explain why mammals of the order *Chiroptera*—that is to say, bats—are more abundant than pigeons. Worldwide, they are second in number only to mammals of the order *Rodentia*, that is to say, rats, squirrels, beavers, chipmunks, and their ilk.

Like Simon de Montfort, I recruited an army to support me in my war against the pigeons. My *Vulgarium numerus infinitus* consisted of the infinity of guests who attended my *dejeuners-massacres*, my luncheon massacres. Back in 1212 the good people of Moissac had used "lumps of meat," along with "fat, oil and other combustible materials" in their struggle to repulse Montfort and his horde. I too opted for a gastronomic strategy, only instead of catapulting comestibles at the pigeons, I fed them to my guests. Then, following a hearty lunch, my anti-pigeon phalanx would clamber up the great Staircase to the Top of the House. There, while the girls and ladies poured the cordials, and the boys helped reload, the men opened fire.

At each volley the sky above the village cloaca would fill with startled pigeons. None, so far as I could tell, ever plunged to earth mortally wounded as the avian extras do in the shooting scene in that French cinematic classic, *Règles de Jeu*. One time a bird did fall to the ground but then, after a moment, it rose, and continued its pursuit of another pigeon with amorous intent. Following each *dejeuner-massacre* I would assure myself that, this time, those dastardly pigeons had learned their lesson. Each time, within twenty minutes of the last guests' departure, the pigeons would return. In spite of such defeats, there were moments when, like Montfort, I believed victory was in sight. Then came the long-ago moment when I was sure I had won!

The great *canicule* of 2003 was roasting the land when a particularly persistent pigeon impinged on my hospitality. *Canicule* is the French word for heat wave, derived from the Latin for the dog days of summer. That year the heat was so intense it caused the pigeon in question to plop over dead. Will this heat wave, I asked myself, give me no reprieve? Now I have a dead pigeon on my hands, but this pigeon had only fainted. After a few moments, it righted itself. It staggered toward the water faucet. It was trying to get at my water!

This was another of those instances that illustrates why I don't write fiction. What novelist could have invented a drama whose plot pivots on the sight of a pigeon fainting? Next thing I knew I was watching the pigeon do something neither Marcel Proust nor Jules Verne could have invented. The pigeon was trying to figure out how to turn on the water spigot. It was like one of our human physicists trying to figure out dark matter. The pigeon knew water was in there, but how to get it out of the spigot? It was struggling with that dilemma when I burst out onto the terrace. "No water for you, you dirty, rotten pigeon!" I screamed. "Get off my property or I'll kill you and eat you!" I elaborated, even though the pigeon knew the worst I ever would do was throw a towel over it.

My life purpose now was to make sure no pigeon ever again got anywhere near my faucet, but how? Suddenly, like a mirage, my heat-addled brain conceptualized the solution. It took the form of a plastic bag. Rushing back into the Loft, I found a plastic bag. I wrapped it round and round the spigot. Columbus had not been looking for America. I was not looking for a break-through in pigeon psychology, but that is how many revolutionary discoveries are made, by accident. In this instance the discovery was that Lauzerte pigeons, unlike New York pigeons, were terrified of plastic bags. This I discovered the next time another pigeon swooped down, confident as an ace fighter pilot zooming in on an aircraft carrier. That was before the pigeon sighted the plastic bag. It halted the pigeon's descent in midair! Were it possible to fly backwards, this pigeon would have done it. The next pigeon to approach likewise recoiled, horrified.

As I festooned the place with dozens of plastic bags, I gave thanks to the petrochemical industry. In addition to manufacturing the synthetic fertilizers that eliminated the pigeons' role in our local agriculture, it produced the plastic bags that terrorized them. In this manner, the sight of those hideous shameless pigeons was supplanted with the sight of dozens of crinkly plastic bags with the names of pharmacies, hardware stores, cheese shops and butchers on them.

Occasionally people would make guarded comments about the cure being worse than the disease "They are effective against the pigeons," I lied. The truth was that the pigeons, having lost their fear of them, had turned the plastic bags to their purposes. When I waved my arms, they no longer took flight. Using their little beaks, they pushed aside the plastic bags like a theater curtain, and hid behind them. I knew I should remove them, but to remove those last plastic bags would be an admission of defeat. Simon de Montfort never admitted defeat, did he? In the end, though, I had to admit that I too had concocted a historical fiction, the better to deny that nonhuman protagonists—not I—were the ones in control.

This long-deferred denouement imposed itself on me in Paris, while visiting Notre Dame Cathedral as part of my historical research. It was, I understand in retrospect, an afternoon of innocence, before first the fire and then the pandemic destroyed what had passed for immutability. Surely there never could come a time when it was not possible to spend a few moments of meditation in Notre Dame, and then loiter maskless in the great parvis in front of the cathedral. It was unthinkable, impossible. The world could never come to that. Then, on Monday, 15 April 2019, came the fire.

News coverage of the Tour de France would propagate into millions of human minds the falsehood that Lauzerte, once upon a time, had been an "important stop on the pilgrimage route to Compostela." News coverage of the conflagration at Notre Dame propagated into the minds of billions the falsehood that it was a "Gothic" cathedral. Historical scruple once again obliges me to point out—however futilely—the truth of the matter. Notre Dame is not now, nor has it ever been, a Gothic cathedral.

Following their conversion to Christianity, the Goths, whose starring role in history came and went with the disintegration of the western Roman Empire, worshiped in the comparatively squat sanctuaries we today call Romanesque churches. Construction of Notre Dame did not begin until centuries later, in 1163, under Louis VII, in the decade after Eleanor of Aquitaine deserted him. For hundreds of years Notre Dame and its sister edifices were known as *Opus Francigenum*—works of the Franks, not the Goths, because that is what they were. No one pretended that the Goths had anything to do with the construction of these marvels of nonmechanical engineering, with their vast windows and soaring arches, until 1550. That year Giorgio Vasari published his immensely influential survey of *The Lives of the Most Excellent Painters, Sculptors, and Architects*.

Whether Europe's great cathedrals were located in Cologne, Germany, or Salisbury, England, or, in France at Paris or Rheims or Chartres or Bourges or Amiens, Vasari detested them all. So far as this fervent neoclassicist was concerned, they one and all were products of the "barbarous German style." To communicate his contempt, Vasari called them "Gothic," after the hordes who ravished the classical Roman architecture he revered so much. For a quarter-millennium it remained a term of derision. Then, on the eve of the Industrial Revolution, "Gothic" started to acquire the breathless connotations it has today. One early sign of the change came when Horace Walpole added the subtitle, *A Gothic Tale*, to his novel *The Castle of Otranto*, and sales soared. Then, in 1831, Victor Hugo published *Notre-Dame de Paris*, the novel far better known today as *The Hunchback of Notre-Dame*.

Some works of literature—*Montaillou*, notably—change the structure of people's thinking. Hugo's novel changed the physical structure of France's architectural patrimony, by unleashing a nationwide process of architectural fictionalization. They called it "restoration." We have its principal perpetrator, a fellow named Eugène Emmanuel Viollet-le-Duc, to thank for all those ancient-looking gargoyles on Notre Dame. The cathedral, as its *violleteur* found it, had no gargoyles, so in the name of "restoration" he plastered the place with gargoyles of his own design. His gargoyles look just like the ones you see in the movies because Viollet-le-Duc took *The Hunchback of Notre-Dame*, not historical accuracy, as his guide. Notre Dame also had no spire, so he topped it with a spire of his own design. During the great fire of 2019, the walls constructed eight hundred years earlier withstood the blaze. Disaster tuned into catastrophe when Viollet-le-Duc's spire, dating only to 1864, burst into flame, then collapsed, bringing down with it the cathedral's roof, enabling the flames to devour the structure's interior.

In the aftermath of the blaze, the role that Viollet-le-Duc's spire played in generating the catastrophe provoked no reconsideration of whether his anachronism, less than two hundred years old, had any business being there in the first place. *Au contraire*, restoring the spire took precedence over efforts to undo the damage it had helped cause. "Notre-Dame's spire to be majestically restored," Radio France International announced. In an episode of the highly influential CBS News program, *60 Minutes*, the restoration of Notre Dame's nineteenth-century spire was equated with the restoration of the cathedral itself. "That spire," it reported. "is going to look as though it has always been there."

The French government had chosen to present the resuperimposition of Viollet-le-Duc's inauthentic spire on the historically authentic parts of the cathedral as tantamount to restoring the cathedral itself. "Notre Dame's Spire: A Masterpiece of Gothic Architecture," proclaimed the Friends of Notre Dame in one of their fund-raising appeals. Subsuming the immense, complicated effort to restore the fire damage in a single, simple historical falsehood served the same purpose as purporting that Lauzerte was a historical stop on the pilgrimage route to Compostela. It facilitated media and public relations, as well as fundraising. It also filled those working on the project with a sense, false but sincere, that recreating the spire was in keeping with their highest ideals of faithfulness to historical accuracy. Many, when asked about their work on the spire, emphasized what a privilege it was to contribute to the reinstallation of this Gothic icon.

That time at Notre Dame, I was forced to confront a historical falsehood of my own invention. "How I loved seeing those plastic bags gyrate in the wind!" I lamented, as I considered my own illusions and the disasters they engendered, including my defeat in the war with the pigeons, "Those plastic bags were my Maginot Line," I ruefully acknowledged, at which point something went splat. Upon inspection I found a large viscous glob of pigeon excrement defacing the brim of my snazzy new Panama straw hat.

I had come to Notre Dame to inspect the spot where Queen Blanche ritually humiliated Raymond VII of Toulouse, only to be humiliated myself. At the same spot where Henry of Navarre also stood on the eve of the Saint Bartholomew's

Day Massacre, the pigeons had visited upon me their retribution. Later, during the great floods of 2016, I acquired irrefutable evidence that the pigeon control network covered the whole of France, not just France Profound. It took the form of a photo I took of the floodwaters of the Seine. In the manner of French paintings like *Liberty Leading the People* by Eugène Delacroix or, more appropriately, *The Raft of the Medusa* by Théodore Géricault, I entitled my snapshot: *Pigeon Orchestrating the Inundation of Paris.* In it the pigeon, in the manner of the *Sorcerer's Apprentice*, urges the deluge ever upwards, even as rising flood waters threaten humanity's cultural heritage in the form of the artworks stored in the basement of the adjacent Louvre Museum. The day will come, that pigeon knows, when his kind will nest where the *Mona Lisa* now hangs. They will court and coo atop the *Winged Victory of Samothrace*.

Back in Lauzerte, I was taught anew the Libby Lesson: "Count on the goodness of your neighbors." In my absence Dominique had contrived a network of pigeon-proof filigree covering the whole of the Top of the House. So cunningly arranged as to be almost unnoticeable up close, it was completely invisible from my desk, but the pigeons could see it. They knew they could not get through it. Also in my absence my neighbor Frédéric had installed an invisible metal grate preventing the pigeons from resuming their loathsome depravities in the cloaca behind our houses, while Lauzerte yet again vindicated one of my fundamental maxims.

The More You Need It, the Closer to Home You Will Find It was the maxim this time. What I needed, following the Notre-Dame pigeon's desecration of my original Panama hat, which I had bought in Panama after sailing through the Panama Canal, was another Panama hat. Hats often were for sale at the Saturday market in front of my House, but wearing a genuine Panama had spoiled me. "These are nice enough," I told the vendor, "but what I truly want on the top of my head is a genuine Panama hat. Heaven knows," I added, "when I shall have the chance to go back there again, let alone get to Ecuador, which as you surely know is where Panama hats are actually woven."

"*Monsieur, ne vous inquiétez pas,*" the hat vendor interjected vigorously, whereupon he threw open a large wooden crate. Inside it was displayed a selection of high-quality Panama hats. I quickly found the hat I wanted. The price he named was so reasonable that this new Panama hat cost me no more in Lauzerte than the original hat had in Panama. For the umpteenth time, things had not turned out for the worst.

In this age of fake news and hyperpartisanship, a commitment to historical evenhandedness obliges me, before concluding the current inquiry, to present the pigeons' point of view. Without their incessant cooing and infernal wooing, the pigeons' official spokesmen could rightfully argue, there could be no new generations of pigeons, hence no continuing supply of pigeon manure, ergo no *pigeonniers*, and so, but for them and their reproductive and excretory activities, Saturday, 17 September 2005, never would have become a notable date in the history of Lauzerte.

On that date, from its headquarters in faraway Paris, the mighty Ministry of Posts, Telegraphs, and Telephones paid homage to France Profound, and to Lauzerte in particular. It did this by printing a stamp commemorating, in capital letters, the PIGEONNIER, and then postmarking its First Day Covers as follows: 82 LAUZERTE. Thanks to the pigeons, Lauzerte's good name now would adorn philatelic collections across France, Europe, and the world. What have you done, that pigeon might have been asking me as it surveyed my nakedness, that in any way compares to our contribution to the renown of the fine old city we find ourselves, after all these centuries, obliged to share with you?

29

PARALLEL LIVES

When I got my House I failed to count on two things, in addition to the pigeons. These were winter and the English. When it comes to winter, insulation can be installed, though insulation's greatest usefulness turned out to be during summer. Without that thick slab of insulation, the Top of my House would turn into an oven when the annual heat waves strike. When winter in all its dank drabness descends, you can stoke your wood-burning stove, and keep your home's fireplaces burning. You can add space heaters, gas heaters, paraffin heaters. When you still have to go to bed clutching your hot water bottle, you can bite the bullet and install central heating.

With great effort and at ruinous expense it is possible to fend off winter, but the English? In his *Parallel Lives*, Plutarch paired the life stories of people who, while living in separate times, shared similar destinies. As I contemplated the lives of the English who came a cropper in France Profound centuries and centuries ago, I likewise found myself witnessing the lives of the English living all around me unfold in a similarly preposterous, often ill-fated manner. The arc of these people's lives traced the Black Prince pattern as all-encompassing presumptuousness in France led to disaster and then flight back to England, or the search for some new place to act out their idea of Englishness.

Edward of the Sliding Swimming Pool's misadventures certainly mirrored Edward the Black Prince's travails. He and

I met at the home of some pleasant French people, the Grimauds. Our host was a successful businessman. Our hostess was a painter. One of her Crucifixions hung in Nice Cathedral. In place of Golgotha, she had chosen the Promenade des Anglais as the scene of Our Savior's death throes. She painted the foliage of the Côte d'Azur with such finesse you could almost smell the flowers. Midst this pleasantness Jesus hung decoratively upon His cross. That night Mme Grimaud made a point of introducing me to Edward. He recently had acquired a residence in the neighborhood. "We are all neighbors now," she said in her charming English. "Isn't that nice, all of us amiably together."

A few afternoons later, my telephone rang. It was Edward, summoning me to dinner that very night. Normally, if one meets someone at someone else's dinner party and wishes to see them again, one invites the hosts along with the new acquaintance, but there was no place for "the French" at Edward's party. It was English-only, except for me. It was one of those moments when currency gyrations made it seem, if you were English, that you could live it up for free in France Profound forever. Just sell your house in England. Use 20 percent of your profits to buy a showplace down here. Put the rest into certificates and annuities, then live like a sahib off the income! Buoyed by the latest cross-Channel bubble, the English people at Edward's that night, a good dozen of them, had bought houses in the area.

The stars of the show were an elderly English couple. Meg and Charles, as these two ne'er-do-wells were known, had been subsisting in these parts for some forty years. After all that time, they still had no house of their own, but Meg had acquired a bit of memsahib French. It was necessary to be firm with "the French," emphasized Meg, as the English around Edward's table nodded appreciatively. When Meg and Charles first arrived in these parts, substantial properties sold for far less than garages do today, yet since they never managed to acquire a property of their own, kind people on occasion lent them their places to stay. This led to the comments one heard periodically, beginning "Poor Meg and Charles—" As in: "Poor Meg and Charles, such a pity. The house where they were staying burned down again." Was it the third or fourth time? No one was quite sure, but it was such a pity. And could you believe it? "The French" who had given them shelter actually held Poor Meg and Charles responsible for these incinerations!

Edward's next telephone call revealed the motive for his last-minute summons to dinner. He would be showing some of his compatriots my House, he announced. They would arrive around lunch time, so I laid out a spread of delicacies ample for twenty. Edward did not introduce me to his friends, as in a body they marched up the stairs, then down the stairs, then out the door. "No, no. Arrangements have been made for luncheon elsewhere," one of them responded dismissively, as though waving away a waiter, when I invited him to partake of the buffet I had prepared.

I never heard from Edward again. Later, Mme Grimaud told me what happened. Another currency crisis had hit. Placements in a certain blue-ribbon Ponzi scheme had collapsed. The smart thing to have done, the experts now agreed, was to have invested in real estate in England or, if you had any, hung on to it. Then came the final straw. "His swimming pool slid down the hill, so he went back to England." She added, amiably as ever: "We did our best to help him, but Edward did not trust the contractors we recommended."

Back in the time of the Crusades, the original Richard's addiction to making war during Lent undid him. My neighbor Richard's insistence on playing keyboard instruments, from the teensiest celestina to the mightiest organ, proved his undoing. Artists go blind. Composers go deaf. It was in keeping with the long-established theme of Englishmen coming to

grief in France Profound that this professional keyboard in-
strumentalist broke his finger, it was said, while playing Lauzerte's beloved organ. At first there was great alarm, but
following careful inspection, the Friends of the Organ Division
of ASAHLP, the Association for the Protection and Promulgation of the Heritage of Lauzerte and Its Periphery, announced
that there was nothing to fear. The Lauzerte organ was not involved in the mishap. The Englishman was not so lucky. It took
more than a year for his hand to heal. By then he had alienated
many of the local French musicians. "He is very English in his
behavior," one of them explained. "He treats us like servants,"
she elaborated.

With Richard, an English maestro, now in their midst, the
English no longer had to listen to "the French" playing Ra-
meau and Fauré, not when they could hear an Englishman
playing Byrd and Elgar. "'No point going to the next concert.
Only the French are performing.' They said it right out loud,
standing right next to me," another French music lover told
me. At another concert I experienced firsthand the deportment
the French music lovers had described. The row where my
musical friends were sitting, with the mayor, was full. "There's
a place for you, over there," the mayor said, pointing one row
back across the aisle. The pew in question was almost empty
except for the woman occupying the seat directly on the aisle.
As I approached, she did not move farther along the bench,
nor would she let me past her. "*Est-ce que je puis passer, madame?*" I courteously inquired.

"Do not speak French to me," she ordered, using the im-
perative mode of address. "Kindly let me pass," I repeated, this
time in English. "These seats are taken," she said. "There's
room for at least five people," I said. I stepped over her, and
took my seat. "Move down there," she said, gesturing toward
a few French people who, in their ritualistic politeness, had ac-
commodated her demand not to sit near her. Beneath the

lordly manner, I came to discover, lurked fear of contamination. The natives were not to be trusted, and as for the food! At the Valence d'Agen market, I once observed an English woman's horror when her husband selected a particular cheese. Though creamy yellow, it is known as *fromage cendré* because ash from the cooking fire is used to preserve it. "Put that down," the woman instructed. "Can't you see? It's dirty." She added, "The children—."

Seated across from me one evening at a Lauzerte dinner party was an English woman now trudging resolutely into the outskirts of old age. She'd been a bright young thing when she fled the London of Twiggy, Carnaby Street, and the Camden Town Communists to rusticate in France Profound. Janna Drake, for that was her name, was an amiable person though, being English, she did spend ten minutes complaining about how funny French food tasted. This caused me to mention that, starting as a mere slip of a lad, I had spent decades listening to the English complain across the globe how funny the food tasted. Whether it was sticky rice, dal baht, guacamole, za'atar, or clam chowder, it all tasted funny to them. When I respectfully requested that we discuss something other than how strange it was that the French ate things the English did not, Janna turned her attention to the French electoral system. "I've lived in France thirty years," this English lady complained, "and the French won't let me vote for president." "If you want to vote in presidential elections," I suggested, "why don't you become a French citizen? I'm sure they would be delighted to have you." Janna looked at me as though, instead of a nationality change, I had suggested a sex change in the days before gender dysphoria became fashionable. "I would never do that," she responded.

For decades my amiable good friend Janna lived in a barn whose ceiling posed exquisite philosophical questions. Is it art if art is not the intent? Is it beautiful when the purpose is only to hold up the roof? Whenever I pondered the intricate web of logs, branches, and beams holding up Janna's Roof, I felt myself in contact with the structure of the universe. Every one of those seemingly random struts both obeyed and reflected the laws of physics. For quite some while our paths had not crossed, but one day there we were, walking along the same side street in Moissac. Janna was coming from her dentist. I was on the way to my Arab barber. "Janna!" I exclaimed, once we finished marveling at the extraordinary coincidence of our meeting in a town almost fifteen miles from Lauzerte, "I need to see your beams." Her reply shocked me. Janna had sold her house. Not to worry, she assured me. The new owner surely would let me see them.

Of course, he was English. The place was as remote as I remembered, but now—next to the beamed house—stood a DIY new concoction. From it emerged, immediately and un-bidden, another Englishman. "We are English here," he in-formed me. "The French are over there. You can't come through here." His next-door neighbor, the new proprietor of Janna's Beams had been a pawnbroker in England. "You must have learned a lot about human nature from the people who pawned stuff with you," I remarked. "Well, since you're inter-ested," he replied, "I will tell you about the man who pawned his iron every month. He'd do all his ironing at the end of the month. Then, when he was finished, he'd bring it back, and pawn the iron again." The quaintness of it charmed me. "You mean, like a steam iron, the kind people use to iron their shirts?" I asked, "Yes," he replied. "Every month he'd pawn it for twelve pound. Then he would pay back the twelve pound, plus interest, so he could do the next month's ironing. I calcu-lated that over the years he paid hundreds to keep his iron in my shop."

As he spoke to me, I gazed at Janna's Beams. They dem-onstrated why even the most vivid recollections must be

fact-checked. In my mind's eye they had been but twigs. A
mass of them, Gulliver-like, held up the roof. In actuality, I
now saw, these supports were Brobdingnagian. A team of in-
terlocking megaliths, they held up that roof the way Hercules
hoisted the sky, only the different beams were so idiosyncratic it was as though the he-men of mythology had gathered there for a superhero convention. In addition to the
Hercules beams, there were the struts of Atlas, also the Si-
syphean buttresses.

Yet more astonishing than the beams, was that here in the
isolation of France Profound, a little cul-de-sac of council
housing had reconstituted itself, down to the nosy neighbor.
No people had established itself in more far-flung spots than
the English, and what did they do once they got there? Whether
the venue was Snooty Ooty in the days of the Raj, or the
European Parliament in a more recent epoch, they dedicated
themselves to impressing upon "the French" and other natives
their differentness, their superiority, their Englishness, meanwhile crowding together, the better to protect and reinforce
that self-same Englishness. The cantonment, the club, this iota
of England Janna and her successors had constructed were, like
autism, parts of a spectrum.

While life must be lived forward, as Søren Kierkegaard
noted, it can only be understood backwards. That certainly
proved true when I was invited to a poolside party. This being
an English get-together, the hostess let it be known I was expected to bring a main dish suitable for fifteen people. I had
just the dish! I once made my fabulous homemade Pesto Pasta
from basil growing on the terrace of my suite at the Old Cat-
aract Hotel in Aswan, Egypt. As I tossed my pesto with the
linguine room service provided, a single light glowed just below in the apartments where President François Mitterrand,
in the company of his mistress, their daughter, and his personal
physician, spent some of the last happy days of his life.

First step: Marshal your ingredients! I already had plenty of pasta, stored in thick plastic bags inside the Louis XV armoire in the Red Room, also a supply of good olive oil. I had garlic. At the Top of the House a bounteous crop of basil waited to be harvested, lovingly. Only Parmesan and pine nuts were missing. Parmesan was not to be had. "We have our own cheeses in France," the cheese monger patriotically informed me, so I used Cantal—a cheese with a hint of grit lurking there behind its rough-hewn finish. It worked fine. Italian pine nuts also were not to be had, so I used French walnuts.

It was a labor of love and now all those English people were going to love my France Profound-variant Pesto Pasta, and therefore love me, but how to transport such a quantity of it? At the supermarket I had bought a box of 100-liter sized plastic trash bags. After filling one of them with the fragrant pasta, I maneuvered that bag inside another bag, then into a third one. There could be no leakage now, plus the bags would insulate my Pesto Pasta, keeping it savory warm during the journey.

The guests were arrayed at tables around the swimming pool when I arrived. "The garbage tip is down the hill," one Englishman called out to me. "It's not garbage," I said. As I explained, the titters started. The hostess lugged the bag into the house. Later a small serving bowl of it was placed at the back of the buffet table. None of the English touched it. At the next Montcuq market, while selecting Reine Claudes, I overheard two passing English women conversing. Though they ignored me, they clearly knew who I was, as—lowering their voices—I heard them utter the words "American" and "garbage bag."

Reliving such events backwards, Kierkegaard-style, I came to understand that what had been true of the English occupying Lauzerte in the Brave Widow Gandillonne's time was still true today. Most of the English did not come here to be nice, to be friendly, to be compassionate or caring. They certainly did not come here in order to eat foreign food from garbage bags. Like the Black Prince, today's suburban bank clerks and High Street shop managers came to France Profound in order to pretend to be what they were not. In most cases this meant a rung or two more elevated on the English social snobbery index.

A number of publications, I discovered, existed to help English people cope with the unfortunate reality that France was inhabited by foreigners. Among the most vexing of these tribulations was the insolent French refusal to speak proper English. Ergo the following headline: "Eight Tips for How the French Could Improve Their English." These publications' personal ads contained entries similar, though not identical to those found in America. "WEM seeks WEF," "WEM seeks WEM." White Males sought White Females, or Males, or couples, or various other permutations. The additional "E" stood for English. "Find Your English Dream Date in France," one ad offered. "Someone of Your Own Race Who Speaks Your Own Language," promised another.

All one had to do was register online, so I did. For my sex-trolling pseudonym I chose: "Francophone Black Dude." Men, Women, Couples, Bi, Trans? I checked All of the Above, adding I was willing both to travel, and entertain visitors. I was all set to press "SEND," when my index finger froze. Fear, not moral scruple, guided me as I pressed "DELETE." What if some of these creeps had shown up in Lauzerte? Even more terrifying: what if some of them lived in Lauzerte? What if I had met some of them at those English-only dinner parties?

The France Profound variant of the anecdote involving the priest, the rabbi, and the mullah who walk into a bar tells what happens when a Canadian, a South African, and an American, me, get to talking. After no more than the second round of aperitifs, they wind up sharing their latest encounters with their English neighbors. "It was a lovely morning." I myself recounted on one such occasion. "I was in an uncharacteristically friendly mood when I saw the English fellow speeding up the hill in a Mini Moke. Our dialog," I continued, "unfolded as follows":

Me: *'Bienvenue à Lauzerte!'*

English fellow: 'Out of my way, fatso Froggie!'

I had spoken to him in French. That was all he had needed.

Their refusal to learn the French language came to annoy me most. As I once publicly remarked in French, knowing in advance the English people at the adjacent table would not understand: *"Les anglais y sont comme des cafards. Retournez un morceau de bois et vous les trouvez."* It was true. The English didn't understand a word of it when I said: "The English hereabouts are like cockroaches. Turn over a log and you find them." Another time, when a Frenchman politely asked if I were English, I snarled back: "Are you Belgian?" It was one thing to put up with the English, quite another to be taken for one. *"Il m'a accusé d'être anglais!"* I exclaimed first in French, and then in English, so even the English would understand: "He accused me of being English!"

These encounters were like the pigeon droppings on the Top of My House. There had to be a way to rid myself of them! Following considerable meditation I came upon a solution Zen-like in its profundity. To avoid problems with the English, avoid the English! Henceforth, I vowed, I would be like an AA alcoholic and saloons. Whenever I saw one, I'd just keep walking. Then came another incident involving another English woman in the church right across from my House, only this time a large animal was involved. She had brought a dog, sheep-like in its dimensions, into the church, then positioned the animal at the corner of the front pew. People had to step over the dog in order to approach the altar.

She's got to be English, I told myself, but then I thought
of my pledge not to get into any more altercations with the
English. Previously, had I found myself forced to make my way
past this woman and her immense dog, I would have said:
"You've got to be English. Only the English could be so utterly, cluelessly, insensitive, and disrespectful." Not now! Without uttering a word, nor even directing a contemptuous glare
at the woman, I exited the church.

Across the Square, at the café, I joined Maître Moret,
Lauzerte's beloved notary. "Curious," I remarked. "A woman
brought her large dog into the church. Then she inconsider-
ately and sacrilegiously placed the dog right near the altar,
blocking everyone's way. I suppose she was English. Anyway,"
I continued, "that no longer is any concern of mine. My con-
tretemps with the English belong to the past, so I'll never know
for sure if she was English," I concluded, except very soon I
would know. I noticed the dog first, waddling across the Square.
At the other end of its leash was the woman whom I heroically
had avoided confronting. Ignoring everyone else at our table,
she chattered away in English with the one Englishman who
was there, at which point my forbearance snapped. "You're the
one who brought the dog into the church," I interjected. "Oh
dear," she responded, acknowledging my existence for the first
time. "It's an American." Her comment was addressed to the
dog. The habitual dialogue of the deaf ensued about the need
to respect the country where one lived, and its people, and their
places of worship.

30

I STAND WITH DE GAULLE

On Thursday, 23 June 2016, my take on the English was entirely vindicated, and not by some petty act of rudeness. The Long March of History proved me right!

Up to then one could have purported that the English, in spite of their idiosyncrasies, were as European as their French neighbors. Me getting into spats with the English, one could have contended, was not their fault. That was before the Brexit vote, following which I now could reply: Look to the facts! Take heed of the facts! I was not the one who brought the dog into the church. I was not the one who hurled insults from the Mini Moke. Nor was it I who voted to give Europe the middle finger, as the English did that day.

"Brexit," like "The Hundred Years' War," was a misnomer. The neologism was derived from "British Exit," but Britain did not spurn Europe. England did. The non-England constituents of the United Kingdom voted to Remain by a majority of more than 56 percent. Outside cosmopolitan London, where the vote was heavily in favor of remaining, some 60 percent of the English had turned up their noses at Europe, and voted to repudiate a half-century of mutually beneficial economic and, increasingly, cultural and political union with their European neighbors.

Outside England the perversity of the English action provoked mirth and wonderment as well as alarm and mystification, yet it was so simple. All England wanted was to keep all the privileges of European Union membership, while shirking all the responsibilities. When the president of France ever so diplomatically informed the English that Brexit "can't come at the expense of the European Union's integrity," the *Daily Express* captured the mood of the nation in capital letters: "Brexit THREAT: Macron says EU's Unity is MORE IMPORTANT than Trade Deal with Britain."

Those ghastly Frenchmen and their conniving continental cohorts, lamented arch-Brexiteer Sir Jacob Rees-Mogg, MP, were out to subject England to "the greatest vassalage since King John paid homage to Philip II in 1200." Nothing had changed in eight hundred-plus years, he added. Rees-Mogg, was right about that, though not in the sense he intended. Here, most unusually, was an Englishman who remembered Philippe-Auguste, but only in order to denigrate "the French" along with all and anything they did. The Member of Parliament for tony North East Somerset failed to mention how that most masterful of French statesman, Philippe-Auguste, had thwarted that most villainous of English tyrants, the usurper King John. It did not occur to him to thank the French king for Magna Carta. Instead, he bore a grudge. After all, if it weren't for upstarts like Philippe-Auguste, the problems "the French" posed never would have arisen in the first place.

"If Philippe-Auguste had lost," pontificated one English academician prior to the Brexit referendum, "the west of France would have been English, the north would have been Flemish, and the east would have been German, but," he conceded regretfully, "he won." Running like a thin red line from the Black Prince up to and including Brexit was the notion that France's very existence was an affront. "There is no inevitability about the French nation as we know it now," the BBC reassured its listeners as the Brexit vote drew near.

The ages-old English contempt for France and, by extension, all of Europe had caused both England's voters and those who governed them to grossly undervalue Europe's strength. It also blinded them to their own vulnerabilities. Following Brexit, economic growth flagged in England; social discord worsened. The scab was torn off the wounds still dividing Ireland. Brexit had given advocates of Scotland's secession from the United Kingdom powerful new proof that the English could never be trusted to act in their common interest. Brexit, instead of undoing Europe, had raised the possibility that the United Kingdom itself might disintegrate. The Brexiteer response, by and large, was: So what? "Most English Tory Voters Would Be Happy to See UK Break Up as Price of Brexit," the *Guardian* reported, citing "research by the Centre on Constitutional Change."

It was another of those moments that illustrated why I don't write fiction, for back in France Profound I yet again was face-to-face with a situation I never could have invented for myself. When I forwarded that article in the *Guardian* to a number of my English neighbors, asking for their comments, they responded as if in one voice. "Frankly, nothing would please me more than to see the Welsh, Scots and Irish go their separate ways," one of them replied. "Europe needs us more than the other way around," remarked another neighbor. "We'll be better off free of those tyrants in Brussels and Strasbourg," averred another. "We don't need them." one posh lady informed me. "They need us." "Of course, I'm against Europe," my very best English friend informed me.

More than any grievance or dissatisfaction, it was the very idea of a competent united Europe that they found so offensive. None of the benefits they got from membership in the European Union diminished their desire that Europe should fail, and their belief that Brexit was the way to get that done!

Once the Europeans were left to their own devices, it was confidently expected, the euro would collapse. Then the European Union itself would disintegrate, and wouldn't that be fun to watch! "It serves them right," declared another English acquaintance. He had lived in France for more than twenty years, and been complaining about "the French" for that same amount of time. Now that Brexit had won, he seemed to expect that his French neighbors finally would accord him the deference he imagined his due.

Even the freeloading English *chômeurs*, I discovered, were Brexit-boosters. The dictionary tells you *chômeur* means "unemployed." While the word does contain that sense, its sociological significance is more specific. In French the fellow seen smoking cigarettes in the café day after day, while other people work, is a *chômeur* in the same sense a cabinetmaker is an *ébéniste*, that an *infirmier* is a nurse. Avoiding gainful employment is his *métier*, his vocation, his *bulot*. *Bulot*, the dictionary also will tell you, is the French word for whelk or sea snail. Mostly, though, it is used in its slang sense, to mean a job. That is because when you get a job in France you crawl into it and stay there, like a sea snail stays in its shell, until it is time for early retirement.

The French social system was not designed to promote idleness among the English, but thanks to membership in the European Union such had been the result. Prior to Brexit the English in France had just as much right as any Frenchman to be a *chômeur*, giving them even more time to complain about "the French," while living off French social benefits. An inflection point came for me when I realized I had not encountered one single English person in France Profound who, in response to Brexit, had said aloud what as an American I would have said, and often did say in the wake of such gratuitous foolishness in America: My country is an Ass. How irremediably, ineradicably English the English were! That was Brexit's great revelation.

Provoked by this absurd and recalcitrant historical recidivism, I decided to do something digital. *I Stand with De Gaulle* was the title topping my online polemic. "Brexit is a self-inflicted catastrophe for the United Kingdom," I wrote. "It is a catastrophe for the cause of an open worldwide human society that transcends tribalism. Most of all," I pointed out, "it is a catastrophe for the losers in England who voted to leave. Ten years from now they will be poorer, more marginalized, angrier and more ignorant. De Gaulle was right," I noted, "when he said the English were not capable of being loyal Europeans. He is still right." On a positive note, I emphasized that the Brexit cloud had its silver lining. The European Union would work much better now that the English, like resentful *chômeurs*, no longer were gumming up the works. "*Vive la Nouvelle Europe!*" I cheerfully added.

Of course, it was not in my character to leave well enough alone. The better to facilitate Brexit, I went on to propose the creation of a volunteer evacuation corps wearing uniforms and helmets with "Brexit Facilitator" inscribed on them. Labeling them in French was to be eschewed, I explained, since the evacuees, being English, would only be confused by "*Facilitateur de Brexit.*" The facilitators would form *condons sanitaires* leading to embarkation zones on the French coast. "The Royal Navy would be standing offshore," I explained, "to evacuate you. Members of the English yachting community could also help. After all, their grandfathers did no less at Dunkirk." Historical exegesis having failed, I had hoped irony would work, but it was all French to them. "Uncalled for," was the epithet most commonly hurled in my direction. "I do wish you Americans would keep your side of the street clean instead of constantly interfering in the affairs of sovereign states," another of my English neighbors responded.

Until then I had shared poor Karl Marx's mistaken belief that class was the most powerful force in English life: Brexit proved us both wrong. Whether they were posh or proletarian, denizens of the Midlands or Montcuq, the watchword was My Country, Right or Wrong, even for those who had not stepped foot in England for decades. As he slaved away on his great abstract opus in the British Museum in London, the class distinctions he saw all around him had misled Marx—hence Marxism—into two fundamental errors. The first was his failure to recognize that people seldom act in their own economic self-interest. If they did, England's Tories would never win an election. Instead, they went from strength to strength because the working class "deference vote" went to them instead of Labour. The second, even more consequential misunderstanding was the failure to recognize that class loyalties did not, and never would supersede nationalism. Since *Das Kapital* was published in 1857, hundreds of millions of humans have died because of nationalism. The nation-state has not withered away. Its grip on humanity has grown stronger, as the Brexiteers' insular scorn for the European Union, one of history's more valiant attempts to transcend nationalism, demonstrated.

"What is it about these island peoples?" I asked aloud one time as, exasperated, I meditated upon the English and their behavior toward others. "Why do they remain so insular even when they leave their islands? Along with the Japanese," I continued, "the English are the most insular people I know. The English," I elaborated, "can be the most wonderful friends. The English language—greatly improved by us Americans, the Irish, the Indians, and other folks—is a gift to the world. They gave us Yorkshire pudding and the steam engine. Their TV murder mystery series have high production values. Still, underneath, something isn't there. You put a Han peasant together with a Kansas farmer and they understand each other implicitly. With the English, it's different."

"Powerful islands. Not just any islands," a Chinese friend of mine at this point interjected. "Powerful islands." I slapped myself on the forehead. He'd pinpointed the missing link! Writing history and witnessing wars had shown me what happens to islands that are not powerful. The Tasmanians weren't insular. The peoples of Newfoundland and of the Antilles were not insular, nor were the Filipinos or the Sri Lankans. Now that I thought of it, island peoples very seldom were insular. Their exposure to sea-born incursion—if the invaders' diseases did not exterminate them first—forced cosmopolitanism upon them. I'd never visited a less insular place, I reflected, than the Indian Ocean island of Mauritius, with its mixture of Indians, Chinese, and Creoles. Hawaii with its rainbow of peoples was not insular. The English could be so insular because for so long they had been so powerful. Even when they lost wars and empires, they remained powerful enough to imagine Brexit was a bright idea, all the more so because it proved England still had the power to disrupt the world.

As of 31 December 2020, the English were well and truly rid of Europe. It was time to let bygones be bygones, but in the new millennium, as much as during the "Hundred" Years' War, it remained *de rigueur* that the foreigner be put in his place. On 21 January 2021, the *Guardian* ran the following headline: "UK Insists It Will Not Grant EU Ambassador Full Diplomatic Status. Foreign Office," the subhead explained, "Says EU Should Not Be Treated as Nation State Despite 142 Countries Granting Bloc this Status."

One discovery life in Lauzerte constantly has thrust on me is that if you leave out the women, you cannot understand anything. I don't just mean Eleanor of Aquitaine or Joan of Arc, but all the fascinating females I got to know delving into what really happened, and trying to understand why: Joan Plantagenet, Blanca of Castille, the Brave Widow Gandillonne, the "little girls and men's wives" of Toulouse. What was true eight hundred years ago is still true today. Inevitably there came the moment when what a woman did, or what was done to her or, most often, a combination of both, crystallized the meaning of an epoch.

I was in my Thinking Nook scanning the latest news flashes on my mobile phone when, thanks to the headline writers of the English tabloids, the latest penny dropped. Today's insight was that the neologisms Brexit and Megxit, like poisonous toadstools, were outgrowths of the same fungus. There always had to be some foreigner to blame—never more so than now as the Brexit woes England had inflicted on the United Kingdom were suppurating more and more. As the Megxit headlines denouncing the non-white foreign female who in her effrontery had dared marry into England's royal family supplanted the Brexit headlines denouncing the Europeans' vile perfidy, each news cycle seemed to bring its new revelation. Today's shocker was that the "American actress" on one occasion had asked to borrow her sister-in-law's lip gloss. At least, I reflected, Megan Markle had not brought a garbage bag full of pasta to her royal in-laws' get-together.

31

HOLES

With France Profound guiding me, I had stood where Richard the Lionheart stood when his character turned into his destiny. I had followed the routes kleptomaniac popes and terrorists on motor scooters took. En route this latest time, I trod paths humans trod tens of thousands of years ago. In so doing I found myself flung back to the future. This past-future fusion took the form of various holes in the ground. What they yielded were insights more precious than diamonds. One of the holes was an ecological-cultural disaster zone repurposed as a tourist attraction. In another of the holes the radiation might fry you if you managed to get down inside it. Some places are intellectually emotive. Others are emotionally instructive. These were both.

   The first hole until recently contained masterpieces dating back some twenty thousand years, but not until September 1940, just months after the Fall of France, did four teenagers discover these fabulous works of art. Less than two hours north of Lauzerte, near a hamlet called Lascaux, they discovered caverns containing more than two thousand paintings, many vast as murals. These works stunned the eye. They also revolutionized our understanding of what it means to be human. In spite of their great age, these paintings were in no way "primitive." After inspecting them, Pablo Picasso declared that the world's artists, including him, had learned nothing new in the intervening eons.

These paintings bespoke a relentless but selective search for exact understanding. Ignoring the local foliage, never depicting the events of everyday life, they focused on the dominant animals of the Pleistocene era—mammoths, aurochs, giant panthers, and hyenas—the way Ptolemy and later Newton did on idiosyncrasies in the motions of the planets. If we can understand these movements, the Lascaux paintings seem to say, we will understand everything. In their attempts to show everything, the Lascaux artists grappled with the same dilemma physicists do today. Scientists call it the Uncertainty Principle. The uncertainty derives from a contradiction built into the process of human observation. You cannot simultaneously measure the precise location and the exact momentum of a subatomic particle. Worse still, the more accurately you do measure one of those properties, the less precise measurement of the other necessarily becomes. The same dilemma holds true in the super-atomic world. That is why in the early days of photography people had to wear head braces while their pictures were taken. It is why portraitists to this day make those they paint sit stone still.

The Lascaux artists found, as quantum physicists did later, that the search for perfect knowledge led to a blur. That did not stop them from trying to transcend our human capacities. In order to depict bison thundering across the prehistoric landscape, they invented the same multiple-image technique Eadweard Muybridge would reinvent in the nineteenth century to depict horses galloping across the American plains. By superimposing multiple moving legs onto animals, these prehistoric innovators prefigured the Italian Futurists of the early twentieth century. Seeking ways both to define their subjects and to portray how they moved, the Lascaux artists also searched out special contours in the cave walls. These they used to create a three-dimensional effect that, when illuminated by flickering torch light, made the animals they painted seem alive. They also were astronomers. Symbols found in the caves, including dots, dashes, diverging lines, converging lines, branching bifurcated lines and parallelograms, seem to have played the same role mathematical notations later would. The animals themselves formed a paleolithic zodiac, linked to their breeding seasons.

These artists left portraits of themselves as evocative as any Rembrandt—or Francis Bacon—would paint. Instead of depicting the human face, they did this by depicting the human hand. Deep into spaces that sunlight never touched, they carried torches, and fuel for their torches, along with the pigments they so carefully concocted. To create portraits of their hands they pressed their own palms against the cave walls. Then, using their mouths and lungs, they turned themselves into human spray cans. Spitting pigment onto the walls, around their hands, they created stencils of who they were.

Most touching are the injured hands—fingers broken or crippled. Physical trauma, these images show, could not quell their need to create. Whatever their injuries, all the hands retain their thumbs. It could not have been otherwise. Those lacking opposable thumbs could not have created such paintings. The crucial importance of thumbs resonates with research suggesting that, as much as our ability to speak and to stand erect, the dexterity of the human hand propelled our species' ascent to power over this planet. Since Lascaux was discovered, other caves with similar handprints have been found as far apart as Patagonia and Sulawesi. The power and intelligence those hands bespeak show there is only one race, the human race. The commonality of those hands, transcending geographical location, proves something else: All those tens of thousands of years ago, human culture was world culture.

These subterranean discoveries unveiled a hitherto unsuspected human past. They also were a revelation of our times. By what we did to those ancient paintings, we showed who we are. At the time the Lascaux paintings were discovered, a new world culture was emerging, creating new paradigms, destroying old ones. In France one of the signal events heralding this new epoch was the opening of Euro Disneyland in the exurbs of Paris. For hundreds of millions of visitors in this new age, the essential sight no longer would be Notre Dame or the Eiffel Tower. Many would drive straight past Paris in order to show their children Disney's fake castles. To date, more than one-third of a billion people have visited that tourist theme park. In the process, the meaning of France, in countless human brains, has been remade. It is part of a worldwide remaking of the meaning of meaning, in which context, provenance, and authenticity no longer matter the way they once did.

Following the Disney paradigm, the Louvre Museum in Paris was also transformed into an attraction, complete with its own McDonald's. The fast-food franchise was located in the Louvre's vast new underground shopping mall, adjacent to its subterranean parking lot. The *Mona Lisa* was to this new drive-in complex, designed by the esteemed American architect I. M. Pei, what Mickey Mouse was to Disney World. After taking their selfies with the world's most famous painting, the thousands crowding the *Mona Lisa* gallery had no need to exit through the gift shop. "The Salon Denon souvenir store," the official English-language Louvre website promises, is "just a few steps away from the Mona Lisa."

While Euro Disney was expanding and the Louvre was being transformed, a parallel parable was unfolding at Lascaux. The Lascaux caverns were opened to the public in 1948. By 1955 a human invasion was wiping out works of art which, until then, had endured undamaged for tens of thousands of years. Besieged by black mold, the paintings in less than ten years had become so contaminated they risked being destroyed entirely by the microorganisms we humans carry with us everywhere we go. These included the bacillus that causes Legionnaires Disease, yet not until 1963 did officials close the cave to the general public.

By then the paintings' brilliant colors had faded like old movie film, so—like old movies—the paintings were "restored." Atop decomposing pigments that had retained their brilliance for at least seventeen thousand years, humans applied modern chemicals that might last—five years, fifty years? There was no need to wait that long; "the efforts to remove the mold," officials soon reported, had destroyed the paintings they were supposed to save, "leaving dark patches and damaging the pigments on the walls." Analyzing the devastation, microbiologists discovered that a hitherto undiscovered species of mold was ravaging the paintings. The newcomer was christened *Ochroconis lascauxensis.* Lascaux, cradle of human creativity, had been turned into a breeding ground for pathogens.

The real Lascaux paintings by then had degenerated to such an extent no tourist could be expected to pay to see them, so its promoters conjured up a fake Lascaux. In the original cave's most spectacular gallery, the Hall of the Bulls, a single unicorn as well as multiple depictions of lions, bison, mammoths, and different extinct varieties of cattle covered the walls. To cut costs and enhance profitability, the Hall of the Bulls was excluded from this supposed replica. It was as though the Sistine Chapel had been left out of a replica of St. Peter's. This faux Lascaux was inaugurated in 1983. By 1988 the heat and glare from the new cave's lighting was degrading the modern pigments on the fake paintings. The fake cave's air-conditioning system had empowered *Fusarium solani,* a previously inoffensive white mold to go on a microbial rampage. Using quicklime in an attempt to repulse the mold caused yet another fungus to cover the cave with black and grey splotches. In an archaeological instant, both the real and the fake Lascaux had turned into those throwaway service-sector consumer commodities whose use and abuse characterizes our age.

Once you destroy the original, you can never recreate it. When the fake is damaged, all you need do is conjure up a newer, bigger fake, then get the influencers busy promoting it. Fake is fungible. That turned out to be Lascaux's great revelation. "This is more than a facsimile," President François Hollande declared on Saturday, 10 December 2016, as he inaugurated the newest fake Lascaux. He was right about that. Semitour, the powerful tourism conglomerate, had transformed Lascaux into its latest theme park. In a French variant on American corporate welfare, the government had footed the bill for this for-profit desecration.

Like that ATM machine outside Montauban, Lascaux had become a paradigm of our current condition. It derived meaning, hence value from the degree to which it corresponded to what people saw on their computer screens, their iPads and, most especially, their cell phones. Lascaux "invites the public to visit a universe firmly focused on technological prowess" was how the official website of "The Lascaux Experience" put it. The possibility of seeing the actual Lascaux paintings had been destroyed forever. This made the public relations campaign to rebrand "The Lascaux Experience" as a futuristic tourist destination all the more vital. A commentary entitled "Why Lascaux Is Not Just Bigger & Better" made the implicit explicit. Fake was better; fake was to be preferred! Who cared that deep within their contaminated caves the actual paintings were moldering like corpses when, at the new "interpretation center featuring state-of-the-art experiential storytelling technology," kids could "create their own personal exhibitions by combining modern art and cave art." The cave might be dying, but the "personal exhibitions" the kids created at this new family-friendly attraction would live forever "on the Lascaux website, via a system activated by guests' scanned entrance ticket." This newest "cave" had an additional advantage. No longer did the paying public have to toil up and down steep steps to see it. This latest Lascaux cave was located entirely above ground.

If, after zigging up to Lascaux, you zag over to the Swiss border, you will come upon another revelatory hole, this one linked literally to "a universe firmly focused on technological prowess." This twenty-first century version of Lascaux is called CERN, an acronym in French for the European Organization for Nuclear Research. At Lascaux, humans attempted to make the world comprehensible by tracing lines deep beneath the earth. Today, at CERN, people are still going down into caves. There they, too, create lines in an attempt to comprehend the nature of the universe. Like the Lascaux grotto, CERN is a cavern where faith and science converge with the human urge to explain and thereby control everything.

Paleolithic humans used ocher, pitchblende, and sputum. Inside CERN, current humans use particle accelerator atom-smashers to create their lines. Where the Lascaux artists sought to explicate the behavior of mammoths or bisons in relationship to the comings and goings of the stars, contemporary scientists seek, shaman-like, to understand how and why quarks and gluons behave as they do. Among the stuff they've found is the Higgs boson, the "God particle" they call it.

It goes without saying I have my own secret cave. Down there I see what no one sees at Lascaux: the real thing. All the prehistoric paintings, palm prints, and lines scratched in my cave are the genuine article. My eyes see what the Paleolithic painters saw. My hands reach out to their hands, as they themselves stenciled them there. My cave is secret for the same reason my secret route to Moissac and my secret vista of Cahors are secret. No one's interested; they can't be bothered. Even when I tell them that this wonderful cave, with its authentic paintings, which is never crowded, is located closer to home and costs less to visit than Lascaux, they shrug. They're taking their kids to Lascaux because that's where all their classmates go. In the former *langue d'oui*, northern France, people drive right past Bayeux and Chartres as they rush to get to Euro Disney. Down here in France Profound, the erstwhile *langue d'oc*, people venerate fake cave art the way people once venerated fake relics.

The name of my secret cave is Pech Merle, located just over an hour's drive from Lauzerte. The devastation of the authentic Lascaux paintings was essential, not incidental to the success of the fake Lascaux. At Lascaux, no one sees the real thing, so tens of thousands throng there. At Pech Merle, the paintings have been protected, so only a few hundred get to see them, even on the busiest days. There is another important difference. For more than fifteen thousand years the Lascaux grotto had been sealed off from the world, so when it was opened, in rushed the pathogens. At Pech Merle, fresh air had circulated through the cave even longer than that. Vegetation and rain also got inside the grotto. The giant tap root of a tree, still there today, descends deep into the cave. This long-term exposure, counterintuitively, saved the Pech Merle paintings because it meant humans were entering a cave that always had been exposed to the outside.

The Pech Merle grotto was discovered well before Lascaux—Pech Merle in 1915, Lascaux not until 1940. A generation earlier, a parish priest in the nearby village of Cazillac, Abbé Barthélemy Taillefer, had devoted his life to saving Lauzerte's past from oblivion. Beginning in 1920, a parish priest in the nearby village of Cabrerets, Abbé Amédée Lemozi, devoted his life to saving Pech Merle from desecration. Like Taillefer, Lemozi brought a sense of reverence to his work, which he imparted to others. The title Lemozi gave his 1929 treatise on his discoveries, *La Grotte temple du Pech Merle, un nouveau sanctuaire préhistorique*, conveyed the sense of spiritual obligation, and also of joy, he brought to his task as, under his guidance, the youths of the village explored their prehistoric sanctuary, carefully and with respect. In 1934, the abbé's acolytes inaugurated what today is called the Amédée Lemozi Regional Museum of Prehistory.

The discovery of Lascaux generated travel posters and ticket sales. The discovery of Pech Merle generated respect and reverence. While the fake Lascaux gets hundreds of thousands of visitors, my secret cave gets hardly any. For a long time, I regretted this, but gradually I have come to be grateful for Lascaux for the same reason I was grateful the *Mona Lisa* is on display in the Louvre. My favorite gallery there—the Ingres gallery—is located right behind the *Mona Lisa*. This being Paris, dominatrix of French art along with everything else, many more of the artist's greatest paintings are on display in the Louvre than ever will be exhibited temporarily in Montauban, yet the Mona mob cares not a fiddle for Ingres. They give his voluptuous odalisques scarcely a glance as they rush first to the *Mona Lisa*, then to the *Mona Lisa* gift shop. It's the same with the traffic jams at Lascaux and the empty parking lot at Pech Merle. The degradation of the one helps preserve the authenticity of the other.

In Ray Bradbury's hopeful, dystopian novel, *Fahrenheit 451*, people subsist deep in the forest, memorizing the great works of literature, so that even after all the books have been burned, Shakespeare and Louisa May Alcott will live in people's minds the same way Homer did in preliterate times. The forest around Pech Merle, for me, is like the forest in *Fahrenheit 451*. Be it in caves or forests, on battlefields or inside my House, each act, good and bad, bequeaths its legacy. One day, in my meditation nook, while meditating on the dialectic of Holes,

I glanced up and saw, as if anew, one of the House's most astonishing features. It is a simple cut in the wood. It looks
more like a square root symbol, √, than a simple letter V.

The atrium of my House is so high, its builders could not
find one tree stout and tall enough to support it, so they used
two trees, slotting one atop the other. Today's builders would
bolt the two vertical beams together, or use some space-age
epoxy. Even more likely, they would tear out the wooden
beams, and replace them with concrete or steel. The masons
of half a millennium ago needed no nails, no screws, just as the
paleolithic painters had no need of acrylic. With utter self-
confidence, they hewed the top of one of those beams and the
bottom of the other so that they wedged together to form that
√-shaped join. For all the centuries since then, those conjoined
beams have stood strong, united, powerful.

Like the single confident unbroken curve tracing the
spine of an aurochs in one of the Pech Merle paintings, this
join is perfect.

32

FOR WHOM THE BELLS TOLLED

It was nine in the morning but the church bells weren't tolling nine. They were ringing three A.M. or maybe three in the afternoon. No one knew anymore. Many blamed Lauzerte's new curé for this discomfiting antisynchronicity. The bells' stately double intonations ceased as soon as the new parish priest arrived. After he said his first Mass they refused for some time to ring at all. Then the bells started sounding the wrong hour while, yet more petulantly, the hands on the clock on the church tower facing my House showed a different wrong time.

"The bells went on strike because the curé is very cruel to his mistress," asserted one person. Others claimed it was because the new curé was so cruel to the son of his mistress. I wanted to take a look at this cleric whose alleged turpitude was blamed for destroying the rhythmic constancy of the bells in my life. An opportunity arose when local choral groups performed a *missa brevis*, a kind of *Reader's Digest* version of a full-blown *missa solemnis*, the curé presiding. With his head of healthy white hair and his strong liturgical voice, he sounded and looked like a man of God; he certainly could have played one on TV. At Communion, I noticed, people preferred to have him hand them the Host, rather than let him put something into their mouths.

Just after Communion, a touching moment occurred. In the pew in front of me a handsome family was partaking of the spiritual nourishment the event provided. The emotional stresses and physical strain of raising a family in the hard-scrabble reaches of France Profound had only just started to reshape the mother's face and remold her body. The father, physically speaking, was located closer to the strapping young soccer player he recently had been than to the graying soccer coach with powerful biceps he might eventually become. It was all they could do to manage their two rambunctious, intelligent little boys. One maybe was five, the other younger.

Finally, the moment came when the older boy no longer could sit still and be quiet. "Papa," he whispered urgently. "Papa!" His father picked up the boy and, holding him close, placed the boy's lips close to his ear. "Papa," the boy said, gesturing around them: "We live?" The boy seemed to sense that the banal repetition he had just witnessed, of people receiving little white wafers from a man in a funny robe, involved mysteries that transcended individual lives. To live was different from simply being alive. Still, he wanted confirmation. "Papa," he repeated, "we live?" It was just a little shadow of a question mark, but he nuzzled his father appreciatively when the father nodded. The father's nod said, "Yes, we live."

As I glanced at these good people, and then at the priest, I remembered Graham Greene's novel, *The Power and the Glory*. No matter how much he drank, the Whiskey Priest could not stop being a priest. The truth about Lauzerte's parish priests, whatever the century, was the truth about humanity. Some were good. Some were bad. Many were boring. A few, even here, were intellectually interesting. One Lauzerte curé did stand-up comedy, though he did it sitting down, in the Café du Commerce, while having a drink. Knowing there would be liquor on his breath when he said Mass, he told René, the café owner, "I'll be doing publicity for you when I breathe on the communicants." An intellectually interesting curé was summoned all the way to Rome, to study Arabic. He had been chosen to be part of the Vatican's outreach mission to Islam.

Unlike his predecessors, the new curé shunned the cafés, also the commonplace pleasantries, as my friend Patrice Brassier discovered when they passed on the Barbacane. "Good day, my father," Patrice said, employing the conventional formula for addressing a man of the cloth. "Address me as 'Monseigneur,'" replied the curé. Distressed that a such a cleric should be entrusted with Lauzerte's spiritual well-being, parishioners wrote to the Bishop of Montauban. The bishop never so much as acknowledged their complaint.

The grumbling did not surprise me. Going back to the time of Jacques of Cahors and the Avignon popes, the faithful hereabouts had been complaining about their clerics. "Of all the great devils who rule the world the lord pope is the major devil; I call him Satan," one devout Christian declared back when Jacques of Cahors sat on the pontifical throne. I had forgotten that for just as long, even the most corrupt clerics—including the kleptomaniac Caursine Pope John XXII—had their defenders. They still did, as I discovered one stifling hot day when I entered the church opposite my House. The Association for Safeguarding and Enlivening the Lauzerte Area's Heritage had organized a cello-organ recital, the latter being the church's great Megan Brothers organ, manufactured in Agen in 1900. This concert occurred during the Saturday market, so after buying preserved duck gizzards from Fred, and shallots and eggs from Sylvain, my favorite peasant vendor, and aged Cantal cheese from Maryline, who on her last vacation trip to America visited Graceland, and not forgetting to collect my complementary bunch of Mr. Orond's superb free parsley, I edged my way toward the Church entrance. The fruit lady's stall was closest to the church's Romanesque side door, so after she personally selected the nectarines she knows

I like best—slightly underripe, with white not yellow flesh—I went inside the church.

It was wonderfully cool inside the nave. The Brahms was soothing, the Fauré more so, but something in my peripheral vision grabbed my attention. Swiveling, I looked back over my left shoulder. The exhibit urging material charity on behalf of the Kwashiorkor-ridden Third World orphans had been removed. A new shrine had been installed on the authority of the Bishop of Montauban. It honored Christendom's corruptest pope, John XXII. Seven centuries after he betrayed every one of Christ's teachings, Jacques of Cahors had been placed on a pedestal in the church in front of my House. I had supposed that Pope John XXII had been disowned by the Church long ago: I was completely wrong about that. Far from being condemned, Jacques of Cahors was being held up as an exemplar of what a model churchman should be in the twenty-first century.

In the public eulogy accompanying the exhibit, the Bishop of Montauban emphasized that veneration of this corrupt killer pope was particularly appropriate hereabouts because John XXII, the better to maximize his revenues, had created the Diocese of Montauban, which included Lauzerte. The bishop went on to praise the Midas pope's father for the money he made through usury. "His son was thus able to benefit from the best education possible, starting with the Dominicans," this official Church statement explained. "Like many of his contemporaries," the bishop's text approvingly continued, "he practiced nepotism on a grand scale and favoritism with regard to his relatives or neighbor. John XXII . . . re-established ecclesiastical discipline," this hagiography added approvingly. By crushing the rights of the local congregations, and arrogating to "himself the appointment of the bishops, until then elected. Another success," it concluded, "was the establishment of a tax system that allowed the Papacy to have abundant and stable resources."

The details the Diocese of Montauban presented might have been extracted from William of Ockham's indictment. The difference was that, after 700 years, those controlling the Church still took Jacques of Cahors, not the Spiritual Franciscans, for their model and mentor. The pontiff who enjoyed the "distinction of being the most popular candidate for the role of Papal Antichrist" was also rehabilitated visually. Glowing with the richness of computer-generated skin tones, this digitally-remastered John XXII had been made to look much younger than he actually had been. Above the image, the following title was displayed in majuscules: "A REFORMER POPE."

In this exegesis, the bishop of Montauban did not mention the murdered Franciscans. He did lay out, frankly and explicitly, his reasons for glorifying a pope famed for his lust for wealth and his delight in violence. Transforming Jacques of Cahors from a killer-kleptocrat into a nice guy, the bishop explained, "provided an opportunity for us to reread history." This enabled a restructuring of "our memory," which in turn allowed the Church to "shape the present we construct from it and, even more, it permits us to envision a common future." Or, as the Inquisitor in *1984* explained: "Who controls the past controls the future: who controls the present controls the past." When I set out to delve into the hearts of France Profound, I never intended to quote George Orwell, any more than I planned to describe La Farge's Minnesota lunette or Francis Bacon's "Screaming Popes." It was just that Orwell's words kept reappearing whenever the big questions reasserted themselves, never more than on that day when I tried to figure out what the glorification of this long-dead tyrant signified.

I was back in my House, climbing the Great Staircase when, for neither the first nor last time, Lauzerte enlightened me. The answer was so simple, a triumph of Ockham's Razor, really. The Jacques of Cahors-John XXII types were still in

control because, whatever the epoch, the Jacques of Cahors-
John XXII types normally were in control. It was an established
pattern: ignoring evil, while revering evil-doers. Gui's gleeful
treatise on inquisitorial terror techniques, far from being disowned, had been revered within the Church generation after
generation. Not content to let it molder away in its original
parchment Latin, devout admirers of the Grand Inquisitor in
the age of the railroad had revived his text. They translated it
into modern languages. They reproduced it on modern printing presses, so that future generations might learn from Gui's
techniques.

John XXII, I discovered, likewise had been revered across
the centuries right up to the moment in the twenty-first century
when, in the church across from my House, he became, just as
he had been 700 years earlier, the object of public veneration.
In 1827, in a volume dedicated to the "remarkable personages"
the Cahors region had produced, the section on the papal anti-
Christ demonstrated how, already for more than 600 years by
then, his crimes had been touted as triumphs. "The pen of a
son of Quercy," it began, "traces with pride the life of this great
man whose birth ennobled the city of Cahors as much as his
papacy honored the Church."

The significance of this essay, as with Gui's treatise, is that
it was not allowed to die. Never repudiated, this paean was republished in 1875 and then, 166 years later, in 1993, without
emendation or qualification. One of the Church's evilest popes
continues to be treated with reverence, as I discovered scanning the works of Abbé Eugène Sol, another of those parish
priests with a literary bent. While Taillefer detailed Lauzerte's past, and Lemozi explored the caves of Pech Merle,
Sol produced volume after volume lauding Quercy. He
lauded its agriculture. He lauded its industry. He lauded its
pope. *Jean XXII, un des plus grands papes de l'histoire* appeared
in 1947. For his efforts he—unlike Taillefer and Lemozi—got

the French equivalent of a knighthood. He was made a chevalier of the Legion of Honor.

The influence of this hagiography of evil transcended Quercy. It extended to the highest sanctum of the Vatican. There the current Vicar of Christ on Earth, Pope Pius XII, held the prose work praising his villainous predecessor in his own hands, and after reading it, he praised it. The future pope and the abbot from Quercy had become friends in Rome, starting in 1900, while both were young men. Sol taught the future pope French. During his three years of study there, Sol and the eventual pontiff often strolled the streets of Rome together, always conversing in French. Their correspondence continued for decades. Nearly half-a-century after they first met, Abbé Sol sent the pope his book lauding John XXII as "one of the greatest popes in history." The pope's response revealed how little the hierarchy's moral calculus had changed across the centuries. Pius XII might have gently chided his old Quercy acquaintance, tactfully suggesting that nepotism, murder and theft were no longer praise-worthy papal proclivities in the twentieth century. Instead, in letters dated 19 July and 8 August 1948, Pope Pius XII praised the author and his book, emphasizing that he "particularly appreciated his erudite researches into the history of his home province."

It was all so clear—so unsurprising—once you understood. No doubt the Bishop of Montauban regretted the Lauzerte curé's alleged indiscretions, just as Innocent III had lamented the moral lapses of the clergy in his time. But as John XXII's own exegesis made clear, the hierarchy's priority was maintaining the privileges and powers of the hierarchy, so "perfect obedience," remained "the greatest good." The same remained true today. Had Lauzerte's controversial curé taken to the pulpit and called for the right of priests like him to marry their mistresses, or for women to become priests, hierarchical punishment no doubt would have been swift, but he had never challenged the Church's authority. He may have sinned; he never disobeyed.

In October 2021, forewarned of the imminent release of an official report that upwards of three hundred thousand children in France had been abused by the Church, the bishop who had lauded Pope John XXII expressed his regret, "as bishop," for what he described as "a widespread evil found more or less everywhere"—*un mal répandu un peu partout.* Just under a year later, it was announced that the bishop, by then seventy-four, was retiring because of his age. The Vatican added he was being sent to "moral sanctuary" not far from Avignon.

The bells began misbehaving when he arrived. It stood to reason they would return to righteous ringing once a good priest replaced him. Finding one required history to turn full circle. In 1799 a high Mass was celebrated right on the Place des Cornières. This solemn *Te Deum*, Abbé Taillefer recounted, "was sung to celebrate France's seizure of Senegal in Africa, and of Santo Domingo in the Caribbean." Senegal would provide the slaves and Haiti the plantations where they toiled. Horror shaped France's colonialist past. Irony would own its recolonialist future, for what greater irony could there be than the arrival in Lauzerte of a parish priest from Africa?

In order to find a virtuous priest, the Montauban diocese had gone all the way to Garoua, Cameroon. "Father Emile Kofor of the archdiocese of Garoua is named to the Lauzerte assembly of parishes," it was announced in August 2017. In addition to Lauzerte, the African missionary would serve as pastor in "the parishes of Saint-Nazaire-de-Valentane-Mongaudon and Saint-Pierre-de-Nazac." One parish was missing from this roster, as was any mention of the priest he was replacing. A subsequent episcopal communiqué clarified matters. The cleric in question was "discharged from the Lauzerte assembly of parishes," it announced, with one exception. "He remains in charge as parish priest of Montaigu-de-Quercy where he lives."

Confronted with accusations of clerical misbehavior, the same bishop who had rechristened Avignon's wickedest pontiff as the "Reformer Pope" had done what bishops from Boston, Massachusetts, to Sydney, Australia, did—what the popes in Rome normally did with the Church's embezzlers, sadists, misogynists, and pedophiles. Rather than acknowledge corruption or punish clerical offenders, the late Pope Benedict XVI, a number of his obituaries noted, had "concealed and transferred known abusive clergy and until his death misled investigators and the public about his direct responsibility for it." This epitomized the norm in Lauzerte, and everywhere else. By then priest shuffling—"the parish transfers of abusive clergy" in order to hide rather than punish their transgression—had become so widespread that the practice had its own Wikipedia entry. Brazil, Austria, Chile, Germany, Ireland, and Italy, along with Poland, the Netherlands, Switzerland, Australia, and the United States—and France—were among the countries, multiple investigations showed, where priest shuffling had been the normal procedure.

In this realm, as in so many others, Lauzerte in its minuscule way revealed what had become of the world.

White missionaries once had brought the Gospel to the unchurched souls of the Dark Continent. Now a Black missionary was bringing Christ's Word to the unchurched natives of Tarn-et-Garonne. In honor of Africa's verdure, both the bishop and Lauzerte's new pastor wore green robes at the solemnities commemorating this watershed event. The mayor and the head of the Gendarmerie were among the notables who welcomed the entry of Lauzerte's first full-time African into the ranks of its elite.

Now that this episode of broken bells and priestly turpitude had run its course, my view of the Place des Cornières was enlivened from time to time by the pleasantly exotic passage of a gentle African who, on his Facebook page, listed his work as "Servant of God," and his favorite music as "Christ Sound." Best of all, the bells were ringing! Every time those bells rang anew, I would stop concentrating on the latest aspect of village life to offend or annoy me. Just while the bells rang, I would remind myself of how privileged I was to be here, and how important it was to be grateful for it.

33

AMBASSADORS OF PROGRESS

Lauzerte is to world events what one of those old-fashioned paperweights is to a snowstorm. Shake the miniature glass globe. Teensy snowflakes swirl just like real snowflakes do, except only twice in my long experience has it ever snowed in Lauzerte; then it didn't stick. Instead, world change at first envelopes you like the drizzle distant storms project. Far off, you see the lightning; then you hear the thunder. Eventually you feel some moisture. It seems nothing much has happened or ever will happen in Lauzerte until the storm smacks you full in the face. That is how it was in the century stretching from Napoléon's defeat to World War One. The very existence of Tarn-et-Garonne was a delayed consequence of the French Revolution. In the decades following its creation, the Industrial Revolution shook the world, though in Lauzerte the temblors once again, were felt indirectly, at a distance.

On the opposite side of the Lauzerte mountain from the little Lendou river flows another, equally unprepossessing stream called the Petite, or Little, Barguelonne. The two rivulets form a hydrological ellipsis encasing the mountain. They then merge into a third glorified gully, ludicrously known as the Grande Barguelonne. It's no grander than some nameless creek in America, yet if you got on an inner tube—a canoe would run aground—and kept following the Grande Barguelonne downstream, you would find yourself traversing a thousand years of history. Starting beneath the mountain where medieval dynasts and religious zealots contended, you would end your downstream paddle right across from those two nuclear reactors that, should they ever malfunction, could kill more people in hours than died in all the centuries of pre-explosives warfare.

We think of history as a flood flowing vast and irreversible, not dribbling along like the Barguelonne, but as the fates of Richard the Lionheart and the Montauban paratroopers demonstrated, history can trickle as well as flood. Sometimes, traversing the rivulets around Lauzerte, I remember the first time I saw the Jordan River. I burst out laughing. Roll on Mighty Jordan! The rickety bridge crossing that fabled stream was no bigger than the little bridges spanning the Barguelonne, and in far worse repair. The Jordan itself was nothing but a ditch—except in our minds, except in our psyches, except in the millennia of myth and religions, and in all the rationalizations people used to trick themselves into believing God was responsible for their mistreatment of other humans, that the evil they did was God's Will.

No product of the Industrial Revolution revolutionized life more than the railroad, yet no railroad would traverse the Barguelonne valley, though traces of the abandoned project to connect Moissac to the south with Cahors to the north via Lauzerte are still visible. This failure to extend the railroad was a decisive event in Lauzerte's modern history—one of those instances when what did not happen mattered most. Lauzerte is "One of the Most Beautiful Villages" in France today because nothing better preserves the past than poverty and isolation. Following the French Revolution Lauzerte lost its administrative power, and the prosperity it generated. Now the Industrial Revolution bypassed it. One by-product would be the preservation of Lauzerte's architectural treasures, including my House.

Things were entirely different less than fifteen miles to the south, in Moissac. There the railroad upended everything. Starting in the seventh century, Moissac Abbey and its clerics had dominated the town, but by 1848, as revolution again swept France and the rest of Europe, the plenipotentiaries of a different faith were dominant in the land. Progress was the new religion, and the "ambassadors of progress," as one chronicler wryly described them, had big plans for Moissac. Its engineers, the Compagnie du Midi announced, were going to demolish the Abbey and its cloister, then run their rail line right through the rubble.

The brazenness as much as the plan itself demonstrated how technology was transforming notions of right and wrong. This proposal for an architectural reenactment of *Caedite Eos* was presented as a worthwhile civic enterprise because, in many people's eyes, it had become as virtuous to ravage the past in the name of Progress as it had been for the papal legates to eradicate "heresy" in the pope's name 650 years earlier. The rail line smashed through Moissac's holy precincts, though following local protests its trajectory was slightly altered. While the monastical refectory and kitchens were demolished, the abbey and its cloister were spared, though barely. To this day the railroad runs straight through the abbatial domain, cutting it in two, destroying the calm of the cloister.

Animating events as the new railroads restructured life was a newly arisen question concerning grapes: which grapes to grow, and what to do with them once they were harvested. Classical antiquity had introduced viticulture; thereafter the most notable thing about wine production in the region stretching from Cahors to Moissac, with Lauzerte at its center, was that nothing changed. Beyond the satisfying alcoholic buzz wine provided there lurked a more fundamental reason why wine production dominated the economy. Wine lasted so much longer than other products did. Decades after it was produced, you could drink fermented grape juice, and it would not poison or kill you.

Wines produced in southwest France had to possess exceptional longevity. Yet again, Eleanor of Aquitaine was the cause. Producing wine for the English market began with her marriage to the English king, and had been dominant in Aquitaine and Quercy going back to the Black Prince's time. Since the local wine was destined for consumption in faraway England, the grapes once processed into wine and placed in wooden casks had to be transported to the coast, then laded onto sailing ships. After transiting the stormy Bay of Biscay, they then were shipped to London, thence to taverns and manor houses across England. By the time, finally, it was decanted, then poured into goblets so some English gentleman could sniff it, swirl it around in his mouth, and then render judgment as to whether the fluids in question were or were not of the proper class, the wine that had started out as grapes grown near Lauzerte was years, sometimes decades old—and you still could drink it!

Perishabilty had been the key economic determinant ever since Caesar wrote his *Commentarii de Bello Gallico*. Now all that changed because the Industrial Revolution revolutionized transport times. Fruits and vegetables as well as people now could be transported overland to other parts of France conveniently, cheaply, and in bulk. This meant that the local produce, when shipped by rail, could reach Paris and the newly industrialized regions of northern France fast, fresh, and edible. As, starting in the mid-nineteenth century, its clever horticulturalists uprooted the old wine grapes and replaced them with *Chasselas de Moissac*—the golden grapes of Moissac—prosperity gripped the land. They called these newly cultivated varieties of table grapes *grains d'or* and it was, truly, as though the region had been sprinkled with gold dust.

The Industrial Revolution also unleashed a revolution in what average people drank. As a result, two separate sectors of grape production emerged, corresponding to the departments of the Lot and of Tarn-et-Garonne. While Moissac boomed producing table grapes, destined to appear on ceramic platters, atop lace doilies, at traditional Sunday lunches all over France, Cahors concentrated on producing everyday wines—*vins ordinaires*—that could be shipped to the new factory towns.

This bifurcation in grape production created the landscape that surrounds Lauzerte today. To the north, toward Cahors, wine grapes cover the hillsides. Heading south, toward Moissac, the vineyards producing table grapes predominate. It is not difficult to tell the difference once you get the hang of it. Table grapes, as their name implies, look like they are being prepared to attend a dinner party. The vines bearing them are spread out elegantly on lattices, the grape equivalents of a finishing school. As for the wine grapes, they look exactly as you'd expect grapes to look that are about to be partially or entirely flayed, then trampled underfoot (or these days crushed mechanically), then left to ooze inside a big, dark, scary oak (or today, stainless steel) vat. As heartless with their wine grapes as the papal legates were with "heretics," local viticulturists inflicted further disfigurement by infecting their wine grapes with *Botrytis Cinerea*, a form of gray fungus. Without this "noble rot," the winemakers asserted, their fermented grape juice wouldn't produce nearly the buzz it does. Table grapes, in contrast, are allowed to develop to the fullness of their natural goodness.

Everywhere he pillaged, Montfort's henchmen had "trampled, cut down, set alight . . . the vineyards," but he was never able to eradicate grape production. The vines flourished too abundantly in Quercy's chalky soil for that, but 650 years later another invader almost succeeded when that other talisman of the Industrial Revolution, the steamship, unleashed the oenological version of the Black Death. Previously *Phylloxera*, tiny predators native to America and related to aphids, had not been able to survive the Atlantic crossing. Now that the journey took weeks instead of months, these microscopic stowaways reached Europe alive, lusty, and hungry. Soon every vineyard in France was in danger.

It was Lauzerte's version of the Columbian Exchange. Having conquered America with its diseases and firearms, Europe in turn was conquered by the potato, tobacco, and greedy little insects. This oenological plague, emanating from America, might have destroyed France's vineyards definitively had not Americans eventually come to the rescue. The heroes in this instance were T. V. Munson and his fellow botanists in Denison, Texas. Their break-through discovery, by 1875, was that the elusive *Phylloxera* fed only on the roots of grape vines, not on their leaves or fruit. Having made that discovery, Munson and his colleagues set to work developing a new variety of vine whose roots were both impervious to the tiny insects' attacks, and hospitable to having the endangered varieties of French grapes grafted on to it.

In gratitude, France in 1888 sent a delegation all the way to Denison, a round trip from Paris of some thirteen thousand miles by ship, railroad, and, in its final stages, stagecoach. There, just a mile from the Oklahoma border, a Knighthood of the Legion of Honor, Agricultural Merit Division, was conferred upon Munson, complete with neck sash and a kiss on both cheeks. A leading freethinker and paradigmatical American of his time, Munson also invented a primitive helicopter. For the first time, Americans had played a decisive role in what happened to and around Lauzerte, though not the last. Soon the age of European dominion would self-destruct. The American Century would replace it.

Phylloxera afflicted wine grapes and table grapes alike, but the consequences differed enormously depending on local circumstances. In Upper Quercy—Cahors, the Lot—the grape plague produced the same dire consequence the potato famine did in Ireland. In 1861, after the railroad but not yet *Phylloxera* had arrived, the population of the Lot peaked at 295,542. Thereafter it fell, and kept falling. By 1962, the lowest point, its population of 149,929 was barely half what it had been a century earlier. Today, with a population of less than 175,000 people, the Lot has 110,000 fewer inhabitants than it did in 1831.

In Lower Quercy—Moissac, Tarn-et-Garonne—the population peaked at 242,250 around 1848. It then also declined, though barely, once *Phylloxera* struck. Its greatest losses came later, as industrialization lured people to the cities. Tarn-et-Garonne's population reached its nadir, 159,559, just after World War One. By 1920 its population was growing again. By 2020 Tarn-et-Garonne's population had risen to an all-time historic high of 262,316. About twenty thousand more people now lived there than had at its peak in the nineteenth century. Some ninety thousand more people lived in Tarn-et-Garonne than in the Lot, which originally had the larger population of the two.

Going back to the Gauls, the Greeks, the Romans, and the Saracens, horticulture had provided a living link connecting the worlds of Classical Antiquity, the Crusades, and later epochs with what Fernand Braudel called "world-historical" events. Now, as their differing population figures demonstrated, it had happened again with the Industrial Revolution. Since it afflicted grape production and only grape production, *Phylloxera* enforced a historic diversification of horticultural production, away from grapes. How successful that diversification was depended on local conditions. Lot's stony limestone plateaux, called *causses*, offered the area around Cahors comparatively few opportunities for diversification. In the gentler terrain extending from Lauzerte south to Moissac, catastrophe bred opportunity.

"Do men gather grapes of thorns, or figs of thistles?" asked Matthew 12:33–7. As it successfully weathered the onslaught of *Phylloxera* in the nineteenth century, and coped with emigration to the cities at the beginning of the twentieth century, the response was, and remained: "Certainly not in Tarn-et-Garonne!" While Cahors stagnated, a wondrous horticultural revolution transformed life in Moissac for the better. Having transcended wine, the local horticulture also transcended the grape, turning Tarn-et-Garonne into a cornucopia yielding bumper crops of peaches, nectarines, apricots, apples, melons, pears, apples, and, *ça va sans dire*, those marvelous Reine Claude plums.

That explained the little department's most counterintuitive distinction. As confected by Napoléon, Lauzerte's home department covered a mere seven-tenths of one percent of the country's territory, yet thanks to this horticultural revolution, it wound up producing one-tenth of all its fruit. This included *Chasselas de Moissac* whose production resumed once the infestation ended. *Pruneaux d'Agen*—plums from the neighboring town of Agen—also were exported far and wide. You can find them today in grocery stores like Fairway, in New York.

By the dawn of the twentieth century, Tarn-et-Garonne's horticultural products enjoyed what, in the newly emerging automobile industry, would be called planned obsolescence. Having bought a bunch of *Chasselas de Moissac*, no one left it in the cellar until it was eight years old, as traditionally was done with Cahors wine. They put the grapes on the dinner table, for all to enjoy. As soon as they were gone, they bought some more table grapes—ditto with all the other tasty comestibles Tarn-et-Garonne now produced.

The differing denouements in the two departments, Lot and Tarn-et-Garonne, derived from one of modernity's most important "world-historical" events. One was the victim of the worldwide wine glut globalization generated. The other benefited from the globalization of eating habits. Together they taught important lessons about the perils of monoculture, and the advantages of economic diversity. They also demonstrated that the Law of Unintended Consequences applied to insects as well as popes and kings. While one department, the Lot, stagnated because the *Phylloxera* infestation had not destroyed its dependence on the grape vine, the other, Tarn-et-Garonne, thrived precisely because it had.

The Moissac rail project came within inches of obliterating sculptural as well as architectural treasures of inestimable importance. Today scholars agree that the Abbey's tympanum forms one of the finest entrances to a religious edifice in the whole of France. More than that, the abbey and its cloister together comprise not just France's, but, as the savant Émile Mâle later put it, Europe's "initial and unsurpassed masterpieces of medieval sculpture." At the time this cultural marvel was almost destroyed in order to facilitate shipments of table grapes, the abbey enjoyed no such respect. After centuries of neglect and desecration, the wonder was that anything of the abbey was left at all. As early as 1042, rival nobles besieged it. Long before Simon de Montfort got there in 1212, a vengeful monk hatched a plot to burn down the abbey. To his everlasting glory, another monk named Anquetil, abbot there from 1085 to 1115, spited his arsonous machinations. Moissac Abbey was ravaged during the wars with the English, in 1430, and again during the Wars of Religion. In 1628, the monks abandoned the precincts. In 1793 rioters ransacked the cloister and the church. The abbey next was turned into a factory producing potassium nitrate, essential for the manufacture of gunpowder.

When humans weren't desecrating it, flood and fire besieged the abbey. So did inept engineering. The roof and the abbey's belfry collapsed a number of times. Repeatedly repaired, repatched, and rebuilt, the upper reaches of the edifice today comprise a jerry-built jumble of ecclesiastical *bricolage*, that useful French term for Do It Yourself. Below, at ground level, are the abbey's wondrous sculptures. Look up, though, and you see the stone turning into rustic brick. The bricks form a multi-windowed facade that terminates with a roof line typical of the region's defining architectural achievement, the pigeon-excrement repository, complete with real-life pigeons "nesting in the hollows of the walls." High above Christ the Redeemer, the pigeons flock and court and relieve themselves. "The cooing of the pigeons," as one French archaeologist lyrically described it, "punctuates with a monotone hum the murmur" of the rites unfolding in the abbey.

By the time the "ambassadors of Progress" took charge in the mid-nineteenth century, Moissac Abbey was but one of countless ruins speckling the land. The Wars of Religion, the Revolution, and, most remorselessly, demographic decline in the rural areas meant that the land was littered with abandoned churches and chapels. "Everywhere we saw the remains of churches or monasteries that were being demolished," lamented François-René de Châteaubriand—famed littérateur and one of the first French ambassadors to the United States—in 1802. In 2002, while exploring abandoned chapels near Lauzerte, I found myself treading on the eye sockets and finger bones of pious, long-dead folk, their remains emerging from the chalky soil of the graveyards of chapels no one tended anymore.

T. V. Munson, a Dust Belt Texan, played a crucial role saving France Profound's vineyards. A New York Jew named Meyer

Schapiro helped make sure the Moissac Abbey and its Sculptures finally got their due. Born in a Lithuanian shtetl, he was brought to America as an infant. Like his near contemporary, George Gershwin, he was raised in Brooklyn. After attending Brownsville's P.S. 84, Schapiro was admitted, at age sixteen, to Columbia University, whereupon the teen was recognized as a prodigy in the field of art history. Guided by his mentor Ernest DeWald, an expert in illuminated medieval manuscripts, Schapiro chose for his postgraduate doctoral research an obscure structure in an obscure town in one of France's most obscure departments, that is to say, Moissac Abbey and Tarn-et-Garonne. DeWald also helped him get a traveling scholarship from the Carnegie Endowment.

In this manner the child of penniless immigrants was able to embark upon the kind of Grand Tour previously the preserve of the kind of well-bred young WASPs encountered in Henry James novels. From July 1926 through October 1927, Schapiro wandered from France to the Holy Land and, via the great sites of Greece and Italy, from Aswan in Upper Egypt to Spain. Although he traveled alone, his constant companion in both mind and spirit was his future wife Lillian, a medical doctor who would live to be 104. While filling notebook after notebook with architectural drawings reminiscent of those Leonardo da Vinci left, the young traveler wrote home to his fiancée constantly, revealing in these letters his deepest thoughts on the research he was conducting. Immersing himself in the same terrain that, getting on for a century later, I today traverse, he also brought his beloved up to date on local goings on. "At Agen," he informed her in a letter from Moissac dated 5 September 1927, "there is a Prune Congress, of the Society of Agriculture of the Agenais. The prune is Agen's main export, its main source of wealth," he elaborated.

The boy from Brooklyn loved Cahors so much it caused him to burst into song. It happened at the Pont Valentré. On his way to the railroad station, he saw "Valentre's towers in the distance, and I spent an hour on the bridge which was never more beautiful to me. As a little boy," he continued, "I would awake in bed and sing for a whole hour. This [happened] again tonight. I do not know when I began to sing. I surprised myself." It seems he also surprised some "huntsmen with black and white dogs." They stood motionless watching the young American singing at the top of his lungs as he "walked up and down the bridge many times, always astonished that there were towers & crenelations & fantastic staircases." In Cahors the young scholar gained insight into what lengths the committed researcher will go to in order to secure his documentation. When a local notable refused him access to his archives, "an abbot of Cahors offered the owner pornographic literature which was instantly devoured. It is thus that we have today some of our most interesting information on the Roman province of Quercy," Schapiro informed his fiancée.

In the dozens of letters he sent her, the young man's prose sang of his love—for the monuments and sculptures he saw in Tarn-et-Garonne and its environs. His greatest love, he declared, always would be "the portal and cloister of Moissac. To be with them is to be happy indeed. And to study their details is to live in perpetual discovery and pride," he assured her. He loved just being "in the beautiful cloister, which is more and more beautiful each day, giving charm to the sunlight and the shade, making silence golden, and revery, an untroubled happiness. The medieval color of the capitals has long faded," he wrote her, but "a delicate pink survives that with the shadowed green of the unorganized flowers and vegetation forms a polychromy as sweet as the most sentimental memory of imagined ancient tones. In the most glaring sunlight," he added, "a deep shade is assured under the arcades and behind the cedars which rise out of court high above the red cloister roofs."

"Cooler, more fragrant, detached from the accidents of the world about," this beloved refuge also provided the focus for what Schapiro described as his "luxurious contemplation." In the sculptured pediments of the cloister's pillars, Schapiro understood, he had discovered a universe. "Its artistic remains can be studied as comparative religion, as folk lore, as design, as technique, as folk psychology, as history, costume, furniture, artifacts, as physical types, and even as architecture, for there are so many buildings domestic, civil, military and religious represented in the capitals." A break-through insight came while observing "the abbey church by starlight. There was such richness of sky [that] the forms of the tower & porch & buttresses" made him feel he was seeing the portal for the very first time. It was different, because in those rich shadows "I recognized no figures as sacred but only the finely serried lines and masses." Thanks to this excision of the sacred, he assured his fiancée, he finally was able to behold the "building's true destiny. And all the days I had beheld it, and worried in it, imperfect accidents of a strange world." He knew by then Moissac had changed his life, and that he would be returning many times. Still, this first departure tore at his soul. It was though he was being torn from a lover's embrace. Describing the end of this first Moissac sojourn, he wrote, "How could I leave it! I could not turn back to see it a last time."

"Daily," he wrote on another occasion, "I learn of more interesting objects in the surrounding country, which I must visit in years to come." Did he ever see Lauzerte? The lack of a rail link protected Lauzerte from "the ambassadors of progress." It also meant its treasures remained undiscovered by many who might have intellectually profited, and been emotionally enriched, from encountering Lauzerte.

Delving beneath the accumulated centuries of misinformation and neglect, and also letting his mind and feelings,

Whitman-style, come to their own conclusions, Schapiro made the key discovery that defied the way people in the twentieth century conventionally understood the history of art: Men, not God, were responsible for Moissac's sculptural marvels. Where others saw rite-like repetition of religious doctrine, and rote-like manipulation of the stone, Schapiro discerned "a new sphere of artistic creation." Thanks to his American Century sensibility, the immigrant boy from Brooklyn perceived at Moissac what had been lost on Europeans, and also on the highly Europeanized American aesthetic elite. Moissac's supposedly static carvings, he demonstrated, were not static at all. They were "imbued with values of spontaneity, individual fantasy, delight in color and movement, and the expression of feelings that anticipate modern art." To compare Moissac's emotive sculptural character studies with the dead-eyed effigies of Innocent III is to see how astute Schapiro's perception was. "This new art, on the margins of religious work," as he put it, "was accompanied by a conscious taste of the spectators for the beauty of workmanship, materials and artistic devices, apart from religious meanings" as defined by the monks and the abbots, the bishops and the pope.

Schapiro's insight afforded historical as well as aesthetic revelation. Like the spiritualism of the "Perfects," the humanism of the Moissac Sculptures flourished "on the margins of religious work"—on the pediments of pillars in the cloister, in the peripheral figures of the tympanum on the facade of the abbey. These depictions bore witness to the vigorous spiritual independence that, denounced as "heresy" a century later, would prompt Innocent III to launch his campaign of spiritual genocide. The Moissac Sculptures were not, Schapiro showed, the product of some "dark age," nor were their creators ciphers. Specific artists, they wanted to be remembered, so they signed their work. Recently, using my cell phone, I photographed one of their marks. It resembled the capital letter "R" turned upside down. This insistence on the individuality of the artist was as modern as Matisse. It was as eternal as the paleolithic handprints on the walls of the cave at Pech Merle.

The Moissac Sculptures reflected an understanding that this physical life we are obliged to live here on Earth is not merely difficult, but in some essential sense materially evil. The world is full of corruption, these figures' facial expressions acknowledge, yet what alternative do good people have except to live within it? The contradiction between God's supposed power and God's alleged goodness haunted both popes and "heretics," as it would Camus and Jean-Paul Sartre. Not even Christ the Redeemer is spared insight into this existential dilemma. From the center of the Moissac tympanum, He peers out with eyes that reflect acknowledgment of humanity's depravities, as opposed to triumph over them.

Hundreds of years before expressionism entered the mainstream of European portraiture, the sculptors of Moissac were masterfully expressing in stone the profoundest of human emotions. Their work also offered deep insights into the historical events that later savaged the region. Neither the pope nor his legates ever provided a consistent definition of the "heresy" they claimed to be repressing, but both this and future "heresy" did share one attribute. It was their attitude toward papal autocracy. Some disputed it. Others disobeyed it. The "Cathars" simply ignored it. Like the early Christians to whom St. Paul wrote his Epistles, these humble people preferred to dwell in small, independent communities. They chose to be guided by the example of their "Perfects," rather than be subservient subjects of the papal empire. The Moissac Sculptures were about a century old by the time the pope launched his Crusade in 1209. They bore witness to a flourishing independence out of which would grow both the spiritual autonomy of the "heretics" and the political autonomy of the Counts of Toulouse. This spiritual independence, as opposed to any particular theological issue, sufficed to bring down upon them papal wrath.

The sculpture of one of the Elders depicted on the Moissac tympanum, apparently the Prophet Jeremiah, has the most unforgettable eyes. They bespeak a stoic distance from the physical world that expresses an acceptance of life's travails so deep as to be, by today's standards, heartbreaking. I thought I would never see another face as expressive of the spiritual dilemmas explored in those works of art until I came upon a photo of Meyer Schapiro himself. It was taken around the time he decided to commit his young life to studying and understanding what the Moissac Sculptures meant.

Those eyes! While Bacon's "Screaming Popes" depict one set of humanity's spiritual possibilities, the Moissac sculpture of the Elder and the photo of the young American scholar bespeak the existence of such a thing as pure love, including love of knowledge for its own sake. I think of Schapiro as kinsman to the Shepherd.

34

GLASS GLOBE WARS

World War One, like the Crusades, was the culmination of what Europe had done to itself. The intent of the Crusades, launched in 1095, had been to seize the Holy Land for Christendom. The unintended consequence was that Christian-on-Christian violence gripped Europe for hundreds of years. Now it happened again, on a gargantuan scale, as Europe's hubris circled back to drench Europe in European blood.

The English called this global projection of arrogance the White Man's Burden. The French called it the *mission civilisatrice*, the notion that it was the God-given right, and duty, of European white men to civilize the rest of the world. To this end they ravaged civilization across the Americas, Africa, and Asia, but nowhere did they do more harm than the harm they did to themselves, starting in 1914. During the Wars of Religion, many more European Christians died killing each other in Europe than ever perished in the wars they launched against the Muslims in the Levant. Now many more Europeans died killing each other in Europe than ever perished in their wars to impose "civilization" on the world beyond Europe.

The practical reason why some twenty million Europeans killed each other on the continent of Europe between September 1914 and November 1918 was the same reason Henry of Navarre used pétards at Cahors in 1580 and Japan would have atomic bombs dropped on it in 1945. It had become possible for humans to do it. The railroad, it turned out, was as wonderfully efficient at transporting adolescent human male soon-to-be corpses to their deaths as it was at transporting the golden grapes of Moissac and luscious Claude Reine plums of Tarn-et-Garonne to Les Halles, the great produce market of Paris.

Today, with one exception, it is possible to wander Lauzerte, appreciating its medieval-seeming décor, without encountering the slightest indication that anything unpleasant ever happened there. The exception is its *Monument aux Morts*, Lauzerte's memorial to the dead. The mass deaths World War One inflicted on Lauzerte, and on all the other cities, towns, and hamlets of France, were too numerous to make historical prettification possible. Memorials to those killed in the greatest of all Europe's bloodlettings cover the land. The simplest monuments in the smallest places, sometimes mere slabs of concrete with only three or four names on them, show how remorselessly a faraway war sucked its victims out of places so remote that, even though it was already the twentieth century, they had war dead before they got electric light bulbs or flush toilets. As befits the town's eminence, Lauzerte's monument is an imposing marble edifice. It has seventy-eight names on it, many of them family names well-known to me. Go stand outside Lauzerte's high school one afternoon as classes are ending. Now imagine taking seventy-eight of those students as they come out of the school, and killing them. Then expand that to encompass every community and family in France.

Lauzerte's monument demonstrates what that ATM memorial in Montauban does: Given enough time, even the worst horrors cease to horrify. Often, without giving humanity's suicidal barbarism a thought, I tell visitors: "The entrance to the Square is just uphill from the *Monument aux Morts*. If you can't find a place for your car at the Place du Château, you can always park on the gravel behind the Monument to the Dead."

The deaths seem more real to me when I take the slow train to Paris. Rattling along the same tracks they took, I think of those boys whose names are on that monument. The railroad epitomized "progress." Progress meant they could take your son and kill him more conveniently than ever before. The railroad-building frenzy of the nineteenth century had created a twentieth-century death-delivery system that funneled them by the millions into the sights of the waiting machine guns, which also were transported from their factories to the killing grounds by rail.

For many of the soon-to-be-dead, this would have been the only time they saw Paris. Paris! Depot of fashion, entrepot of culture, turnstile of death. A glimpse, maybe, of that marvel of modern progress, the Eiffel Tower, then Onward! They died after being caked in their own feces, after wading through the sludge of decomposed bodies, after weeks or months in those fetid trenches.

To feel the full horror of what nationalism did to all the nations of Europe, listen to the "La Marseillaise" as Hector Berlioz orchestrated it. At the end, the boys who would never reach puberty—the boys whose high-pitched voices have yet to break—sing as they too march joyously into the cannon fire. Every time I hear the Berlioz version, it makes me shiver. It reminds me how the myth of the Pied Piper never ceases to provide illumination.

The advent of World War Two confirmed Braudel's observation concerning the asynchronicity of historical time. The almanacs tell us World War Two began on Friday, 1 September 1939. That was true if you were Polish, but if you were American, it did not begin until Sunday 7 December 1941, when the Japanese bombed Hawaii, which the United States had annexed just forty-three years and five months earlier. In Lauzerte, World War Two began even later—before dawn on

Sunday, 11 November 1942, as Hitler, disregarding and disrespecting the collaborationist Pétain regime, seized military control of the whole of France.

Lauzerte in this instance too was like a little glass globe. In the far distance, the lightning was visible as Europe exploded. Then the thunder was heard as the Nazi Panzers outflanked the Maginot Line, though initially the chief consequence of the Fall of France in June 1940 was a change in atmospherics. The erstwhile Kingdom, Empire, and Republic of France was now called *l'État français*. On the coinage of the collaborationist French State, *Travail, Famille, Patrie*—Work, Family, Country—replaced Liberty, Equality, Fraternity.

Another difference was that for the first time since the popes held sway in Avignon, the orders from on high did not emanate from Paris. They came from the thermal spa town of Vichy, 225 miles northeast of Lauzerte, headquarters of the regime established after France surrendered to the Germans. From Vichy, Marshal Henri Pétain, abetted by the most notorious of the Nazi collaborators, Pierre Laval, administered some 40 percent of the country's territory, while retaining authority over France's vast colonial empire. In newspaper reports Vichy France was called Unoccupied France. It would better have been called Self-Occupied France. By assuming the functions a German army of occupation otherwise would have had to shoulder, the Pétain regime freed up Hitler's forces to go on the attack in North Africa, and to invade Russia. Initially Vichy, which administered Corsica, was also able to prevent France's strategic overseas territories, stretching from the Caribbean across North Africa to the Far East, from supporting the Allies.

Lauzerte's elected city council resigned rather than take orders from the new regime. From Vichy, a Special Delegation was appointed to run the town. Known by its French initials, the D.S. in January 1942 passed a lick-spittle resolution assuring "the chief of the French State, the venerated Marshal Pétain, of their admiration," while also "expressing their thanks and support for his work redressing the national condition." After servilely "pledging him their total and respectful devotion from this, their little part of the country," the message concluded: "Vive Lauzerte! Vive la France! Vive Pétain!" In June 1943 the D.S. unanimously approved a motion "to place in the town hall, in witness of its respect and loyalty, a bust of His Excellency Marshal Pétain."

"Il nous faut faire confiance au maréchal," was the watchword in those times. Any cause for confidence in Marshal Pétain was shattered as German forces, meeting no resistance, occupied "unoccupied" France. Hitler ordered the takeover because he knew what Simon de Montfort had known 730 years earlier. A nullity like Baldwin could not be trusted with Caylus, any more than Pétain could be trusted with Paris. Even within France Profound, Pétain lacked legitimacy. As soon as the chance arose, every locality, Lauzerte included, would turn into a new Lolmie.

Present and past rhymed in another way. The arrival of tens of thousands of German troops did not quash resistance. It intensified it. In Lauzerte the nucleus of the Resistance had begun to form in mid-1941. It consisted of a network of whispered contacts linking *Lauzertins* with fellow *resistants* in the neighboring communes of Bourg-de-Visa and Montagu-de-Quercy. By spring 1942 it included handfuls of people with names similar to those still heard today. Étienne Lafargue headed the Resistance in Lauzerte, aided by Henri Segonne, code name "Ysr," and Julien Pax, a future mayor whose code name was "Lulu."

They formed elements of what would become the Eighth Company of the Secret Army in Tarn-et-Garonne. It was part of what the Allied command called the F.F.I., the French Forces of the Interior. By 1943 the Resistance in Tarn-et-Garonne counted 352 armed partisans, including a number of women. By 1943, 301 local boys and men also had joined the local *milice*, the dreaded paramilitaries who worked hand in glove with the Gestapo. Each recruit swore "to combat democracy, dissidence, and the Jewish leprosy." That did not stop their neighbors from sheltering Jews by the hundreds all over Tarn-et-Garonne. In Moissac, a large building overlooking the Tarn River was turned into an orphanage where more than five hundred Jewish children found safety. Today it is the Hotel & Spa le Moulin de Moissac, the town's largest. Moissac also became headquarters of the Jewish Boy Scouts of France—*Eclaireurs Israelites de France*—once the Germans seized control in Paris. Though *Eclaireur* can be translated as scout, Pathfinder gives a stronger, deeper sense of the existentialist transformation these young people underwent, from big-city Boy Scouts to resourceful guerrillas.

"Be Prepared" could have been the motto in November 1942 as hundreds of Jewish children were whisked out of Moissac before the Gestapo could get to them. Issued counterfeit identification papers, some were sent to hide in the mountains. Some joined village innkeepers, or lived with farming families for the duration. Others were enrolled in boarding schools. "The principal was waiting for us, and right away instructed us what to do if the Germans would come," one of them remembered, "He knew that we were the Jews in hiding." Yad Vashem, the World Holocaust Remembrance Center, includes Moissac in its acknowledgments of the "Righteous Among the Nations." Moissac saved many Jews; Lauzerte saved but one human being from the Holocaust. In the Yad Vashem database, the orphan Lauzerte sheltered for the duration of the war is listed as "Lindenblatt, First Name Unknown."

What is known—the only truly important thing to know—is listed next: "Survived the Shoah."

To the frustration of many, the strategy of the French government-in-exile, led by General Charles De Gaulle, was for the Resistance to lie low until the Allies were ready to invade. While waiting for orders to act, *resistants* concentrated on hiding weapons, ammunition, and government vehicles from the Germans. Their efforts were constantly stymied by their neighbors. As a result of denunciations by French collaborators, approximately two-thirds of the hidden vehicles were seized. The remaining vehicles, along with the hidden weapons and ammunition, would be waiting when orders came to launch attacks on the Germans.

There were also logistical preparations to be made. By the autumn of 1943, groups based in Lauzerte were scouting parachute drop zones. The closest one, six miles away near the hamlet of Bouloc, was well chosen; it is a parachuting school today. In April 1944 the Allies dropped seventy-six containers, holding six tons of armaments, near Lauzerte. Local partisans, including a school teacher from Saint-Amans-de-Pellagal, helped a Lauzerte trucker, Pierre Capitaine, to recover and hide the arms and ammunition.

General Dwight D. Eisenhower later estimated that the F.F.I. tied down eighteen German divisions that otherwise might have blocked the Allied landings in Normandy, or turned the tide during the Battle of the Bulge. The Resistance in Tarn-et-Garonne can take credit for helping to immobilize one of them. Initially no German forces were needed in Tarn-et-Garonne. The detested Vichy police did the dirty work, but by April 1944 the Resistance, just as planned, had become disruptive enough for the Nazi high command to transfer an entire division to Montauban, and not just any division. The name of this elite SS Division, "Das Reich," evoked the *führer*'s dream that the state he created would last a thousand years.

Little Tarn-et-Garonne had been the bait, and Hitler's High Command had bitten. With only eight weeks to go before the D-Day landings, an entire SS division found itself stranded twenty miles from Lauzerte. With the Allies now advancing in Normandy, the strategic objective of the local Resistance was to keep the Germans mired. The effort succeeded. Had it been able to move by rail, the "Das Reich" division could have reached the Normandy front in three or four days. Instead, stymied by resistance attacks on the rail line, it was obliged to move more than 12,000 soldiers and their materiel over France Profound's narrow two-lane roads. Moving that way disabled the steel treads on its thirty-seven Panzer and fifty-five Panther tanks. Its fourteen hundred other vehicles broke down frequently or ran out of gas.

Moissac saved many hundreds of Jews; Lauzerte saved one human being from the Holocaust. Those Jewish boy scouts, supplied by the Americans, derailed a German ammunition train; they captured its commander, along with fifty-six German soldiers. Lauzerte, ever Lilliputian, would contribute but a pin-prick to the campaign of harassment against the Germans.

In July 1944, a company of U.S. commandos, parachuting into the region, landed almost on Lauzerte's doorstep. "Vincent," the resistance leader, was far from the last local in trouble spots around the globe to be astounded by the sheer quantity of stuff Americans carried with them. "These thirty or forty American paratroopers," noted Vincent, whose real name was Jean Douet, came "heavily harnessed and over-equipped, draped in canteens and other unneeded accessories, lugging with them canvas bags of all kinds, [also] padded overcoats in the middle of August, food rations, toilet paper."

Burdened down with their "huge amount of equipment," ignorant of the local terrain and conditions, they would have been "unable to survive . . . without volunteer guides, and the help and support" people in the local resistance provided.

Six hundred years earlier, the Black Prince had marched on nearby Lolmie. Now the avant-garde of the world's newest global empire found itself installed, thanks to the help of these "volunteer guides," at the Château de Charry, some seven miles from Lauzerte. Taking charge of their deployment, the leaders of the local resistance hid the Americans in a spot so remote neither the Germans nor their collaborators could find it. Even today, in peace time, guided by G.P.S., the Château de Charry is difficult to locate. After traversing a gauntlet of twisting upland lanes, one finds the chateau much as the Americans did some eighty years ago, shrouded by the encompassing forest, surrounded by a stone wall, guarded by an iron gate.

Vincent was at the Cafe Étienne in Lauzerte's Faubourg d'Auriac one night when, he later told his son, "there was a knock on the door of the restaurant. In silence, weapons in hand, we waited for the two men outside to make themselves known." Explaining the urgency of the situation, the visitors revealed that "thirty Americans were waiting at the bottom of Lauzerte mountain." They had decided to attack a railroad bridge twenty miles away at Lamagistère. They needed the *Lauzertins* to guide them there.

A few days earlier, with the help of some Jewish refugees from Poland, Vincent had tried unsuccessfully to engineer the desertion of a number of young Poles forcibly conscripted into the Wehrmacht. He had been unable to get in contact with them because he could find no way to penetrate the glass spikes and barbed wire surrounding the German camp. On this same foray he had come within a hundred yards of the heavily-defended bridge which the Americans, sight unseen, had chosen as their objective. Vincent warned them of the difficulties, but "the Americans who conferred at length confirmed their intention to fulfill their mission."

Having failed to dissuade the Americans, Vincent facilitated their plan. He and four other members of the Lauzerte resistance "took, in their black Citroën, the head of a long column of many trucks and cars which transported the men and important loads of tools and explosives." The Americans thought big, Vincent noted. For them, "it was not a question of sabotaging a railway line, as the 8th Company was accustomed to do, but of blowing up the entire structure, which presupposed the use of the very heavy quantities of high explosives" they brought with them.

Over the next seventy hours ensued a calamity which, in its microscopic way, defined what war mostly is: pointless acts of violence producing gratuitous mayhem and needless death. Getting to the site the Americans selected was an ordeal of men and vehicles—including Vincent's tiny Citroën—threading their way across empty tracts and along unpaved lanes, all the while knowing a barking dog or a Vichy sympathizer could betray their presence at any moment. Once they got there, the Germans opened fire before the Americans could get close enough to detonate their plastic explosives. In the melee several of them fell into the river, only to be rescued half-drowned. Others were pinned down in the cross-fire "but, saving their ammunition, the Germans soon stopped firing. There were probably only a few men at this isolated post," Vincent recalled, but the element of surprise had been lost. Finding themselves in complete disorder, both French and Americans "gathered around two haystacks near a flour mill, the Americans dragging two or three of their exhausted comrades with them."

"The return was pitiful," Vincent elaborated. It was broad daylight when their "wretched cohort," as he described it, finally reached the rendezvous point. The convoy transporting the Americans had disappeared, Only the little Citroën and the *Lauzertins* guarding it remained. The following night, at great risk to themselves, Vincent and some others repeated the dangerous journey to Lamagistère, in order to rescue one "wounded *resistant* who had been abandoned there and three Americans lost in the fields whom their leader never expected to see again."

Like so many tales *Lauzertins* tell each other, the story of the disastrous Lamagistère foray was provided a happy ending. Thanks to the *Lauzertins* and their neighbors, Vincent related, the Americans learned their lesson. "Instructed by experience, they no longer undertook badly prepared operations against unevaluated objectives." *Au contraire*, the Americans thenceforth took the *resistants* of France Profound for their model. "The 8th Company henceforth remained their touch stone," he noted with satisfaction, "and they were with us some time later at the liberations of Moissac, Albi, Lacaune and the Montagne Noire in the days of combat and triumph that would soon follow."

To the end of his life Jean Douet—the erstwhile Vincent—remembered the Americans' missteps. Douet's son Pierre never forgot the generosity of the American troops. The bomber jacket one American gave him long remained a treasured possession. It had a zipper, the first the boy had seen. It was, he recalled in an account published in 2008, "certainly one of the first zippered military jackets to be worn by a civilian in France."

Those paratroopers were among the first Americans ever to lay eyes on Lauzerte. They surely were the first Americans to bear arms there, but the revelatory personage in this minuscule catastrophe was not French, German, or American. A Spaniard initially known only by his code name "Mosquito," this valiant *resistant* was the only one killed in the course of the Lamagistère fiasco. Earlier he had fought as an artillery captain in the Republican Army during the Spanish Civil War.

When the war ended with Franco victorious in April 1939, just five months before the outbreak of World War Two, "Mosquito" was among more than 475,000 Spanish opponents of fascism who fled to France. Under Pétain, thousands were forced into internment camps; some 200,000 were forced to return to Spain. Many others, like "Mosquito," found a warm welcome and a new life in the remoter parts of France, not excluding Lauzerte.

The most notable of the nearly five thousand Spanish exiles to find refuge in Tarn-et-Garonne was the last president of the Republic of Spain, Manuel Azaña Díaz, who established his headquarters in the center of Montauban at the Hotel du Midi. After the Fall of France in June 1940, Mexico intervened to prevent the Vichy France authorities from handing over the republican statesman to Franco. It proclaimed the Hotel du Midi its consulate, conferred Mexican citizenship on the former Spanish president, and bestowed upon him the rank of ambassador. Azaña was protected by this diplomatic immunity, but when he died of natural causes in November 1940 the Pétain regime refused to let the Spanish Republican flag be displayed at his obsequies. Thousands paid their respects as the last Spanish president, his casket draped in the Mexican flag, was buried in a Tarn-et-Garonne graveyard, where he remains to this day.

The Spaniard "Mosquito," the sole fatality of the American-French foray, had found a new life even closer to Lauzerte, near the neighboring village of Montcuq. There he became a stalwart of the resistance, and an esteemed friend to many, and also a respected military leader who trained the Lauzerte *resistants* in the manufacture and use of high explosives. "Mosquito," the Spaniard, was killed while leading the French-American attack on the bridge. When Vincent and the others returned the following night to Lamagistère, they made sure to retrieve his body; the next day it was given a respectful burial in Montcuq.

His French friends never forgot their Spanish comrade's valor. Honoring his sacrifice, they inscribed the name "Mosquito" on no less than three memorials, but those who had been touched by his life's "unique and touching journey" were not satisfied. Determined to establish his true identity, a son of Spanish refugees named Charles Farreny undertook the patient search that bore fruit a full seventy years after the disastrous foray that cost "Mosquito" his life. Though some had known "Mosquito" as Emmanuel Salvador, the investigation established that his full name was Salvador Estrada Dilmer. On 16 August 2014, the seventieth anniversary of his death, his full name at last inscribed on his tomb stone, "Lieutenant Mosquito, whose burial in the Montcuq cemetery had remained anonymous for seventy years, finally found a name and a past. During an emotional ceremony," a local press report continued, "Charles Farreny retraced the life and arrival in France of this Spanish Republican who came to fight and die alongside the local Resistance."

It took another five years for "Mosquito" to be accorded the recognition—"*Mort pour la France*"—seen on countless other tomb stones. Like being classified as One of the Most Beautiful Villages, or certified as a stop on the Compostela pilgrimage route, the approval of Paris is required before even the humblest memorial in the remotest village can bear that inscription. Finally, in 2019, the encomium "*Mort pour la France*" was officially conferred on him by the National Office for Veterans and Victims of War. The honor did not do "Mosquito" full justice, for he had died in pursuit of a loftier purpose than mere nationalism. After Franco triumphed in Spain in 1939, many Spaniards like him continued fighting fascism wherever they could, from France Profound to the Russian front. His death, among hundreds of thousands of others, demonstrated that the second world war was, among many other things, a European civil war.

Every nation in Europe had its fascists, ranging from England's Black Shirts to Norway's quislings, as well as its *resistants*. A generation later, in a cafe in Melilla, the Spanish enclave on the Mediterranean coast of Morocco, I met one of the Spaniards who had fought on the opposite side, for the Nazis. A giant map of Europe covered the wall behind the bar. It showed a blue arrow plunging across Europe into the heart of Russia. The legend, in Spanish, read: "From Spain to Russia: 5000 kilometers with the Blue Legion." The Légion Azul, the most ultra of the ultra-fascist units to see combat on the Eastern Front, fought shoulder to shoulder with the Nazis to the end.

Standing beneath the map depicting the exploit that all these decades later still made him proud, the proprietor greeted me warmly. There were guitars for the patrons to borrow whenever they wished to burst into song. All nationalities were welcome. "Come in!" he called to them, when some Moroccans appeared shyly at the door. "Welcome!" This man would have been fighting for the Nazi cause in Russia around the same time his countryman was killed fighting against them in the course of that Lauzerte foray.

Distracting a few German machine gunners on one bridge demonstrated what saving one Jew in one village did. In war, there are no inconsequential events. The Germans guarding the bridge at Lamagistère were among the many thousands of German soldiers who never would defend Germany as the Allies advanced on Hitler's bunker. In Mosquito's case, too, context helped provide the measure. His side had been defeated in Spain, he had been killed, but today Spain is a democracy. As a legacy of the fascist triumph in Spain, Lauzerte today has a notable sprinkling of residents with Spanish—mostly Catalan—surnames. Descendants of those who found refuge on the Lauzerte mountain following Franco's victory, they have significantly enriched the life of the town.

In pinprick attacks, the *resistants* picked off the Germans by ones, twos, and threes. Attempting "to break the spirit of the population," SS troops murdered one-third of the population at the hamlet of Marsoulas. At Tulle, also about ninety-four miles north of Lauzerte, all males between the ages of sixteen and sixty were arrested; 99 were hanged in public, 149 sent to Dachau. At Argenton-sur-Creuse fifty-six civilians, including women and children, were killed. Oradour-sur-Glane was the Beziers this time. The killer giving the *Cadeat eos* order was Sturmbannführer Adolf Diekmann, commander of the 1st Panzergrenadier Battalion of the Der Führer SS-Panzer-Division. First the entire population, including children and old people, was ordered to proceed to the Place du Champ-de-Foire, the local version of the Place des Cornières. There the Germans divided the people into two groups. Men and boys were herded at gunpoint into barns and sheds, where the German troops opened fire on them. The living and the dead then were covered with bales of hay, which were set ablaze. Only six of the male victims survived. One of them later described seeing his neighbors writhing in the flames, their legs twitching as, wounded but still alive, they were burned to death.

The killers locked the girls and woman of Oradour-sur-Glane inside the village church. There they gave *bricolage* new meaning by turning the nave of St. Martin into a Do-It-Yourself Auschwitz. After their container of poison gas exploded, filling the church with thick black smoke, the SS troops threw wood and hay, as well as wooden pews and anything else combustible they could find atop the suffocating women and children, and burned them too. Next, cripples and invalids who not been able to take themselves to the Place du Champ-de-Foire were rounded up and killed. Six vacationers who happened to be bicycling through town were also seized and killed, as were fifteen Spaniards and eight citizens of Germany's ally, Italy. Later, the charred bodies of a baker, his wife, and their three children were found roasted to death in the baker's oven.

Like the Montauban ATM massacre site, the village of Oradour-sur-Glane is one of the most important historical sites in the whole of France. This is because it shows history exactly as it happened. After Liberation, General de Gaulle ordered that Oradour-sur-Glane stay as the Germans left it. Go there today, and you see the church, the oven. To see what Sturmbannführer Diekmann and his storm troopers did there is also to see what Simon de Montfort and *Vulgarium Numerus Infinitus* did. History repeated itself in another way. The Nazi commander wound up as Simon de Montfort did. Killed less than three weeks later, he got to Normandy too late for his death to make any difference. By stymieing the Nazi advance, the massacred civilians of Oradour-sur-Glane, 643 in total, had saved at least that many Allied combatants. Today a new village stands next to the destroyed one.

General Heinz Lammerding, Das Reich's divisional commander, later was convicted of war crimes, but in addition to being a crime, this slaughter of civilians was a military mistake. Bogged down in France Profound, the "Das Reich" division never again played a significant role as the Allied forces advanced, inexorably, in the direction of Hitler's bunker. His decision to occupy "unoccupied" France had the unintended effect of hastening Hitler's own suicide, but then everything the *führer* did, when viewed through the prism History provides, was suicidal.

The Oradour-sur-Glane massacre took place on 10 June 1944. No monument marks the site seventy-eight miles to the west, near a hamlet called Le Vert, where on 12 June 1944, *resistants* murdered fifty-five disarmed German soldiers. After forcing them to dig their own graves, the killers poured quick lime on the corpses' faces. The massacre might have remained secret forever, but in 2020 and again in 2023, Edmond Réveil, a teenager at the time, and now nearing his hundredth year, divulged the details. "It was wrong to kill them," he said. "I am satisfied that it no longer is a secret."

In all, 801 men and women bore arms for the French Forces of the Interior in Tarn-et-Garonne, including Lauzerte. Of those, forty-four were killed in combat and thirty-nine shot or hanged; seventeen died after being deported. Pierre Loubradou, a leader of the Lauzerte commandos, was seized by the Germans, deported to Buchenwald, and then transferred to the Mittelbau-Dora slave labor camp. In April 1945 he and more than one thousand others, starving and sick, were forced on to a train. At a place called Gardelegen, they were forced off the train, into a barn.

Just as Europeans liked to pretend it was only the Germans, the Germans liked to pretend it was only the Nazis. What befell that lad from Lauzerte proved otherwise. The Gardelegen massacre of 13 April 1945 was not ordered by Hitler. Trapped in his Berlin Bunker, he would be dead just seventeen days later, his corpse then burned. The Gestapo had nothing to do with it; like the rest of the Nazi apparatus, it was in its death throes by then.

The townsfolk of Gardelegen were the ones who locked them in the barn and, aided by the town firemen, set it on fire. Once Joan Plantagenet had provided the living link between Quercy and her brother Richard's grotesque, futile massacres in the Holy Land. Now, in the form of the burned corpse of Pierre Loubradou, Lauzerte had a direct link, horribly and ironically, to a signal crime of the twentieth century. The horror was that his murder was so gratuitous. The irony was that rescue was so close. Less than forty-eight hours later, on 15 April 1945, US Infantry liberated Gardelegen. Sorting through the 1,016 corpses, they discovered eleven prisoners were still alive: seven Poles, three Russians, and one Frenchman, though not Pierre Loubradou.

Not all prisoners were so unfortunate. On a list of those from Lauzerte who managed to escape from Germany, I found the name Martial Paris—my Mr. Paris! The genial old gentleman who at every Saturday market provisioned me with poultry and wisdom had escaped, then lived long enough to provide a living link to a time which, thankfully, I was born too late to see. Surely, it later occurred to me, Mr. Paris in his youth had an older friend who could have seen Leon Gambetta, if not taking off from Paris in his hot air balloon, perhaps strolling his namesake boulevard in Cahors. That man in turn could have had a friend who once laid eyes on Napoléon, maybe that time in Montauban. How many handshakes would it take?

When I tried to calculate it, I was surprised. As few as a dozen, certainly no more than twenty, was the number it would take to shake hands my way back to 1291, and so be able to go out my front door, walk around the corner, knock on her door, and let the Brave Widow Gandillonne know how her example guided the women of Lauzerte during this latest foreign occupation. One of them, Huguette Vernais, survived deportation, and made it back alive to Lauzerte, where she rose to the rank of postal inspector. People in Lauzerte long remembered the heroics of a *Lauzertine* named Elise Lafargue, though not for what she did to the Germans. Just as Lauzerte was being liberated, two *resistants* got into a fight. In those final days, the pent-up frustrations frequently burst into fisticuffs, or worse. One *resistant* was menacing the other with his revolver when, by interposing herself, this courageous woman prevented a possible killing.

World War Two, having begun late there, ended early in Lauzerte—nearly eleven months early, on 11 June 1944 to be exact. A particular incident marked the moment. It involved the use of a telephone. That day Bernard Labarde, a member of the Vichy-appointed Special Delegation, was taken into custody by the Resistance. They claimed he had been observed making a telephone call to the *milice*, the most detested of the Nazi collaborators. Somewhere else, he might have been shot on the spot, but when Labarde protested that he had not telephoned the *milice*, his captors decided to investigate. They discovered the telephone call had been made by a distraught woman trying to reach the gendarmes, not the *milice*, in Moissac. The Vichy councilman was set free.

The partisans now decided who went free or was arrested in Lauzerte, so long as they had public support. When they also detained Edmond Delcer, the council president Vichy imposed on Lauzerte, another uninventable denouement ensued. People all over Lauzerte demanded his release. Delcer, the villagers pointed out, was not some opportunist who threw in his lot with the collaborators, milked it for all he could, then scuttled and ran. He had fought the Germans and been captured by the Germans. He was a prisoner in a POW camp in Germany when the Vichy regime was established. He was freed after agreeing to serve as the president of the Vichy-appointed Special Delegation in Lauzerte. As a result, an honest soldier got his freedom. Instead of some fascist thug, Lauzerte got a local boy to act as intermediary between the collaborationists in Vichy and, in due course, the Germans themselves. As the *Lauzertins* put it, he concerned himself "with administration, not politics."

President Delcer, as Vichy styled him, knew what both Raymond VI and Raymond VII had known. Obsequiousness—this time in the form of that "bust of His Excellency Marshal Pétain"—often protected the people better than pride.

So also, once again, did the tactics of inaction. In the whole of 1944, Delcer called but one meeting of the D.S. Respected though he was, Edmond Delcer had had enough. Vowing he never wanted to lay eyes on Lauzerte again, he vanished—like the Shepherd of Montaillou—at the moment his life had become truly a revelation.

V-E Day, marking Germany's unconditional surrender, would come on Tuesday, 8 May 1945, but people in Lauzerte had seen with their own eyes that the war was truly won and done the previous August 1944. That was when a good forty German soldiers entered Lauzerte—as prisoners, not conquerors. They were held in the turreted redoubt behind my House that I see from my Loft every time I sit down to write. A prison then, it later became the headquarters of the Gendarmerie.

Throughout this latest historical ordeal, the spirit of the Lauzerte Charter continued to animate civic life, as events showed in December 1943 when the German police searched a local home. They had reason to be suspicious. It housed the café where the American paratroops would be welcomed. It belonged to two of Lauzerte's most stalwart *resistants*: Elise Lafargue and Étienne. The Lauzerte authorities—Vichy-appointed though they were—vigorously protested the intrusion on grounds first promulgated in the Lauzerte Charter in February 1241. The raid was impermissible, they argued, since the Germans "could undertake the search of a private residence only in the presence of the members of the Lauzerte administration," and none had been present. "They must also explain the motive for their search [beforehand], and also identify all and any persons who had denounced them to the local police," and they had not done that either. The Lafargues had been forewarned; the search party found nothing. All the Germans got for their trouble was a formal complaint to the highest official in the department.

Running through war as it did in peace was the leitmotif horticulture provided. One of the rare instances when the Vichy-appointed council directly challenged their superiors involved a dispute over who got to sell melons in Lauzerte.

Once a democratically chosen council was reinstated, it voted a sum of 5,800 francs—one-eighth its total budget—to help those who had been deported to Germany reconstitute their lives, and their orchards. A year later, 1946, it authorized the larger sum of 6,150 francs to cover the costs of feeding the German prisoners. Once the Jewish orphans were spirited into the countryside, a number of them enjoyed growing plums and grapes so much that they adopted horticulture as their vocation. Some of those whose lives had been saved would wind up on kibbutzim in mandatory Palestine, soon to become Israel.

In war as in peace, unoccupied or occupied, formulaic or not, politeness prevailed in Lauzerte. When the authorities asked them to name names, the Lauzerte council provided the names of just two collaborators. It politely requested that one of those persons not be permitted to return to Lauzerte "in his own interest as much as the public's." In the second case it was suggested that, temporarily, the person in question "be forbidden access to the commune of Lauzerte" because such a return would both "pose a grave risk to his person" and "cause trouble among the ensemble of the population." In 1945, as in 1241, the objective was not vengeance. It was the maintenance of civility—*civilité*, like *civilisation* itself derived, as in English, from the Latin *civitas*, for city.

French Revolution, Industrial Revolution, two world wars: The universe had turned somersaults, but Lauzerte had not changed very much. The main difference, this time, was that they had not taken the children, so there was no need for a second Lauzerte monument to the dead. They just added three names to the ones already there. Like the missing railroad earlier, that lack of an additional *Monument aux Morts* was a revelation.

The memory of what happened in Lauzerte during World War Two might have been lost entirely but for the stalwart efforts of my long-time friend and neighbor, Patrice Brassier. Inspired by Abbé Taillefer's example, he spent years accumulating facts about Lauzerte. Many of his most precious discoveries came as he talked about their lives, at the end of their lives, with those who witnessed World War Two and the changes overtaking Lauzerte following the war.

Thanks to Brassier's *Chroniques Lauzertines de la Gandillonne à la Resistance*, the stories of both the Vichy collaborator Edmond Delcer and of *resistants* like the Lafargues were not lost, and the names of hundreds of others were preserved. Published by the City of Lauzerte, his compendium did not fail to display the official emblem of "*Les Plus Beaux Villages de France*" on its cover.

35

TRIUMPH OF THE
TRAFFIC CIRCLES

For hundreds and hundreds of years, Lauzerte's mountaintop location dictated what Fernand Braudel called *Les Structures du Quotidien*—the structures of everyday life. Protected by their mountain's steep slopes, Lauzerte's butchers, bakers, and ironmongers, as well as its clerks and clerics, enjoyed a degree of security the surrounding valleys could not provide.

Its elevation also isolated the town from the transformations of the nineteenth century, epitomized by the railroad. During the first half of the twentieth century, too, Lauzerte continued to subsist in its own historical time zone. So rare were the new technological amenities of twentieth-century life that in 1923, when an automobile crashed into a tree in the Middle Village, the spectacle attracted crowds of onlookers. Photographs of the event still circulate today. Only following World War Two did most people in Lauzerte get indoor toilets. Lauzerte well and truly entered the twentieth century—the century of the automobile and the airplane— only as the twenty-first century was getting underway.

As ever, the Law of Unintended Consequences held sway. In this instance, it was the unforeseen need for parking spaces that, just since I started living there, changed Lauzerte as irrevocably as the "Hundred" Years' War did. Since I got my

House, the mountaintop—once the very reason for Lauzerte's existence—has ceased to be the municipal locus. The town's economic and administrative activities have migrated downhill, drawn ineluctably to the flat places where cars can park. The notions shop where I got my daily newspaper until I started getting my news digitally, and the little *épicerie* where I got my morning croissant have disappeared. The last of the mountaintop barbers had an exquisite set of scissors, clippers, and combs. Waiting for their haircuts, the old men talked about being shipped off to fight at Dien Bien Phu. "Forty-one days on that boat," one of them marveled, "Marseilles to Haiphong."

At the tree-shaded gravel area behind the *Monument aux Morts*, where men both old and young once played *pétanque*, the France Profound version of *bocce*, the clank of the metal balls is no longer heard. The place is now a parking area. The new *pétanque* pavilion, at the bottom of the mountain, has klieg lights so they can hold nightly tournaments when it's too hot to play in the daytime, plus its own parking spaces. At the Saturday market, I still can get a week's supply of most of the comestibles I need, from *maigret de canard* to *cabecu*, but it's not the availability of duck steak and goat cheese that lures people up to the Place des Cornières every weekend. The Saturday market has turned into an attraction. People congregate there to see and be seen, and catch up on the local gossip. They also come for the free internet access both cafés provide. The old peasant who once purveyed the best Swiss chard in the universe has retired; a newly arrived vendor sells sushi.

One morning up in the Loft, as I made coffee, I sensed something had changed; it wasn't until I awoke the next morning that I understood. The little yellow postal vans that had been annoying me for twenty-six years had disappeared. *La Poste*, too, had migrated down the hill, to a new location with a big parking area for the postal vans. For decades I had been complaining about those vans, though I couldn't call them that.

The French language has no exact word for "van," so they call them "baby trucks," *camionette* being to the French word for truck, *camion*, what bassinet is to basin. More recently the tax office—560 years after the Lord of Duras looted it— relocated to a lowland location. The Gendarmerie led the way decades earlier.

Farther down the mountain, in the Middle Village, the insurance office has closed. The pharmacy has relocated. The Casino grocery store, Lauzerte outpost of the national food chain, disappeared long ago, eventually to be replaced by a part-time civic museum. The butcher shop is also gone. Though only in his fifties, he had to quit, the butcher explained, because by working he imperiled his retirement benefits. The Crédit Agricole bank maintains its Lauzerte wealth extraction monopoly. How else would it pay the fines it incurs for supporting rogue regimes? "Credit Agricole Fined $800 Million for U.S. Sanctions Violations," the BBC reported back in 2015. Without so much as lifting their shoulders, they later sold off their Greek subsidiary, after losing billions, for one euro.

Curious about the bank's apparition in the crime columns, I asked a teller there why Crédit Agricole preferred international felons to honest clients like me. It was like the time in Metz when I asked the ticket agent for a ticket to Montauban. In reply, this haughty young woman, straight out of her bank teller training course, resorted to the standard all-purpose rejoinder of the French functionary: "*Ce n'est pas mon problème, monsieur.*" She already was deeply annoyed because—can you believe it?—I had walked into the bank and, just like that, asked for some of my own money. Well! In that case I would have to come back next Tuesday, and remember, *monsieur*, you only can withdraw as much as we allow.

For more than a year recently, customer service at Crédit Agricole branches throughout the region was curtailed even more drastically than usual while the offices were extensively refurbished. Thanks to these embellishments, the bank personnel now disdained their clients in even greater comfort, at a more effective remove. As before, clients were obliged to stand behind a line while they waited to be acknowledged, but now there was, in addition, a glass wall. "Be sure to tell them how they make you stay behind the glass wall, and what happens when you try to get their attention," a neighbor urged me, and then described what happened to him. A busy professional, the owner of substantial real estate, he had significant deposits there. After waiting for some time, he crossed the line; he opened the door in the glass wall. "The same young woman who had been refusing to acknowledge my existence for twenty minutes," he related, "wagged her finger at me. *'Pas permis,'*" she told him, not permitted, and continued ignoring him. He then added the kind of telling detail Peter of Vaux-de-Cernay would have taken care not to omit. "She was wearing ear buds," he told me. "She was listening to some podcast, and I had the temerity to distract her. She never removed the ear buds."

When I asked this friend if I could use his name, Dr. Amr Sultan replied, "Please!" He added: "I just don't understand why they treat us this way." "It is most understandable," I replied, "So far as they are concerned, it is their money, not yours. How would you react if people kept walking into your office and asking for your money?" More recently, I was informed that if I wanted access to any of my funds, I would have to provide, after thirty-three years a customer, new proof that I was who I claimed to be. A mere passport no longer sufficed, I was furthermore informed.

The view from my House onto the town Square never ceases to epitomize Lauzerte's evolving imagination of itself as a charming vestige of a charming past, never mind it never truly existed, and wasn't exactly charming. My hillside garden provides a more accurate *aperçu* on what really has been happening to Lauzerte, and the rest of the world, since I got there. The path leading to my garden is now known as the Chemin des Horts, *horts* being an old-fashioned term cognate to horticulture. Giving it that fancy name was one more example of Lauzerte trying to prove it was up-to-date by appearing medieval. On the way to my garden, I used to pass an enclosure where a neighbor kept his pack of spotted Dalmatians. Whenever the dogs sensed me coming, they'd set off a symphony of yelps. A canine version of Terry Riley's serialist composition, *In C*, their yelping would reach a crescendo when I came into view, then continue, in a yelp-diminuendo, after I passed.

Then came the day when I heard no yelping. While time, or so it seemed, stood still for me, those dogs' lives had been unfolding like a speeded-up video, in dog years. Midway upon my journey along that same path, I more recently observed a boy no older than sixteen bounding up the mountain. As magnificent as any pedigreed Dalmatian, he took the mountain in effortless, self-absorbed strides. Could this perfect specimen, I wondered, possibly be like the Dalmatians—fated to grow old, to be silenced, to die?

Changing the village décor did not impede ongoing changes in the structure of events. During my time there, Lauzerte, like every spot on this planet, has been reshaped by three inter-related world forces. These are Americanization, globalization, and recolonialization. From my garden, I now am able to observe phenomena long familiar in places like Dallas and New Jersey. Spreading like Lascaux mold, local versions of the "ranch" houses that earlier defaced America now splotch the countryside. Lauzerte also has acquired its own patch of exurban sprawl.

All-powerful Paris, as usual, is to blame. Paris purported its policy was to preserve the past by prettifying places like Lauzerte, but emplacing those traffic circles produced an entirely contrary result. In just a few years the Bottom Village, with one of those traffic circles as its nexus, has supplanted both the Medieval City and the Middle Village to become the town's primary commercial center. As if to prove it, Lauzerte's Bottom Village welcomes you with a flashing, billboard-sized LED digital display sign. It announces the time and predicts the weather, while simultaneously updating motorists on pending dog shows and soccer matches.

Epicenter of the Traffic Circle conurbation is Lauzerte's ever-more snazzy supermarket. Thanks to Intermarché, as it styles itself, you don't have to drive to Cahors or Montauban anymore to stock up on light bulbs and toilet paper, but just like in America you have to get in your car to do it. It would be nice if a little shuttle bus connected the top of the mountain with the Middle and Bottom villages, but none exists. Lauzerte, in truly twenty-first-century fashion, has an American-style lack of public transportation. Were there a way to get to the airport without driving, and then having to pay to park your car, that would be even nicer, but no such link exists. This leads to another helpful hint. Make a point of staying on friendly terms with the village bores. They, experience has taught me, are more likely than the stimulating conversationalists to come get you at the airport.

Intermarché's commitment to post-literate communication heralds the future. Someday, its signage promises, even in Lauzerte people will be liberated from having to read! Its post-literate emojis announce, inter alia, the availability of two amenities not traditionally provided by French grocery stores: toilets and loyalty cards. One time, atop one of the supermarket's color-coordinated trash bins, I found a novel by Émile Zola. Appropriately enough, its title was *L'argent*—Money. Someone had wanted to throw it away, but had second thoughts. Or was it a guilty conscience? As if to emphasize the transitional character of our times, this work of literature was balanced on the cusp, but had not yet been pushed into the dustbin of history. I took it home, of course.

Intermarché's very name connotes digital splendor as it subliminally links its sports equipment section, children's apparel aisle, and plastic lawn furniture display to the life-style marvels proffered by the internet. Other amenities include a seafood selection that would be the envy of both the poached salmon and gefilte fish districts of Manhattan. To paraphrase a Chinese sage—Deng Xiaoping, not Confucius—this is Americanization with French characteristics, and it's terrific! The fishmonger in the supermarket wears a natty sailor's outfit. "I used to be in the merchant marine," he explained. "I love the sea and all its produce." It also boasts a cheese section where you could watch for movie stars, were it located in Beverly Hills rather than Lauzerte. In addition to the everyday cuts of meat, its butchers offer guinea fowl, squab, and rabbit, and at least fifty varieties of *charcuterie*.

The continuity here is that whether they are selecting *gigot*—leg of lamb—at the supermarket or choosing between white and yellow nectarines at the Saturday market, people in Lauzerte continue to care deeply about what they put in their mouths. If Freud's personality types could be applied to nations, France would be oral. The French language is another important example of the fixation on what use, precisely, people put to their lips, their tongues, and their oral cavities.

In addition to the relocated pharmacy, the Bottom Village's amenities include a garden center, an auto repair shop, a restaurant, a new notions shop. Right there, you additionally can get propane for your kitchen stove. You can have your keys copied. There's an optician. Before the last of the old pastry shops up on the mountain closed, Lauzerte was renowned for its macaroons. Now, once again, it is. A local lad has proven himself to be a *pâtissier* of genius, an advent stirring as much civic pride as if he'd turned into a soccer star. He has located his pastry shop in the Bottom Village, not the Middle Village or the Medieval City as his father or grandfather would have. Also located there is the one commerce absolutely essential to everyday life, but long missing from Lauzerte. Thanks to the credit card devices installed on the pumps, it finally became possible right here in Lauzerte to get gas 24/7, a generation after it did in America.

The advent of the traffic circle reflected and accelerated the structural changes overtaking everyday life in Lauzerte. It also helped explain why I no longer see eccentric and confused old people wandering around the Place des Cornières. One old creature always wore a shapeless house dress and too much lipstick. Her hair made her look like she'd just had tea with Medusa. She would cadge cigarettes. She loved cigarettes! Another of these odd old folks was named Émilion. Émilion was a little slow, and slightly crazy. He would beg you for a beer. Then, when you bought him a beer, he would kiss your hand. Only while he imagined he was kissing your hand, he actually was slobbering all over it.

I wasn't expecting guests, but one night I heard my door bell ringing, insistently. A boy of seven or eight stood there. He said he was scared. He pointed to the interval of darkness separating the Place des Cornières from the street lights down by the *Monument aux Morts*. He grasped my hand tightly as I walked him through darkness to the light. As soon as we got there, he let my hand drop. He scampered away, but not before I'd asked what scared him. "Émilion might get me," he said. Had his parents told the boy that Émilion was the bogeyman, so he better behave! Or had his playmates, in some Lauzerte version of *Lord of the Flies*, singled out Émilion as the focus of their prepubescent viciousness? Today that boy would be in his thirties. No Émilions remain in Lauzerte to scare his children, if he has any. All the old folks, as they say in Latin America, have been disappeared.

The age of invisible old folks reached Lauzerte when giant building cranes were maneuvered into place on the other side of the mountain, beyond the second of those intrusive traffic circles. After the natural foliage was scraped away, engineers laid down a foundation bigger than the mountaintop expanse upon which the original Lauzerte was built. This new self-contained complex was the biggest construction project in the town's history—bigger than the Lauzerte fortress was before it was demolished, as ordered by Paris, some four hundred years ago.

Lauzerte already had a fine mountaintop retirement home, located near my House. The *maison de retrait* where Émilion and dozens of other old people lived respected its surroundings. It had a lovely garden, and a chapel. Its modern facilities occupied some of Lauzerte's finest old Quercy stone buildings. An edifying example of how old architecture could be repurposed to serve new needs, it provided the old people who lived there with life-affirming views from its glassed-in terraces. Since they could see us, we could see them. In a France where, as in America, old people more and more must be kept out of sight, the situation had to be remedied.

The great heat wave of 2003 revealed how immensely the structure of French family life had changed. For weeks, not one day passed when it did not go above 30 degrees centigrade. Then came the nights when it never went below thirty. Government statistics later verified that in the course of the *canicule* some twenty-thousand old people died prematurely, abandoned by their families. It was summer, time for the *grande vacance*. This annual nationwide assertion of the right to indolence increasingly posed a problem. Whatever to do with *mami* and *papi* while on vacation?

Now that they were gaga and incontinent, they hardly could be allowed to travel with the rest of the family in their overcrowded camping car to that overcrowded camp ground where every August the young ones paddled around in that bacteria-infested wading pool while the teenagers sneaked into the adjacent pine barrens to lose their virginity. As in America, caring for the elderly no longer was a labor of love, let alone a sacred duty. It had become an embarrassment. True, these old folks once changed our diapers and now that their diapers needed changing? The fundamental sociological changes the great heat wave of 2003 revealed took the form of those twenty-thousand corpses their families found upon the September *rentrée*. People already had started leaving their pets in kennels. Now their parents and grandparents, more and more, were being stashed in *maisons de retraite*, and not just during the holidays.

While the heat wave was killing all those old people, it was accelerating the growth of France's retirement home industry. As in other service-sector industries, standardization was the key to growth, consolidation the ticket to profitability. Today, that nice retirement home where Émilion and the others lived, nestled into the community, is a ruin, the artifact of a bygone era. The last time I passed the place I looked in the windows. The kitchen, the bedrooms, the chapel were dirty, untended, filled with broken furniture and discarded utensils. Down at the bottom of the mountain, the new containment camp for the elderly, like the globalization of the produce in the supermarket and the arrival of our African curé, demonstrated how the unfolding of History transforms even the obscurest spots, along with every aspect of human life.

Lauzerte already had the internet and its new shopping hub. Wednesday, 6 January 2016 marked the date when Lauzerte totally and entirely entered the twenty-first century, because that was the day Lauzerte's old people finally were subsumed into the structures, psychological as well as material, of the new epoch. As always, civility prevailed. Volunteers among the local population made sure all the old people were politely evicted from their former *maison de retrait* and escorted to the new one.

Lauzerte's new old folks' exclave was the latest example of how Lauzerte, like all successful polities, survived by reinventing itself. With the advent of gunpowder, Lauzerte ceased being useful as a fortress. Following the Revolution, it ceased to be a significant administrative center. In the age of the Eiffel Tower, it was too remote for factories, just as later it was too small for a hospital, which was just as well since hospitals lost money. Elder care, in contrast, was profitable, and in this instance Lauzerte's remoteness was an asset, since the function of retirement homes—admitted or not—was to keep the inexorability of the aging process out of sight.

Already classified as one of The Most Beautiful Villages in France, and inscribed as an official stop on the Pilgrimage Route to Santiago Compostela, now also glamorized by drone for the viewers of the Tour de France, Lauzerte had become a trailblazer in twenty-first-century old folks' storage. This helped explain why Lauzerte, while losing barbers and butchers, was gaining medical professionals. Lauzerte had five doctors now, also a podiatrist, and their number was growing. One doctor already lived right next door to me. Another doctor recently bought a house on the Place des Cornières. With the waiting room and consultation clinic on the ground floor, and living quarters on the upper stories, Lauzerte's fine old Quercy edifices have turned out to be ready-made for practitioners of the medical arts.

One dappled afternoon, perched on the Staircase above the √-cleft, I made a sketch map of how the structures of everyday life had changed in Lauzerte just since I got there. The ziggurat still stood at the center, its apex the Place des Cornières, but flanking it now were two separate, distinct additions to the agglomeration. On one side, amoeba-like, that traffic circle its nucleus, throbbed the Bottom Village. On the opposite side of the mountain now stood Lauzerte's proto-necropolis, the place where the soon-to-be-dead people were stashed. My sketch map revealed the logic of this schema. All that was new and lively had been positioned to one side of the mountain. There was no way the old folks, confined to their opposite side of the mountain, could get anywhere near the cheese section, the new pastry shop, the garden center, but the old folks' exclave, my sketch map revealed, was conveniently located right nearby Lauzerte's walled cemetery.

Though no shops or services are to be found there, the second traffic circle does boast a sculpture made from one of our epoch's defining products—cast-off junk. Celebrating Lauzerte's recently reinvented past, this thirteen-foot-tall, metal assemblage is entitled "The Pilgrim." Though the sculpture has what are meant to look like legs and arms, and carries a pilgrim's stave, it—most appropriately—has no head, therefore no brain, hence no possibility of historical memory. The town has been quick to incorporate this totem of a nonexistent past into its celebrations of the present. When Lauzerte wins a championship, "The Pilgrim" is dressed in the team's colors—red leggings, blue jersey, but of course no helmet or cap since there is no head.

New manifestations of Lauzerte's nonexistent past are constantly appearing underfoot. Only the other day I happened to look down, and for the first time noticed that the Place des Cornières and its approaches have been newly adorned by miniature versions of Point Zero in Paris. Round and shiny, these bronze medallions commemorate the town's place on the Santiago pilgrimage route. They look like they have been there for hundreds of years.

Unconsciously, organically, Lauzerte has been reconstituted to please the eye and suit the convenience of a newly arrived demographic cohort of historical protagonists. These were the *neo-ruraux*. Parisians and other foreigners, these New Rustics' lifestyle of choice was the State of Nature, plus All Mod Cons, and this New Lauzerte, communal cognate to the New Lascaux, certainly fit the bill. It looked so medieval, yet there was this terrific supermarket right down the hill! Never forget, it is a major stop on the Pilgrimage Route to Compostela, but if you prefer speedier travel, the TGV from Montauban gets you to Paris in three-and-a-half hours, and Toulouse airport is less than an hour away. Catch a morning flight and you can be back in New York that same afternoon.

No term is more essential to the *neo-ruraux* conception of what life should be than "authentic," yet when they looked around them, authentic *Lauzertins* were like the "heretics" of three-quarters of a millennium ago. Their ancestors, viewing the greed and viciousness of the Avignon papacy, were shocked, and frightened. This was not the Christianity into which they were born. "We old folks are shocked at the changes of life in the village," Armand Lafargue told Patrice Brassier in 2012. In an earlier epoch this man would have been respected as a village elder; now he was just one of the elderly.

The newly installed medieval décor did not evoke any past that *Lauzertins* like him could recognize. *Au contraire*, it symbolized the denaturing of life, the destruction of the past. "There are fewer gatherings," Armand Lafargue continued. "Before there were soirees, lottos, beauty contests." He especially missed the *brassages intensifs*, the intensive social intermingling of earlier times. "People sat in front of their open doors in order to take the air. Others strolled from one neighbor's to the other, or in reverse depending on the hour and the day."

They had pensions now. They had modern medical care, but within the hearts of these authentic *Lauzertins* gnawed the understanding that in Lauzerte, as in so much of the rest of the world, the old were considered eyesores. "There are no more old people," Jean-Louis Chanuc, a retired tinsmith told Brassier. Asked who was to blame, Lafargue replied: "Those most responsible for this are the TV and the car."

One balmy autumn evening, this time out on the Top of the House, with the rhythms of Schubert's op. 100 converging where I sat, I made another of my lists, this time of some of the "world-historical" events I needed no television set to see, because I could see them unfolding from and often within my own House. They included the conflict between Christianity and Islam and the moral and sexual crisis within the Catholic Church, along with the English insularity that produced the Brexit crisis, and the perpetual struggle between Paris and France, including the *gilet jaune* and pension protests, as well as the worldwide cultural impact of Americanization. Here in France Profound, as in so many other places, people to one extent or another wanted to live as they imagined Americans did, even as globalization and the worldwide migration of peoples were transforming the structure of life in America itself in ways that frightened and angered many Americans.

Next, I found myself listing some other, more basic forces that constantly displayed themselves whether I was peering out my windows, or delving into what happened hundreds of years ago. These included the persistence in human affairs of the Seven Deadly Sins, especially pride, greed, avarice, and lust. Whatever the epoch, also on display was the deep egotistical yearning inside all humans for both earthly gratification and eternal paradise, combined with the faith, contrary to all evidence, that such things are anything other than meaningless concepts unrelated to any reality, individual or universal. Finally, to my list, I added that damnable ineradicable human urge to find explanations for things, explanations for everything! Would this obsessive human need to understand, linking everything from Lascaux to CERN, ever leave us humans in peace?

What made this deep urge so human is that the answers people crave do not need to be right. The power of the Pied Pipers back then, like the power of fake news purveyors in the COVID Age, rested not on the lies they told, but on the need of their followers to believe. While we never do find the One True Cross or the one irreducible subatomic particle, the perpetual quest for absolute knowledge leads to us humans acquiring lots of stuff: axes, inquisitions, telescopes, alloys, doctrines, sextants, algorithms, apps. These we use to order pizza and find exoplanets, arrange sexual trysts with strangers or, contrarily, kill them by remote control. As both ancient history and the latest news flashes show us, all humanity's achievements—shameful or sublime—derive one way or another from our failure to find absolute truth. Today, as in Simon de Montfort's time, the quest for truth does not produce truth, as intended. It produces power. How we use it depends on us.

Whatever the epoch or ego, whether the scale was cosmic or microcosmic, my Balzac-style wanderings inevitably led me, over and over again, to the discovery that the Law of Unintended Consequences reigns supreme, never loosening its grip. That cosmic protagonist Napoléon Bonaparte did not intend to die on an island in the South Atlantic Ocean, yet that was the unintended consequence toward which his actions, from Egypt to Muscovy, propelled him. Enacting my own microscopic destiny, I intended my House to be the place where I would find freedom—escape!—from all my decades of observing, then chronicling world events, and then trying to make sense of them. I never intended to spend years observing, then chronicling, and then trying to make sense of the interconnections of the cosmic and microscopic the Lauzerte prism captured, but the unintended consequence was that the House made me do it.

Another time, in the Thinking Nook, I recalled something I. B. Singer had told me years earlier. I was just back from Ethiopia. "Ah," he said, "you came back alive." One of the reasons Mr. Singer was a great writer was that, like that pope-inquisitor, Jacques Fournier-Benedict XII, "He knew how to bring forth the lambs." Whenever I was with Mr. Singer, I found myself telling him things I otherwise would not have dared say aloud, even to myself. I gave him the article I had written about the people in Ethiopia starving to death. How could any writer be equal to such an event? "I only got fifteen percent of it," I confessed. "Ah," the Nobel Prize winner replied, "I have never been able to get more than three percent of it."

What remains to be said is that all the depravities of history and all the defects of human nature cannot negate a parallel reality: without empathy we understand nothing, and without contextualization we are lost. As the Shepherd knew, life is worth living, no matter when, no matter what happens. Life is the great prize we each of us possesses. More than that, life is the only gift. The seeming eternal is but an icicle on a sunny day, the sun beckoning us to put aside our petty concerns with the epistemologically nonexistent and, for this moment, come bask in its warmth as salamanders do.

ENVOI
UNTO US THE DEAD IMPART THE SWEETNESS OF LIFE

The last time I saw their little girl she was eleven. She was coming out of the house with her mother, Françoise, who is a doctor. Though Françoise has the bone structure of a Paris mannequin, she started out as a farm girl. At that time her mother still tended the family farm just outside Lauzerte. Her local accent helped her patients confide in her. If people hereabouts got AIDS, or bled too much, or their husbands made strange demands, or when it was just a wrenched ankle that wouldn't come right, they came to Françoise.

Françoise's spouse, Frédéric, a nurse, was Lauzerte's secular incarnation of the popular idea of Saint Francis of Assisi. Only instead of the beasts and birds of the field, his flock consisted of the old complaining sick people, the suffering and ungrateful children of the countryside, the confused and frightened of all ages. On his visits, he made sure they took their medicine. He took them to the toilet. He washed and comforted them. He took only an hour for lunch, startling to people in France Profound. While Frédéric every day traversed the countryside—hundreds of miles per week, thousands per month—Françoise tended to her patients on the ground floor of their house. The entrance is right next to mine, so I often would see the patients coming and going. I'd see the stout peasant grandmas, and the drop-out girls who had made foolish choices, or no choice. I'd see distraught parents. Mostly they were mothers, but the fathers also grasped their sick child's wrist tightly, holding on to them tight, lest disease snatch them away.

Over the many years that I have been their neighbor, Frédéric and Françoise have endured many misfortunes. One time, Frédéric was grievously injured when, speeding, he tried to pass another car and misjudged the distance. There was a murder in their extended family. It was a homicide almost American in its gratuitousness: a bungled robbery, a shot in the dark. Françoise and Frédéric sheltered the wife and children of their dead relation in their house on the Place des Cornières until they found a way to live again on their own.

It never will be a cliché to say that nothing hurts more than the death of a child. Françoise and Frédéric dedicated their lives to healing the sick, and now that little girl I saw coming out the door was dying and they could do nothing. That last time I saw them together, Françoise was not holding her daughter's wrist tight, like the parents who knew that in spite of their fears, their child was going to get better. Françoise held her daughter's hand without insistence. I was giving another of my parties. This time I had commandeered a swimming pool. Surely, I suggested, the little girl would enjoy the swim, and the chance to meet some other children.

Françoise smiled at me. No, unfortunately, that would not be possible. In French, the word most often used for "unfortunately" is *malheureusement:* unhappily. This time the meaning was exact. Today I marvel at her composure, but until I came to appreciate the enormity of her goodness it had seemed to me Françoise's smile was artificial. It was not artificial. It was practiced. How could your smile not be, when every day it greeted dozens of suffering people? The next I heard the girl was dead. She was just past the age of the little girl with the watering can in the Renoir painting. I still see her, outside their front door, taking her mother's hand. She stood there just for a moment, under the vaulted arch, as her mother responded to the American's question.

On my bedroom floor, one flight down from the Loft, I often sleep with the shutters shut. Each of the great windows there has its set of shutters; each panel is the size of a New York dining room table. They swivel open on cast iron pivots and clamp shut with handcrafted cast iron levers. Iron latches keep them from slamming against the house when high winds blow. The shutters help keep in the heat in winter. They help keep out the heat in summer, but the most important insulation they provide is psychological. When I just have to have some distance from Lauzerte, I close all the shutters. It's not nearly as effective as an escape to Barcelona, but it helps.

The shutters muffle the sounds rising from the Square. They do not silence it, so on Saturdays the sounds of the peasants and merchants arriving for the weekly market in the Place des Cornières are the first sounds I hear. It used to be that old Mr. Legume, the vegetable vendor, always arrived first, just after five A.M. One time my friend and namesake Tim Curtis, who was doing anthropological research at Aix-en-Provence, arrived for a visit with his latest girlfriend. She was an exotic Mediterranean beauty from Marseilles named Amélie. After kissing me on both cheeks, Amélie announced she was half-Jewish and half-Muslim, that she was a former lesbian, but now, she added, with a beatific smile in Tim's direction, she was bisexual. She announced she was going to make ratatouille. She would use my kitchen.

The preparation of Amélie's Ratatouille was an epic. She might have been Mme Curie discovering radium as she announced each new discovery in her unforgettably enticing high-pitched voice, a mixture of Beijing opera and Piaf. Mr. Legume, thrilled, would get a kiss on the cheek each time she discovered the perfect artichoke, or the most precious little pepper. The announcement of her greatest discoveries was reserved for Tim. She pronounced his name as though it were a French name. "*Teem!*" she would cry out in ecstasy, brandishing aloft the paradigmatical stalk of celery, the veritable Platonic ideal of it, as though it were a scepter: "*Regarde!*"

We formed a basket brigade to transport the purple eggplant and the ivory-colored eggplant, variously oblong and oval, along with the many different tribes of onion and factions of zucchini and clans of tomatoes, and the necklaces of fresh garlic, and the giant fennels, and the armsful of pungent fresh herbs across the Square, into my House, up the staircase and into the kitchen. By the time Amélie started preparing her ratatouille, a Noah's Ark of produce overflowed my six-foot-long Quercy farmhouse kitchen table. On both the wood-burning and the propane stoves, waiting like bridegrooms, stood the cook pots and the stew pots—enameled and cast iron, tall and wide, lidded and unlidded. Beside them, like groomsmen in attendance, were the sauté pans and the casseroles. Attending back farther were the glass storage jars and clay confit pots.

Were I a troubadour, I would have composed a vegan Song of Roland to describe first the preparation, and then the many evolving pungencies of Amélie's Ratatouille. Then, expanding my epic, I would sing also of the many lives the merest taste of her preternatural elixir transformed, but not now, not here. This is the moment, instead, to concentrate on the remarkably vivid silhouette of Mr. Legume. Amélie never came back to Lauzerte, but Mr. Legume never stopped hoping that someday a dark-tressed beauty once again would bathe him in kisses as she extolled the magnificence of his produce. For years afterwards, when I came down to the Square every Saturday, he would shout: "*Ah, la ratatouille! La ratatouille!*" In terms of personal appearance, he was pockmarked and partially toothless, but what a becoming fellow he was, nonetheless! Mr. Legume radiated the rustic joy of being.

One time a famous European magazine, *GEO*, sent a photographer to Lauzerte. Everyone was excited. Then everyone forgot as more than a year passed and nothing happened. Finally, the story ran. The photo in the magazine, which showed the Place des Cornières on market day, used darkness to define the bright side of Lauzerte's spirit. The rich colors of the pears and plums, or the sheen on the vegetables, or the brilliance of the sunflowers were not what made this photo so remarkable. It was the blacked-out section of the photo that revealed so much. The photographer had positioned herself so as to photograph one of the market vendors in eclipse. The dark silhouette of this human being against the sun was all you could see, yet you could tell right away, it was Mr. Legume! The joy, the energy, his vibrancy grabbed you, and kissed you on both cheeks. He disappeared from the Square years ago, but I still see him. I still hear him: *"Ah, la ratatouille! La ratatouille!"* "Papi suffered terribly at the end," his daughter-in-law told me when I ran into her one market day in Lauzerte's nearby, rival village, Montcuq. She added: "He was joyous up to the end."

On Saturday market mornings I can see from my bedroom window if the poultry lady has a guinea fowl for me. I can tell whether Mr. or Mrs. Fishmonger will sell me my oysters this week. I say Mr. or Mrs. because these days such couples no longer go to market together. In this age of car loans and flat screen TVs, they double their income by the husband tending one market, the wife another. When I first got My House, it wasn't like that. Fred the Foie Guy and his wife Marie-Hélène were there together. Now they work separate markets. It's the same with Mr. and Mrs. Fishmonger. Whichever one of them is working Lauzerte this week, their sole and salmon and mussels are always briny fresh, plus, thanks to them, Lauzerte boasts the handsomest fishmonger couple in the whole of France Profound! When I first bought oysters from them, they were barely out of their teens. They were gorgeous as any film-screen Romeo and Juliet, but sturdier and smarter—not the kind of folks to let some dumb nurse or father confessor make them take a sleeping draught. How could they, when they must rise before dawn to carry their oysters, their mussels, their boulots, all the way over to Lauzerte from Arcachon, beyond Bordeaux on the Atlantic coast?

When I first met them, he was cuter that Alain Delon in his prime. Today, his magnificent mane of white-streaked black hair would have made Cesar Romero envious. He also has brilliant movie star–type teeth, so when he laughs his one gold tooth sparkles. If you imagine that the young Leslie Caron had been a fishwife, and then grew up to become Mme de Pompadour, you have an idea of how his wife looked then, and how she looks today. Like her husband, she does not hide her age. She, too, now has white streaks in her pompadour. She has grown into such a great beauty for the same reason he keeps getting handsomer and handsomer. Each, instead of denying it, has embraced the beauty that comes with age.

Looking down from my windows I also see the damage denial does, notably to women's hair, because from this height and angle I can see the tops of their heads. Women, I have observed, do not go bald the way men do. Instead of an expanding bald spot, there is a steady thinning all over the tops of these ladies' heads, as that shocking red hair dye so beloved of women in rural France first brutalizes their hair and then, the more they use the dye, and the more insistently they tease their hair, makes them go bald. In conjunction with the white face powder that, attempting to conceal them, emphasizes their wrinkles, that red Medusa-stiff fringe of fake-red hair surrounding their faces forms a mask, as defining as the mask in a Greek play. It defines that period in a woman's lifecycle that unfolds after her youth has been lost irretrievably to work and childbirth, but before she must cover her encroaching baldness with a cap or a wig. It is that time after the children leave, but before widowhood.

In addition to living people, I also hear the voices of dead while I am inside My House. If I ever tried to enumerate the dead, first on the list would be my friend Jean-Paul. "Just like the Pope," he told me. He came to my rescue one of those days when I had to get somewhere and the little Volvo Tim Curtis had sold me for seventy-five dollars in Brussels refused to start. Jean-Paul raised the hood, inspected the engine, then asked me to go get a spoon. I came back with one of those big old farmhouse soup spoons they used to sell, tied up with a piece of old string, for one franc a dozen at junk sales. Jean-Paul used the spoon to create an arc between the spark plug and the starter, and *voila*! The little Volvo coughed itself into life.

One time Jean-Paul asked if I had any American money. At school the teacher had assigned his son's class a show-and-tell on America. The boy had the idea of showing his classmates some American money. I went into the house, and came out with a dollar bill. As Jean-Paul held this mythic object up to the light, examining both sides of it, as if some rarified fetish of exotic origin and great cultural and anthropological significance were being displayed, passersby pressed around him, eager to catch a glimpse of the fabled currency. One and all were stunned by the immensity of my generosity when I announced that the kid could keep it. It came as an anticlimax when I explained that one dollar was worth less than a euro, though all of them were too polite to show their amazement that something so famous and so American could be of such little value.

"He hanged himself," Sylvain the ironmonger told me one time when I mentioned I hadn't seen Jean-Paul in a while.

"He had a lot of debts." What sum of money could have caused a fellow like Jean-Paul to take his life? Sylvain named a sum that amounted to about eight thousand dollars. The Lauzerte garbage man also committed suicide. He looked like a garbage man. Grubby, hairy, and pot-bellied, a well-chewed cigar clenched between his tobacco-stained teeth, he wore a none-too-spotless singlet rather than a proper shirt as he went about his duties. Thanks to him, Lauzerte was always so clean! However big the communal dinner held in the Square, no matter how many ceramicists or florists or dog lovers showed up for the annual pottery, flower, or dog show, by the following morning the Square once again would be spic-and-span, not a cigarette butt or crumpled paper plate in sight.

His work should have filled him with pride. All Lauzerte's pretensions—including its proudest, its claim to being one of the Most Beautiful Villages in France—depended on how it was always so *propre*, both in the French sense of spotless, and in the English-language sense, proper. Did no one ever think to thank him? While he was alive it never occurred to me to thank him for carting away all the plastic bags of waste I generate. Now, whenever I see his successor sanitation worker, Yves, I make a point of thanking him for keeping everything so tidy. I started doing that in Lauzerte, and now I thank garbage men in New York, too, and wherever else the opportunity presents itself. I thought of Mr. Poubeaux years later, when the president of Brazil pinned medals on the trash pickers of São Paulo, proclaiming them heroes of the environment. Mr. Poubeaux deserved to get a medal in Lauzerte. Who knows what his fate might have been had he been so honored?

Sometimes I would discuss psychology with a nice German named Frederick: "Just like the king," he told me. At the Saturday market Frederick sold wicker baskets that, when queried, he conceded he himself had not actually woven. He had been a psychotherapist back in Germany. Our acquaintance began when I bought a particularly handsome basket from him. The news of this event, like all human transactions in Lauzerte, became the subject of widespread commentary. Françoise the cheese monger right away saw what had happened, and spread the word: "The American has purchased a new basket."

I still use the basket, though Frederick the German psychologist is long gone. Like the luckiest and most intelligent of the *neo-ruraux*, he figured out in time that there are better things to do with life than being a pretend basket artisan. I hope he went back to psychotherapy because Frederick was insightful and compassionate. During one of our conversations, he told me something I've never forgotten. "Suppressing catharsis is a killer," he explained didactically though gently, in his combination kindly Germanic uncle-Herr Professor style. "Human beings need to resolve conflicts, not deny they exist."

In France Profound in general and Lauzerte in particular life is all about denial—most of all the denial that anything unpleasant might ever unfold in this supposedly delightful place where the winters are as drab as people's lives and, going back to the Wars of Religion and beyond, conflict has been the norm. Scarcely anyone I know and like in Lauzerte has not been engaged, at some point, in some ferocious groundless conflict with someone else I know and like over some petty issue or another. Why only this week, via email, came the news that Mme de Renzy's book club was riven into irreconcilable factions, each accusing the other of perfidy and ill will as well as cultural illiteracy and bad taste.

The American I admired most in France Profound was Ambassador Arthur Hartman. As US ambassador in Moscow, he played a key role in keeping the dissolution of the Soviet Union detached from Cold War politics. Later he'd been enormously respected as the US ambassador to France. Then, one time, I got back to Lauzerte, and found Hartman was at war with the cultured German fellow he had helped start an

annual program of classical music concerts. How had the dip-
lomat and the musicologist come to be at daggers drawn? I
never knew because, by then, I had trained myself not to care.
Oh, at first, I tried to be like Solomon. I listened carefully to
contending plaints, striving honestly to make an honest judgment. Nowadays I just say: "Please stop. These endless Lauzerte controversies bore me. Anyway you're both wrong."

Though I met him only once, near the top of my listing
of the dead also would be that magnificent African bicyclist
who arrived unannounced on my staircase one afternoon. His
racing bike slung over his shoulder, he bounded up those stairs
as though that bicycle were a handkerchief. He was a relation
of Mrs. Bevington, my neighbor in New York as well as Lauzerte. An artist-architect of Belgian and Congolese origin, she
and her Scots husband, Alistair, owned a whole string of houses
running down the Rue de l'Ancienne Gendarmerie. They
bought them for a song back in the 1970s, before Lauzerte had
indoor plumbing. Like me, the Bevingtons had wound up in
Lauzerte by chance. She had relations in Lamagistère, the same
town where the Lauzerte-American maquis had targeted the
railroad bridge. They were on the way there when they saw
Lauzerte, perched up on its mountain.

Mrs. Bevington one time asked me if some of her relations
from Lamagistère might attend my then-annual, now-defunct
Open House. That's how the bicyclist wound up climbing my
staircase. The young man biked the entire distance, mostly uphill, just over twenty miles. Upon arrival he wasn't sure where to
stow his bike so, having pedaled straight up the mountain, he
carried his bike all the way up to the Loft, not pausing for breath.
"He drowned in the Atlantic Ocean," Mrs. Bevington later told
me, "off the African coast, on a trip to find his roots there. He
was a powerful swimmer yet the riptide took him."

A similar fate befell Marielle and Jacques Buchholtz, who
lived glamorously in their manor house in the hills overlook-

ing Lauzerte. Their estate was called Chartron. Among its wonders was an unusual half-timbered dovecote perched on classic pillars, a kind of Parthenon for pigeons and their feces. Instead of the conventional statuary array of nymphs, satyrs, goddesses, and nude lovers, their formal garden was populated with glass pylons. The pylons by day glinted in the sun. At night they showered you in moonlight.

Jacques and Marielle were the Christo of Lauzerte. Lauzerte had them to thank, doubly, for the curious upturned paving stone at the edge of the Square. Thanks were due, first of all, for the humanity of the sculpture itself. It immediately turned itself into a polyvalent socially interactive cultural platform upon which children played, behind which lovers kissed, and from which, as previously noted, Tosca took flight. Even greater thanks were due for another reason. Innovative, yet in harmony with its surroundings, this sculpture precluded the construction of some grotesque modernesque hideous monstrosity in the middle of the Place des Cornières, like the ugly numbers defacing so many other village squares.

One of the final Buchholtz projects was the transformation of the old Café Central into the postmodern Le Puits de Jour. A triumph of textural eclecticism, this new rendition of an old space made you appreciate anew the adaptability as well as the beauty of Lauzerte's traditional architecture. Until it was overlaid by the kitschy comfy tacky bric-a-brac that clutters all French cafés, this place was so stark yet so inviting that the Style Section of the *New York Times* would have cooed over it. Their son, Matthieu, ran the café. He was the one who told me about how all they ever found was one of his mother's shoes. Fresh from New York, I bounded into the café, and said to Matthieu, "How are your parents? I can't wait to see them!"

The last time Marielle put on those shoes, she and Jacques were headed back to Lauzerte from Bilbao, Spain. It was the moment when everyone everywhere just had to have been to

Bilbao. You scarcely dared show your face at a fundraiser in SoHo or an opening on the Ile Saint-Louis had you not inspected with your own eyes the titanium-clad edifice that Frank Gehry had designed to house the Guggenheim Museum's Basque Country franchise. Some friends offered Marielle and Jacques a lift to Bilbao in their private airplane. They got killed on the way back. A sudden storm brewing up out of the Atlantic grabbed them. The Atlantic Ocean most of the time seems such a domesticated body of water, as we fly back and forth across it, swim in it, or go sailing on it. Then it rears up, and takes Marielle and Jacques and their friends. It might have been a paper plane so far as the Atlantic Ocean was concerned, just as that bicyclist might have been nothing more than a rag doll when, from underneath, that same Atlantic Ocean grabbed that powerful young man.

Another of the dead I remember fondly ran a depot for dry cleaning. You would give her your dry cleaning. She in turn entrusted it to the dry-cleaning van that made the circuit from village to village the same way the Lauzerte priest made the circuit of the outlying churches that no longer have congregations big enough to support their own parish priest. The dry-cleaning depot lady's own clothes were always dirty. She was extraordinarily beautiful. She would have been a most beautiful girl, then gorgeous as a young woman. In maturity she had those striking good looks that characterize women who are yet more beautiful at fifty than they were at twenty-five.

Her husband never wore shoes. Let the winter drizzle chill the paving stones of Lauzerte and make them slippery. Let the summer sun turn them into burning coals. It was of no matter to him. He would stride along, his bare feet unwashed, his magnificent seedy consort beside him. Cleaned up and dressed up, she could have been a duchess and he, hence, a duke.

Like my neighbors' daughter, they died of cancer. So did Mme Dessart, who lived in the other house abutting mine, the

half-timbered one the tourists always photograph. Alain
Chauve, my veterinarian neighbor who loved being mayor of
Lauzerte even more than he loved delivering breech-birth
calves and treating indisposed poodles, which are hunting dogs
here, at the end was allowed to stop his cancer treatment. He
left the hospital and came home to die in Lauzerte, the place
he loved more than life itself. Look at a map of Lauzerte, and
you will see that the very layout of the town reflected our may-
or's passions. The Rue de la Mairie and the Rue de l'Ancienne
Gendarmerie—Ex-Police Station Street and City Hall Street—
encase the Place des Cornières in a kind of ellipse. The same
could be said of the former mayor's *vie sentimentale*. The house
of Alain's wife, a bookish attractive blonde, was located steps
away from the Place des Cornières on the Rue de la Mairie.
The house of his mistress Gloria, a kindly and spiritual-looking
woman whom Goya might have sketched, was also located steps
away from the Place des Cornières, on the Rue de l'Ancienne
Gendarmerie, also known as the Rue de Garrigues.

Hardly a person in Lauzerte, me included, had not benefited from some good deed of his. He had been defeated in
his last campaign for mayor, but everyone loved him and respected him, including the man who defeated him. Alain, lovely
man, spent his last public days in Les Puits de Jour, the café
Jacques Buchholtz designed for his son. There he received the
affectionate and respectful farewells of all who passed. In his
last days, as throughout his life, Alain Chauve was *brave*, and
now he was brave too, courageous and calm as the fine autumn
sunlight, glinting off the Quercy stone, blessed him, and us too.

The ugliness of the world rebukes the poets. It does not stop
them being poets. After their little girl died it was the same
with Françoise and Frédéric. Physician, heal thyself! No, this
had been so much crueler. Heal thy daughter! This horrible
rebuke did not stay them. To this day they continue healing

other peoples' children. On his fortieth birthday Françoise hosted a big birthday bash for Frédéric at her family's farm. Inside, Françoise's mother's barn was transformed into a yummy wonderland of all that is delicious to eat and delightful to drink in France Profound. A local restaurateur confected hundreds of exquisite petits fours for the occasion. Others brought foie gras, and extracted treasured wines from their cellars. I brought a Spanish ham all the way from La Boqueria, the great covered market just off the Ramblas, in Barcelona. While the women served up the cassoulet and the homemade rillettes, outside in the field the menfolk were slowly roasting, over open fires, the most succulent lamb I would ever taste. Then it rained! How it rained! That was the best part. Laughing and rushing, everyone crowded into the barn, while the slashing rain pounded on the high roof above us.

One day I saw Frédéric engaged in what in America might be called art therapy. On to the surface of three separate wooden boards he was applying different shades of paint, all of them blue. Sometimes I wonder at the poverty of language. How can we call so many different colors by the same name? I said that to Frédéric, and then pointing to the separate panels, added: "I love your triptych, how the rhythms of the different blues relate to each other." It wasn't a triptych so far as Frédéric was concerned. As he explained it, he was just testing different shades of blue for his shutters, which needed repainting. "Well, to my eyes it is a triptych," I said, "so give it to me." To this day Frédéric's Triptych hangs in my entry hall. Visitors assume it's some modern work I've carted over from America, like the nearby abstract expressionist work of art—the one that my frozen pipes, not Jackson Pollack, created.

One day Frédéric asked me what I knew about Colombia, the country in South America, not the university in New York. Quite a lot, it turned out, as I recently had done a series of articles on that country for *Rolling Stone* magazine. He and

Françoise, he informed me, were going to Colombia to adopt a child. I was ready to get busy. "I know someone in the President's office in Bogotá," I said. "He could put you in touch with . . ." "You don't need to be helpful all the time," Frédéric responded. They returned from South America with two extraordinarily well-formed little boys. They were brothers, shy and wide-eyed. The elder brother wore big round glasses that magnified the curiosity in his eyes. Handsome as child movie stars, they had very dark skin. Along with the problem of finding a family willing to keep the two brothers together, their African origins explained why until then it had been impossible to find homes for them. They might have been orphans forever, there in the great landlocked city of Santiago de Cali, jewel of the Valley of Cauca, until out of nowhere—out of France Profound, actually—Françoise and Frédéric appeared. They carried them home to their great stone house, adjacent to mine, on the Place des Cornières.

From the start Juan and Christian refused to converse in Spanish, as though persisting in the language of their past would be a transgression against their future. More polite than the other children, they always would say "*Bonjour, monsieur*," when they passed me in the Square. These days, having grown up to be handsome young Frenchmen, they gravely shake hands when we meet. Another time, toiling back up the mountain from my hillside garden, I saw the older boy strolling hand in hand with one of the village girls along the Chemin des Horts, a dreamy look on his face, a flattered smile on hers. They promenaded past me up the mountain, effortlessly as courting gazelles. This was the same spot where, earlier, I had noticed the Dalmatians were gone.

Juan had become a pastry chef. Christian trained to be an electrician, but after all the training and expense, Christian announced he did not want to be an electrician. He wanted to be a pharmacist. Lauzerte is becoming as bad as America, I told

myself. In France, qualifying to be a pharmacist, like everything else, is a long, complicated process, strewn with bureaucratic pit-falls. The boy will fail his tests, and then sit around
complaining just like American kids, I told myself. Françoise
suspended her practice, and moved with Christian to an apartment in Toulouse so she could coach him as he prepared for
his examinations. I never doubted the outcome. I had seen similar dramas unfold too often to doubt it. I certainly was not
going to raise the subject when I got back to Lauzerte.

Then one day, following my latest return from America,
Frédéric mentioned that Françoise's patient and loving coach-
ing had turned the trick. Christian had done very well on
the examinations. Once again, things had not turned out
for the worst! He was going to be pharmacist after all, but it
turned out I had it wrong, "A nurse," Frédéric told me, "not a
pharmacist. He's going be a nurse—" "Just like his *papa*," I
interjected. "Bravo!" They would be going away for a few
weeks, Frédéric added, to Colombia. "They boys agree they
should meet their mother. What happens after that is entirely
their decision. She is a nice woman, though life has not been
kind to her." Things not only had failed to turn out for the
worst. They had turned out wonderful!

I like to say nothing that happens here can surprise me, so just
a few weeks ago I was astonished to realize that, after Frédéric
and his family, I now have become the senior resident of the
Place des Cornières. When I checked the departmental cadasters in Montauban, I also found I have occupied my House
longer than almost anyone else in its recorded history. The past
never was static the way we imagine it to be, those old documents showed. They revealed something else. Affordable as it
seemed by New York standards, I had paid much more for my
House than anyone else in the entire history of Lauzerte had
paid for a house up to that time. So there I was, defined by the

cadasters they started keeping back in 1241—freest-spending of the free-spending *neo-ruraux*.

Down in the Studio I keep a photo of a dead man I never knew. It's one of those photographs country folk used to have made of themselves before there were Polaroids, let alone selfies. Judging from the man's attire, the photo dates back to the period between the World Wars. I bought that photo for the frame at a junk sale. I was going to throw the photo in the trash: I found I couldn't do that. This was all that was left of him. I could not do that to another human being, so now we share the House, he and I, along with all the others from all the others times who have lived here, and will live here with us centuries and centuries from now.

In the photo he tilts his eyes upward, at a jaunty angle. His eyes sparkle as he sees something ahead, but what? In this photograph of an anonymous, forgotten dead man I have come to perceive a portrait of hope and trust as unforgettable as Bacon's portraits of rage and megalomania are. You can tell from the jaunty fedora the fellow in the photo is wearing, and the stage-set suit, that these were photographer's props, yet he has the most wonderfully prophetic gaze. It seems to me, sometimes, that he is foreseeing wonderful, wonderful things.

ACKNOWLEDGMENTS

Countless people in France Profound merit my fulsome acknowledgment of all they did to inspire and then help realize this book, but first of all, in faraway New York, it is my joy as well as my duty to acknowledge the help of my editor, George Gibson. Editors are like translators in war zones. A good one can save your life. A bad one can get you killed.

When my neighbors in France Profound asked why everything was taking so long, I told them to blame my editor. "Most editors are mere nuisances. You just ignore them, but not this one! His every suggestion makes the book better." Also at Grove Atlantic, I wish to thank Emily Burns for the great care she took with the manuscript. None of this would have happened had Judy Hottensen, with Morgan Entrekin's support, not brought George and me together. I offer thanks as well to Deb Seager and her energetic team.

This book flows out of a relationship with France going back more than sixty years. So first of all I should acknowledge the contribution my father, Paul J. Allman, made when he took me on my first visit to the country in 1960. Back then the currency was marked NF—for New Francs. Signs everywhere urged *"Paix en Algerie."*

Across the many decades since then, none have immersed me more deeply in the life of France than the family of Chantal Marie Françoise Courant, including her children Christopher, Anthony, Nathalie, Timothy, and Ben, and her sister Marie-Pierre Bardin. Her son Timothy played an especial role in making this book possible by selling me, for $75, his little Volvo hatchback. Its odometer had more than three hundred thousand kilometers on it by the time it broke. It must have accrued another hundred thousand as I explored all the nooks and crannies of France Profound I could find, then drove this rusted indestructible little marvel of a mechanical wreck to the heart of Marrakesh, Morocco, via the Rock of Gibraltar. In the course of these explorations, Daniel and Martine Rocchi, at the Moulin de la Font, were especially helpful as I explored the rills where Eleanor of Aquitaine, her son Richard, and her daughter Joan once trod.

I became friends with Chantal and her husband, Australian ambassador Peter Curtis, in Laos, as I did with the French ambassadorial couple, Thea and Andre Ross, as well as with Princess Moune Souvanna Phouma and her husband, Perry Stieglitz. Starting in 1968, and lasting for decades to come, these friendships in due course migrated to France where they continued to enrich my understanding of the country. It was thanks to them, also during my visits with Vessa and Wilfred Burchett, that I developed the idea of one day having a house of my own in France. That dream—hence this book—became a possibility thanks to Tina Brown and my work as foreign correspondent for *Vanity Fair* magazine, the only time before or since when this freelance writer was paid a living wage. Also from that early war correspondent phase dates my friendship with Charlie de Nerciat, who at that time was a correspondent for Agence France-Presse, and his wife, Mary. They turned out to be, when transposed to France Profound, the Baron and Baroness Charles Antoine Andréa de Nerciat with one of the family châteaux located right near Lauzerte, and it was not just any château. The Château de Piquecos played a memorable role in the history of Lauzerte, and of France, as it also did in this book.

Lewis Lapham and Sir Harry Evans helped deepen my experience of the country by sending me on assignment in France, as did the editors of the *Washington Post*. The legendary foreign correspondent Jonathan Randal shared his long-term knowledge of the country, and on a 1970 visit he presented me to Walter Lippman, who as a young man had crossed paths with Woodrow Wilson and Ho Chi Minh at the 1919 Versailles peace conference. That same day, I ran into James Baldwin in Le Drugstore on the Rue de Saint Germain de Pres. The day after that I met Captain Kong Le, the exiled Lao neutralist. Like so many of the people acknowledged here, he was a source of practical wisdom as well as insight into the way history works, "Always buy yourself a book of Metro tickets," the patriot who had overthrown a CIA-backed regime in Vientiane told me. "It saves time and money, especially if you wind up staying longer than expected." The Laos loop reappeared decades later when the erstwhile CIA station chief in Vientiane, Larry Devlin, showed up in Lauzerte. He stole my copy of the *International Herald-Tribune*, but we had Jackie Kennedy in common,

Adumbrations of Lauzerte, it turned out, had entered my life even before I reached Indochina. It happened one night in Kathmandu, in 1967; I was a Peace Corps volunteer in Nepal. It was an amazing sight—this debonair gentleman ordering a bottle of champagne in the lobby of the Soaltee Hotel. Who could he be? He was Jean Français, the French ambassador to Nepal, and more than thirty years later, at a dinner given by my long-time neighbor Justin Downes, we met. He and his Magyar wife, Ildiko, world renowned for her patchwork, had wound up in Lauzerte too. I also wish to acknowledge the generosity of spirit shown by Donna and Arthur Hartman, another ambassadorial couple who wound up in the Lauzerte area.

Among the very first people I got to know in Lauzerte were Hugo Gordon and his mother, Janet Watson. Like many of the people acknowledged here, they remain friends to this day. Among my neighbors on the Place des Cornières, Tim Abadi and his family, and Pierre Dessarts and his, along with our indefatigable ironmonger, Sylvain Solignon, were loyal and helpful from the start. Marie-Christine and Alistair Bevington, fellow New Yorkers, were neighbors who became friends, as was Nean Stoddart, who spent nearly three years painting me. No one has ever had better neighbors than Libby Pratt and Craig Resnick. Their neighborly attributes, in addition to lively wit and culinary excellence, included their swimming pool, which they put at my disposal. Those natational privileges—essential to writing books during the France Profound summertime—have since been assumed by Yael and Justin Prough.

Among my neighbors on the Place des Cornières, Nicole Dardelou and René Beziat, and Françoise Ducasse and Frédéric Berthaux occupy very special places in the gallery of my esteem. Another deeply cherished neighbor is Gloria Curiel, supremely elegant and ever serene. To live in Lauzerte is to encounter the prominent and productive Rey family, and their good works. Christian and Bernard Rey both have served in our city government, Bernard as mayor. Another mayor whose aid I must acknowledge is Jean-Claude Giordana. As mayor he bore many burdens—none heavier than the giant suitcase I was struggling to get out of my car, having come directly to Lauzerte from New York. "Let me help you," the mayor offered, and so he did, lugging this monstrous carry-all to my House, then into the House, and up the stairs.

In addition to the unforgettable and beloved Alain Chauve, others connected with the mayor's office whose help I wish to acknowledge include Sandy Communal, Ombeline

Joliet, and their colleagues, who are always so helpful to me. Equally so have been Jean-Claude Martinez. Jacques Jofre, Annie Berthelo-Frouen, and the other members of Les Amis de Lauzerte. In addition to accumulating and preserving precious information concerning Lauzerte's past, they have created a charming museum devoted to life in Lauzerte. It includes authentic reproductions of those two traditional centers of life in Lauzerte: the family kitchen with its fireplace and plain Quercy farm table, and the schoolroom with its desks, including inkwells, and charts and maps. No one should leave Lauzerte without visiting it.

Les Amis de Lauzerte also have published *Les Petits Histoires de Lauzerte*, a fascinating and useful compendium of historical information. In them they preserve the memory of a score or more of the enterprises that once thrived on the mountaintop. Almost all of them have migrated or disappeared, but when I first arrived, George Mercadier's barbershop, obliquely facing the Square, was still in operation. Just around the corner, at their Tabac—notions shop—Ginette and Robert Pardo provided me with cigarettes, before I stopped smoking, and my daily newspaper, until the CIA stole it. The memory of Pierre Bonnet's superb macaroons still adds sweetness to life in Lauzerte.

The countryside surrounding Lauzerte is studded with châteaux, manor houses, farmhouses and, yes, hovels, where reside so many others who taught me so much about human nature, as well as the life and times, present and past, of France Profound. Doyenne of this esteemed horde of benefactors is Madam Nicole de Renzy Martin. By having twins, her daughter Sophie and her son-in-law David Long caused me to acquire a new nickname, perhaps to be revealed ulteriorly, in a successor tome. It was a privilege to know Christine and

Paul Grimaud. I remember fondly Patrick Bretons who, proudly practicing his English idioms, one time asked me: "Is everything under control?" I could not prevent myself from bursting out laughing. "Patrick," I emphatically reminded him, "things are never, ever under control! Not once in your life have they been or will they ever be under control." Life in Lauzerte would have been not nearly so sonorous without the lilt provided by our international songstress and all-around glamour queen, Isabelle de Valvert, and Georges Tapie, "the hardest working man in show business."

My fellow New Yorker Jedd Novatt introduced me to Pierre Passemard, the wily operative who got me to buy the House, after ten minutes of reflection in the Café Central, during a momentary stopover while rushing from New York to Cairo. Today it is the Café Musical Le Puits de Jour. Its empresario of electronic amplification, Matthieu Buchholtz, is the son of my cherished friends, the sculptor-ceramicists Jacques and Marielle Buchholtz. Novatt also introduced me to Patricia and Dominique Darnière. Without them, my House and my life—and this book—would have been far less interesting.

Amidst the flux of life in Lauzerte, the human constancy of Lauzerte's market is notable. "Have you been to Iowa?" inquired Frédéric Noyer, aka Fred the Foie Gras Guy, the first time we met. I hadn't, still haven't, but he had, and after many global journeyings had decided to build his life in Lauzerte, with ducks. Every Saturday I practice my English with Fred in order to keep up my past participles; they tend to deteriorate after a few months living in French. Frédéric Noyer began attending the Lauzerte market in 1988, two years before I got there, and is still there every Saturday. Maryline Ortalo started offering her superb cheeses and charcuterie from the Auvergne in 1990. Her aged Cantal remains the most memorable to be found anywhere. No oysters are brinier than those purveyed by Estelle and Cyril Foucher, who also began attending the Lauzerte market in 1990. They shuck dozens of them for me every Saturday during the season, kind people. I admire Joel Vigouroux for his plums and his wine. I revere him for his good cheer in the face of terrible adversity.

Maurice Capmas was the dean of the peasant-philosophers whose vegetables, fruit, and wisdom have made the market such a focus of my life in Lauzerte. When I first conversed with Maurice, his accent made me imagine he was speaking Occitan, not French. "Maurice," I called to him recently, "why don't you bring your produce to the market anymore?" "I'm ninety-two," he responded, "time for a break." Diagonally across the Square, little Lionel Lauture and his mother Michele cheerfully tolerated my insistent queries as to when the guinea fowl would be ready. Right next to them Monsieur and Madame Cachard always saved a bottle of their homemade tomato sauce for me. Everyone already used tractors by the time I got to Lauzerte, but Cachard also kept a donkey. "For the company," he explained.

On the opposite side of the Square, Angel and Pepita Font provided transcendent Swiss chard. Each customer also was presented with a complimentary bouquet of parsley. Later habitués of the weekly market include Serge Bonnet and his goat cheeses, also Quentin Baroche—a Jean-Paul Belmondo look-alike, but much taller—along with his spicy peppers and beefy tomatoes. Down the hill, Christian and Françoise Larroque baked the world's best bread. How I would miss their bread when I was not in Lauzerte! Most people become acquainted with the amiable brothers, Leo and Carl Carumi, while buying fruits and vegetables from them at local markets, including Lauzerte. Others have had the privilege of hearing these young polymaths perform Haydn, Mozart, and Beethoven at our local concerts.

Françoise Lamouroux, empress of bons mots as well as dairy products, occupies the most exalted echelon of this peasant pantheon, along with Martial Paris and Monsieur Legume.

Sometimes, in the course of my work, someone asks me how I can be so at ease conversing with kings, presidents, and prime ministers. "The life of every rickshaw puller and seamstress is a source of fascination for me," I would respond. "Well," I would add, "kings, presidents, and prime ministers have interesting lives too."

Certainly there are no uninteresting lives in Lauzerte. The following people are listed by name only simply because they are too interesting! If I added a single detail, an individual sentence would lead to the creation of a paragraph, a book—a life, then dozens of lives! Suffice it to observe that those mentioned hereafter include felons as well philanthropists, people who have rescued me and cheated me, insufferable snobs and persons of unaffected humility. One of them helped put men on the Moon but became notorious from Thailand to Texas for an entirely different reason. One of my closest friends I later discovered was a confidence man, jailed for stealing money from his friends, though not from me; I had been taken in too many times by then! Then there was the poor lady, crushed to death by one of our Lauzerte truck drivers, just shy of her hundredth birthday. The vast majority of them, though, are good people who led good lives and did good to me.

What all of the following have in common is that, one way or another, they contributed to the creation of this book: Jill Morgan; Raymond Burton; Victoria Sharples; Michael Morison; Ejaz Ahmed; Vincent Douglas; Therese de la Rue; Caroline Kristoffersen; Blanche Fourmachat; Bosco the Boston Terrier; Jane Oehr; Steve Branton; Paule Clos-Arceduc; Nuria and Enric Almiron; Janna Drake; Christophe Estrade;

Helen and Emmanuel Raft; Momoe and Edmund Downes; Arthur Watson; Sophie Gordon; Viv, Nikki and Frankie Abadi; Carole LeBars; Lise and Klaus Othman; Daphne Morgan-Barnicoat; Jeanne McCaul; Garry Stark; Keith Macfarlane; Paul Muller; Dr. Amr Sultan; Anne, Penny, and Edward Kynoch; Dr. Sylvie Pradines; Nicolas, Maëva et Laëtitia Darniere; Livia and Oscar "Flash" Gordon; and Didier Broult. As always and inevitably my thanks go to Dr. Sui ChengZhong for his quirky keen insights.

Right now, the people most on my mind are those whose names I cannot remember. These include the long-haired fellow with bad teeth who saved me when both the steering and brakes failed on my car on the steepest of Lauzerte's uphill slopes. His face, his medieval features, made his face unforgettable. He looked like he had just stepped out of a tapestry. Sifting through those forgotten names of people I remember so vividly I recall how good the original proprietors of the Café Central were to me. He was the one who sawed up the logs in the cave. She was so helpful and gentle, plus—essential for an American—they produced ice! What were their names? What has become of them? In life as well as history the search never ends.

Meanwhile, Lauzerte in its minuscule, particular way goes on reflecting the tumults of the times. At our weekly Gourmet Nights, I noticed only recently, plastic cups and plates have disappeared; so have throw-away knives, forks, and spoons. *Lauzertins* now must bring their own nonplastic utensils, or pay an additional fee to use those the vendors provide. Just as it did during the struggle against the English, or in World War Two, Lauzerte is doing its bit, in this instance to contain the effects of climate change.

SOME WORDS ABOUT
MY SOURCES

PATTERNS IN THE CARPET

The information, the knowledge, and dare I hope, the wisdom to be found in this book derive from several distinct sources.

The most copious and consequential set consists of the thousands of interactions I have had over the decades with human beings who live, or have lived, both in the general vicinity of Lauzerte—the combination village-city where I have owned a house since 1990—as well as elsewhere in the world. The most obsessive diarist could not maintain a record of all the encounters that have shaped this book. Were one to exist, the individual notations would be incomplete for understanding, like trust and friendship, evolves gradually, emerging from many events, on many occasions. Henry James wrote about the pattern in the carpet. Understanding Lauzerte and its people, and understanding the history that has made it and its inhabitants who and what they are, has been like taking a multitude of strands and weaving them together. The resulting book has many patterns. It also has some raggedy edges, as real life always does.

FAULKNER AND FRANCE PROFOUND

A second, though by no means secondary source of information is the geological, physiological, horticultural, meteorological, and architectural context that enveloped me as I had the life experiences that led me to write this book. This is a history in which limestone, wine, disease, and plums are as much protagonists as kings, clerics, and common people. William Faulkner's observation that "The past is never dead. It's not even past," applies to my everyday physical surroundings in Lauzerte. I have had to learn to read the stones of the old buildings I pass every day, while also appreciating that the newest constructions—retirement homes, supermarkets—are revelations in their own way. Among the seemingly pristine surroundings of vineyards and sunsets, it is also vital to perceive where railroad culverts once existed, or Roman squat toilets were.

One vital discovery has been the power that décor exerts over events and people, how it keeps shaping events and molding lives. I bought my House because the mountain was scenic and the square charming. Only gradually did I come to understand how such physical features continued to determine what Lauzerte was, and who the people living there were, long after their original purpose disappeared.

Then there is the power of a place's psychological décor. Just since I have been there, Lauzerte's various claims to being one of the most beautiful villages in France or to have been a historic stop on an ancient pilgrimage route have shaped events, including the town's evolving sense of itself, as much as the heat waves and advent of the internet have.

KIERKEGAARD WAS RIGHT

One of the more pervasive insights quantum physics provides is that the observed is nondetachable from the observer. The master artists who painted the caves in the area around Lauzerte up to twenty-thousand years ago, like the scientists of today, had to cope with that profound and annoying reality. "Even with perfect instruments and technique," as one scientific paper acknowledges, "the uncertainty is inherent in the nature of things." This means that no matter how hard we try, we no more can detach the reality we observe and attempt to portray from the circumstances of us observing it than we can detach our living selves from the external world. That Siamese twin-like condition has applied equally to me and this book. Learning about Lauzerte has been—inescapably, nondetachably, whether I wanted it or not—to learn new things about myself, and hence to find myself changing.

This has led to me reconsidering a comment Søren Kierkegaard made his diary in 1843. While it "must be lived forwards," he observed, "Life can only be understood backwards." Immersed professionally and personally in some of recent history's most

melodramatic events, I long considered comments like Kierkegaard's to be excuses made by those who preferred ivory towers to
the real-life cut and thrust of events. Writing this book—to put it
more precisely, becoming the person able to write this book—has
shown me I was wrong. Kierkegaard was right.

A SURFEIT OF SOURCES

This brings us to the books, manuscripts, memoirs, documents,
chronicles, and other written or printed sources that constitute the
book's formal documentation. The citations that follow are necessarily selective. Take for example, documentation on Eleanor of Aquitaine, her children and marriages, one of their legacies being the
promulgation of Lauzerte's first city charter. In English alone, Eleanor has inspired thousands of books, many fictional, some factual,
most an unreliable amalgam of the two. Their subtitles help explain
why she remains a figure of such fascination: "Queen Eleanor,
Independent Spirit of the Medieval World," declares one. "Crown
Jewel of Aquitaine," "Heroine of the Middle Ages," "Queen and Legend," announce others. "Eleanor of Aquitaine, Queen of the Troubadours and of the Courts of Love" hints at another reason she fascinates
so many. "The Scarlet Raptures of Eleanor of Aquitaine" shouts it.

To cite the books that imparted the knowledge that forms the sub-
structure of this book would require me to provide dozens of lists far
longer than that one. Just for starters it would have to include the
dozens of books consulted on such subjects as the hydrology of
France, the disasters of the Valois dynasty, the politics of the medieval
papacy, and the evolution of France's national infrastructure.

THE SAGE OF CAZILLAC

Some of the chapters required copious notation, as they involved
extensive historical and at times scientific research. Others, based entirely on personal experience, required none. While citations of
specific books are sparing, one work has been of fundamental importance. Around the turn of the last century, Lauzerte and all
those who care about Lauzerte were blessed by the presence in Cazillac, one of Lauzerte's attendant villages, of a parish priest named

Barthélemy Taillefer. Born in 1856 just over thirty miles south of Lauzerte in the village of Verdun-sur-Garonne, he spent most of his adult life in Cazillac, just six miles east of Lauzerte, dying there in 1937.

Those were days when the tiniest hamlet had its village curé; it was a tradition for some of these clerics to devote their ample spare time to scholarship. The abbé's scholarly endeavors culminated, in 1902, in the publication in the departmental capital, Montauban, by a printer named Edouard Forestié, of an extraordinary book, entitled *Lauzerte: Essai Historique*. Just as Lauzerte has rows of handsome arcades, two noteworthy churches, one of them containing a world-class organ and the other a rococo altar worthy of a French Bernini, it was likewise blessed by the abbé's book. His Cazillac vantage point—close, but not too close—had given him just the right perspective. Neither obsessed with civic trivia and score-settling, nor condescending in the manner of a work composed from the perspective of Cahors or Montauban, let alone Paris, might have been, the abbé's opus also was structurally felicitous. Many nearby towns were older than Lauzerte. Others had become more important, but the abbé recognized that Lauzerte provided what every historian wants. This was what the beloved American history book writer Barbara Tuchman described as a way "to narrow the focus to a manageable area."

For the Abbé of Cazillac, the beloved focus was a particular set of centuries. Founded during one of Europe's most tumultuous periods, Lauzerte thrived for approximately six hundred years, until another supremely tumultuous epoch arrived. By destroying the town's importance, first the French Revolution and then the Industrial Revolution conferred on Lauzerte a priceless benefit. Its ensuing irrelevancy, decline in population, and comparative poverty preserved its extraordinary architectural and physical ambiance. The frame was there, and the Abbé of Cazillac filled it. Astutely avoiding foundational myths and modern boosterism, he confined his study to those six centuries when Lauzerte played a definite, albeit minuscule, role in the world of great big history books. This meant that his book, unlike so many other such tomes, was blessed with a beginning, a middle, and an end. When it came to ferreting out fact, he himself was as relentless as any Inquisitor. Had he not hunted down the last known surviving copy of Lauzerte's Charter of 1241, eventually finding it in the chateau of another of my neighbors, the Marquis of d'Escayrac, its full text might have been lost forever.

By the standards of Toulouse or Bordeaux, Abbé Taillefer of Cazillac and his printer and friend Edouard Forestié were mere rustics, yet together they produced a volume whose quality would do any Left Bank bibliophile proud. The typeface, the proofreading, the simple but expressive line illustrations and, where appropriate, the translations from the original Occitan all were first class. So, also, was the abbé's textual narration, composed in vivid, never fussy, French. I often pass Cazillac, the obscure hamlet where he labored so long on his research and writing. Then as now there is nothing much to Cazillac, really, except for the little church, a house or two, and some stables, now serving as tractor sheds, yet pride of place endures. In France Profound villages lacking natural or architectural distinction, the French obsession with controlled beautification seems all the stronger. From spring through autumn, Cazillac's roadside planters make the place look like a flower show.

Cazillac, like so many other details of my life in France Profound, became important without me noticing it. This is because, I gradually came to understand, it shows how beautifully the independent human intellect can bloom, no matter how obscure its flowerpot. Sometimes, as I slow down for the Cazillac speed bumps, I think of how, after preaching to the local farm folk who, even today, seldom open a book, the abbé would return to his scholarly labors, and I am filled with admiration. The Abbé of Cazillac initially was of interest to me because of the book he wrote. Now he is important to me because of who he was. I have grown to love the man, as I have so many other of my neighbors. He shows us every life is worth living, provided we make it worthwhile. His remains rest in the grave yard at Cazillac.

I owe thanks to my neighbor, Patrice Brassier, for introducing me to Abbé Taillefer's book, and also for his own contributions to rescuing Lauzerte's past, including its recent past, from oblivion. His *Chronologie de l'histoire de Lauzerte* (2012) and, especially, his *Chroniques Lauzertines de la Gandillonne à la Resistance* (2014) are treasure troves!

Pervading this book is the presence of the renowned twentieth-century historian, Fernand Braudel. Of that esteemed savant's vast opus, this narrative draws principally on his two-volume work, *The Identity of France*, especially *Volume I: History and Environment*, their American, English-language editions dating from 1989 and 1991, respectively. More important than any citation, though, is my own evolving understanding of what Braudel understood, and communicated to so many others, including me: History, like life itself, must live and breathe in order to have meaning. More than that, history is life, encompassing all who have lived and will live, including us.

Dix siècles de vie littéraire en Tarn-et-Garonne, Association des Amis de la Bibliothèque Central de Pret de Tarn-et-Garonne, Marcel Maurières et al. (1988) contains a vast miscellany of what people have written about the area over the past thousand years but, it bears repeating, the House itself has been the primary source for this book. Its eaves, its cave, its stone work, its pillars, what I see through its windows never cease answering my questions, and posing new ones.

AI AND I—AND EVERYONE ELSE

At first gander this may seem like a capricious bibliography, but I have good reason for including so many obscure citations. The reason is that so many of these illuminating sources of information are obscure no more! The digitization of the world's knowledge is another example of how Lauzerte, in its Lilliputian way, epitomizes the cosmos. Discoveries that once might have required years of ferreting through obscure archives now can be found through on-line (though often also exhausting and time-consuming) searches. Only as I was preparing these notes did I come upon the memoir of a French aristocrat in the court of Henry of Navarre. He directly quotes the king referring to Lauzerte, twice. This constitutes irrefutable documentation of the importance the little town had acquired in the four centuries or so separating its foundation from Navarre's arrival on the scene in 1580.

While standard sources of authentic information remain absolutely essential, websites and podcasts are now also important fonts of knowledge. Many honorable people are constantly expanding knowledge in ways that never will never wind up in print. While new fonts of knowledge proliferate, old sources of knowledge are becoming easier to find and read than when they were first published hundreds of years ago. Roger de Hoveden, who died in 1290, was still applying quill to parchment around the same time the Brave Widow Gandillonne was counting her chestnuts. Today his *Annals*, in both English and the original Latin, are far more accessible to a general audience than they ever were when he—and she—were alive. Earnest works of scholarship like *The Spiritual Franciscans*, by David Muzzey, published in 1907, might otherwise have been lost to the world, except now you can download them!

My use of foreign-language citations—overwhelmingly in French, but also in Spanish—is likewise a sign of things to come. Ready or not, like it or not, chatbot is but part of an early generation of thingamajigs that, before you know it, will translate any document in any language into any other language. In this new era, in which the capacity both to search for the truth and to generate falsehoods constantly expands exponentially, the responsibility of the author (in distinction to the writer) is to separate the wheat from the chaff, the authentic from the false that more and more parades itself as "history." This I have spent countless hours attempting to do. One result is that many otherwise unknown sources are included. Another is that I have left out some supposedly standard sources, which, upon investigation, proved to be little more than compendiums of what today we call fake news.

NOTES

CHAPTER 1   44°15'4" NORTH, 1°08'18" EAST

As I point out in this chapter, *France profonde* means different things to different people, but one thing is certain. It is not Paris! All agree it refers to the France apart from Paris, the Paris elite, and its fads and follies. For some the term can seem condescending, an epithet the haughty Parisians use to denigrate the rest of the country. For others, it indicates a rustic strength of character that endures, and sometimes prevails, whatever Paris does or wants. See for example: Michel Dion, *La France profonde* (1988).

France Profound as opposed to *France profonde* as I use it refers to the specific France of which the town of Lauzerte is paradigm and epicenter. It combines the virtues of both the Reine Claude plum and the Brave Widow Gandillonne, while displaying a spectrum of ironies and follies that would do Paris proud. As used in this book, the term also connotes the force, strength, identity, and idiosyncrasies of the area extending from Lauzerte across the traditional regions of Aquitaine, Quercy, and Languedoc.

Unlike France Profound, Faulkner's Yoknapatawpha County is fictional, hence the relationship is analogous. Yoknapatawpha County formed the background for Faulkner's novels *Sanctuary* and *Requiem for a Nun*, published in 1931 and 1951. His famous comment about the past being never dead comes from *Requiem*.

On 4–11 August 1789, less than two months following the 17 July Fall of the Bastille, in a series of nineteen proclamations abolishing feudalism known as the August Decrees, the National Constituent Assembly decreed all places, as well as people equal. The provinces, like the nobility, were formally abolished in Article Ten. See *A Documentary Survey of the French Revolution*, ed. John Hall Stewart (1951).

Quercy traditionally is divided into two distinct areas. *Quercy blanc*, also called *Bas-*(or lower) *Quercy*, largely corresponds to the present-day

department of Tarn-et-Garonne. Upper or *Haute-Quercy* largely corresponds to the present-day department of the Lot. Lauzerte lies athwart
their geographic transition zone. Books on Quercy range from touristy
pamphlets to Guillaume Lacoste's massive *Histoire générale de la Province
de Quercy*. First published in 1883, then republished in 1968, its four enormous volumes are now available online. Jean Lartigaut's *Histoire du Quercy*
was published in 1993.

Jean Froissart's *Chroniques*, more than a million words long, were published in four books between 1322 and 1400, and forever after have been a
font of myth as well as fact. Written in prose as opposed to poetic form, it
deals with what later, and erroneously, was called The Hundred Years'
War, along with other subjects.

Fernand Braudel discussed his concept of historical time among other subjects in a filmed interview, now available on line. See France, Ministère de
l'Éducation nationale, Institut national de l'audiovisuel, "Fernand Braudel et
les différents temps de l'histoire," 30 October 1972. Oswyn Murray discusses
Braudel's sense of time in his introduction to *Memory and the Mediterranean*,
trans. Siân Reynolds (2001).

"President Emmanuel Macron—Berated, Despised, Contemned": "Ma-
cron Faces an Angry France Alone," headline on article by Roger Cohen,
New York Times, 16 March 2023. "Un homme contre un peuple," Serge
Halimi, *Le Monde diplomatique*, February 2023.

England, ever insular, kept itself eleven days—not a mere hour—distant
from the continent until 1752: Robert Poole, "'Give us our eleven days!':
Calendar reform in eighteenth-century England," *Past & Present*, Oxford
Academic, 5 December 2014.

The Antic Disposition Theater Company performed *Henry V* in front of
my House on 4 August 2015. See *Quercy Local: The Region's Free Magazine
in English*, no. 20, July–August 2015.

Quercy's status as a realm of transitions is treated in *Observations sur la
géographie et l'histoire du Quercy et du Limousin*, by Léon Lacabane, which
dates back to 1860.

Concerning my maps being printed between 1790 and 1808: While the
provinces were abolished in 1789, the original French departments, including the Lot, were established the following year, on 4 March 1790.

See *Réforme administrative ou révolution: La création des départements 1789–1790*, Documentary compendium, Departmental Archives, Conseil Général de Yvelines (1989).

Origins of the town's name: *Guide de Lauzerte: Promenade dans l'histoire*, by Rino Bandoch, also published in 1989, outlines the various theories.

Dictionnaire des pièges et difficultés de la langue française, by Jean Girodet, is a source of delight and education for anyone charmed, annoyed, or simply bewildered by the manifold contradictions of the French language.

CHAPTER 2   DISCERNING THE FACE OF THE SKY

I extend my thanks here to Mme Sandy Communal, Lauzerte municipal historian, for her help in understanding the history of my House and "the many faces it has presented to the world." *Maisons de Quercy et du Perigord*, by Alfred Cayla (1973) provides an overview of the region's domestic architecture. Also of interest are:

"Cahors, une maison de la fin du XIIIe siècle," Frédéric Épaud.
"Pans de bois antérieurs à 1450 dans les régions du sud-ouest,"
   Anne-Laure Napoléone, in *La Construction en Pan de Bois*, ed.
   Clément Alix (2013).

Historically "goat's cheese as opposed to cow's cheese takes pride of place," but opinion is far from unanimous, and thanks to globalization, the discussion long ago transcended France Profound. "Is goat cheese better than cow cheese?" The *Times of India* asked in its 14 September 2020 edition. "4 Reasons Goat Cheese Is Better Than Cow Cheese," responded *Stylecraze—Women's Fashion, Beauty And Wellness Community* in a 30 May 2023 posting. Medical specialists tend to agree: There were at least "6 Reasons You Should Switch to Goat Cheese," *Prevention* magazine argued as far back as 22 July 2015.

"*Compromis de vente*" is an example of how the meanings of French words can shift when they migrate into the English language. In French, the word continues to describe an agreement between two contracting parties; it does not necessarily have the pejorative sense of compromising ideals or objectives as it often does in English.

In this section I refer to the following articles:

"The Revolt Within," T. D. Allman, *Harper's Magazine*,
　　September 1984.
"One Tough Corie," T. D. Allman, *Vanity Fair*, February 1988.
"The Crushing Wheel of China," T. D. Allman, *Vanity Fair*,
　　October 1989.
"King Kohl," T. D. Allman, *Vanity Fair*, December 1990.

"German POWs in 1945." The information of the POWs comes from
Brassier's *Chroniques Lauzertines*.

"Pyrénées Mountains . . . Pic du Midi." Hercules and other details are
presented in *Le Pic du Midi de Bigorre et son observatoire: Histoire scientifique,
culturelle et humaine d'une montagne et d'un observatoire scientifique*, Jean-
Christophe Sanchez (1998).

The concern over "nuclear towers . . . chronic source of environmental con-
cern" was reported in the following articles: "Centrale rale nucléaire de
Golfech: la Garonne contaminée sur une 'centaine de kilomètres,'" Lauriane
Nembrot, *franceinfo*, 9 February 2023; "L'état de la centrale de Golfech in-
quiète toujours les riverains," Institut Supérieur de Journalisme de Toulouse,
Le Journal Toulousain, 30 April 2013.

"Poet as well as master mariner" refers to *A Passage to India: Canto in XXV
Stanzas*, by Paul J. Allman (1969).

"Red sky at night, shepherd's delight": The Jesus comment appears in
Matthew 16:2b–3 of the King James Bible.

Bricolage, meaning Do-It-Yourself is an example of French being pithier
than English.

In *Moby Dick, or The Whale* (1851), Herman Melville has Ishmael state that
"a whale-ship was my Yale College and Harvard."

CHAPTER 3　THE CONSTANT PROSCENIUM

La Depeche du Midi, 22 July 2022, announced the Lauzerte transit of the
famous bicycle race: "Tour de France: Les amateurs ouvrent la route vers
Lauzerte." The drone video showing the House, and providing the false
narrative of Lauzerte history can be accessed at https://www.youtube.com
/watch?v=CkhpbLeQ5nA.

The Church of St. Barthélémy and its origins are described in "Lauzerte," *Dictionnaire des Paroises du Diocese de Montauban,* Pierre Gayne (1978).

"One of the Most Beautiful Villages." The official website of the program explains the process by which communities like Lauzerte apply for the classification: https://www.les-plus-beaux-villages-de-france.org/fr/. Its section on Lauzerte recycles the various distinctions claimed for the village: https://www.les-plus-beaux-villages-de-france.org/fr/nos-villages/lauzerte/.

"L'éboulement des remparts," *Les Amis de Lauzerte,* November 2022 newsletter, explains how the "Garden of the Pilgrims" came to be invented in 1994.

For an understanding of how and why the "Pilgrimage Route to Compostela as it currently exists was invented by Generalissimo Francisco Franco's economic advisers," see "Revival of the Pilgrimage to Santiago de Compostela: The Politics of Religious, National, and European Patrimony, 1879–1988," Sasha D. Pack, *The Journal of Modern History,* 82, no. 2 (June 2010), "The Pilgrimage to Santiago de Compostela, Spain"; also "The Pilgrimage to Santiago de Compostella, Spain," John B. Wright, *Focus on Geography* (March 2014).

Lauzerte's "official status as a halting place on the Pilgrimage Route": The *Agence française des chemins de Compostelle* administers this newly contrived status in a manner similar to the way Lauzerte's status as one of the most beautiful village is controlled. See https://www.chemins-compostelle.com/qui-sommes-nous. Also "Chemins de Saint-Jacques-de-Compostelle: les chiffres clés du périple en Occitanie," *Le Journal Toulousain,* 19 April 2023. According to news reports, in good years some four thousand pilgrims traverse Lauzerte on the way to Compostela: "Lauzerte marche du bon pied avec les pèlerins de Compostelle," *La Depeche du Midi,* 23 May 2015.

Louis XIII ordained that the Lauzerte château, along with all other such redoubts, "be razed and demolished; even ancient walls shall be destroyed." "In June 1622 some 7,000 royal troops, backed by five cannons and four artillery pieces, seized control of Lauzerte, and drove out its Protestants" is mentioned in Brassier, *Chronologie.* See also: "Il y a 400 ans, le roi Louis XIII mettait l'Occitanie à feu et à sang," Pascal Palas. *Actu.fr Occitanie Tarn et Garonne,* 14 July 2022.

Lauzerte and its neighboring place names are showcased in *Lauzerte: Bouloc, Cazes-Mondenard, Durfort-Lacpelette, Montagudet, Monrbarla,*

Saint-Amans-de-Pellagal, Sainte-Juliette, Sauveterre, Trejouls, Christian-Pierre Bedell (2007).

The reference to the cluster bombs comes from "Laos Finds New Life After the Bombs," T. D. Allman, *National Geographic*, August 2015.

CHAPTER 4   OF WASPS AND WOMBS

For two fascinating expositions of figs, wasps, and "obligate mutualism," see:

> "Fig Wasps & Pollination," F. Kjelberg, S. van Noort, and J. Y.
>   Rasplus, in *The Fig: Botany, Production and Uses,* ed. Ali Sarkosh
>   et al. (2022).
> *Obligate Pollination Mutualism,* ed. Makoto Kato and Atsushi
>   Kawakita, Ecological Research Monographs (2017).

I here offer my homage to Mme Nicole de Renzy Martin, and my deep thanks for the vast amount of wisdom, as well as personal memories, she has shared with me, starting with personal discussions in 1991 and continuing across the decades.

As noted earlier, when it comes to Eleanor of Aquitaine's life, marriages, and legacy, the printed sources are too vast to cite individually. Among contemporary works, Alison Weir's books, notably *Eleanor of Aquitaine: A Life,* are consistently useful.

The law changing the British and Commonwealth order of succession is United Kingdom Statutory Instruments, 2015 No. 894 (C. 56), The Succession to the Crown Act 2013 (Commencement) Order 2015.

CHAPTER 5   FRYING PAN BOY

When it comes to the plethora of sources, ranging from the generally accurate to the absurdly false, what is true of Eleanor of Aquitaine is equally true of her son, King Richard I of England, whom nobody called the "Lionheart" while he was alive. In the century following his death at Châlus in 1199, at least nine chroniclers dealt with Richard's life, his family relations, his exploits during the Crusades, and his sexuality.

Among them I have relied on *Chronica magistri Rogeri de Hoveden,* which appeared in various forms up to 1291, and the *Chronicles* of Guillaume de Nangis, which were augmented by other chroniclers following his death in 1300. See:

> *The Annals of Roger de Hoveden: Comprising the History of England and of Other Countries of Europe from A.D. 732 to A.D. 1201*, Roger of Hoveden, trans. Henry T. Riley (1853).
>
> Roger of Hoveden, *Gesta Regis Henrici II & Gesta Regis Ricardi Benedicti Abbatis*, ed. William Stubbs (1867).

The *Chronique latine de Guillaume de Nangis, de 1113 à 1300, avec les continuations de cette chronique de 1300 à 1368*, as edited by the French statesman François Guizot in 1825, is now accessible online.

The dean of contemporary scholars dealing with Richard and his epoch is John Gillingham. His general work, *Richard the Lionheart*, published in 1978, was augmented by *Richard Coeur de Lion: Kingship, Chivalry and War in the Twelfth Century*, in 1994. In the chapters dealing with Richard, I have relied on his work, as well as the various chronicles and the sources I additionally cite, including for "He cost me much," *Henry the Young King, 1155–1183*, Matthew Strickland (2016). See also:

> *Richard Coeur de Lion in History and Myth*, ed. Janet L. Nelson (1992).
>
> *Lionheart and Lackland: King Richard, King John and the Wars of Conquest*, Frank McLynn (2012).
>
> *History of King Richard the First of England*, Jacob Abbott (1877).
>
> "King Richard I of England Versus King Philip II Augustus," Historynet.com, 23 August 2006.

The comments about "all wounded, either in our bodies or in our hearts," and other details from the Muslim side come from the Kurdish jurist Bahā' ad-Dīn Yusuf ibn Rafi ibn Shaddād, and his richly detailed biography of Saladin, *The Rare and Excellent History of Saladin*, translated by D. S. Richards (2002). See also: *Arab Historians of the Crusades*, ed. Francesco Gabrieli (1969).

"The devil is loose," the King of France warned John Lackland. Several versions of this famous comment exist. Pierre Gosset, *Histoire du Moyen-Âge* (1876) has Richard *déchaîné*, unchained, as opposed to *lâché*, let loose.

All concur he was called the devil. None of Richard's contemporaries refer to him as the Lionheart. The epithet, it would appear, only came into use many hundreds of years later. The earliest references in print I could find to "Richard Cœur de Lion" in French, and to "Richard the Lionheart" in English, dated back only to 1553 and 1694. They were:

> Annales & croniques de France depuis la destruction de Troye jusques au temps du roy Louis onzième Nicole Gilles et Denis Sauvage (1553).
>
> *THE GREAT HISTORICAL, Geographical and Poetical DICTIONARY. BEING A Curious Miscellany OF SACRED and PROPHANE HISTORY. Containing, in Short, the LIVES and Most REMARK-ABLE ACTIONS Of the Patriarchs, Judges and Kings of the Jews; Of the Apostles, Fathers, and Doctors of the Church; Of Popes, Cardinals, Bishops, [et]c. Of Heresiarchs and Schismaticks, with an Account of Their Principal Doctrines; Of Emperors, Kings, Illustrious Princes, and Great Captains; Of Ancient and Modern Authors; Of Philosophers, Inventors of Arts, and All Those who Have Recommended Themselves to the World, by Their Valour, Virtue, Learning, Or Some Notable Circumstances of Their Lives. Together with the Establishment and Progress Both of Religious and Military Orders, and the Lives of Their Founders. The Genealogy of Several Illustrious Families in Europe. The Fabulous History of the Heathen Gods and Heroes. THE DESCRIP-TION Of Empires, Kingdoms, Common-Wealths, Provinces, Cities, Towns, Islands, Mountains, Rivers, and Other Considerable Places, Both of Ancient and Modern Geography; Wherein is Observed the Situation, Extent and Quality of the Country; the Religion, Government, Morals and Customs of the Inhabitants; the Sects of Christians, Jews, Heathens and Mahometans. The Principal Terms of Arts and Sciences; the Publick and Solemn Actions, as Festivals, Plays, [et]c. The Statutes and Laws; and Withall, the History of General and Particular Councils, Under the Names of the Places where They Have Been Celebrated. The Whole Being Full of Remarks and Curious Enquiries, for the Illustration of Several Difficulties in Theology, History, Chronology and Geography,* Louis Moreri and Edmund Bohun (1694).

Since these are works of reference, the terms no doubt had been in use for some time before they were published, but the fact remains that the first documented uses of the term to describe King Richard I of England come more than three hundred years after his death.

"King Henry II, had ravaged the child Alys." The claim was spread by Gerald of Wales, who wrote in the century following these alleged depravities. See

Gerald of Wales: De principis instructione/Instruction for a Ruler. Reports of Richard being rebuked for the "sin of sodomy"; then, "receiving absolution, [he] took back his wife." No gold at Châlus; Richard's death: *Chronicon Anglicanum*, Ralph of Coggeshall (1224), Robert Bartlett (2018). Richard's sexuality, his refusal to marry Alys, his relations with Blondel de Nesle and Bérengère are explored in *Sodomy, Masculinity and Law in Medieval Literature: France and England, 1050–1230*, by William Burgwinkle (2004).

See also: *Richard I, Coeur de Lion: A study of Sources and Variations to the Year 1600*, Bradford B. Broughton (1966); "The Unromantic Death of Richard I," John Gillingham, *Speculum*, January 1979.

The comment about the Plantagenets being "a dreadful blood line, celebrated for its violence, its love of women, its inveterate betrayals of sons by fathers, fathers by sons, brothers by brothers," comes from *Les Comtes de Toulouse (1050–1250)*, Jean-Luc Déjean (1979). Déjean's book provides essential information, used throughout this book, concerning the Counts of Toulouse, and their place in the historical structure of their times.

For the preparation of *rillettes* in an American kitchen see "Duck rillettes a delectable addition to your holiday party table," Lynda Balslev, *Chicago Sun-Times*, 6 December 2022.

"The Embalmed Heart of Richard the Lionheart (1199 A.D.): A Biological and Anthropological Analysis," by Philippe Charlier et al., was published in *Scientific Reports*, 28 February 2013; see also "Science Reveals Secrets of the Lionheart's Heart," *Los Angeles Times*, 1 March 2013.

Richard's lack of Englishness was asserted in the *Guardian*, 14 September 2013, by Justin Cartwright. The article's headline stated that the "English King Whose Coat of Arms Adorns the National Football Side's Shirts Was Not in Fact English at All."

The *Telegraph* took a whack at him in a 4 April 2014 story entitled "Cruel, Anti-English and Almost Certainly Gay: Meet the Real Richard the Lionheart," by Dominic Selwood.

Sir Walter Scott's fantasies concerning Richard are discussed in *The Talisman* (1825), edited by J. B. Ellis and published in 2009. See also Edward Said's comments in his book *Orientalism* (1978).

For information on the bronze statue of Richard, see:

Art in Parliament: The Permanent Collection of the House of Commons: A Descriptive Catalogue, Malcolm Hay and Jacqueline Riding (1996). The statue continues to require repair: "Richard Coeur de Lion Conservation Work," U.K. Parliament, 17 August 2009.

CHAPTER 6   IN BOUVINE'S UNSEEN WAKE

For Louis VII's life as a whole, as opposed to his status as Eleanor's first consort, consult *Louis VII et son royaume*, Marcel Pacaut (1964). *Louis VII*, Yves Sasier (1991) is also useful.

His son's administrative innovations, including expansion of armed forces and the bureaucracy, are explained in *The Government of Philip Augustus: Foundations of French Royal Power in the Middle Ages*, John W. Baldwin (1991), and in *Philip Augustus: King of France 1180–1223*, Jim Bradbury (1997).

The source for "They loved each other so much," and other such comments is the *Annals* of Roger de Hoveden: *Gesta Regis Henrici Secundi et Gesta Regis Ricardi Benedicti abbatis*, edited in two volumes by William Stubbs (1867).

The importance of the Battle of Bouvines, Sunday, 27 July 1214, is discussed in "The Consequences of Bouvines," by John W. Baldwin and Walter Simons. *French Historical Studies* (Spring 2014). The various comments by historians to the effect that "without Bouvines there is no Magna Carta," come from a 26 July 2014, BBC broadcast by Hugh Schofield subtitled: "Exactly 800 years ago on Sunday, in a field next to what is now the airport of Lille, a battle was fought which determined the history of England."

"Realization" of modern France:

WARGAME DEVELOPMENTS—COW 2015: The Conference of Wargamers, 19 July 2015, is worth accessing at: http://soawargamesteam.blogspot.com /2015/07/10th-12th-july-knuston-hall.html.

Map showing Philippe-Auguste's advances: *Les conquêtes territoriales de Philippe Auguste, entre son avènement (1180) et sa mort (1223)*, 14 April 2006, Wikipedia Commons.

CHAPTER 7   THE SLEEP OF REASON
PRODUCES MONSTERS

For an overview of the Franks, and the emergence of France, see *Histoire des Francais pendant le regime feodal (987–1780)*, Theophile Lavalle (1865).

The uses and abuses of papal powers, including excommunication and annulment, are considered in *Innocent III: Vicar of Christ or Lord of the World?* James M. Powell (1963).

As a papal legate informed Count Raymond VI of Toulouse in 1208, "He who dispossesses you will be counted virtuous; he who strikes you dead will earn a blessing." *Massacre at Montségur*, Zoé Oldenbourg (1966) is the source here. Oldenbourg also provides a source of information in the following chapters concerning Simon de Montfort.

For the legacy of the 1076 excommunication of the Holy Roman Emperor, see "25 janvier 1077: 'Aller à Canossa,'" Jean-Marc Daniel, *Le nouvel Economiste*, 26 January 2018; for Hitler's discomfort with Mussolini, "Mussolini Muscles In," G. E. W. Johnson, *The North American Review*, August 1934.

Laval met Stalin in Moscow, 1935. No less an authority than Winston Churchill, in *The Second World War, Volume 1: The Gathering Storm*, vouches for the Laval-Stalin encounter being the first known instance when the phrase was used.

Ingoborg of Denmark's fate was discussed in *Ingeburge de Danemark, reine de France, 1193–1236*, by Hercule Géraud, Académie des Inscriptions et Belles-Lettres, 11 August 1844. A more recent consideration is "Le Cauchemar d'Ingeburge, épouse bafouée de Philippe-Auguste," Marie Petitot, *Plume d'histoire*, 3 February 2018.

1202 Sack of Constantinople: "The spoils were so great" and other comments come from Geoffrey of Villehardouin, *La Conquête de Constantinople* (1213). Edward Gibbon's observations come from *The History of the Decline and Fall of the Roman Empire, Volume I* (1781).

The full transcript of the "Address," by John Quincy Adams "Celebrating the Anniversary of Independence, at the City of Washington on the Fourth of July 1821," is available at the University of Virginia, Miller Center, "Presidential Speeches, John Quincy Adams Presidency."

"Que le Seigneur Pape trouve de l'argent et des soldats, qu'il oblige sur-
tout les Anglais a rester en paix, et l'on verra." Innocent III's exchanges
with Philip II, and much other information on the king's activities in this
and other chapters come from *Philippe Auguste: Le conquérant*, Georges
Bordonove (1983).

To the misfortune of the region's inhabitants, Simon de Montfort ravaged
the area around Lauzerte in 1212. To the edification of future generations, he was accompanied by a gifted young chronicler, a Cistercian monk
named Peter of Vaux-de-Cernay. His fascinating account, translated and
edited by W. A. Sibly and M. D. Sibly, was published as *The History of the
Albigensian Crusade* (1998). Peter of Vaux-de-Cernay's commentaries provide vivid descriptions of the area, and of the events unfolding there, at the
time Lauzerte was being founded. They provide indispensable documentary source material throughout this book.

For the origins and effects of the myth, see *The Pied Piper: A Handbook*,
Wolfgang Mieder (2007); also, *The Pied Piper of Hamelin at the Crossroads
of History, Religion and Literature*, Julian Scutts (2015).

For information on Innocent III, his writings, actions, and times, see:

Histoire du pape Innocent III et de ses contemporains, four volumes,
 Frédéric Hurter (1838).
Le pape Innocent III et la France, Raymonde Foreville (1992).
De Miseria Condicionis Humane of Pope Innocent III, ed. Robert E.
 Lewis (1978).
"The Sobering Story of the Pope Who Begged for Help from
 Purgatory," *ChurchPOP*, 1 November 2015.
"Saint Lutgarde, Saint of the Day," *Daily Compass*, 16 June 2020.
The Papacy and Crusading in Europe, 1198–1245, Rebecca Rist
 (2009).
The Deeds of Pope Innocent III, James M. Powell (2004).

The original of the portrait, which, Giorgio Vasari observed, "was so lifelike and true it frightened everyone who saw it" is in London. The famed
portrait in the Borghese Gallery in Rome is a copy. See *Raphael's Portrait of
Pope Julius II*, Cecil Gould (1970).

The Sleep of Reason Produces Monsters (1798). *El sueño de la razón produce
monstruos* was forty-third of the eighty aquatints in the series, *Los Caprichos*, that Francisco Goya produced for a Madrid newspaper between

1797 and 1799. An analysis is found in *Francisco de Goya, Los Caprichos*, Rafael Casariego (1988). *Goya*, by Robert Hughes (2003), places *Los Caprichos* in context.

Bacon's paintings and their context: "Francis Bacon's 'Screaming Pope' Embodied Postwar Anguish," Katie White, *artnet news*, 1 February 2022, describes how this series came to be painted. See also, "Francis Bacon: The Papal Portraits of 1953," *Museum of Contemporary Art San Diego* (1999) and "Visceral and Unsparing: Why Francis Bacon's portraits of Screaming Popes and Lovers Live On," broadcast by Nick Glass, CNN, 28 July 2019.

"6-inch tall, hard plastic model" of Innocent III sold out quickly: See "Pope Innocent III Figure, Item Number: AU11147: SOLD OUT—FOR INFORMATIONAL PURPOSES ONLY," *Entertainment Earth*, Sun Valley, California, sales website, accessed 20 June 2023.

CHAPTER 8 *CAEDITE EOS*

"Never did God make a scribe," "From near and far they come" and other details on the papal invasion come from William of Tudela, *Song of the Albigensian Crusade* (1213).

A Most Holy War: The Albigensian Crusade and the Battle for Christendom, by Mark Gregory Pegg (2008), in addition to providing important information on the papal massacres, places these events in their moral as well as historical context. See also, *La Croisade contre les Albigeios et l'union du Languedoc à la France, 1209–1249*, P. Belperron (1944).

Massacre of 22 July 1209, at Beziers, *Caedite Eos*. Arnaud-Amaury, Abbot of Cîteaux, boasted of the massacre in his report to the pope. He is first credited with uttering the phrase in question by Caesarius of Heisterbach, writing a dozen or so years later. See *Caesarius, The Dialogue On Miracles*, translated from the Latin and edited by Henry von Essen Scott and C. C. Swinton Bland (1929).

Jacques de Vitry's comments on the death of Innocent III, and other useful information derive from his *Histoire des Croisades*, (c. 1225), translated into French by François Guizot (1825).

Comments on supposed heretics being "folk near and dear to us," and on Innocent III doing "as much evil to the Catholics as to the heretics, and much other useful information come from *L'histoire de France depuis les temps les plus recules jusqu'en 1789: Racontee à mes petits-enfants*, Vol. 1, François Guizot (1809), especially Chapter XVII: "Les Croisades: Leur declin et leur fin." Guizot's grandchildren must have been precocious. His history today would be considered a university-level text.

The papal massacre was "one of the great pivotal moments in world history." Mark Gregory Pegg makes this vitally important point in *A Most Holy War*.

CHAPTER 9   *VULGARIUM NUMERUS INFINITUS*

Here, too, the descriptions of Montfort's massacres, how Raymond-Roger was seized in flagrant breach of his safe-conduct, and the Abbot of Cîteaux conferring on Simon de Montfort "the government of the territory for the glory of God, the honor of the Church and"—lastly—"the suppression of heresy" come from Peter of Vaux-de-Cernay's eyewitness accounts.

CHAPTER 10   SECRET ROUTES

"Never was a more attractive young man born," and Innocent III's other comments on the future Raymond VII: "Raymond VII of Toulouse: The Son of Queen Joanna, 'Young Count' and Light of the World," Laurent Macé, in *The World of Eleanor of Aquitaine: Literature and Society in Southern France between the Eleventh and Thirteenth Centuries*, ed. Marcus Bull and Catherine Léglu (2005).

Accounts of Baldwin's life and death; including being captured at Lolmie, and being hanged from a walnut tree come from Zoé Oldenbourg's *Masacre at Montsegur*, as does the observation that Montfort's "writ only ran where he stood armed from head to toe, his men behind him; not an inch further" and that his death produced an outburst of popular rejoicing. For other details, also see *The Albigensian Crusade* by Jonathan Sumption (1978).

Flaubert's tale was first published as

   Un coeur simple, Gustave Flaubert (1877), eventually as
   A Simple Soul, Gustave Flaubert, Project Gutenberg Translation
      (2006).

Fibonacci, *Liber Abaci* (1202), "The Book of Calculation," was revised 1227. The first complete English translation: *Fibonacci's Liber Abaci*, Laurence E. Sigler (2002), came nearly eight hundred years later.

CHAPTER 11   THE REMEMBERED MONTFORT

The description of the 25 June 1218 death of Simon de Montfort, of the catapult being loaded, fired, and reloaded, and the statement that "If one may seek Christ Jesus in this world by killing men and shedding blood, by fostering evil and snuffing out good; by slaughtering women and slitting children's throats——why, then he must needs wear a crown, and shine resplendent in Heaven!" come from *The Song of the Albigensian Crusade*. Sumption describes "heavy blocks of masonry" hurtling down on the attacking forces. One of them "struck Simon on the head and killed him." William of Puylaurens was the one who wrote: "The man who inspired terror from the Mediterranean to the British Sea fell by a blow from a single stone."

For information on the sons of Simon de Monfort, including his namesake, and on the Model Parliament and its legacy, see:

> *The First English Revolution: Simon de Montfort, Henry III and the Barons' War*, Adrian Jobson (2012).
> *Simon de Montfort and the Rise of the English Nation*, Darren Baker (2018).

For "testicles cut off and hung on either side of his nose" and other details:

> *Chronicles of the Mayors and Sheriffs of London 1188–1274*. Account of A.D. 1264–65.
> "Simon de Montfort Called Together Knights and Burgesses 750 Years Ago—Creating the First Parliament of Elected Representatives," *Telegraph*, 20 January 2015.
> "Simon de Montfort: The Turning Point for Democracy That Gets Overlooked," BBC News, 19 January 2015.

CHAPTER 12   EVERYTHING THAT RISES

The artist himself explained his intentions regarding "The Adjustment of Conflicting Interests." His "Description (original by artist)," John La Farge, *Moral and Divine Law*, "c. 1903 Oil on canvas, permanently fixed to wall

Supreme Court Chamber, East Wall Installed circa 1905," appears in *Minnesota State Capitol: Overview of the Fine Art*, Minnesota Historical Society (2015). With thanks to Beau Berentson, Director of Communications and Public Affairs, Minnesota Judicial Branch.

For context: *America in the Gilded Age: From the Death of Abraham Lincoln to the Rise of Theodore Roosevelt*, Sean Dennis Cashman (1984).

Proof La Farge was depicting Count of Toulouse: Metropolitan Museum of Art, "The Adjustment of Conflicting Interests: Count Raymond of Toulouse Swears at the Altar to Observe the Liberties of the City; Color Study for Mural, Supreme Court Room, Minnesota State Capitol, Saint Paul." The Met website, accessed 21 June 2023.

See also "A Socrates for St. Paul," *New York Times*, 26 May 1905.

Joan Plantagenet's marriages, motherhood, warfare, and death are described in Puylaurens's *Chronicle*.

The lives of Eleanor of Aquitaine's daughters, including Joan Plantagenet, are discussed in the following works:

"Les filles d'Aliénor d'Aquitaine: étude comparative," Edmond-René
   Labande, in *Cahiers de civilisation médiévale* (1986).
The Daughters of Henry II and Eleanor of Aquitaine, Colette Bowie
   (2014).
"Shifting Patterns in Angevin Marriage Policies: The Political
   Motivations for Joanna Plantagenet's Marriages to William II of
   Sicily and Raymond VI of Toulouse," Colette Bowie, *Les straté-
   gies matrimoniales (ixe–xiiie siècle)*, ed. Martin Aurell (2013).

CHAPTER 13   OF ALL HER ILK

The details of Blanca's metamorphosis into Blanche, her domination of her son and daughter-in-law, and her historical importance can be gleaned from the following works:

Blanche de Castille, Gérard Sivéry (1990).
La Reine Blanche, Régine Pernoud (1992).
Histoire de Blanche de Castille, Elie Berger (1895).
"Blanche de Castille, mère aimante, belle-mère tyrannique,"
   Charlotte Chalin, *GEO*, 6 January 2021.

Books on Louis IX's misadventures include:

La Septième croisade et le vrai Louis IX: 1248–1254, Gaëlle Audéon (2022).

Louis IX's captivity, care by the eunuch Sabih Almoaddhami, relations with the Sultana are described in *Le Collier de Perles*, Bedr-Eddyn (1226–27). Extracts in French translation by E. DuLaurier, *Acadamie des Inscriptions et Belle-lettres* (1887), digitized by Marc Szwajcer.

Louis IX: Tragedie en cinq actes, M. Ancelot (1819). A "Tragedy in Five Acts."

Descendants of Eleanor and Blanche:

Eleanor of Aquitaine: The First Grandmother of Europe, John G. Gurley (2016).

"Celebrities You Had No Idea Were Related to Royals," Constance Gibbs, *SheKnows*, 28 February 2019.

CHAPTER 14   SWEARING ON THE ALTAR

The governmental organization of the town is documented in
Coutumes de Lauzerte, Émile Rébouis, Bulletin de la Société Archéologique de Tarn-et-Garonne (1886).
For a contrast with neighboring localities see also:

Lauture et Cazillacc: Histoire de ma paroisse, Abbé Barthélemy Taillefer (1899).
Les coutumes de Montcuq, Abbé Barthélemy Taillefer (1912).

Finding and preserving the surviving text of Lauzerte's 1241 charter was among Abbé Taillefer's great achievements. His translation of the charter from Occitan into French, presented in *Lauzerte: Essai historique*, provides the source for discussions of the charter and its significance.

The development of the planned townships of Quercy and the rest of France Profound is related in the following volumes, among others:

L'histoire des bastides, Catherine Rèfre (2016).
L'aventure des bastides du Sud-Ouest, Gilles Bernard (1998).

The chartering of Lauzerte and some of its sister towns is presented in the essay:

Cinq Coutumes Tarn-et-Garonne: Larrazet, Angeville, Fajolles,
   Lauzerte et Valence d'Agen, Emile Rebouis, Ariviste Paleoégraphe,
   Membre de la Société Archéeologique de Tarn-et-Garonne:
   Montauban. (Imprimerie et Lithographie Forestié, 1886).

CHAPTER 15   UNINVENTABLE DENOUEMENTS

Letter to a Friend," Petrarch, cited in *Readings in European History,* J. H.
Robinson (1904), digitalized in Fordham University's *Medieval Sourcebook*: "Petrarch: Letter Criticizing the Avignon Papacy."

For information on Domingo Félix de Guzmán, the formation of the
Dominicans, and their militarization and corruption, including their terror campaign in Quercy, also on Peter Seila incarnating the Dominicans'
dark transformation, see:

Heresy, Crusade, and Inquisition in Southern France, 1100–1250,
   Walter L. Wakefield (1974).

Gui's Interrogation techniques are detailed in the following texts:

Practica Inquisitionis Heretice Pravitatis, Bernardus Guidonis (1866).
   Original Latin text.
Manuel de l'inquisiteur: practica officii inquisitionis heretice pravitatis
   (1926). French translation.
The Inquisitor's Guide: A Medieval Manual on Heretics, Bernard Gui,
   trans. Janet Shirley.
"Bernard Gui: Inquisitorial Technique (c.1307–1323)," English
   extract, *Medieval Sourcebook,* ed. Paul Halsall.

Regional origins of the Avignon popes:

Avignon of the Popes: City of Exiles, Edwin Mullins (2007).
The Right of Spoil of the Popes of Avignon, 1316–1415, Daniel Willi-
   man (1988).

The *noblesse de la robe* versus the *noblesse de l'epée*:

La science des personnes de la cour, de l'épée et de la robe, Henri Philippe
   de Limiers (1752).
La Robe contre l'épée?; la noblesse au XVIIe siècle, 1600–1715,
   Christophe Levantal (1987).

Jacques de Molay and persecutions of the Templars:

Jacques de Molay: le crépuscule des templiers, Alain Demurger (2002).
Jacques de Molay: le dernier grand-maître des templiers, Philippe Josserand (2019).

CHAPTER 16   OUR QUERCY POPE

John XXII as "Papal Antichrist," see *Apocalypticism in the Western Tradition*, Bernard McGinn (1994).

Pope and the murdered Franciscans, their execution:

The Spiritual Franciscans, David Muzzey (1907).
The Spiritual Franciscans: From Protest to Persecution in the Century After Saint Francis, David Burr (2001).
Later comments by the Archbishop of Marseille:
Antiquité de l'église de Marseille, et la succession de ses évêques, adressées au clergé seculier et regulier, & aux fidèles de son diocése, pour leur instruction, vol. 2, Henri François Xavier de Belsunce (1747).

Condemnation of John XXII:

Guillaume d'Occam: sa vie, ses œuvres, ses idées sociales et politiques, Léon Baudry (1949).
William of Ockham: Questions on Virtue, Goodness, and the Will, ed. Eric W. Hagedorn (2021).

"Of all the great devils who rule the world the lord pope is the major devil; I call him Satan; the lord kind of France is the second devil . . ." The image of Pope John XXII, the Sacred Lamb and Satan is to be found in *Vaticinia de Summis Pontificibus*, an illuminated manuscript dating from the late 1300s:

https://www.bl.uk/catalogues/illuminatedmanuscripts/ILLUMIN .ASP?Size=mid&IllID=51683

CHAPTER 17   LOVING THE SHEPHERD

The principal sources here are:

The *Register* of his inquisitions left by Jacques Fournier, the future Pope Benedict XII, and discovered by Jean Duvernoy, the archivist who translated it.

Le Registre d'inquisition de Jacques Fournier, évêque de Pamiers, 1318–
    1325: manuscrit Vat. Latin no 4030 de la Bibliothèque vaticane,
    publié avec introduction et notes par Jean Duvernoy (3 vols., 1965).
    Republished 2004.
Le registre d'Inquisition, ed. Jean Duvernoy (1965), original text;
    1968 French version.
Inquisition à Pamiers, interrogatoires de Jacques Fournier: 1318–1325,
    choisis, traduits du latin et présentés par Jean Duvernoy (1966).

The two, significantly different versions of Emmanuel Le Roy Ladurie's
vastly influential book, the original in French and the "considerably
abridged version, less than half the length of the original" in English.

Montaillou, Village Occitan de 1294 à 1324, Emmanuel Le Roy
    Ladurie (1975).
Montaillou, The World Famous Portrait of Life in a Medieval Village,
    Emmanuel Le Roy Ladurie (first U.S. edition, 1980).

See also:

Les Archipels Cathares: Dissidence chretienne dans l'Europe medieval,
    Ann Brenon; pref. de Jean Duvernoy (2000).
Defining Heresy: Inquisition, Theology, and Papal Policy in the Time of
    Jacques Fournier, Irene Bueno (2015).

Duvernoy honored:

"Montaillou: le Centre historique Jean-Duvernoy a été inauguré,"
    La Depeche du Midi, 19 August 2021.
"Jean Duvernoy (1917–2010)," Mairie de Montaillou (2010).
"His search was humble," *Actualités Unitariennes*, 25 August 2010.

CHAPTER 18   BRAVE WIDOW GANDILLONNE

Spellings of the Brave Widow's name vary. The spelling here follows the
usage in Abbé Taillefer's *Lauzerte: Essai historique*.
    A book has been written about this succulent plum. *La Reine-Claude*,
Alain Audubert (1995).

There also are two museums dedicated to plums in the Lauzerte vicinity:

Le musée du pruneau à Granges-sur-Lot;
Ferme et musée du pruneau à Lafitte sur Lot.

The life of Queen Claude is recounted in:

> *Claude de France: première épouse de François Ier, mère de Henri II,*
> Henri Pigaillem (2006).
> *Claude de France, femme de François Ier, 1499–1524,* Jean Alexis Neret
> (1942).

Abbé Taillefer's accounts and Brassier's *Chronologie* provide the main sources
here.

CHAPTER 19   THE BLACK PRINCE SYNDROME

For the basic outline of the tale Shakespeare never told, see:

> *Edward, the Black Prince: Power in Medieval Europe,* David Green
> (2007).
> *The Black Prince and His Age,* John Garvey (1976).
> "The Epitaph of Edward the Black Prince," Diana B. Tyson,
> *Medium Ævum* (1977).
> "The Illness of Edward the Black Prince," A. S. MacNalty. *British
> Medical Journal* (1955).

Also:

> *The English in the Twelfth Century: Imperialism, National Identity, and
> Political Values,* James Gillingham (2000).
> *The Hundred Years' War, The English in France, 1337–1453,* Desmond
> Seward (1978).
> *La Guerre de cent ans,* J. Vincent (1954).
> *Gascony under English Rule,* E. C. Lodge (1926).

"English simply abandoned the struggle":

> This comment comes from "Les temps feodaux" in the *Encyclopédie
> autodactique Quillet* (1958), Tome III.

CHAPTER 20   BRIDGE OF THE DEVIL

Cahors: the Lot river and its Roman past:

> "The Lot," *Three Rivers of France: Dordogne, Lot, Tarn,* Freda
> White (1952).
> The "old Roman road from La Rochelle to Nîmes via Cahors" is
> mentioned in "The French Isthmus," Braudel, *Identity,* vol. 1.

In this France Profound version of Faust, Satan strikes his usual bargain:

"La Légende du Pont Valentre," *Légendes Quercynoises*, Tante
    Basiline (1960).

See also:

Cahors au cours des siecles, Jean Fourgous (1944).
Les pays de la moyenne Garonne, Pierre Deffontaine (1931).
Le vieux Quercy, Eugène Sol (1929).

CHAPTER 21 EVEN ANCIENT WALLS SHALL BE DESTROYED

Lauzerte, Cahors, and the eruption of religious war:

Guerres de religion en Quercy, E. Gabie (1906).
The Huguenot Struggle for Recognition, Nicola Sutherland (1980).
The Wars of Religion in France, 1559–1576, J. W. Thompson (1909).
The French Wars of Religion, A. A. Tilley (1919).
*The King's Army: Warfare, Soldiers and Society during the Wars of
    Religion in France, 1562–1576*, James Wood (2002).

Best-selling etching, *The Massacre at Cahors*:

Le Massacre faict à Cahors en Querci le xix Novemb. 1561, Jacques
    Perrissin, originally published by Nicolas Castellin and Pierre
    Le Vignon.
The Trial of Jan Hus: Medieval Heresy and Criminal Procedure,
    Thomas A. Fudge (2013).

CHAPTER 22 WORTH A MASS

Henry of Navarre's references to Lauzerte are found in:

Henri IV en Gascogne, 1553–1589, Charles de Batz-Trenquelléon
    (1885).
Recueil des lettres missives de Henri IV, Vol. I, ed. Jules Berger de
    Xivrey and Joseph Gaudet (1843).

The vast literature concerning Henry of Navarre includes:

History of Henry the Fourth: King of France and Navarre, John S. C.
    Abbott (2009).

Henri IV: Roi de Navarre et de France, Hélène Tierchant (2010).
Henri IV, Jean-Pierre Babelon (2009).
France in the Age of Henry IV, Mark Greengrass (1986).

Interesting information on his mother, Queen Jeanne of Navarre, is to be found in:

Histoire de Jeanne d'Albret, reine de Navarre, Théodore César Muret (1862).
Mémoires et poésies de Jeanne d'Albret (Queen of Navarre), Alphonse de Ruble (1893).
Queen Jeanne and the Promised Land: Dynasty, Homeland, Religion and Violence in Sixteenth-Century France, David Bryson (1999).
Queen of Navarre: Jeanne d'Albret 1528–1572, Nancy Roelker (1968).

The venerable historian Robert Knecht, the son of French parents, has produced a respected body of work on this period in English. It includes:

Catherine de' Medici (1998).
The French Renaissance Court (2008).
The Valois: Kings of France 1328–1589 (2007).
The French Religious Wars 1562–1598 (2002).
The Rise and Fall of Renaissance France: 1483–1610 (2002).

Some works on the decline of the Valois dynasty include:

The Duke of Anjou and the Political Struggle During the Wars of Religion, Mack Holt (2002).
Catherine de Medici: Renaissance Queen of France, Leonie Frieda (2004).
Catherine de Médicis, Ivan Cloulas (1979).
La reine Margot et la fin des Valois (1553–1615), Charles Merki (1905).
Catherine de Medici and the Ancien Régime, N. M. Sutherland (1966).

As for the famous massacre, see among many others:

The Massacre of St Bartholomew and the European Conflict: 1559–1572, Nicola Sutherland (1973). "The Saint Bartholomew's Massacre in the Provinces," Philip Benedict, *The Historical Journal* (1978). See also "The Dynamics of Protestant Militancy: France 1555–1563," by the same author.
Tocsin pour une massacre: La saison des Saint-Barthélemy, Janine Estebe (1968).

The St Bartholomew's Day Massacre: The Mysteries of a Crime of State, Jouanna Arlette (2007).

Descent of Henry of Navarre from Robert of Clermont:

Archives curieuses de l'histoire de France depuis Louis XI jusqu'à Louis XVIII, ou Collection de pièces rares et intéressantes, ed. Jean Louis Félix Danjou and L. Lafaist (1839).

"The Assassination of Henry IV," an engraving by Gaspar Bouttats, would be as popular, and profitable, as "The Massacre of the Huguenots in Cahors":

Ravaillac, le fou de Dieu, Janine Garrisson (2013).
Ravaillac, l'assassin d'Henri IV, Jean-François Bège (2014).

CHAPTER 23   JERRY-BUILT BY BONAPARTE

I dedicate this chapter to my friends-for-life Charlie and Mary—the Baron and Baroness—Charles-Antoine Andréa de Nerciat. I met him drinking in journalist hang-outs in Beijing and Bangkok, and she's a baroness from Shanghai via Canada, yet I learned more from them about Montauban than any textbook taught me.

For geographical information on "our hydrographically denominated department of Tarn-et-Garonne" see:

"Le Quercy," *Les fleuves de France: La Garonne*, Louis Barron (1891).
Nouveau dictionnaire complet géographique de la France, Briand de Verzé (1842).
Le Tarn-et-Garonne: histoire, sciences, industrie, commerce, agriculture, viticulture, idiome, moeurs, coutumes, assistance, anciens monuments, instruction, bibliothèque, archives, musées, sociétés savantes, démographie, E. Forestié (1902).

Also:

Departement de Tarn-et-Garonne, Abel Hugo (1835).
"Tarn-et-Garonne," *Geographie illustre de la France*, Jules Verne (1879).
Dictionnaire des communes du Departement de Tarn-et-Garonne, Adolphe Joanne (1881).
Le Tarn-et-Garonne, Syndicate d'Initiative (ESSI), Montauban (1932).

Voyage littéraire et archéologique dans le département de Tarn-et-Garonne, Alexandre Du Mège (1828).

"To attack Montauban is to court disaster." Louis XIII and Napoléon at Montauban, and other details on the city's history, see:

Histoire veritable de tout ce qui s'est fait & passé dans la ville de Montauban, Messieurs de Rohan, de Soubize, and de la Rochelle (1527).

Histoire de la ville de Montauban divisée en deux livres. Dont le premier contient plusieurs matieres curieuses. Et le second, un sommaire de toutes les guerres de religion, Henri Lebret (1902).

Montauban: le sense de l'histoire, Dominique Porte and Didier Taillfer (1994).

Histoire de Montauban sous la domination anglaise et jusqu'à sa réunion à la couronne de France, Jean Ursule Devais (1843).

The Huguenots and the Revocation of the Edict of Nantes, H. M. Baird (1895).

Histoire de Montauban, ed. Daniel Ligou (1984).

Montauban would humiliate the young king when its Protestant defenders successfully defied his siege:

"La 'Geneve française,'" Janine Garrison, in *Histoire de Montauban*, ed. Daniel Ligou (1984).

Beyond Belief: Surviving the Revocation of the Edict of Nantes in France, Christie Sample Wilson (2011).

For a vast overview of the paradoxical connection between male descent and female power, immerse yourself in:

La France, les femmes et le pouvoir, 3 vols., Elaine Viennot (2006).

CHAPTER 24 PARIS IS THE PATTERN

To document France's domination by Paris would require recapitulating the history of Europe, and much of the rest of the world as well.

For details on the regional and linguistic policies emanating from Paris, see:

French Language Policies and the Revitalisation of Regional Languages in the 21st Century, ed. Aurélie Joubert and Michelle A. Harrison (2018).

"Pourquoi Notre-Dame est le point zéro des routes françaises?"
Paris Secret, 29 September 2022.

"2016, naissance de la grande région," *Petite histoire des collectivités
régionales*, La Region Occitanie, accessed 25 June 2023.

"La nouvelle région Languedoc-Roussillon-Midi-Pyrénées
s'appellera 'Occitanie,'" *Le Journal du Dimanche*, 24 June
2016.

Chapter 25   Incunabula of the ATM

For sequence of photos of the Montauban massacre site, go to:

https://www.google.com/maps/@44.0237955,1.3417089,3a,75y,345
.3h,82.89t/data=!3m7!1e1!3m5!1sUcO7Xh5CRO9_m2Q0P5L5
PQ!2e0!5s20091001T000000!7i13312!8i6656?hl=en.

Details of the victims and their lives are provided by the Association Francaise des Victimes de Terrorism in the following entries:

France—Assassinats de Mohamed Legouad & d'Abel Chennouf
(Montauban)
France—Assassinat d'Imad Ibn Ziaten (Toulouse)
France—Tuerie devant l'École Ozaar Hatorah

For further details on the killings, see:

"Montauban-Toulouse. Trois exécutions, une même arme," *La
Depeche du Midi*, 17 March 2012.

"La même arme utilisée pour abattre les militaires de Toulouse et
Montauban," *Le Parisien*, 16 March 2012.

Relating to the encounter with the Montauban paratroopers in Iraq:

"Saddam Wins Again: Letter from Baghdad," T. D. Allman, *New
Yorker*, 17 June 1996.

Chapter 26   The Voice in the Loft

"When Lauzerte lost its status as a seat of justice":

"Assemblée Nationale, Suite de vendredi 29 janvier, Suite de de-
crets," *Journal de Versailles*, 2 February 1790.

Many sites quote Feynman. This one provides both the complete text and a video of Feynman himself making that famous comment:

"Richard Feynman: Knowing the name of something and knowing something," rAmg website, 29 September 2015: https://ramjeeganti.com/.

Encounter in the Salvadoran forest:

"Rising to Rebellion: Inside El Salvador," T. D. Allman, *Harper's Magazine*, March 1981.

Oxygenation that made current life possible:

"The Great Oxidation Event: How Cyanobacteria Changed Life," *American Society for Microbiology*, 18 February 2022.

For Cambodia epiphany, see:

"Sihanouk's Side Show," T. D. Allman, *Vanity Fair*, April 1990.
"Cambodia, Nightmare Journey to a Doubtful Dawn," T. D. Allman, *Asia*, March/April 1982.

CHAPTER 28   THE PIGEONS ARE CROWING

"Ambiguous undulations" comes from:

"Sunday Morning," Wallace Stevens, *Poetry Magazine of Verse*, Vol. VII, No. II, November 1915.
"Lauzerte and its pigeonniers," are described in *Pays de Serres en Quercy, Office de Tourisme Intercommunal, Lauzerte* (2023).

Origins of pigeonniers are explored in:

Pigeonniers en Midi-Pyrénées, Michel Lucien (2014).
Pigeonniers de France: histoire économique et sociale, technique architecturale, conseils de restauration, Dominique Letellier (1998).
From Le Pigeonnier, Dirk Bogarde (1995) deals with the actor's life in France.

"Marvelous Pigeon Manure," is lauded on the *Pigeon Talk* website, accessed 24 June 2023.

Goths, Gothic, and *Opus Francigenum,* and how they have come to be confounded, and the role Vasari, Walpole, and Victor Hugo played, see:

"De l'"opus francigenum" à l'art gothique," Les Anecdotes de l'Histoire,
    15 March 2021.
Qu'est-ce que l'architecture gothique? Arnaud Timbert (2018).
The Lives of the Most Excellent Painters, Sculptors, and Architects,
    Giorgio Vasari (1550).
The Castle of Otranto, Horace Walpole (1764).
Notre-Dame de Paris: 1482, Victor Hugo (1831).

Viollet-le-Duc presented his rationale for his actions in:

Projet de restauration de Notre-Dame de Paris, Jean-Baptiste-Antoine
    Lassus (1843).
Notre-Dame de Paris et la nouvelle sacristie, Jean-Baptiste-Antoine
    Lassus and Eugène Viollet-le-Duc (1867).
Fire and Spire: Viollet-le-Duc's anachronistic spire, source of the
    worst damage in the blaze, spire turned into centerpiece of
    "restoration."
"An exact replica of Notre Dame cathedral's spire will be rebuilt
    starting this summer," Eleanor Beardsley, NPR's *All Things
    Considered,* 5 May 2023.
"Notre-Dame's spire to be majestically restored by end of year,"
    Radio France International, 15 April 2023.
"Recreating Notre Dame's Iconic Spire," CBS's *60 Minutes
    Overtime,* 9 April 2023.

Spire called Gothic masterpiece, made focus of fund-raising:

"Notre Dame's Spire: A Masterpiece of Gothic Architecture,"
    Friends of Notre-Dame de Paris, the official 501(c)(3) charity
    leading the international fundraising efforts to rebuild and restore
    Notre-Dame Cathedral," Spring 2023.

CHAPTER 29   PARALLEL LIVES

Lauzerte's beloved organ is described in:

"Historique de l'Instrument paroisial," Louis Salesse, *LAU-
    ZERTE, Eglise Saint Barthélemy,* Association des Amis des Orgue
    de Lauzerte (A.A.O.L.), 1999.

English-only dating apps are lauded in:

> "The Perfect Dating-Site for Expats Living in France," *Quercy Local: The Region's Free Magazine in English*, no. 16, September–October 2014.
> Contempt for the French is reflected in "Summer, Scavenging & Scaring the French!" *Quercy Local*, no. 15, July–August 2014.
> "Eight Tips for How the French Could Improve Their English," the *Local*, 11 September 2018.

CHAPTER 30   I STAND WITH DEGAULLE

"Brexit," like "The Hundred Years' War," was a misnomer.

> *Results and Turnout at the EU Referendum*, The Electoral Commission.
> *Report: 23 June 2016 Referendum on the UK's Membership of the European Union*, The Electoral Commission.
> "EU Referendum: Full Results and Analysis," *Guardian*, undated fact sheet, available online.

The "west of France would have been English, the north would have been Flemish, and the east would have been German," BBC News, 26 July 2014.

"Brexit THREAT":

> Macron says EU's Unity is MORE IMPORTANT than Trade Deal with Britain," Tom Parfitt, *Daily Express*, 27 August 2018.
> Rees-Mogg comment, *Express*, 12 July 2018.
> "Most Conservative Voters in England Would Be Happy to See the UK Break Up as the Price of Brexit," *Guardian*, 8 October 2018.
> "UK Insists It Will Not Grant EU Ambassador Full Diplomatic Status," *Guardian*, 18 January 2021.
> "Meghan Markle, Kate Middleton and . . . Lip Gloss?" Jessica Bennett, *New York Times*, 24 January 2023.
> "Kate Middleton and Meghan Markle Had Some Weird Tense Drama Over Lip Gloss," *Cosmopolitan*, 6 January 2023.

CHAPTER 31   HOLES

For a thorough yet concise overview of Lascaux as it originally existed, and of the extraordinary hand stencils found in such caves, see:

"Lascaux Cave Paintings: Discovery, Layout, Meaning, Photographs of Prehistoric Animal Pictures," and "Prehistoric Hand Stencils: Types, Characteristics, Meaning of Oldest Handprints and Stencilled Hands," both accessible in *Encyclopedia of Stone Age Art*, at visual-arts-cork.com.

For reports on the contamination of Lascaux, see:

"Two new species of the genus Ochroconis, O. lascauxensis and O. anomala isolated from black stains in Lascaux Cave, France," *Fungal Biology*, May 2012.
"Debate Over Moldy Cave Art Is a Tale of Human Missteps," Molly Moore, *Washington Post*, 1 July 2008.
"Lascaux's 18,000 Year-Old Cave Art Under Threat," Laurent Banguet, *Phys.org*, 23 June 2011.

"Lascaux Experience" and presidential visit:

"François Hollande inaugure Lascaux 4, une nouvelle réplique de la grotte, *Le Monde*, 10 December 2016. The sub-headline announces: "This project has the ambition to make the visitor relive the 'same sensations' as the four teenagers who had discovered the prehistoric cave in 1940."

For a basic yet rigorous explanation of these inherent observational ambiguities, see Department of Physics and Astronomy, Georgia State University, "The Uncertainty Principle," *HyperPhysics*, 14 December 2021.

To compare the Lascaux artists with the greatest artists of the future, start with:
Leonardo da Vinci: The Complete Paintings and Drawings, ed. Frank Zoellner (2012).
Similarities between the Louvre and Disneyland:
Once Upon an American Dream: The Story of Euro Disneyland, Andrew Lainsbury (2000).
I. M. Pei: The Louvre Pyramid, Philip Jodidio, I. M. Pei, and Yann Weymouth (2009).

CERN and the God Particle:

The God Particle: If the Universe Is the Answer, What Is the Question?
Leon M. Lederman and Dick Teresi (2006).

The Higgs Boson: Searching for the God Particle, Scientific American
Editors (2012).

Higgs: The Invention and Discovery of the 'God Particle,' J. E. Baggott
(2013).

Pech Merle:

La Grotte temple du Pech Merle, un nouveau sanctuaire préhistorique,
Amédée Lemozi (1929).

La fabuleuse histoire de la grotte du Pech-Merle, Maryse David (2018).

Pech-Merle de Cabrerets, L.-R. Nougier and R. Robert (1954).

CHAPTER 32 FOR WHOM THE BELLS TOLLED

For clerical details on Lauzerte and the Diocese of Montauban, see:

"700 ans de la création du diocèse de Montauban," Conference of
Bishops of France, 4 July 2017.

"En 2017, quatre diocèses célèbrent leurs 700 ans," Malo Tresca, *La
Croix*, 31 May 2017.

"Le nouveau curé en poste," *Le Petit Journal*, 29 August 2017.

"Le père Emile Kofor, notre nouveau curé," *La Depeche du Midi*, 3
September 2017.

Publications of the Diocese of Montauban dealing with Lauzerte, its
foundation, organization, and personnel include:

"Ensemble paroissial de Lauzerte"

"700 Ans: Le catalogue de l'exposition sur les 700 ans du diocèse de
Montauban"

"Notes historique"

"Abbé Emile Kofor"

All are available on the diocesan web site: https://www.diocese
-montauban.fr/.

Priest shuffling:

"Predator Priests Shuffled Around Globe," CBS News, 14 April 2010.

"SCANDALS IN THE CHURCH; Bishop Tells of His Role in
Shuffling," Associated Press, 3 May 2002.

"Parish Transfers of Abusive Catholic Priests," Wikipedia article.

Details on Abbe Sol and Pius XII, and continuing veneration of John XXII:

"Le Chanone Sol," J, Fourgous, in *Le vieux Quercy*, E. Sol (1969)
"Jean XXII," in Personnages Remarquables des Departements
   Francais: Le Lot (1827, 1875 & 1993)
Jean XXII, un des plus grands papes de l'histoire, E.Sol (1947)

For details on sex scandals and clerical changes within the Diocese of
Montauban, see:

"Tarn-et-Garonne. Abus sexuels de l'Église: Mgr Bernard Ginoux
   'demande pardon comme évêque' et parle d'un 'mal répandu un
   peu partout,'" *La Depeche du Midi*, 5 October 2021.
"L'évêque de Montauban Mgr Bernard Ginoux a démissionné,"
   Mikael Corre, *La Depeche du Midi*, 1 October 2022.
"French Catholic Church in Upheaval Following Sexual Abuse
   Revelations," Radio France International, 8 November 2022.
"About 333,000 children were abused within France's Catholic
   Church," *Associated Press*, 5 October 2021.
"The French Catholic Church Acknowledges a Staggering
   Pattern of Sexual Abuse," *Economist*, 9 October 2021.

CHAPTER 33   AMBASSADORS OF PROGRESS

The rickety Allenby Bridge is described in "Hopes and Fears Bridge the
Jordan River," Sarah Helm, *Independent*, 13 August 1992.

The reasons "no railroad would traverse the Barguelonne valley" are reported in:

"Histoire de la ligne fantôme Cahors-Moissac," *La Depeche du Midi*,
   22 December 2022.
"La ligne fantôme Cahors-Moissac," lecture by Georges Ribeill,
   Société des Études du Lot, 16 December 2022.

The phrase "ambassadors of progress" comes from:

"Moissac et le chemin de fer," *Tramways à vapeur et chemin de fer en
   Tarn-et-Garonne*, Jean-François Loock—Saint-Vincent Lespi-
   nasse septembre 2002/avril 2019. See also:
"Moissac. Lorsque le cloître faillit disparaître sous les rails," *La
   Depeche du Midi*, 11 March 2021.

Fernand Braudel discussed the concept of "world-historical" events in his *Leçon inaugurale*, 1 December 1950, College de France (1951).

"Producing wine for the English" and its context are presented in *Wine & The Vine, An Historical Geography of Viticulture and the Wine Trade*, Tim Unwin (2005). For modern developments, there is:

> *Wine Globalization: A New Comparative History*, Kym Anderson and Vicente Pinilla (2018).

Phylloxera and the Columbian Exchange:

> "The Great Wine Blight," Matthew Lyons, *History Today*, 4 April 2022.

The role of T. V. Munson and his fellow botanists in curbing the epidemic is presented in:

> *Grape Man of Texas: Thomas Volnay Munson & The Origins of American Viticulture*, Sherrie S. McLeRoy and Roy E. Renfro (2008).

For the comparative demography of the departments of Lot and Tarn-et-Garonne, see:

> SPLF, *Site sur la population et les limites administrative de France*, Departements actuels 82 Tarm-et-Garonne; 46 Lot.

Pruneaux d'Agen:

> "In France, the Prune Holds a Noble Station," Florence Fabricant, *New York Times*, 31 October 2001.
> "La route du pruneau de France," *Les pepites de France*, 29 August 2022.

For accounts of Moissac and Moissac Abbey, see:

> *Moissac et le Moissagais*, Marguerite Vidal (1955).
> *L'Abbaye et les cloitres de Moissac*, Ernest Rupin (1897).
> *Abbaye de Moissac:39 gravures et 1 plan*, Auguste Anglès (1933).
> *Etudes archéologiques description portail église St Pierre Moissac*, Abbé J-B Pardiac (1859).
> *Les gloires de Moissac en Quercy*, Pierre Testas (1949).

Regarding Meyer Schapiro and Moissac Abbey, his classic is:

> *The Sculpture of Moissac*, Meyer Schapiro, photographs by David
>   Finn (1985).
> Fascinating insights into the scholar and his work are provided by:
> *Meyer Schapiro Abroad: Letters to Lillian and Travel Notes*, Daniel
>   Esterman (2009).

See also:

> "What Did Meyer Schapiro Do? An Introduction to the Great
>   Humanist Art Historian," Blair Asbury Brooks, *Artspace*
>   (8 August 2014).
> Identification as Jeremiah: *Vidal, Moissac et Le Moissagais*, cover
>   photograph and frontis page.

CHAPTER 34   GLASS GLOBE WARS

I again offer my thanks to Patrice Brassier for his decades of research, and
for the results it produced in *Chroniques Lauzertines de la Gandillonne à la
Resistance* (2014) and *Chronologie de l'histoire de Lauzerte: Des origins à 1798*
(2012).

Idyllic décor:

> *Lauzerte: Itineraire d'une bastide*, Office de Tourisme Quercy
>   Sud-Ouest (2021).

Books dealing with France's supposed superiority, hence right to "civilize" the world, include:

> *La haute mission civilisatrice de la colonisation*, J. W. Hay (1895).
> *Mission to Civilize: The French Way*, Mort Rosenblum (1986).
> *Mission civilisatrice: le rôle de l'histoire coloniale dans la construction de
>   l'identité politique française*, Dino Costantini (2008).

Communal role of France's Monuments to the Dead:

> *The Construction of Memory in Interwar France*, Daniel J. Sherman
>   (1999).
> *Comprendre le monument aux morts: Lieu du souvenir, lieu de mémoire,
>   lieu d'histoire*, Franck David (2021).

"La Marseillaise" and Hector Berlioz:

La musique Française de la Marseillaise à la mort de Berlioz, Paul Landormy (1944).

For an overview of *L'État français*, consult:

Vichy France: Old Guard and New Order, 1940–1944, Robert O. Paxton (1972).

Details on Moissac's role in saving Jewish children, and information on the Jew sheltered in Lauzerte are accessible at the Yad Vashem Data Bank.

Information on World War Two in the Lauzerte area:

La résistance en Tarn et Garonne, Louis Olivet and André Aribaud (1995–2008)
Livre 1 : Cinquantenaire de la libération de Montauban
Livre 2 : Contre l'oubli
Livre 3: Avant que mémoire ne meure
Livre 4: Afin que mémoire demeure
Livre 5: La mémoire : Heurs et malheurs

Eyewitness account of "Vincent" on U.S. paratroopers as related to his son:

"LE 15 AOÛT 1944 Echec de l'opération de destruction d'un pont de chemin de fer au lieu-dit Roudes (Lamagistère). Relation directe qu 'en a faite Jean Douet (Vincent), participant à l'opération et qu'a recueillie son fils Pierre Douet." Text in Book Four, above.

"Mosquito" and The Legacy:

"The painful past of Spanish Civil War refugees in France, 80 years on," *France24*, 9 February 2019.
"Franco refugees still haunted by the past: 'We were cold, hungry and scared,'" Ros Coward. *The Guardian*. 9 February 2019.
"Mosquito, capitaine de l'armée espagnole, inhumé en terre montcuquoise," La Dépêche du Midi, 2 November 2020.

Das Reich Division:

2nd SS Panzer Division Das Reich—Drive to Normandy, June 1944, Philip Vickers (1999).

Das Reich: The March of the 2nd SS Panzer Division Through France, June 1944, Max Hastings (2013).

Das Reich, la division maudite: De Montauban au front de Normandie par Tulle et Oradour: La barbarie SS, Michel Peyramaure (2014).

Europe against itself:

Hitler's Spanish Legion: The Blue Division in Russia in WWII, Gerald R. Kleinfeld (2014).

Fire and Blood: The European Civil War, 1914–1945, Enzo Traverso (2016).

German massacres:

Martyred Village: Commemorating the 1944 Massacre at Oradour-sur-Glane, Sarah Bennett Farmer (2000).

Silent Village: Life and Death in Occupied France, Robert Pike (2021).

Paradour-sur-Glane: autopsie d'un massacre: le drame heure par heure, Robert Hébras (1992).

French massacre:

"Témoignage—Edmond Réveil: On avait honte, mais est-ce qu'on avait le choix? " *La Vie Correzienne*, 17 May 2023.

"French Resistance Fighter Goes Public About Execution of German P.O.W.s," Constant Méheut, *New York Times*, 17 May 2023.

"Témoignage. 'Je suis content que ça ne soit plus un secret.' Edmond Réveil, résistant, révèle l'exécution de soldats allemands en 1944 en Corrèze," Nicolas Chigot, *France Info: Nouvel Aquitaine*, 16 May 2023.

Mittelbau-Dora killings:

A History of the Dora Camp: The Untold Story of the Nazi Slave Labor Camp That Secretly Manufactured V-2 Rockets, Andre Sellier (2003).

Le livre des 9000 déportés de France à Mittelbau-Dora, Laurent Thiery (2020).

CHAPTER 35   TRIUMPH OF THE TRAFFIC CIRCLES

"Structures of everyday life":

Les structures du quotidien: le possible et l'impossible, Fernand Braudel (1979).

The Structures of Everyday Life: The Limits of the Possible, vol. 1 of *Civilization and Capitalism, 15th-18th Century*, Fernand Braudel, trans. (like his other major works) Siân Reynolds (1985).

Analyses of Lauzerte's current situation:

"Renouer les liens entre ville et paysage à Lauzerte," André Viviane, *Report* from Centre de Recherches sur l'Habitat, Ecole Nationale Supérieure d'Architecture de Paris Val de Seine, 8 February 2018.

"Lauzerte: mécanismes de revitalisation d'un bourg rural en crise," Geneviève Schetman-Labry, *Revue géographique des Pyrénées et du Sud-Ouest* (1992).

"Automobile crashed into a tree in the middle village."
"L'Accident," *Les Amis de Lauzerte*, Spring 2023.

"*La Poste*, too, had migrated down the hill."
"La nouvelle Poste inaugurée," *La Depeche du Midi*, 7 December 2018.

"Credit Agricole Fined $800m for US Sanctions Violations," BBC News, 20 October 2015.

Dr. Amr Sultan replied, "Please!" Personal discussion, 6 June 2023.

Proliferation of traffic circles in France and elsewhere:

"Le rond-point en France: approches plurielles d'un objet géographique émergent," Serge Bourgeat and Catherine Bras, *GeoConfluences*, 16 May 2023.

"Le rond-point, symbole d'un mal français," Eric Treguier, *Challenges*, 21 December 2018.

"Les ronds-points: une France qui ne tourne pas rond," Pierre Robert, *Contrepoints*, 4 June 2022.

"The 'Quiet Roundabout Revolution' Sweeping U.S. Cities," Dian Ionescu, *Planetizen*, 5 December 2022.

"One of the Most Amazing Trends You've Never Heard of: The
Rise of the Roundabouts," Andrew Van Dam, *Washington Post*,
25 November 2022.

Intermarché:

"Histoire des Mousquetaires," *Les Mousquetaires* (https://www
.mousquetaires.com/notre-groupement/notre-histoire/).
"Top 10 Supermarket Retail Chains in France," Steve Wynne-
Jones, *ESM European Supermarket Magazine*, 29 March 2023.

Maison de retrait; creation of new retirement complex:

"Le chantier de l'Ehpad est dans les délais" *La Depeche du Midi*,
12 March 2015.
Information from Mme Jeanne McCaul, April 2023.
"Les EHPAD (établissements d'hébergement pour personnes âgées
dépendantes)," *Republique Francaise: Portail national
d'information pour les personnes âgées et leurs proches*, 11 January
2023.

Falsely claims its inmates to be "fully integrated into local life with participation in the activities of the town [including] exchanges with the
child-care nursery, the school, and the various associations present in
the village:

"Historique de l'etablissement," Lauzerte Maison de Retrait
(https://www.maisonderetraitelauzerte.com/historique-de-l
-%C3%A9tablissement/).

Books on the heat wave of 2003 include:

*Canicule 2003: Origines sociales et ressorts contemporains d'une mort
solitaire*, Victor Collet (2005).
*Expérience gériatrique de la canicule 2003: recommandations pour les
soignants en charge de personnes âgée*, Clara Bitchev (2004).
*Surmortalité liée à la canicule d'août 2003: suivi de la
mortalité (21 août—31 décembre 2003), causes médicales des décès
(1–20 août 2003)*, Denis Hémon and Éric Jougla (2004).
"20,000 morts en quelques semaines: retour sur la terrible canicule
de l'été 2003," *FranceInfo*, 25 May 2023.
"Canicule 2003: température, durée, date," *Le Journal des Femmes
Santé*, 13 October 2022.

Quotations from Jean-Louis Chanuc and Armand Lafargue:

> *Chroniques Lauzertnes de la Gandillonne à la Resistance*, Patrice Brassier (2014).

"Diocese of Montauban":

> *Dictionnaire des paroises du Diocese de Montauban*, Pierre Gayne (1978).

ENVOI: UNTO US THE DEAD IMPART THE SWEETNESS OF LIFE

Colombia reports:
> *Busted: Stone Cowboys, Narco-Lords, and Washington's War on Drugs*, T. D. Allman et al. (2002).
> "Colombia: Parts 1 & 2," T. D. Allman, *Rolling Stone*, June and July 2002.

The dark silhouette . . . was Mr. Legume:

> "Quercy, un pays rude au charactere bien trempe," photo by Catherine Hanriette, *GEO*, July 2002.

Henna "can cause hair damage . . . may cause hair loss."
> "Is Henna Hair Dye a Bad Idea? Here's What the Experts Have to Say," *Healthline*, 30 September 2021.

Ambassador Arthur Hartman:

> "Arthur A. Hartman, U.S. Ambassador to Soviet Union, Dies at 89," *New York Times*, 18 March 2015.
> "Arthur A. Hartman, d'une «élégante simplicité»," *La Depeche du Midi*, 22 March 2015.

Fate of Jacques and Marielle Buchholtz:

> "Pour Jacques, et pour Marielle," *La Depeche du Midi*, 22 October 1998.

"Everyone loved him and respected him, including the man who defeated him":

> "Hommage: « Jardin du pèlerin, Alain Chauve »," Mayor Bernard Rey, *Mairie de Lauzerte*, August 2010.

"Lauzerte. Le jardin du pèlerin conservera le souvenir," *La Depeche du Midi*, 9 August 2010.

"Lauzerte. Décès d'Alain Chauve," *La Depeche du Midi*, 28 December 2009.

My House on the cadasters:

"Plan cadastral de Lauzerte Place des Cornières 113," *France Cadastre*, Department of Tarn et Garonne.

The article concerning the author's long residence in Lauzerte:

UN ÉCRIVAIN AMÉRICAIN À LAUZERTE." *Le Petit Lauzertin*, September–December 2022.

INDEX